MAKE YOUR *NEXT ADVENTURE* A
*MOUNTAINRAIL ADVENTURE!*

CALL: 866.820.7782
OR VISIT: MTN-RAIL.COM

# TOURIST TRAINS
# GUIDEBOOK
### SIXTH EDITION

KALMBACH BOOKS

**Kalmbach Books**
21027 Crossroads Circle
Waukesha, Wisconsin 53186
www.KalmbachHobbyStore.com

Published in 2017
21 20 19 18 17    1 2 3 4 5

Printed in the United States

ISBN: 978-1-62700-409-1
EISBN: 978-1-62700-410-7

Front cover photo: Great Smoky Mountains Railroad by Joshua Scott
Back cover photo: Leadville, Colorado & Southern Railroad

**Editor:** Randy Rehberg
**Book Design:** Tom Ford

Library of Congress Control Number: 2016943637

# Using the guidebook

*Tourist Trains Guidebook* describes 525 excursion trains, dinner trains, trolley rides, railroad museums, and historical depots across the United States and Canada. The sites are described in either full-page reviews or shorter listings.

*Trains* magazine staff and contributors reviewed 200 of the top attractions. Their reviews provide an in-depth look at each location. They describe what each train ride or museum offers and give you an idea of when to go for the best experiences. They also point out nearby activities that are worth doing and what you shouldn't miss to make your visit most enjoyable.

Another 325 unique attractions are presented in capsule descriptions that offer a concise look at each site and provide contact information.

We have included the most up-to-date details possible for every attraction. However, due to the many factors that can affect a tourist train or museum, we recommend that you contact any site before planning your visit. Steam engines may not be running, schedules and prices may change, and museums may be under renovation.

While almost every attraction has a website, many of them post their most current information and upcoming events on Facebook.

in this edition, the sites are organized into 12 geographic regions. Each region includes a list of sites and a handy locator map. You can browse a region's listings by state or province, where you'll find the shorter entries first followed by the full-page reviews. Each grouping is listed in alphabetical order. You can also look for an individual site using the index at the back of the book.

# Contributors

The following people provided reviews of the tourist train sites: Kevin Andrusia, Bryan Bechtold, Marvin Clemons, Dave Crosby, Steve Glischinski, John Godfrey, Cody Grivno, Scott Hartley, Patrick Hiatte, David Hoge, Frank Keller, Tom Kline, G. Wayne Laepple, Robert LaMay, Elrond Lawrence, David Lustig, Rob McGonigal, Jackson McQuigg, Alexander Mitchell IV, Steve Patterson, Mark Perri, Mark Perry, Jeff Terry, Ralcon Wagner, Jim Wrinn, and Karl Zimmermann.

# Contents

# Introduction

Welcome to a world of exploration, fun, and adventure. This guidebook will open a window into North American railway history, it will lead you to sacred places, and it will put you on board some of the oldest and coolest trains in some of the most beautiful locations around. Think of this guide as a key to unlocking something special.

I have used this guide for years to help find railroad attractions during business trips, while on vacation, and to make the most of my time. We've tried to provide as much helpful information as possible following in-the-field visits.

You'll be amazed at the number of venues and the wide range of experiences that are available. There are train rides that are about scenic wonders, train trips that are about bird watching, excursions that include cuisine as well as beverages, and even trains that take you to a gold mine.

Many venues include annual special events that bring Thomas the Tank Engine or the Polar Express to life. Some allow passengers to join the crew in the locomotive, and some even feature programs that put you in the engineer's seat.

Whatever you're looking for as far as a railroad attraction, it is probably in here. So, start turning pages. Get out those yellow sticky notes. And start planning. The train is ready and waiting. All aboard!

*Jim Wrinn*

Jim Wrinn, Editor
*Trains* magazine

# REGION 1

Naugatuck Railroad, page 14

# REGION 1

## CONNECTICUT

1  Connecticut Antique Machinery Association
2  Connecticut Eastern Railroad Museum
3  Connecticut Trolley Museum
4  Danbury Railway Museum
5  Essex Steam Train
6  Naugatuck Railroad
7  Shore Line Trolley Museum
8  SoNo Switch Tower Museum

## MAINE

9  Belfast & Moosehead Lake Railway
10  Boothbay Railway Village
11  Cole Land Transportation Museum
12  Downeast Scenic Railroad
13  Maine Narrow Gauge Railroad

14  Oakfield Railroad Museum
15  Seashore Trolley Museum
16  Wiscasset, Waterville & Farmington Railway Museum

## MASSACHUSETTS

17  Berkshire Scenic Railway Museum
18  Cape Cod Central Railroad
19  Chatham Railroad Museum
20  Edaville USA
21  Lowell National Historical Park
22  Shelburne Falls Trolley Museum

## NEW HAMPSHIRE

23  Ashland Railroad Station Museum
24  Café Lafayette Dinner Train
25  Conway Scenic Railroad
26  Gorham Historical Society Museum
27  Hobo Railroad
28  Mount Washington Cog Railway
29  Potter Place Railroad Station
30  Sandown Depot Museum
31  Silver Lake Railroad
32  White Mountain Central Railroad
33  Winnipesaukee Scenic Railroad

**NEW YORK**

34 Adirondack Scenic Railroad
35 Arcade & Attica Railroad
36 Brooks Alco Railroad Display
37 Buffalo, Rochester & Pittsburgh Depot Museum
38 Catskill Mountain Railroad
39 Central Square Station Museum
40 Cooperstown & Charlotte Valley Railroad
41 Delaware & Ulster Railroad
42 Empire State Railway Museum
43 Hyde Park Railroad Station
44 Martisco Station Museum

45 Medina Railroad Museum
46 New York Museum of Transportation
47 New York Transit Museum
48 North Creek Railway Depot Museum
49 Railroad Museum of Long Island
50 Railroad Museum of the Niagara Frontier
51 Rochester & Genesee Valley Railroad Museum
52 Salamanca Rail Museum
53 Saratoga & North Creek Railway
54 Trolley Museum of New York

**RHODE ISLAND**

55 Newport & Narragansett Bay Railroad

**VERMONT**

56 Shelburne Museum
57 Vermont Rail System

# CONNECTICUT

## Connecticut Antique Machinery Association

The association features an operating 3-foot-gauge railroad that is powered by a 1925 Baldwin locomotive that was used in the sugar cane fields of Hawaii. A variety of other locomotives and rolling stock fills out the collection. The site contains six other exhibits dedicated to antique industrial and agricultural machinery. It is open Wednesdays through Sundays May through October.

**LOCATION:** 31 Kent-Cornwall Road (Route 7), Kent
**PHONE:** 860-927-0050
**WEBSITE:** ctamachinery.com
**E-MAIL:** form on website

## Connecticut Trolley Museum

Founded in 1940, this museum offers a narrated 3-mile, round-trip trolley ride. Its collection contains passenger and freight streetcars, interurban cars, elevated railway cars, service cars, and other rail equipment. A fire equipment museum and motor coach museum are also on site. The museum is open April through October with Winterfest taking place in November and December.

**LOCATION:** 58 North Road, East Windsor
**PHONE:** 860-627-6540
**WEBSITE:** ceraonline.org
**E-MAIL:** office@ceraweb.org

# Danbury Railway Museum

This museum contains 70 pieces of equipment representing 11 different northeastern railroads and includes unique pieces such as a New Haven Railroad Mack FCD railbus. Vintage train rides in the yard include a spin around an operating turntable. The 1903 station features displays and a model layout of the Danbury yard. It is open year-round but closed on Mondays and Tuesdays during winter and on most holidays.

LOCATION: 120 White Street, Danbury
PHONE: 203-778-8337
WEBSITE: danburyrail.org
E-MAIL: form on website

# Shore Line Trolley Museum

The museum features a collection of 100 vintage transit vehicles. A 3-mile round-trip trolley ride takes you along the area's scenic shore. Along the way, the trolley stops in the yard, where you can take a brief guided tour of the carbarn exhibits. You can also take a more comprehensive self-guided tour. The shop overlook allows you to view any restoration activities, and the station building contains additional exhibits. It is open May through October, with daily operations June to September.

LOCATION: 17 River Street, East Haven
PHONE: 203-467-6927
WEBSITE: shorelinetrolley.com
E-MAIL: office@shorelinetrolley.org

# SoNo Switch Tower Museum

This 1896 New Haven Railroad switch tower has been restored, complete with an original armstrong 68-lever mechanical interlocking machine. Located next to the Northeast Corridor main line, the unique museum is open Saturdays and Sundays May through October.

LOCATION: 77 Washington Street, South Norwalk
PHONE: 203-246-6958
WEBSITE: sonotower.org
E-MAIL: info@westctnrhs.org

# Connecticut Eastern Railroad Museum

Robert LaMay

For anyone interested in seeing what takes place in a 1900s-era railroad village, this would be the place to visit. Located on the original site of the Columbia Junction freight yard and roundhouse, the Connecticut Eastern Railroad Museum is one of the few railroad museums to have a roundhouse complete with an operating standard gauge 60-foot armstrong turntable.

**CHOICES:** The museum features a variety of restored buildings including a station, section house, freight house, and crossing shanties. Numerous working projects occur every week throughout the museum's operating season. It houses several diesel locomotives, various railcars, and a steam locomotive. Tour guides are also on hand to show and explain the Ghost Train story and other tales of railroad history. The museum offers train rides along a section of the original Air Line Route.

**WHEN TO GO:** The museum is open weekends from May into October. A variety of events take place during the season, such as music concerts, night photo shoots, and Metal Fest in May—a full day of blacksmithing events and demonstrations.

**GOOD TO KNOW:** With museum supervision, kids of all ages can ride on a replica 1850s pump car. You can also pretend that you are the engineer and sit in the engineer's seat of a New Haven Railroad FL9 passenger diesel locomotive.

**WORTH DOING:** Willimantic is situated in the Last Green Valley, designated as Quinebaug and Shetucket Rivers Valley National Heritage Corridor. The valley contains seven state forests and five state parks. During Walktober, there are more than 100 guided walks and special events, including one at the Connecticut Eastern Railroad Museum.

**DON'T MISS:** Train rides are available if there is demand for them. The fare for the round trip from Columbia Junction to Bridge Street is $3.

**GETTING THERE:** Located about 30 miles east of Hartford in downtown Willimantic, the museum can be easily reached via numerous state roads such as Routes 6, 66, 32, 195, and 2. Once downtown, turn onto Bridge Street (Route 289 South), take a quick right, and follow the railroad tracks down a dirt road to the museum entrance.

**LOCATION:** 55 Bridge Street, Willimantic
**PHONE:** 860-456-9999
**WEBSITE:** cteastrrmuseum.org
**E-MAIL:** info@cteastrrmuseum.org

# Essex Steam Train & Riverboat

Valley Railroad Company, Roger Charbonneau Jr.

**The Essex Steam Train, operated by the Valley Railroad Company, is unusual in offering a train ride that can be combined with a connecting riverboat excursion, providing scenic views of the Connecticut River from both rail and water. The 12-mile rail round trip from Essex station to Deep River and Haddam takes about an hour, while the rail-water package lasts 2.5 hours.**

**CHOICES:** The Essex Steam Train is hauled by locomotive No. 40, which dates from 1920, or the far newer Chinese-built No. 3025, while the *Becky Thatcher*, a replica of a three-deck Mississippi-style riverboat, handles the water excursion. A number of seasonal events take place, including the diesel-powered Eagle Flyer, a wildlife-viewing excursion in February, as well as sunset cruises on Saturdays and a lunch train. On some weekends, a caboose is available for rides.

**WHEN TO GO:** Trains operate from the historic 1892 Essex depot May through late October. Day Out with Thomas weekends take place in spring, and Santa Special (afternoons) and North Pole Express (evenings) trains run in November and December. Spring and fall are fine times to visit, with the leaves either a new green or brilliant autumn colors.

**GOOD TO KNOW:** Essex is a historic seaport village, with lots of white-clapboard New England charm. The Victorian Goodspeed Opera House in nearby East Haddam presents productions of classic musical comedies.

**WORTH DOING:** Nearby Gillette Castle is a whimsical faux-medieval mountaintop estate built of local fieldstone and completed in 1919 for actor and playwright William Gillette, most famous for his portrayal of Sherlock Holmes. Visit it on your own or as a train-ferry-hiking package offered by the railroad.

**DON'T MISS:** The diesel-hauled Essex Clipper Dinner Train operates seasonally and offers a four-course dinner. One of its dining cars is a special treat: the heavyweight Pullman parlor car *Wallingford*, built in 1927 for the New York, New Haven & Hartford.

**GETTING THERE:** Essex is located on Route 9 just 3 miles from I-95.

**LOCATION:** 1 Railroad Avenue, Essex
**PHONE:** 800-377-3987 or 860-767-0103
**WEBSITE:** essexsteamtrain.com
**E-MAIL:** info@essexsteamtrain.com

# Naugatuck Railroad

Scott Hartley

Today's Naugatuck Railroad runs over 19.6 miles of former New Haven Railroad, between Waterbury and Torrington, a line built by the original Naugatuck in 1849. The tracks follow the railroad's namesake river for the entire route. The Naugatuck Railroad, part of the Railroad Museum of New England, offers regularly scheduled train service over a 9-mile portion of its line, and periodic special excursions over other segments.

**CHOICES:** Departing the 1881 Thomaston station aboard 1920s heavyweight coaches or a 1950s streamlined Budd RDC, you cross two trestles over the Naugatuck River, see century-old New England brass mills, and roll high across the face of giant Thomaston Dam. Operating locomotives include U23B 2203 (the last domestic U-Boat built by General Electric) and EMD FL9 New Haven 2019 (the only FL9 still operating on original NH trackage).

**WHEN TO GO:** Excursions run on Sundays and Tuesdays from Memorial Day through September, with Saturday departures added in October. The fall colors peak in early to mid-October, and this is the most popular time to ride the Naugatuck's trains. Easter Bunny Express trains run the Saturday before Easter, Northern Lights Limited and Santa Express trains run weekends late November through December, and wine-tasting and Chocolate Decadence Tour trains run throughout the year.

**GOOD TO KNOW:** Built in 1881 by the original Naugatuck Railroad, the brick Thomaston station is being restored. The station features a display track of historic New England railroad rolling stock.

**WORTH DOING:** Thomaston offers a pleasant New England downtown with historic mills, restaurants, and a picturesque opera house. Nearby Litchfield has large 18th century homes, shops, and restaurants. Waterbury's Mattatuck Museum shows visitors the history of Connecticut's brass industry.

**DON'T MISS:** At Thomaston station, you can see an electro-pneumatic interlocking machine used by the New Haven and recently installed 1920s semaphore signals.

**GETTING THERE:** Take I-84 to Waterbury and then Route 8 north to Exit 38.

**LOCATION:** 242 E. Main Street, Thomaston
**PHONE:** 860-283-7245
**WEBSITE:** rmne.org
**E-MAIL:** form on website

# MAINE

## Belfast & Moosehead Lake Railway

Excursion trains depart from City Point Railroad Museum in Belfast, run to Waldo, and return. You can enjoy the 70-minute trip aboard a coach, an open-air car, or a caboose. Special fall and pizza trains also operate. The season runs from Memorial Day weekend through October.

**LOCATION:** 13 Oak Hill Road, Belfast
**PHONE:** 207-722-3899
**WEBSITE:** brookspreservation.org
**E-MAIL:** form on website

## Boothbay Railway Village

A 2-foot-gauge steam train takes you around a re-created historic village with several stations and an engine house. A railbus also operates. Exhibits show the history of Maine's narrow gauge railroads, and various pieces of rolling stock and equipment are on display, as are more than 50 antique or classic vehicles. It is open daily from Memorial day weekend through mid-October.

**LOCATION:** 586 Wiscasset Road, Boothbay
**PHONE:** 207-633-4727
**WEBSITE:** railwayvillage.org
**E-MAIL:** form on website

## Cole Land Transportation Museum

The museum houses 200 antique land transportation vehicles and 2,000 photographs of life in early Maine. Its railroad collection includes one of the first Bangor & Aroostook diesels, a Canadian Pacific section shack, a Maine Central caboose, and a relocated station. It is open daily May until November.

**LOCATION:** 405 Perry Road, Bangor
**PHONE:** 207-990-3600
**WEBSITE:** colemuseum.org
**E-MAIL:** form on website

## Oakfield Railroad Museum

Exhibits in the restored Oakfield station include hundreds of photographs dating to the beginning of the Bangor & Aroostook Railroad in 1891, vintage signs, signal lanterns, railroad maps, and telegraph equipment. A restored caboose, handcar, and motor car are also displayed. It is open summer Saturday and Sunday afternoons.

**LOCATION:** 40 Station Street, Oakfield
**PHONE:** 207-267-5882
**WEBSITE:** oakfieldmuseum.org
**E-MAIL:** oakfieldmuseum@pwless.net

# Downeast Scenic Railroad

Downeast Scenic Railroad

The Downeast Scenic Railroad offers a 90-minute round-trip excursion that travels along the former Calais Branch of the Maine Central Railroad from Ellsworth to Ellsworth Falls, and then to Washington Junction and back. Along this stretch of the Calais Branch Line, you'll see Little Rocky Pond, Green Lake, marshes, and glacial deposits including massive boulders. You may even see ospreys, eagles, and deer.

**CHOICES:** The train is pulled by a vintage diesel locomotive. Seating options include restored passenger coaches from the 1910s, an open-air car made from a log car, and a caboose. You can reserve tickets, but specific seats are not assigned, so arrive early to pick out your seat. The open-air car has picnic tables for dining al fresco, and well-behaved dogs are allowed on this car.

**WHEN TO GO:** The railroad runs excursions on weekends starting Memorial Day weekend. That weekend, service begins with one trip each day. From the end of June to mid-October, two trips are offered. The Touch-A-Train event in June gives you a close-up look at the equipment.

**GOOD TO KNOW:** At Washington Junction Yard, the recently rehabilitated wye turns the train for the return trip to Ellsworth.

**WORTH DOING:** The coast is less than an hour away, where you can visit Mount Desert Island and Acadia National Park. Activities in the area include hiking, kayaking, and whale watching. Also, while in the area, be sure to indulge in fresh lobster and other seafood and homemade blueberry pie in many of the local restaurants.

**DON'T MISS:** At Washington Junction Yard, the staging area for the railroad, you'll be able to see vintage maintenance-of-way equipment and diesel locomotives.

**GETTING THERE:** Ellsworth is 24 miles east of Bangor. From there, take Highway 1A straight into Ellsworth. The boarding location is behind the Maine Community Foundation building located at 245 Main Street, where you can park as well.

**LOCATION:** 245 Main Street, Ellsworth
**PHONE:** 866-449-7245
**WEBSITE:** downeastscenicrail.org
**E-MAIL:** form on website

# Maine Narrow Gauge Railroad & Museum

Jeff Terry

The Maine Narrow Gauge Railroad runs along the Eastern Promenade fronting Casco Bay. Excursions offer spectacular views of ferries, sailboats, cruise ships, lobster boats, and freighters as well as the many islands that dot the bay. The museum helps preserve Maine's 2-foot-gauge railways.

**CHOICES:** The railroad operates diesel-powered trains with historic open-window coaches and open-sided excursion cars. Most of the railroad's equipment once operated on two of Maine's famed two-footers: the Sandy River & Rangeley Lakes and the Bridgton & Harrison. You can tour the museum and see several beautifully restored passenger coaches, including *Rangeley*, the only 2-foot-gauge parlor car ever built. Also on display is a railbus used on the Sandy River and Bridgton & Harrison Railroads.

**WHEN TO GO:** The museum is open daily May through October. Various special events, including a Polar Express train, take place throughout the year.

**GOOD TO KNOW:** The museum is continuing preparations for a move to Gray, 25 miles north of Portland. Currently, all trains are diesel powered until locomotive No. 7 returns to service.

**WORTH DOING:** The Portland waterfront is a busy area for tourists, and there are many other attractions in the area, including excellent seafood restaurants and shops constructed in Federal-style architecture.

**DON'T MISS:** Ride on the water side of the train for the best views. A walking and bike path follows the line for its entire length, which makes taking action photos easy.

**GETTING THERE:** Amtrak's *Downeaster* makes several daily trips between Boston and Portland. I-95 passes just west of the city.

**LOCATION:** 58 Fore Street, Portland
**PHONE:** 207-828-0814
**WEBSITE:** mainenarrowgauge.org
**E-MAIL:** info@mainenarrowgauge.org

# Seashore Trolley Museum

Karl Zimmermann

Founded in 1939, the Seashore Trolley Museum is touted as the oldest, largest electric railway museum in the world. Its international collection includes more than 250 transit vehicles, mostly streetcars, and virtually every major United States city that operated trolleys is represented. Much of this equipment is under cover in three exhibit carbarns.

**CHOICES:** Included in the museum admission is a streetcar ride over the 2 miles of rebuilt trackage. This ride, a treat for all the senses, is the best way to relive the trolley and interurban experience. If just riding isn't enough, you can take advantage of the Be a Motorman program and actually operate a trolley. In the visitor center, you can view an exhibit chronicling the way trolleys changed life in Maine and their relevance to the contemporary world.

**WHEN TO GO:** The museum is open seven days a week from Memorial Day through Columbus Day, weekends in May, and for the balance of October. In early December, the museum opens for Kennebunkport's Christmas Prelude, with rides and refreshments. There are a number of additional special events, including sunset ice cream rides on summer weekends and pumpkin patch trolleys in September.

**GOOD TO KNOW:** On Transit Weekend in October, the museum brings out rapid transit cars, buses, and trackless trolleys that do not usually operate.

**WORTH DOING:** Kennebunkport and adjacent Kennebunk are resort towns with Atlantic beaches and old-world New England charm. There are antique shops, galleries, restaurants (lobster a specialty), and opportunities for whale watching and other sea-related activities.

**DON'T MISS:** The restoration shop is open to the public. From elevated walkways, you can watch the painstaking work on the cars going forward.

**GETTING THERE:** The museum is located just a few miles from I-95 (the Maine Turnpike) off Exit 25. Amtrak's Boston-Rockland *Downeaster* stops in Saco, about 8 miles away, where taxis are available.

**LOCATION:** 195 Log Cabin Road, Kennebunkport
**PHONE:** 207-967-2800
**WEBSITE:** trolleymuseum.org
**E-MAIL:** form on website

# Wiscasset, Waterville & Farmington Railway Museum

Wayne Laepple

Operating over a portion of the original WW&F Railway, which was abandoned in 1933, the WW&F is a faithful re-creation of a segment of the original Wiscasset, Waterville & Farmington, one of Maine's five 2-foot-gauge common carrier railroads.

**CHOICES:** Steam and diesel trains operate from Sheepscot station to Top of the Mountain, passing the flag stop station at Alna Center. A journey on the WW&F takes riders back to the early years of the last century, when the railroad carried the commerce and the people of the inland region to the seaport town of Wiscasset. Visitors are welcome to tour the railway's shops, where volunteers maintain and rebuild rolling stock, using traditional skills and techniques. A Model T Ford railcar also operates regularly.

**WHEN TO GO:** The museum is open every Saturday year-round, and on Sundays from Memorial Day weekend through mid-October. Steam-hauled trains run in July, August and October, with diesel trains running in April, May, June, and September.

**GOOD TO KNOW:** No. 9, a Portland Company engine built in 1891, was recently returned to service, having last run in 1933, and is the regular power on weekend trains during the summer months.

**WORTH DOING:** The mid-coast region of Maine features plenty of attractions, lodging choices, and restaurants. Nearby attractions include scenic Boothbay Harbor, Boothbay Railway Village, Owl's Head Transportation Museum, Maine Maritime Museum, and L.L. Bean.

**DON'T MISS:** The museum holds annual spring and fall work sessions, when members lay track, work on equipment, paint buildings, and build structures over long weekends. Vistors are welcome to join in.

**GETTING THERE:** Alna is located north of Wiscasset, approximately 50 miles northeast of Portland. The museum is on Cross Road, just off Route 218 about 4.5 miles from Wiscasset and Route 1.

**LOCATION:** 97 Cross Road, Alna
**PHONE:** 207-882-4193
**WEBSITE:** wwfry.org
**E-MAIL:** info@wwfry.org

# MASSACHUSETTS

## Chatham Railroad Museum

This restored country depot is situated on its original site. Museum exhibits feature hundreds of railroad artifacts from the Chatham Railroad Company and other railroads, including a restored 1910 New York Central caboose and telegraph instruments. It is open Tuesdays through Saturdays mid-June to mid-September.

**LOCATION:** 153 Depot Road, Chatham
**PHONE:** 508-945-5100
**WEBSITE:** chathamrailroadmuseum.com

## Edaville USA

This is a family fun park with a 2-mile train ride through a 1,300-acre cranberry plantation. It operates both a steam engine and a diesel locomotive. There is a variety of amusement rides and an indoor play area. Special events include National Cranberry Festival, Christmas Festival of Lights, and others.

**LOCATION:** 5 Pine Street, Carver
**PHONE:** 508-866-8190
**WEBSITE:** edaville.com
**E-MAIL:** info@edaville.com

## Lowell National Historical Park

The park includes a variety of structures related to industry, 5.6 miles of canals, and restored mill buildings. It displays a Boston & Maine 0-6-0 Manchester locomotive built in 1910, a combine car, and several open-air trolleys. Trolley tours as well as several boat tours are available, except in winter. You can also take in the National Streetcar Museum, which is across from the park's visitor center.

**LOCATION:** 246 Market Street, Lowell
**PHONE:** 978-970-5000
**WEBSITE:** nps.gov/lowe
**E-MAIL:** form on website

## Shelburne Falls Trolley Museum

The museum features a 15-minute ride on restored trolley car No. 10, which was built in 1896. For an added fee, and with a little instruction, you can become an instant motorman and run No. 10 yourself. Pump car rides are also available. The museum displays railroad and trolley artifacts, a steam locomotive, and a caboose. It is open Saturdays, Sundays, and holidays late May through October.

**LOCATION:** 14 Depot Street, Shelburne Falls
**PHONE:** 413-625-9443
**WEBSITE:** sftm.org
**E-MAIL:** trolley@sftm.org

# Berkshire Scenic Railway Museum

Scott Hartley

The Berkshire Scenic Railway Museum operates its Hoosac Valley train ride between North Adams and Adams, a distance of approximately 4 miles, on the onetime New York Central North Adams Branch. The organization's museum is located approximately 30 miles south of North Adams in the beautifully restored New Haven Railroad station at Lenox.

**CHOICES:** Berkshire Scenic operates on Saturdays, Sundays, and federal holidays from Memorial Day to late October, with four trains each day. The hour-long ride is aboard a former Boston & Maine Budd Rail Diesel Car, and features narration of the various scenic and historic locales seen from the train. Special event trains also are offered. BSRM's museum and the majority of its collection are located at Lenox, which is open to visitors on Saturdays from Memorial Day to Labor Day weekends. Exhibits include a train dispatcher's console, a replica block station, several vintage diesel-electric locomotives, and a wooden baggage car.

**WHEN TO GO:** New England's famed fall foliage peaks in this region in early October. During this time, expect crowded roads and high lodging rates. It is less congested at other times.

**GOOD TO KNOW:** Lodging is available in North Adams and in the Pittsfield/Lenox/Lee area. The Berkshires feature many cultural and natural attractions. Fine dining as well as fast-food chains can be found throughout the region.

**WORTH DOING:** The museum's 1903 Lenox station contains an impressive collection of local railroad historical artifacts, and offers a short "Jitney" train ride within the grounds.

**DON'T MISS:** The Western Gateway Heritage State Park in North Adams includes two museums: the North Adams Museum of History and Science and the Visitor's Center and Museum, which features exhibits on the nearby 4.75-mile Hoosac Tunnel.

**GETTING THERE:** North Adams is located at the intersection of Massachusetts Routes 2 and 8. Lenox is near Highways 7 and 20, south of Pittsfield. Amtrak's *Lake Shore Limited* Boston Branch stops daily at Pittsfield.

**LOCATION:** 10 Willow Creek Road, Lenox (museum);
98 Crowley Avenue, North Adams (depot)
**PHONE:** 413-637-2210
**WEBSITE:** berkshirescenicrailroad.org and
hoosacvalleytrainride.com
**E-MAIL:** forms on websites

# Cape Cod Central Railroad

Cape Cod Central Railroad

The Cape Cod Central operates diesel-powered scenic excursions and meal trains, which also include lunch and brunch outings. It runs from Hyannis over 27 miles of the former Old Colony Railroad. Along the way, you'll pass cranberry bogs, sand dunes, forests, and marshes until reaching the Cape Cod Canal.

**CHOICES:** For evening dining, passengers can select the Friday Cape Cod Dinner Train, which features multiple courses served in candlelight. For less formal service, a shorter ride, lower fares, entertainment for children, and a children's menu, the Sunday Yankee Clipper Brunch Train and weekday Colonial Lunch Train both offer three-course meals.

**WHEN TO GO:** Trains run from mid-May through October in various combinations and with varying frequencies. Sea breezes mean that Hyannis typically remains temperate throughout the operating season, but visiting outside of summer may minimize crowds. The Polar Express operates in November and December from the Buzzards Bay depot.

**GOOD TO KNOW:** Hyannis is quintessential Cape Cod, with all the sun, sand, salt— and tourists. Whale watching, beaching, fishing, golfing, and biking are among the available outdoor activities. The John F. Kennedy Hyannis Museum is located in town.

**WORTH DOING:** An ideal accompaniment to the train ride is an hour-long boat tour of Hyannis harbor and the Kennedy compound offered by Hy-Line Cruises.

**DON'T MISS:** The Cape Cod Dinner Train offers one decided advantage—in addition to the cuisine—over the other Hyannis departures, excursions, and lunch and brunch trains. While the other trains are all 2 hours in length and run briefly along the Cape Cod Canal, only the 3-hour dinner train crosses it on a lift bridge into the town of Buzzards Bay. This bridge features outstanding aesthetics and was the longest of its kind when completed in 1935.

**GETTING THERE:** Hyannis is located on the Atlantic Ocean at the elbow of Cape Cod, 70 miles from Boston. Hyannis and the Cape Cod Central depot are easily accessed from Highway 6 or Highway 28. Buzzards Bay is at the southwest end of the Cape Cod Canal and also accessed from Highway 6.

**LOCATION:** 252 Main Street, Hyannis
**PHONE:** 877-726-7245
**WEBSITE:** capetrain.com
**E-MAIL:** form on website

# NEW HAMPSHIRE

## Ashland Railroad Station Museum

The museum was built by the Boston, Concord & Montreal Railroad as a station around 1869. It is one of the state's best preserved examples of a 19th century passenger station. The museum contains rail artifacts and photo displays. Occasionally, an excursion train stops at the museum. It is open Saturdays during July and August.

**LOCATION:** 69 Depot Street, Ashland
**PHONE:** 603-968-7716
**WEBSITE:** aannh.org/heritage/grafton/ashland.php

## Gorham Historical Society Museum

The 1907 former Grand Trunk Railroad station houses a museum that exhibits rail and local historical items. It displays a 1911 Baldwin steam locomotive, a 1949 F7 diesel locomotive, and several boxcars. Operated by the Gorham Historical Society, the museum is open Wednesdays through Saturdays late May into October.

**LOCATION:** 25 Railroad Street, Gorham
**PHONE:** 603-466-5338
**WEBSITE:** gorhamnewhampshire.com
**E-MAIL:** gorhamhistoricalsociety@gmail.com

# Potter Place Railroad Station

The Potter Place station, which was built in 1874, features striking Victorian Stick-style architectural elements. Listed on the National Register of Historic Places, the station includes a preserved station master's office and exhibits on local history. This historical site also includes a Central Vermont caboose and freight house, both from the early 1900s, as well as a general store and schoolhouse. It is open weekends late May to early October.

**LOCATION:** 105 Depot Street, Andover
**WEBSITE:** andoverhistory.org
**E-MAIL:** pres@andoverhistory.org

# Sandown Depot Museum

Located in a former 1874 Worchester, Nashua & Portland Railroad depot, the museum displays two 1914 Maine Central Railroad flanger cars, an 1880s velocipede, a restored 1958 speeder, and various railroad exhibits. It is open Saturdays May through September.

**LOCATION:** 6 Depot Road, Sandown
**WEBSITE:** sandownnhdepot.org
**E-MAIL:** form on website

# Silver Lake Railroad

Situated just south of North Conway, the Silver Lake Railway offers a 55-minute round trip through this scenic area. From the open-air cars, passengers can see a variety of scenery, from mountains to swamps, as well as an occasional moose. The railroad's museum displays a range of vintage equipment and buildings, including a restored 1941 diner, which you can use for picnics. It is open weekends July to September. Train rides are by donation.

**LOCATION:** 1381 Village Road, Madison
**WEBSITE:** silverlakerailroad.com
**E-MAIL:** silverlakerr@yahoo.com

# Café Lafayette Dinner Train

Café Lafayette Dinner Train

The Café Lafayette Dinner Train provides a top fine-dining experience while traveling through the lush forest and open fields of the Pemigewasset River Valley, which is surrounded by mountains that bear witness to New Hampshire's nickname—the Granite State.

**CHOICES:** The 20-mile round trip follows an ex-Boston & Maine right-of-way that once ran into nearby Lincoln. As the scenery rolls by, diners enjoy a five-course meal. Entree selections change on a regular basis, with orders taken onboard and then prepared to order. Menu items often highlight local ingredients, including blueberries and maple syrup, in season, and salad greens and herbs are grown in the train's adjacent garden.

**WHEN TO GO:** Café Lafayette operates seasonally, mid-May through October. Runs occur on Saturdays and Sundays in May and June, then Tuesdays, Thursdays, Saturdays, and Sundays late June to late October. An expanded schedule is offered for the fall foliage season, mid-September to the end of October, which is an especially scenic time to visit. Book early as demand at this time of year is high.

**GOOD TO KNOW:** Café Lafayette began operation in 1989, making it America's longest continuously operating dinner train under the same name and in the same location, where the train is parked on its own siding.

**WORTH DOING:** There is much to do in the area as the nearby Hobo Railroad operates a number of excursions, as does the Conway Scenic Railroad, which is 40 miles east. Hiking and other recreational activities are found in the White Mountain National Forest and along the Appalachian Trail.

**DON'T MISS:** Enjoy dining under the dome of the *Granite Eagle*. This 1952 Pullman-built car ran on the Missouri-Pacific's *Texas Eagle* and then on the Illinois Central's popular *City of New Orleans*.

**GETTING THERE:** The Café Lafayette Dinner Train is located just west of I-93 at Exit 32 on Route 112.

**LOCATION:** 3 Crossing at River Place, Route 112, North Woodstock
**PHONE:** 603-745-3500
**WEBSITE:** cafelafayettedinnertrain.com
**E-MAIL:** form on website

# Conway Scenic Railroad

Scott Hartley

Here is a New England excursion train ride bursting with great scenery and Yankee character. The setting is in the Mount Washington Valley in the charming village of North Conway. With three different trips to choose from, this railroad offers a bounty of great journeys.

**CHOICES:** Two Valley Train excursions are offered: a 55-minute, 11-mile round trip to Conway and a longer 21-mile round trip to Bartlett. Valley Train passengers have lunch and dinner options aboard the Chocorua. The Notch Train carries passengers from North Conway into the rugged Crawford Notch on a 5-hour round trip, as the first trains did more than 130 years ago. Passengers may choose from coach or first-class service, which includes lunch aboard the Hattie Evans. Vintage diesel locomotives pull most trains, but some midweek Valley Trains take place on a Budd Rail Diesel Car.

**WHEN TO GO:** Valley Trains operate excursions April through December, and the Notch Train runs mid-June through mid-October. Nothing is better than an autumn train ride in New England, but special trains operate throughout the year. For a change of scenery, try riding through snow-covered woods during December.

**GOOD TO KNOW:** Stick to the right side of the Notch Train as it ascends Crawford Notch and crosses the Frankenstein Trestle (named for artist Godfrey Frankenstein, not because it's a monster trestle) and Willey Brook Bridge for excellent views of bluffs, ravines, and streams. Also look for the Elephant's Head rock formation. The later in fall you travel, the fewer colors you'll see, but the better the vistas are from the train.

**WORTH DOING:** The surrounding Mount Washington Valley and White Mountain National Forest offer four seasons of recreational activities, attractions, and spectacular scenery.

**DON'T MISS:** Well, you can't miss the Victorian station in North Conway. Take some time to appreciate this structure that's been at work as a railroad depot since 1874.

**GETTING THERE:** The Conway Scenic Railroad is less than a 3-hour drive from Boston. From Boston, take 1-95 to Route 16, which runs to North Conway.

**LOCATION:** 38 Norcross Circle, North Conway
**PHONE:** 800-232-5251 or 603-356-5251
**WEBSITE:** conwayscenic.com
**E-MAIL:** info@conwayscenic.com

# Hobo & Winnipesaukee Scenic Railroads

David Lustig

Boston & Maine's 72-mile White Mountain Branch from the state capital of Concord north to Lincoln long served paper mills and other forestry companies, but the railroad abandoned this route as those businesses shut down. Fortunately, the entire line has survived, and two tourist train operations on the northern 54 miles keep portions busy for visitors throughout the year.

**CHOICES:** The Hobo Railroad offers 15-mile round trips on the north end of the branch to the many tourists who visit the White Mountain region. Trains out of Lincoln follow the scenic Pemigewasset River south, crossing numerous trestles and passing such locations as Grandma's Crossing and Swimming Hole Bridge, before changing directions at the Jack O'Lantern Resort near Thornton. Farther south, on the shores of its namesake lake, the Winnipesaukee Scenic Railroad offers trains out of Meredith and Weirs Beach to and from Lakeport, always in view of New Hampshire's largest lake. Trains include open-window coaches, as well as cabooses on the Winnipesaukee. Two rare Alco 660-hp diesel switchers work with newer EMD locomotives to power the two railroads' trains.

**WHEN TO GO:** Both railroads operate weekends from May through mid-June, and daily through the summer. The daily operations continue through the fall foliage season on the Hobo, while the Winnipesaukee reverts to a weekend schedule. Santa Claus and Polar Express trains run during late November and December.

**GOOD TO KNOW:** Lake Winnipesaukee is a major summer vacation destination, and the White Mountains also attract large crowds in summer and early October for fall foliage.

**WORTH DOING:** To see more of Lake Winnipesaukee, daytime and dinner cruises are available from Weirs Beach and other towns. You can explore the quaint shops, antique stores, and historic buildings of Meredith. There is much to do in the White Mountains, from hiking and kayaking to viewing covered bridges, waterfalls, and wildlife.

**DON'T MISS:** Try a hobo picnic lunch, complete with a souvenir bindle stick.

**GETTING THERE:** For the Hobo, take I-93 to Exit 32. For the Winnipesaukee, take I-93 to Exit 23. The drive through the center of New Hampshire is beautiful year-round.

**LOCATION:** 64 Railroad Street, Lincoln (Hobo)
154 Main Street, Meredith (Winnipesaukee)
**PHONE:** 603-745-2135
**WEBSITE:** hoborr.com
**E-MAIL:** info@hoborr.com

# Mount Washington Cog Railway

Karl Zimmermann

England may have invented the railroad, but the United States invented the mountain-climbing cog railroad. The first such successful cog—a standard railroad with flanged wheels but with the addition of a gear engaging a toothed "rack" rail in the center of the tracks—was the Mount Washington Cog Railway, which opened in 1869 and has been in operation ever since. The trip takes you to the top of 6,288-foot Mount Washington, infamous for its bad weather but famous for its vistas when the clouds part.

**CHOICES:** Sit back and enjoy the views during the trip to the summit and back. On a clear day, you can see four states, Canada, and the Atlantic Ocean. The trains operate on a steep track that resembles a ladder plunked down on the mountainside. The diesel-powered run up the mountain allows visitors a full hour at the summit.

**WHEN TO GO:** Excursion trains operate late April through November—daily from late May through October and weekends only the remainder of the schedule. Reservations are recommended. In fall, the White Mountains are always spectacular. During November, trains run only halfway to the summit.

**GOOD TO KNOW:** Though most trips are now powered by the railroad's biodiesel-powered engines, from Memorial Day weekend through October, one trip a day, usually the first, is operated with one of the railroad's coal-burning steam locomotives.

**WORTH DOING:** Explore the mountains. Mount Washington State Park is at the summit and contains hiking trails, an observatory, a visitor center, and the stone Tip Top House—a hotel built in 1853 and restored as a museum. The surrounding White Mountain National Forest offers a variety of recreational activities.

**DON'T MISS:** View the railway's original cog engine, *Old Peppersass*, which is on display at Marshfield Base Station. The railway's museum there has recently been enhanced and made more comprehensive and interactive.

**GETTING THERE:** The Cog Railway is a pleasant drive from Boston, Hartford, New York, or Montreal. It is 90 miles from Portland off Route 302. From Bretton Woods, follow Base Road for 6 miles to the railway.

**LOCATION:** 3168 Base Station Road, Marshfield Station
**PHONE:** 800-922-8825 or 603-278-5404
**WEBSITE:** thecog.com
**E-MAIL:** info@thecog.com

# White Mountain Central Railroad

Dave Crosby

The White Mountain Central Railroad is part of the popular family-owned Clark's Trading Post amusement park deep in New Hampshire's White Mountains. The railroad offers 30-minute excursions across the Pemigewasset River over a 1904 Howe truss railroad covered bridge that was moved from the Barre & Chelsea Railroad in Vermont.

**CHOICES:** Once a center for the logging and paper industries, the region now caters to tourists and skiers. Six decades ago, the Clark family added a 1.25-mile railroad to their small amusement park and acquired an impressive collection of geared steam locomotives. Admission to the still-growing park includes the train ride as well as other activities. During July and August, the train is usually powered by steam locomotive No. 6, a Climax geared engine built in 1920. At other times, a 1943 GE diesel switcher is used. The park includes a variety of rides, museums, and displays.

**WHEN TO GO:** Operations are daily from mid-June through the end of August and on weekends in late May, early June, September, and October. The best fall foliage usually occurs in early October, which is also the peak tourist season.

**GOOD TO KNOW:** Lodging, including motels and B&Bs, and restaurants can be found in Lincoln and the surrounding communities. Rates will be the highest during fall, so reservations should be made far in advance for this season.

**WORTH DOING:** The White Mountain National Forest is worth visiting any time of year for camping, hiking, history, and scenic drives.

**DON'T MISS:** The star attractions of the park's operating locomotive fleet are the Beebe River Lumber wood-burning, two-truck Climax, which was recently rebuilt. Also operational are a Baldwin 2-4-2T, a Porter 0-4-0T, and the only known Reo railbus. Other geared locomotives in the collection include an International Shoe two-truck Heisler and a Woodstock Lumber Shay.

**GETTING THERE:** From I-93, take Exit 33, and go south 1 mile on Route 3 (Daniel Webster Highway). In fall, driving along the Kangamangus Highway from Conway offers exceptional views and plentiful wildlife.

**LOCATION:** 110 Daniel Webster Highway, Lincoln
**PHONE:** 603-745-8913
**WEBSITE:** whitemountaincentralrr.com
**E-MAIL:** info@clarkstradingpost.com

# NEW YORK

## Brooks Alco Railroad Display

Located at the Chautauqua County Fairgrounds, this display features an Alco-Brooks 0-6-0 locomotive built in 1916, a Delaware & Hudson wood-sided boxcar, a wooden New York Central caboose, and other railroad artifacts.

**LOCATION:** 1089 Central Avenue, Dunkirk
**PHONE:** 716-366-3797
**WEBSITE:** dunkirkhistoricalmuseum.org
**E-MAIL:** contact@dunkirkhistoricalmuseum.org

## Buffalo, Rochester & Pittsburgh Depot Museum

The brick station is being restored as it was in 1911 with separate men's and women's waiting rooms, a baggage room, and a station agent's desk. It is open Saturdays during the summer and hosts various events including an annual ice cream social.

**LOCATION:** 395 S. Lincoln Avenue, Orchard Park
**PHONE:** 716-662-7002
**WEBSITE:** wnyrhs.org

## Central Square Station Museum

The museum has various pieces of rail equipment on outdoor display including two 0-4-0 steam locomotives, a 1929 Brill car, a circus car, a streetcar, and a GE diesel switcher. Indoor exhibits are housed in an early 20th century depot. It is open Sundays June through October.

**LOCATION:** 132 Railroad Street, Central Square
**WEBSITE:** cnynrhs.org/CentralSq.html
**E-MAIL:** contact@cnynrhs.org

## Cooperstown & Charlotte Valley Railroad

Regular excursion and a variety of special trains travel between Milford Depot and Cooperstown Dreams Park. In the restored 1869 Milford depot, you can view an array of railroad displays. Regular excursions run on Thursdays during summer, and theme trains throughout the year. Railfan Day takes place in August.

**LOCATION:** 136 E. Main Street, Milford
**PHONE:** 607-432-2429 or 607-286-7805
**WEBSITE:** lrhs.com
**E-MAIL:** wendy@lrhs.com

# Empire State Railway Museum

Through photos, films, and artifacts, the museum highlights the history of railroads that served the Catskills. The museum, located in a refurbished 1899 Ulster & Delaware Railroad station, is also restoring several railway cars and a 1910 2-8-0 locomotive. It is open weekends and holidays from Memorial Day through October.

**LOCATION:** 70 Lower High Street, Phoenicia
**PHONE:** 845-688-7501
**WEBSITE:** esrm.com
**E-MAIL:** ovondrak@yahoo.com

# Hyde Park Railroad Station

Built in 1914, the Hyde Park Railroad Station is listed on the National Register of Historic Places. You can tour the restored station, which was designed by the same architects who designed Grand Central Station, and view displays on the area's railroading history. It is open weekends and holidays during summer and on Monday evenings year-round.

**LOCATION:** 34 River Road, Hyde Park
**PHONE:** 845-229-2338
**WEBSITE:** hydeparkstation.com
**E-MAIL:** milotsukroff@netscape.net

# Martisco Station Museum

This restored 1870 New York Central station contains two floors of local railroad artifacts. On the first floor of this Victorian-style brick structure, you'll enter a replica of a small-town railroad station. Items are displayed outside as well. It is open Sunday afternoons May until October.

**LOCATION:** 5085 Martisco Road, Marcellus
**WEBSITE:** cnynrhs.org/Martisco.html
**E-MAIL:** contact@cnynrhs.org

# New York Museum of Transportation

The museum exhibits various trolley cars, a steam locomotive, a caboose, and rail artifacts, as well as highway and horse-drawn vehicles. Trolley rides from the museum take you to Midway station, where you can connect with a diesel train or track car that takes you to the nearby Rochester & Genesee Valley Railroad Museum. The NYMT is open Sundays year-round.

**LOCATION:** 6393 E. River Road, Rush
**PHONE:** 585-533-1113
**WEBSITE:** nymtmuseum.org
**E-MAIL:** info@nymtmuseum.org

# New York Transit Museum

Located in a 1936 subway station, the New York Transit Museum features restored subway cars and other exhibits related to urban transit. Exhibits highlight elevated rail lines and the construction of New York City's first subway line. The museum also offers special subway tours and events during the year. It is closed Mondays.

**LOCATION:** Boerum Place at Schermerhorn Street, Brooklyn
**PHONE:** 718-694-1600
**WEBSITE:** nytransitmuseum.org

# North Creek Railway Depot Museum

Step into the North Creek Depot Museum, and you'll relive a piece of presidential history. The depot is where Theodore Roosevelt learned he had become president upon the death of President McKinley. The museum features an exhibit on this event as well as displays on area history, the Adirondack Railroad, and other railroads. The museum complex includes a restored freight house, an engine house, and a working turntable. The Saratoga & North Creek Railway also boards from the depot's platform. It is open June into October.

**LOCATION:** 5 Railroad Place, North Creek
**PHONE:** 518-251-5842
**WEBSITE:** northcreekdepotmuseum.com
**E-MAIL:** director@northcreekdepotmuseum.com

# Railroad Museum of Long Island

The Railroad Museum of Long Island has two locations: Greenport and Riverhead. Greenport, situated in a Victorian-style Long Island Rail Road freight station, exhibits photos and artifacts of Long Island rail history. It displays an 1898 snowplow and a 1927 wooden caboose. An operating tower and turntable are also on site. At Riverhead, the museum restores its rolling stock and displays several steam locomotives and various railcars. A miniature train ride also operates around the site. Both sites are open on weekends.

**LOCATION:** 440 Fourth Street, Greenport; 416 Griffing Avenue, Riverhead
**PHONE:** 631-477-0439 (Greenport) or 631-727-7920 (Riverhead)
**WEBSITE:** rmli.us
**E-MAIL:** info@rmli.us

# Railroad Museum of the Niagara Frontier

Housed in a restored Erie Railroad freight depot, which was built in 1922, the museum contains a collection of artifacts that recognizes the region's railroading heritage. Also on display are several industrial locomotives, an Erie caboose, and a New York Central caboose. The museum is open summer Saturdays.

**LOCATION:** 111 Oliver Street, North Tonawanda
**PHONE:** 716-694-9588
**WEBSITE:** nfcnrhs.com
**E-MAIL:** museum@nfcnrhs.com

# Rochester & Genesee Valley Railroad Museum

The Rochester & Genesee Valley Railroad Museum is housed in a restored 1918 Erie Railroad depot. Inside, you'll see the original ticket agent's office, waiting room, and artifacts. You can also inspect various early diesel and steam locomotives, freight cars, and passenger cars. It is open Sundays May through October. Start your visit at nearby New York Museum of Transportation and take a train, trolley, or track-car ride over to the RGVRRM.

**LOCATION:** 282 Rush Scottsville Road, Rush
**PHONE:** 585-533-1431
**WEBSITE:** rgvrrm.org
**E-MAIL:** form on website

# Salamanca Rail Museum

This Buffalo, Rochester & Pittsburgh depot has been fully restored right down to the telegraph key in the ticket office, and it includes a ladies retiring room and a baggage room. Artifacts and photos show the history of railroads in western New York and Pennsylvania. A boxcar, a crew camp car, and two cabooses are on display. The museum is open Tuesday through Sunday and weekends during winter.

**LOCATION:** 170 Main Street, Salamanca
**PHONE:** 716-265-2109
**WEBSITE:** facebook.com/salamanca-rail-museum-171739779583682

# Trolley Museum of New York

The museum operates a trolley ride aboard No. 358, a restored 1925 trolley, from Kingston to the banks of the Hudson River, where you can enjoy a picnic lunch. With a stop at the museum, you can learn about trolleys and see them being restored. The museum's collection dates back to the early 1900s. The museum is open weekends and holidays May through October.

**LOCATION:** 89 E. Strand Street, Kingston
**PHONE:** 845-331-3399
**WEBSITE:** tmny.org
**E-MAIL:** admin@tmny.org

# Adirondack Scenic Railroad

Karl Zimmermann

**The Adirondack Scenic Railroad offers excursions behind classic diesel locomotives over 69 miles of the former New York Central's Adirondack Division from Utica to Big Moose.**

**CHOICES:** For serious riders, the railroad offers day-long excursions from Utica to Big Moose, with a stop at Thendara, up to four times a week from mid-July through mid-October. Roughly half allow layover time in Thendara to visit the resort town of Old Forge (reached by a railroad-provided shuttle bus), where possibilities include a 2-hour cruise on the Fulton Chain of Lakes and a visit to the Goodsell Museum. Shorter round trips, either south to Otter Lake or north to Big Moose, run from Thendara June through mid-October.

**WHEN TO GO:** The brilliant foliage of fall makes that season a fine time to ride.

**GOOD TO KNOW:** The railroad offers a smorgasbord of themed trains throughout the year, including dinner, beer and wine, train robbery, and haunted history trains. It's also possible to paddle down the Moose River and ride the Otter Lake train back from Whitewater to Thendara, with canoes or kayaks transported in the baggage car.

**WORTH DOING:** Thendara and Big Moose are deep in the Adirondacks, replete with natural beauty. The region's history is presented at the Adirondack Museum in Blue Mountain Lake. Adirondack Park offers 2,000 miles of hiking trails and hundreds of miles of kayaking routes.

**DON'T MISS:** The Adirondack Scenic Railroad shares Utica's grand 1914 Union Station with Amtrak, making it among the few excursion railroads with national rail connections. Take time to look through this historic station.

**GETTING THERE:** Served by multiple Amtrak trains each day, Utica also has excellent highway access, being located right on the New York State Thruway (I-90). Lake Placid is 30 miles from the Adirondack Northway (I-87).

**LOCATION:** 321 Main Street, Utica
**PHONE:** 800-819-2291
**WEBSITE:** adirondackrr.com
**E-MAIL:** form on website

# Arcade & Attica Railroad

Arcade & Attica Railroad

When steam engine No. 18 blows its whistle, you get a real blast from the past. The Arcade & Attica Railroad offers the last remaining steam locomotive excursion in New York. This scenic ride rolls through countryside that has changed little since the line was formed in the early 1880s.

**CHOICES:** On the 14-mile, 2.5-hour round trip, you can ride aboard steel heavyweight coaches that were built around 1915 or an open-air gondola observation car (just watch out for soot). In the Arcade station, you can view historic photographs, artifacts, and operating model railroad layouts. A 1920s boxcar and caboose are also on display.

**WHEN TO GO:** Regular steam excursions run on weekends May through September. During July and August, additional rides take place on Wednesdays and Fridays, and there is a special extended schedule in October for viewing fall foliage. Murder mystery, Halloween, Christmas, and childrens' special trains also run during the season. Diesel locomotives operate in December as well as on some special trains.

**GOOD TO KNOW:** While snacks and beverages are available on the train, General George's Famous Hot Dogs and ice cream are available for purchase at the Curriers depot, the halfway point.

**WORTH DOING:** A Civil War reenactment takes place during the season that includes a battle with Union and Confederate troops fighting on and off the train. At the encampment, you can see how soldiers and civilians lived in the 1860s.

**DON'T MISS:** On the 15-minute stopover at Curriers depot, watch No. 18 run around for the return trip to Arcade. You can even take pictures and talk to the crew. Then, for a unique experience, hop in the gondola, which is now coupled to the front of the engine, for the ride back.

**GETTING THERE:** Arcade is located about an hour's drive south of Buffalo. The museum is located 3 miles east of Route 16 on Main Street at Railroad Avenue.

**LOCATION:** 278 Main Street, Arcade
**PHONE:** 585-492-3100
**WEBSITE:** aarailroad.com
**E-MAIL:** aarailroadny@yahoo.com

# Catskill Mountain Railroad

Karl Zimmermann

The Catskill Mountain Railroad operates a segment of the former Ulster & Delaware Railroad, which later became New York Central's Catskill Mountain Branch. The train runs from Kingston west towards Stony Hollow, in the foothills of the Catskill Mountains.

**CHOICES:** The Kingston City Limited, powered by an Alco RS1 built in 1950 for Illinois Terminal, boards at the Westbrook Lane station and features open cars and ex-Long Island Rail Road coaches.

**WHEN TO GO:** The Kingston City Limited runs on Saturdays from Memorial Day through Labor Day, with special event trains in spring and during October, November, and December. CMRR also hosts a visiting steam engine at least once a year.

**GOOD TO KNOW: :** For children, the CMRR runs an Easter train in the spring, Pumpkin Patch Express from late October into November, and the Polar Express in November and December.

**WORTH DOING:** Nearby uptown Kingston, the first capital of New York State, offers many stores and restaurants.

**DON'T MISS:** A short drive west is the restored Phoenicia depot, which opened in 1900 and is now home to the Empire State Railway Museum. Farther west is the Delaware & Ulster Railroad, which offers excursions from Arkville.

**GETTING THERE:** The railroad is easily accessible from Exit 19 of the New York State Thruway (I-87). The Westbrook Lane station for the Kingston City Limited is virtually right there.

**LOCATION:** 149 Aaron Court, Kingston
**PHONE:** 845-688-7400
**WEBSITE:** catskillmtrailroad.com

# Delaware & Ulster Railroad

Karl Zimmermann

The Delaware & Ulster Railroad's 24-mile round-trip excursions of roughly 2 hours run from Arkville north to Roxbury, with much of the ride along the East Branch of the Delaware River, across rolling fields and through small towns in the heart of the Catskill Mountains.

**CHOICES:** In addition to the scenic excursions aboard open cars or ex-Pennsylvania Railroad coaches, the D&U also operates a luncheon train, the Rip Van Winkle Flyer. While the Flyer doesn't have a set schedule, operating only if a group has made a booking, the public is welcome on these occasions whenever there's available space, which there most often is. Motive power for the excursion and lunch trains is generally an Alco RS36 resplendent in its original Delaware & Hudson livery.

**WHEN TO GO:** The Delaware & Ulster operates on Saturdays and Sundays from Memorial Day through October, with Thursday and Friday trains added in July and August. There's no more spectacular time for a visit than during the fall foliage season.

**GOOD TO KNOW:** The Rip Van Winkle Flyer is a handsome, five-car Budd-built streamliner, featuring an ex-New York Central parlor-observation car and a dome diner that began life as a Missouri Pacific dome coach.

**WORTH DOING:** The Catskill Scenic Trail lies along 26 miles of the former Catskill Mountain Branch right-of-way. It passes through seven towns and connects with hundreds of miles of other trails. The four-season trail is used by hikers, bicyclists, cross country skiers, and horseback riders.

**DON'T MISS:** The depots at both Roxbury and Arkville offer displays of photographs and artifacts highlighting the history of the Ulster & Delaware. From Mount Tremper, just a short drive away, the Catskill Mountain Railroad offers excursion over another piece of the Ulster & Delaware.

**GETTING THERE:** Arkville is a 43-mile drive on Route 28 from Exit 19 on the New York State Thruway (I-87). Route 28 passes right by the depot.

**LOCATION:** 43510 Route 28, Arkville
**PHONE:** 800-225-4132 or 845-586-3877
**WEBSITE:** durr.org
**E-MAIL:** form on website

# Medina Railroad Museum

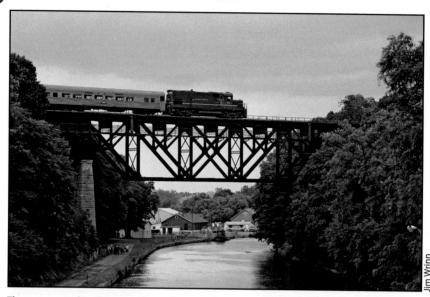

Jim Wrinn

The area east of Buffalo provides a pleasant distraction with small towns, farms, and a relaxed existence. Here, you'll find a museum located inside one of the largest surviving wooden freight houses around. You will also have the opportunity to ride a streamlined passenger train.

**CHOICES:** The old New York Central freight house is huge—301 feet long and 34 feet wide—and contains memorabilia, models, and artifacts. Enter the Union Station archway, and you'll see displays dedicated to the trains, such as the *Empire State Express* and *20th Century Limited*, and railroads, including the Pennsylvania Railroad, that helped develop the area. On a former New York Central main line, you can ride in 1947 Budd coaches pulled by a historic Alco Century diesel locomotive. The trains run on select days.

**WHEN TO GO:** The museum is open year-round Tuesday through Sunday. Specials that leave from the museum include fall foliage trips, Halloween trains, and Polar Express rides.

**GOOD TO KNOW:** Ask about the bridge at Lockport, which, according to legend, was built upside down so as to limit the size of barge traffic on the competing Erie Canal.

**WORTH DOING:** For a unique experience, take a one-of-a-kind ride in a mule-drawn packet boat on the Erie Canal.

**DON'T MISS:** In the museum, watch a large HO scale model railroad in action. The prototypical railroad layout measures 14 feet by 204 feet. Also, take a close look at the lobby, which is refinished as the freight depot office.

**GETTING THERE:** Medina is situated between Buffalo and Rochester, not far from Lake Ontario. From Buffalo, take I-90 east to Route 77. Continue north on Route 77/63 to downtown Medina. There, turn left onto North Avenue and then turn right onto West Avenue.

**LOCATION:** 530 West Avenue, Medina
**PHONE:** 585-798-6106
**WEBSITE:** medinarailroad.com
**E-MAIL:** mrrmuseum@yahoo.com

# Saratoga & North Creek Railway

Scott Hartley

The Saratoga & North Creek Railway operates passenger trains over 56.5 miles of the former Delaware & Hudson Railway's Adirondack Branch, connecting S&NC's namesake cities of Saratoga Springs and North Creek. The northern part of the line follows the Hudson River, which is a scenic, rushing whitewater stream at that spot.

**CHOICES:** S&NC features two levels of service, standard and Diamond class, the latter in full-length dome cars. Meal service is offered on select Pullman table departures. In addition to the Saratoga to North Creek trains, the railroad runs the shorter North End Local from Thurmond to North Creek. Operating twice a day on July and August weekends, this service is designed especially for visitors to the Lake George area.

**WHEN TO GO:** Trains operate Saturdays and Sundays from early May through Columbus Day, with additional departures in peak season. Fall colors are spectacular, making autumn a choice time to ride. The Polar Express operates in November and December.

**GOOD TO KNOW:** The S&NC makes connections at Saratoga Springs to and from Albany and New York City with Amtrak's *Adirondack* and *Ethan Allan Express*.

**WORTH DOING:** Both Saratoga Springs and North Creek offer ample recreational opportunities. Nestled in the Adirondack Mountains, North Creek is a hub for outdoor activities such as hiking and kayaking the Hudson River. Just a few miles away, you'll find the historic Barton Garnet Mines. With its historic downtown, Saratoga Springs is a city of elegant homes and quality restaurants. At its historic track, thoroughbreds race from mid-July through August.

**DON'T MISS:** Leave time to visit the North Creek Depot Museum, which contains exhibits about the Adirondack region and Theodore Roosevelt's train ride to be sworn in as President of the United States.

**GETTING THERE:** Both Saratoga Springs and North Creek are easily accessible from the Adirondack Northway (I-87).

**LOCATION:** 26 Station Lane, Saratoga Springs
**PHONE:** 877-726-7245
**WEBSITE:** sncrr.com
**E-MAIL:** customerservice@premierrails.com

# RHODE ISLAND

## Newport & Narragansett Bay Railroad

Along scenic Narragansett Bay, the railroad operates several different train rides between May and December. On Saturdays, the Grand Bellevue provides dinner in elegantly restored 1940s Budd dining cars. Other offerings include a lunch train, ice cream train, and murder mysteries.

**LOCATION:** 19 America's Cup Avenue, Newport
**PHONE:** 401-295-1203
**WEBSITE:** trainsri.com
**E-MAIL:** info@trainsri.com

# VERMONT

## Shelburne Museum

Outside the museum, you'll see the 1890 Shelburne passenger station, locomotive No. 220, which pulled the trains of four presidents, and an 1890 private luxury car. Other historic buildings, a steamboat, and more than 200 horse-drawn vehicles are displayed at the museum. It is open daily May through December and Wednesday through Sunday January through April.

**LOCATION:** 6000 Shelburne Road, Shelburne
**PHONE:** 802-985-3346
**WEBSITE:** shelburnemuseum.org
**E-MAIL:** info@shelburnemuseum.org

# Vermont Rail System

Scott Hartley

**Vermont Rail System, through its Green Mountain Railroad division, operates regular fall foliage excursions and numerous charters that are open to the public throughout the state.**

**CHOICES:** Fall foliage excursions make two round trips out of Chester on Tuesdays, Thursdays, Saturdays, and Sundays. The 2-hour ride travels west to Okemo Mountain in Ludlow, past farms, through historic villages, climbing steep grades through rock cuts. Friday evening dinner trains travel the same route. VRS runs summer excursions out of Burlington on special weekends, including a Mother's Day brunch from Burlington to Middlebury, a rail and sail train ride with lunch on Lake Champlain's *Spirit of Ethan Allen* cruise boat, and Father's Day trains. The railroad offers chartered public train rides throughout the state that benefit many organizations and charities. Other services include live music trains, Halloween parties, visits with Santa Claus, and trips from White River Junction's Glory Days Festival in September.

**WHEN TO GO:** Vermont is world-famous for its spectacular fall foliage, and VRS's fall foliage excursions is scheduled to offer the best views of that color.

**GOOD TO KNOW:** Train operations and special charters change from year to year, so be sure to check the website before planning your visit.

**WORTH DOING:** Chester has two districts in the National Register of Historic Places to explore, including the area surrounding the depot.

**DON'T MISS:** Green Mountain Railroad's former Rutland Railway Alco RS1 No. 405 has operated in Vermont since it was built in 1951, and makes regular appearances on the fall foliage trains.

**GETTING THERE:** Chester is located in south-central Vermont. Take Exit 6 from I-91 and drive 10 miles north on Route 103 to Chester. Burlington's station is located downtown near the shore of Lake Champlain. Use Exit 14 from I-89 and go west on Route 2.

**LOCATION:** 563 Depot Street, Chester; 1 Main Street, Burlington
**PHONE:** 800-707-3530
**WEBSITE:** rails-vt.com
**E-MAIL:** passenger@vrs.us.com

# REGION 2

**DELAWARE**

1 Wilmington & Western Railroad

**DISTRICT OF COLUMBIA**

2 Smithsonian National Museum of American History

**KENTUCKY**

3 Big South Fork Scenic Railway

4 Bluegrass Scenic Railroad

5 Historic Railpark & Train Museum

6 Kentucky Railway Museum

7 My Old Kentucky Dinner Train

8 Paducah Railroad Museum

17 National Capital Trolley Museum

18 Walkersville Southern Railroad

19 Western Maryland Scenic Railroad

**NEW JERSEY**

20 Black River & Western Railroad

21 Cape May Seashore Lines

22 Delaware River Railroad

23 Maywood Station Museum

24 New Jersey Museum of Transportation

25 Whippany Railway Museum

34 Greenville Railroad Park and Museum

35 Harris Tower Museum

36 Horseshoe Curve National Historic Landmark

37 Kiski Junction Railroad

38 Lake Shore Railway Museum

39 Lehigh Gorge Scenic Railway

40 Ligonier Valley Rail Road Museum

41 Ma & Pa Railroad Heritage Village

42 Middletown & Hummelstown Railroad

43 New Hope & Ivyland Railroad

**MARYLAND**

9 B&O Railroad Museum

10 Baltimore Streetcar Museum

11 Bowie Railroad Museum

12 Chesapeake Beach Railway Museum

13 Ellicott City Station

14 Gaithersburg Community Museum

15 Hagerstown Roundhouse Museum

16 Irish Railroad Workers Museum

**PENNSYLVANIA**

26 Allegheny Portage Railroad

27 Allentown & Auburn Railroad

28 Bellefonte Historical Railroad Society

29 Colebrookdale Railroad

30 Electric City Trolley Museum

31 Everett Railroad

32 Franklin Institute Science Museum

33 Friends of the Stewartstown Railroad

44 Oil Creek & Titusville Railroad

45 Pennsylvania Trolley Museum

46 Pioneer Tunnel Coal Mine & Steam Train

47 Portage Station Museum

48 Railroad Museum of Pennsylvania

49 Railroaders Memorial Museum

50 Reading Railroad Heritage Museum

51 Rockhill Trolley Museum

**52** The Stourbridge Line
**53** Steam into History
**54** Steamtown National Historic Site
**55** Strasburg Rail Road
**56** Tioga Central Railroad
**57** Tunnels Park & Museum
**58** Wanamaker, Kempton & Southern Railroad
**59** West Chester Railroad
**60** Williams Grove Railroad

**VIRGINIA**
**61** C&O Railway Heritage Center
**62** Crewe Railroad Museum
**63** Eastern Shore Railway Museum
**64** Fairfax Station Railroad Museum
**65** O. Winston Link Museum
**66** Rappahannock Railway Workers Museum
**67** Richmond Railroad Museum
**68** Suffolk Seaboard Station Railroad Museum
**69** Virginia Museum of Transportation

**WEST VIRGINIA**
**70** Cass Scenic Railroad State Park
**71** Durbin & Greenbrier Valley Railroad
**72** New River Train
**73** Potomac Eagle Scenic Railroad
**74** Princeton Railroad Museum

## Wilmington & Western Railroad

Wilmington & Western Railroad

**The Wilmington & Western is one of the premier tourist railroads on the East Coast. Attractive equipment, historic steam locomotives, and a scenic route through Delaware's Red Clay Valley make this line a must-see when visiting the mid-Atlantic.**

**CHOICES:** The Wilmington & Western offers two trips from Greenbank Station: a 90-minute round trip to the Mount Cuba picnic grove or a 2.5-hour round trip covering the entire 10-mile line to Hockessin. The train's vintage coaches have adjustable windows, and an open-air car is available during the warmer months. Power is provided by steam or diesel locomotives. A doodlebug also operates. A large variety of special events take place, including dinner trains, murder mysteries, train robberies, and twilight trains.

**WHEN TO GO:** The W&W operates excursions beginning in April. Fall foliage and winter holidays see steam excursions nearly every weekend. Mid-October through early November is prime season for autumn leaves in the Red Clay Valley. December is Santa Claus Express time, with the focus on families and fun.

**GOOD TO KNOW:** Baltimore & Ohio SW1 diesel locomotive No. 8408 has returned to operation after a multi-year restoration, and steam locomotive No. 98 operates on select days.

**WORTH DOING:** Nearby attractions include a tall ship, the *Kalmar Nyckel*, Longwood Gardens, and Winterthur, a 1,000-acre estate featuring a 175-room house that showcases antiques amidst meadows, woodlands, and an expansive garden.

**DON'T MISS:** To beat the heat, try the Christmas in July event with a visit from Santa himself.

**GETTING THERE:** Greenbank Station is about 4 miles southwest of downtown Wilmington on Route 41, close to I-95. Amtrak's Northeast Corridor trains provide service to downtown Wilmington.

**LOCATION:** 2201 Newport Gap Pike, Wilmington
**PHONE:** 302-998-1930
**WEBSITE:** wwrr.com
**E-MAIL:** form on website

# DISTRICT OF COLUMBIA

## Smithsonian National Museum of American History

National Museum of American History

The National Museum of American History features the landmark transportation exhibition "America on the Move." Eighteen multimedia dioramas, each re-creating a specific time and place using artifacts, images, and sound, demonstrate how road and rail transportation shaped America, from before 1876 to 2000.

**CHOICES:** Must-see exhibits include the massive Southern Railway No. 1401, a 280-ton passenger locomotive built in 1926; *Jupiter*, a Baldwin-built narrow gauge 4-4-0; and a 19th century streetcar. The museum also displays *John Bull*, one of the oldest surviving steam locomotives in North America. This 1831 English-made locomotive is displayed on a vintage iron truss bridge that once served the Philadelphia and Reading Railroad.

**WHEN TO GO:** The museum is open every day of the year except Christmas Day. Spring sees the renowned cherry trees in bloom at the nearby Tidal Basin. The Smithsonian Folklife Festival, a huge outdoor exposition of living cultural heritage, takes place each year around Independence Day on the National Mall.

**GOOD TO KNOW:** The museum's west wing is being renovated. While some exhibits have moved or closed, the renovation does not affect the transportation displays.

**WORTH DOING:** Explore the National Mall, where you can visit the Washington Monument, Lincoln Memorial, Jefferson Memorial, and several war memorials.

**DON'T MISS:** Listen to the re-created conversation between the fireman and engineer of Southern No. 1401 as they discuss their upcoming run. Take a full-immersion multimedia journey around Chicago's famous loop as it was in 1959 aboard L car 6719.

**GETTING THERE:** Public transportation is the best option. The Metrorail subway offers convenient access to the museum from its Smithsonian and Federal Triangle stations. A DC Circulator bus loops around the museums.

**LOCATION:** 1300 Constitution Avenue NW, Washington, D.C.
**PHONE:** 202-633-1000
**WEBSITE:** americanhistory.si.edu
**E-MAIL:** info@si.edu

# KENTUCKY

## Historic Railpark & Train Museum

Bowling Green's restored Louisville & Nashville depot contains a rail museum featuring two floors of interactive exhibits. On guided tours, visitors can explore railcars including a post office car, diner, sleeper, business car, and E8 locomotive. The site is open year-round. Escape games are also available.

LOCATION: 401 Kentucky Street, Bowling Green
PHONE: 270-745-7317
WEBSITE: historicrailpark.com
E-MAIL: info@historicrailpark.com

## Paducah Railroad Museum

Operated by the Paducah Chapter of the National Railway Historical Society, the museum displays equipment and memorabilia from railroads including the three that served Paducah. It operates a locomotive simulator, includes replicas of a waiting room and freight office, and has section cars, tools, and an operating signaling system. A steam engine, caboose, and baggage car are displayed a block away. It is open Wednesdays through Saturdays.

LOCATION: 200 Washington Street, Paducah
PHONE: 270-908-6451
WEBSITE: paducahrr.org

# Big South Fork Scenic Railway

Big South Fork Scenic Railway

In the 20th century, short lines and branches brought forth coal for use nationwide, and one of the primary locations was Stearns, home of the Kentucky & Tennessee short line. The coal is gone now, but the K&T has been reborn as a scenic railroad.

**CHOICES:** The railway offers 3-hour trips through the Daniel Boone National Forest and Big South Fork National River and Recreation Area on the former Kentucky & Tennessee Railway. The train follows mountain streams, passes through a tunnel, and crosses a bridge as it descends 600 feet to the floor of the river valley. The ride includes a layover at the restored mining camp of Blue Heron.

**WHEN TO GO:** The railroad runs regular excursions on a varied schedule from April through October. During November, 2-hour excursions run to the Big South Fork gorge. The Banjo Boogie Express, Moonshine Limited, Halloween, Christmas, and other specials operate during the season. Spring is especially beautiful in this part of the Appalachians because of all of the blooming plants that inhabit the mountains.

**GOOD TO KNOW:** The bridge over Roaring Paunch Creek is unique. It was constructed in 1937 from a used railroad bridge. The line crossed the creek at an angle. The bridge's girders were offset in the opposite direction, so it was placed upside down, and the ties and track then added.

**WORTH DOING:** The McCreary County Museum, which is housed in the Stearns Coal and Lumber Company headquarters that was built in 1907, exhibits many facets of Appalachian life including the coal and lumber industries.

**DON'T MISS:** Take the walking tour of the Blue Heron Mine at the end of the run. Built in 1937, this mine and coal tipple operated until abandoned in 1962. The mine was restored with ghost structures (representations of where the actual buildings stood) and oral history exhibits by the National Park Service as part of the Big South Fork River and Recreation Area. You can also camp, hike, fish, and raft the river.

**GETTING THERE:** Stearns is 70 miles from Knoxville, Tenn., and 120 miles from Lexington. From Knoxville, take I-75 north to Exit 141. Take Route 63 west to the junction with Route 27. Take Route 27 north to Stearns. Turn left on Route 92 and travel west 1 mile to the depot.

**LOCATION:** 100 Henderson Street, Stearns
**PHONE:** 800-462-5664
**WEBSITE:** bsfsry.com
**E-MAIL:** info.web@bsfsry.com

# Bluegrass Scenic Railroad & Museum

Bluegrass Scenic Railroad

**The railroad offers 90-minute, 11-mile round-trip excursions over former Southern Railway track through the heart of Kentucky's Bluegrass region.**

**CHOICES:** The diesel-powered trains are made up of vintage coaches from the 1920s and 1930s. Accommodations include four commuter-style coaches with vinyl bench seating and two first-class coaches featuring plush reclining seats and air-conditioning. Many trips have a special theme, which include Civil War train robberies, Pumpkin Patch trains, and Santa specials. Locomotive cab rides are also available. You can view outdoor displays of railcars, equipment, and a rare watchman's shanty. Inside the museum, exhibits showcase artifacts from Kentucky's railroad history.

**WHEN TO GO:** The grounds of the museum are open every day, so you can inspect or photograph equipment when you like. The museum's indoor displays are open on Saturdays and Sundays from mid-May through October, with excursions also operating on those Saturdays and Sundays.

**GOOD TO KNOW:** While in Bluegrass Country, you can tour its noted horse farms and bourbon distilleries.

**WORTH DOING:** Minutes away from the museum are several other local attractions that include the Aviation Museum of Kentucky and the Wildside Winery and Vineyard. If you like smaller trains, visit the Nostalgia Station Toy Museum in downtown Versailles. It is housed in a restored 100-year-old Louisville & Nashville Railroad depot and contains numerous antique toy trains.

**DON'T MISS:** The museum has a large collection of locomotives and rolling stock in various stages of restoration. Interesting cars include U.S. Army boxcars, a Seaboard safety car, and a Louisville & Nashville bay window caboose.

**GETTING THERE:** From Versailles, proceed south and west on Highway 62 for approximately 1.5 miles. Turn right onto Beasley Road into Woodford County Park. The museum is on the left after you cross the tracks.

**LOCATION:** 175 Beasley Road, Versailles
**PHONE:** 800-755-2476 or 859-873-2476
**WEBSITE:** bluegrassrailroad.com
**E-MAIL:** form on website

# Kentucky Railway Museum

Kentucky Railway Museum

Housed in a replica of the original New Haven station, the Kentucky Railway Museum has more than 50,000 items in its collection and more than 120 locomotives and pieces of rolling stock. The museum also operates excursions on 17 miles of former Louisville & Nashville track.

**CHOICES:** The museum's excursion trains take you on a 22-mile, 90-minute round trip through the scenic and historic Rolling Fork River Valley between New Haven and Boston. Diesel operating power includes ex-Monon BL2 No. 32 and ex-AT&SF CF7 No. 2546. You can ride in open-air or air-conditioned coaches.

**WHEN TO GO:** The museum is open year-round, and excursions take place April through December. Trains run on weekends throughout the season with Tuesday and Friday runs added during summer. Spring and fall scenery is nice, with temperatures in the 70s and low 80s.

**GOOD TO KNOW:** Steam engine No. 152 was built in 1905, is listed on the National Register of Historic Places, and was designated the official steam locomotive of the Commonwealth of Kentucky. It is currently out of operation due to maintenance.

**WORTH DOING:** Abraham Lincoln was born nearby, and historical sites to visit include his birthplace, boyhood home, and the Lincoln Museum. Mammoth Cave National Park, Fort Knox, the General George Patton Museum, and My Old Kentucky Home State Park are also close by.

**DON'T MISS:** The museum offers special excursions that include dinner trains, murder mystery trains, locomotive cab rides, train holdups, Santa trains, and days out with Thomas the Tank Engine. A 1940s weekend also takes place.

**GETTING THERE:** The museum is about 45 miles from Louisville and 65 miles from Lexington. If driving from Louisville, take I-65 south to Exit 105, Route 61 to Boston, and then Route 52 to New Haven. From Lexington, take Highway 60 west to the Martha Layne Collins Parkway. Take the parkway to Exit 21 and then Route 31E to New Haven.

**LOCATION:** 136 S. Main Street, New Haven
**PHONE:** 800-272-0152 or 502-549-5470
**WEBSITE:** kyrail.org
**E-MAIL:** info@kyrail.org

# My Old Kentucky Dinner Train

R. J. Corman

**My Old Kentucky Dinner Train operates in 1940s dining cars on 16 miles of former Louisville & Nashville track between Bardstown and Limestone Springs. The passenger waiting room is located in Bardstown's former limestone freight house, which dates from 1860 and is on the National Register of Historic Places.**

**CHOICES:** The train offers both 2-hour lunch and dinner trips, as well as murder mystery, Valentine's Day, North Pole, and other special event trains. Trains are pulled by two ex-Southern FP7s. The Budd-built lightweight cars are of AT&SF, C&O, and PRR ancestry, including the former C&O No. 1921 that operated on President Dwight Eisenhower's funeral train. Two restored depots, Deatsville and Limestone Springs, can be seen on the line.

**WHEN TO GO:** The train operates year-round, and the scenery is especially nice in spring and fall, with temperatures in the 70s and low 80s.

**GOOD TO KNOW:** Founded in 1780, Bardstown is Kentucky's second-oldest city and features a mix of old and new inns, restaurants, and shops. Several local distilleries give tours, and the Kentucky Railway Museum is 15 minutes away.

**WORTH DOING:** The area is rich in history and includes Abraham Lincoln's birthplace and his boyhood home. The Civil War Museum at Old Bardstown Village is dedicated to the war's western theater. The village also contains 11 historic log cabins. The Women of the Civil War Museum and several other museums are also nearby.

**DON'T MISS:** The train passes through part of the Bernheim Forest, a private 14,000-acre nature preserve, a habitat for a variety of trees, vegetation, and wildlife. While in the forest, the train passes slowly over the 310-foot-long, 60-foot-high Jackson Hollow timber trestle built for predecessor Bardstown & Louisville Railroad in 1860.

**GETTING THERE:** Bardstown is about 40 miles south of Louisville and 55 miles southwest of Lexington. When driving from Louisville, take I-65 south to Exit 112 and then Route 245 east. From Lexington, take Route 60 west and then the Martha Layne Collins Parkway.

**LOCATION:** 602 N. Third Street, Bardstown
**PHONE:** 502-348-7300
**WEBSITE:** kydinnertrain.com
**E-MAIL:** info@rjcorman.com

# MARYLAND

## Bowie Railroad Museum

This museum consists of a renovated freight station, switch tower, waiting shed, and caboose. The station and tower contain photos and artifacts. The museum is open Tuesday through Sunday. The Old Town Bowie Welcome Center and Interactive Children's Museum is next to the railroad museum.

LOCATION: 8614 Chestnut Avenue, Bowie
PHONE: 301-809-3089
WEBSITE: cityofbowie.org
E-MAIL: pwilliams@cityofbowie.org

## Chesapeake Beach Railway Museum

From 1900 until 1935, the Chesapeake Beach Railway carried passengers to the Chesapeake Beach resort in cars such as the *Dolores*, which is on display. Housed in the original station, the museum exhibits photographs and artifacts of the railroad and the resort. It is open daily April through October and on weekends in March and November. Special events also take place throughout the year.

LOCATION: 4155 Mears Avenue, Chesapeake Beach
PHONE: 410-257-3892
WEBSITE: cbrm.org
E-MAIL: cbrailway@co.cal.md.us

## Ellicott City Station

Located on the B&O Railroad's historic Old Main Line, Ellicott City Station could be the oldest surviving railroad station in the country. The main depot building was completed in 1831, and the freight house was built in 1855. The museum displays a replica of the first horse-drawn passenger railcar, the *Pioneer*, and a 1927 caboose. Joint admission with the B&O Railroad Museum in Baltimore is available. It is open Wednesday through Sunday year-round.

LOCATION: 2711 Maryland Avenue, Ellicott City
PHONE: 410-461-1945
WEBSITE: borail.org/ellicott-city-station.aspx
E-MAIL: sitemanager@borail.org

# Gaithersburg Community Museum

The museum features permanent and rotating exhibits in a restored 1884 B&O freight house. Also on display are a B&O Budd Rail Diesel Car, a 1918 Buffalo Creek & Gauley steam locomotive, and a C&O bay window caboose. You can also visit the adjacent History Park and restored station, which is now a MARC station. The museum is open Tuesday through Saturday.

LOCATION: 9 S. Summit Avenue, Gaithersburg
PHONE: 301-258-6160
WEBSITE: gaithersburgmd.gov
E-MAIL: museum@gaithersburgmd.gov

# Hagerstown Roundhouse Museum

Located near the roundhouse site in a historic building, the museum presents local rail history through artifacts, photos, and model train layouts. A Baldwin diesel, two Western Maryland cabooses, and a Hagerstown & Frederick trolley are on display. It is open Friday through Sunday year-round.

LOCATION: 296 S. Burhans Boulevard, Hagerstown
PHONE: 301-739-4665
WEBSITE: roundhouse.org
E-MAIL: info@roundhouse.org

# Irish Railroad Workers Museum

Located a short walk from the B&O Railroad Museum, this preserved set of five 1840s rowhouses pays tribute to Irish immigrants who settled in Baltimore to help build the Baltimore & Ohio Railroad and work in its nearby shop complex. Free tours highlight this and other historic locations in the neighborhood. Open Fridays through Sundays.

LOCATION: 918-920 Lemmon Street, Baltimore
PHONE: 410-347-4747 (during museum hours) or 410-669-8154 (after hours)
WEBSITE: irishshrine.org
E-MAIL: info@irishshrine.org

# B&O Railroad Museum

Alexander Mitchell IV

**With nearly 200 locomotives and railcars and hundreds of thousands of smaller artifacts, the B&O Railroad Museum contains one of the largest and most diverse collections of railroad history in a unique, 40-acre setting.**

**CHOICES:** The museum occupies several vintage buildings, including a fully covered roundhouse and turntable built in 1884. The domed roundhouse is a distinctive feature of Baltimore's skyline. The museum houses the largest collection of 19th century locomotives in North America. Later steamers and diesels are well represented, and passenger cars and freight cars round out the collection.

**WHEN TO GO:** The museum is open year-round, with special events scheduled throughout. Train rides are offered Wednesday through Sunday April through December and weekends in January.

**GOOD TO KNOW:** Allow at least a half day for a full tour of the museum and include a 20-minute train ride along the first commercial mile of railroad track laid in America. Combined admission to the nearby Ellicott City Railroad Museum, the oldest railroad station in America, and Mount Clare Museum House, a colonial Georgian plantation house, is also available.

**WORTH DOING:** The museum is in a residential neighborhood just west of downtown and the city's major stadiums. Baltimore has a host of other attractions, including the Baltimore Streetcar Museum, Civil War Museum (in the President Street Station), National Aquarium, Fort McHenry, and the nearby Edgar Allan Poe House.

**DON'T MISS:** Free tours are offered at the Irish Railroad Workers Museum, a set of 1840s rowhouses only 2 blocks away, on Fridays, Saturdays, and Sundays.

**GETTING THERE:** The museum is only a few minutes off I-95 by car. The Orange Route of the Charm City Circulator connects the Museum with downtown and Inner Harbor. MARC commuter trains connect Washington, D.C., and Baltimore on weekends.

**LOCATION:** 901 W. Pratt Street, Baltimore
**PHONE:** 410-752-2490
**WEBSITE:** borail.org
**E-MAIL:** info@borail.org

# Baltimore Streetcar Museum

Alexander Mitchell IV

Since 1968, the Baltimore Streetcar Museum has operated its distinctive and unique collection of streetcars and other transit equipment. You can relive a piece of Baltimore's history by hopping on one of the city's original streetcars for a 1-mile ride.

**CHOICES:** The museum's streetcar ride takes you along the former right-of-way of the Maryland & Pennsylvania in the Jones Falls Valley and passes a historic freight house and roundhouse before turning on a loop for the return trip. On a guided tour of the car house, you can view 13 historic Baltimore streetcars, ranging from a horse car to the last PCC that ran in Baltimore. You'll also see three Philadelphia streetcars (one a snowsweeper), a replica Baltimore PCC (originally a San Diego car), and several buses.

**WHEN TO GO:** The museum is open on Sunday afternoons April through December and also on Saturday afternoons June through October. Special events, such as Santa's Streetcar, take place throughout the year. Summers in Baltimore can be excessively hot and muggy.

**GOOD TO KNOW:** Admission to the museum also includes unlimited streetcar rides and guided car house tours. A family admission plan is also available.

**WORTH DOING:** Baltimore is full of interesting things to see including the picturesque Inner Harbor, National Aquarium, and the USS *Constellation*. The historic Mount Vernon neighborhood, with the Walters Art Museum, Meyerhoff Symphony Hall, art galleries, and eclectic shops and restaurants, is a short distance to the south.

**DON'T MISS:** In the visitor center, you can view historical displays as well as a short video about the trolleys and streetcars that ran in Baltimore from 1859 to 1963.

**GETTING THERE:** The museum is two blocks west of the major north-south streets of Charles Street and Maryland Avenue. It is a short walk from Amtrak's Penn Station, and weekend service between Washington and Baltimore) is now available on MARC commmuter trains. MTA Light Rail also serves Penn Station. A downtown Circulator bus service connects Federal Hill and downtown with Penn Station on its Purple Route.

**LOCATION:** 1901 Falls Road, Baltimore
**PHONE:** 410-547-0264
**WEBSITE:** baltimorestreetcar.org
**E-MAIL:** form on website

# National Capital Trolley Museum

National Capital Trolley Museum

**Inspired by streetcar buildings of the past, the National Capital Trolley Museum's visitor center provides an educational and entertaining look at the history of the region's streetcar systems, complete with an authentic trolley ride.**

**CHOICES:** The museum is divided in three halls. In the Main Hall, you'll learn about the history of local streetcar systems, watch several silent films starring streetcars and actor Harold Lloyd, and see a model electric railway. Conduit Hall contains exhibits that explain how streetcars were powered. In Streetcar Hall, you get a close-up look at a variety of trolleys in the museum's collection. Unlimited trolley rides are included with admission.

**WHEN TO GO:** The museum is open weekends year-round as well as on select Thursdays and Fridays April through November. In summer, the museum offers special programs for children that include activities such as storytelling and crafts.

**GOOD TO KNOW:** Opportunities to ride a boat tram from Blackpool, England, occur on most Saturdays in warm, dry weather and during the Calvalcade of Street Cars each April and September. The museum has a newer exhibit that tells the story of the 20th century comic strip Toonerville Folks, which was centered on the Toonerville Trolley.

**WORTH DOING:** Downtown Washington, with its wealth of cultural and historic attractions, is just 14 miles away.

**DON'T MISS:** Look In Streetcar Hall, look for CTCo 09, one of two remaining specialty cars that swept the snow from streetcar tracks in the nation's capital.

**GETTING THERE:** The museum is located in Northwest Branch Park, about a 20-minute drive from the Capital Beltway and adjacent to the Inter-County Connector toll highway. Bonifant Road is 5.5 miles north of I-495.

**LOCATION:** 1313 Bonifant Road, Colesville
**PHONE:** 301-384-6088
**WEBSITE:** dctrolley.org
**E-MAIL:** facebook.nctm@gmail.com

# Walkersville Southern Railroad

Walkersville Southern, Randy Srba

**The Walkersville Southern Railroad takes you on a pleasant 8-mile, 70-minute round trip through woods and farmland, past a restored century-old lime kiln, and across the scenic Monocacy River.**

**CHOICES:** Trains depart from the original Pennsylvania Railroad station pulled by one of the railroad's collection of switchers, which includes a 1939 Davenport gas-mechanical, a rare 1942 EMD model 40 four-wheel diesel and a GE side-rod 45-tonner. Passengers may ride in former Long Island Rail Road coaches, a covered open-air car, or a caboose. Walkersville Community Park, with covered picnic stands, is located near the depot.

**WHEN TO GO:** From May through October, there are two departures on Saturdays. In October, there are additional trips on Sundays. Dinner trains run on some holidays and on two Saturdays every month May through November. Trains that combine a mystery adventure with dinner run on select dates. Special events are scheduled throughout the year and include Wild West train robberies. For kids, there are bunny trains, teddy bear picnics, superhero trains, and Santa trains. Visiting steam trains are also scheduled on several weekends.

**GOOD TO KNOW:** The railroad has restored to service an additional 3 miles of track north of Walkersville, which is usually used for dinner trains and specials.

**WORTH DOING:** For Civil War buffs, Gettysburg and Harpers Ferry are about an hour away. The railroad also conducts a Civil War reenactment weekend. Historic downtown Frederick is just down the road.

**DON'T MISS:** The railroad's museum occupies a former ice plant and features rail artifacts from the line and a model railroad.

**GETTING THERE:** The railroad is 50 miles from Baltimore or Washington, D.C. From Baltimore, take I-70 west to Exit 53B near Frederick. Follow Route 15 north for 6 miles and then turn right onto Biggs Ford Road. Travel about 2 miles and look for a tall grain elevator, which is adjacent to the station.

**LOCATION:** 34 W. Pennsylvania Avenue, Walkersville
**PHONE:** 301-898-0899
**WEBSITE:** wsrr.org
**E-MAIL:** admin@wsrr.org

# Western Maryland Scenic Railroad

Dave Crosby

Of all the Appalachian railroads, the Western Maryland was one of the most beloved because of its excellent steam power and beautiful mountain setting. Today, the trip out of Cumberland on the main line, with a short detour the last few miles onto a branch into Frostburg, is one of the best parts of the so-called "Wild Mary."

**CHOICES:** Traveling through the mountains of western Maryland, this 32-mile round trip takes you from Cumberland's restored Western Maryland Railway station to an 1891 Cumberland & Pennsylvania depot in Frostburg. You'll ride aboard restored coaches pulled by a 1949 Baldwin 2-6-6-2 steam locomotive or a vintage diesel engine. Regular excursions offer first-class seating, parlor car, dining car, premium coach, and standard coach. Dining car seating is available on Saturdays and most Fridays and Sundays. It includes reserved seating with a meal cooked on board. The railroad also offers murder mystery, wine tasting, Christmas, and other special trains.

**WHEN TO GO:** Trains run year round. The height of the fall color season is especially beautiful, and reservations are required for fall excursions.

**GOOD TO KNOW:** When the train arrives in Frostburg, you have a 45-minute layover. Be sure to find a good spot to watch the locomotive change directions on the turntable. You will also have time to walk down Main Street for shopping or quick dining.

**WORTH DOING:** The Western Maryland station houses the Chesapeake & Ohio Canal National Historical Park's Cumberland Visitor Center, where you can learn more about the C&O Canal.

**DON'T MISS:** Stick to the right side of the train. Leaving Cumberland, the train passes through the Narrows, a gap in the mountain that also allows the highway and parallel CSX (the former B&O) an escape to the west. Just beyond is famous Helmstetter's Curve, a classic horseshoe curve. From here on, views remain mostly on the right side as the train makes its way 1,300 feet higher into the mountains. Open vestibules are found throughout the train.

**GETTING THERE:** When driving, Cumberland is about 2.5 hours from Baltimore, Washington, or Pittsburgh. From either direction, the Western Maryland station is easily reached from Exit 43C off I-68 in downtown Cumberland.

**LOCATION:** 13 Canal Street, Cumberland
**PHONE:** 240-920-6273
**WEBSITE:** wmsr.com
**E-MAIL:** trainmaster@wmsr.com

# NEW JERSEY

## Cape May Seashore Lines

Ride the original equipment operated in south Jersey by the Pennsylvania-Reading Seashore Lines, the Reading Company, and the Pennsylvania Railroad on 30-mile round-trip excursions between Richland and Tuckahoe.

LOCATION: Reading Avenue and Mill Road, Tuckahoe

WEBSITE: capemayseashorelines.org

E-MAIL: conductor@capemayseashorelines.org

## Maywood Station Museum

This station has been restored, inside and out, to preserve its Victorian style. The station museum features local history and railroad artifacts. Also on display are a restored caboose that contains additional exhibits and a New York, Susquehanna & Western Alco S2 diesel locomotive. It is open on a limited schedule April through December.

LOCATION: 269 Maywood Avenue, Maywood

WEBSITE: maywoodstation.com

E-MAIL: info@maywoodstation.com

# Black River & Western Railroad

Karl Zimmermann

The Black River & Western, which also hauls freight, hosts 90-minute passenger excursions (operated by the nonprofit Black River Railroad Historical Trust) over a short segment of the former Pennsylvania Railroad's Flemington Branch between Flemington and Ringoes.

**CHOICES:** In addition to standard excursions that operate on Saturdays and Sundays from Memorial Day through Labor Day, various family-friendly special trains are offered at other times of year. These include the Easter Bunny Express, Pumpkin Train, Trick or Treat Express, and the North Pole Express. Summer excursions board at both Ringoes and Flemington, while theme trains board at Flemington only. Most special-event trains and many summer excursions run with ex-Great Western Railway 2-8-0 No. 60, and the balance with diesels.

**WHEN TO GO:** Each season on the BR&W has its own charm. For a special treat, catch one of the summer excursions or special trains to WoodsEdge Farm, 2.5 miles west of Ringoes over recently restored rails toward Lambertville.

**GOOD TO KNOW:** Flemington is a mixture of quaint and commercial, with 60 percent of its buildings on the National Register of Historic Places. At Ringoes, a Jersey Central baggage car houses a display of railroad artifacts and a model railroad.

**WORTH DOING:** Northlandz, an extraordinary model railroad rich in spectacle, is located in Flemington. With 8 actual miles of track, dozens of trains moving at once, and 35-foot-tall model mountains, it's acres of whimsical fun.

**DON'T MISS:** Just across the Delaware River in Pennsylvania is the New Hope & Ivyland Railroad, which makes it easy to ride two excursion trains in the same day. Almost as close is the Delaware River Railroad in Phillipsburg, N.J.

**GETTING THERE:** Flemington is roughly 35 miles from Philadelphia and 50 miles from New York City. Ringoes is about 15 miles farther from each city. Both Ringoes and Flemington are located just off Route 202.

**LOCATION:** 80 Stangl Road, Flemington; 105 John Ringo Road, Ringoes
**PHONE:** 908-782-6622
**WEBSITE:** blackriverrailroad.com
**E-MAIL:** info@blackriverrailroad.com

# Delaware River Railroad

Dave Crosby

**Ride along the scenic Delaware River in western New Jersey from Phillipsburg to Carpentersville aboard one of only two operating steam locomotives in the state.**

**CHOICES:** The Delaware River Railroad operates several theme trains in addition to the standard excursions along the Delaware River. They include Great Pumpkin, Corn Maze, and Mine Train specials, which are fun for the whole family, while the Warren County Winery Train offers more adult fare on its trip to two local wineries. The railroad also hosts Thomas the Tank Engine and Polar Express events.

**WHEN TO GO:** Beginning in May, regular excursions operate on Saturdays and Sundays through October. Autumn provides particularly breathtaking views of the changing leaves along the Delaware River. Late and early season trains are pulled by diesel locomotives.

**GOOD TO KNOW:** Every year, the railroad rehabilitates additional trackage and adds to the length of the excursion. Current trips operate as far south as Riegelsville, which makes for a 20-mile round trip.

**WORTH DOING:** Across the river, nearby Easton, Pa., features a historic downtown with activities the whole family can enjoy such as visiting the Crayola Museum and the National Canal Museum.

**DON'T MISS:** Having been served by five different railroads, Phillipsburg is rich in railroad history. A short distance away, the Phillipsburg Railroad Historians offer a miniature train ride several times during summer.

**GETTING THERE:** Situated on the Delaware River, Phillipsburg is located along the New Jersey–Pennsylvania border. It is easily reached by automobile via Route 22 or I-78. The station is just off Main Street in Phillipsburg.

**LOCATION:** 99 Elizabeth Street, Phillipsburg
**PHONE:** 877-872-4674 or 908-454-4433
**WEBSITE:** nyswths.org
**E-MAIL:** ccotty@fastwww.com

# New Jersey Museum of Transportation

New Jersey Museum of Transportation

**The museum is home to many rare pieces of equipment, and it offers a short ride on a narrow gauge train on the grounds of Allaire State Park.**

**CHOICES:** Besides looking at the equipment on display, you have the opportunity to tour the museum's shops and see the progress on various restoration projects. The train travels through the scenic state park, which is home to the Manasquan River.

**WHEN TO GO:** The vintage locomotives run weekends spring and fall, with daily operations during summer. During the Railroader's Weekend in mid-September, all the equipment in running shape operates. The Christmas Express, which started more than 30 years ago, begins running in late November and continues into December.

**GOOD TO KNOW:** Founded by one of the oldest all-volunteer railroad preservation groups, the museum began as the Pine Creek Railroad in 1952, using rail salvaged from sand pits.

**WORTH DOING:** In the park, you can explore Allaire Village, a historic 19th century ironmaking town. The park also contains hiking and biking trails.

**DON'T MISS:** Look for the Ely-Thomas Lumber Company Shay locomotive. While currently undergoing restoration, it is one of the smallest Shays left in existence.

**GETTING THERE:** The museum is located in Allaire State Park, not far from the ocean. It is easily accessible from the Garden State Parkway or I-195 off Exit 31B. Signs show the way to the park.

**LOCATION:** 4265 Atlantic Ave, Wall
**PHONE:** 732-938-5524
**WEBSITE:** njmt.org
**E-MAIL:** office@njmt.org

# Whippany Railway Museum

Whippany Railway Museum, Steve Hepler

**The Whippany Railway Museum, which is housed in a restored 1904 freight house, displays a large selection of historic locomotives and rolling stock. Much of the collection focuses on New Jersey railroading.**

**CHOICES:** The Whippany Railway Museum operates several themed and special event excursions throughout the year including caboose rides, Easter trains, and pumpkin trains. Excursion passengers may choose to upgrade seating to the restored Jersey Coast club car. The museum's collection features a 110-year-old Baldwin 2-8-0 steam locomotive (Southern Railway No. 385), a D&H caboose, a railbus, and several vintage diesels including an RS1. Among the structures on the grounds are a Morristown & Erie Railroad passenger station that is made of fieldstone and a wooden water tank. Interior exhibits change each year to highlight a different railroad.

**WHEN TO GO:** The Whippany Railway Museum is open Sundays April through October. Special excursions run on select dates throughout the year.

**GOOD TO KNOW:** The museum grounds are adjacent to the Morristown & Erie Railroad, an active freight hauler. Steam locomotive No. 4039 (former U.S. Army 0-6-0 No. 4039 and ex-Virginia Blue Ridge Railway No. 5) is undergoing restoration for return to operation.

**WORTH DOING:** The town of Whippany plays host to a number of outdoor recreational activities such as the Patriots Path hiking and biking trail.

**DON'T MISS:** Be sure to check out the former DL&W club car No. 2454 as well as former Morris County Central/Pennsylvania Railroad caboose No. 981590, which are undergoing restoration.

**GETTING THERE:** Whippany is in northeast New Jersey, about 20 miles from Newark. It easily reached via I-80, I-78, or I-287. The museum is located at the intersection of Routes 10 and 511 (Whippany Road) in Whippany.

**LOCATION:** 1 Railroad Plaza, Whippany
**PHONE:** 973-887-8177
**WEBSITE:** whippanyrailwaymuseum.net
**E-MAIL:** info@whippanyrailwaymuseum.net

# PENNSYLVANIA

## Allegheny Portage Railroad

This national historic site preserves the remains of the Allegeny Portage Railroad. You can explore the 900-foot Staple Bend Tunnel, the first railroad tunnel built in the United States, visit the engine house, or take a hike. The Staple Bend Tunnel is about 25 miles southwest from the site's main location. From the parking lot, it is a 2-mile hike or bike ride to the tunnel. The site conducts a large number of special events.

LOCATION: 110 Federal Park Road, Gallitzin
PHONE: 814-886-6150
WEBSITE: nps.gov/alpo
E-MAIL: form on website


## Allentown & Auburn Railroad

Diesel-powered round trips to Topton over the 4-mile former Reading Railroad Kutztown Branch leave from the historic 1870 depot. Trains operate roughly 40 times per season, with most departures scheduled around special, seasonal, or holiday events. The ride lasts roughly an hour, and an open car is added in warm months.

LOCATION: 232 Railroad Street, Kutztown
PHONE: 570-778-7531
WEBSITE: allentownandauburnrr.com
E-MAIL: form on website


## Bellefonte Historical Railroad Society

The society operates train rides in fall and winter. While destinations vary, all trains depart from the historic 1889 Bellefonte station. Fall foliage trains travel along Spring Creek and through the Bald Eagle Valley. Family-friendly Halloween and Santa Express rides also operate, using restored 1920s and 1940s passenger coaches.

LOCATION: 320 W. High Street, Bellefonte
PHONE: 814-355-1053
WEBSITE: bellefontetrain.org
E-MAIL: info@bellefontetrain.org


## Franklin Institute Science Museum

The museum features the Train Factory, an interactive exhibit showcasing Baldwin's experimental locomotive No. 60000, which has been at the museum since 1933, and two other locomotives. You'll explore railroad technology as you journey through the exhibit and even take No. 60000 for a test run. The museum is open year-round.

LOCATION: 222 N. 20th Street, Philadelphia
PHONE: 215-448-1200
WEBSITE: fi.edu
E-MAIL: guestservices@fi.edu

## Friends of the Stewartstown Railroad

This group works to preserve and promote the currently inactive Stewartstown Railroad, a 7.4-mile bucolic rural country short line founded in 1885. Open houses, featuring track speeder rides, are held at the railroad's 1914 brick Stewartstown station.

LOCATION: 21 W. Pennsylvania Avenue, Stewartstown
PHONE: 717-654-7530
WEBSITE: stewartstownfriends.org
E-MAIL: friendsofstrt@hotmail.com

## Greenville Railroad Park and Museum

This railroad museum displays Union Railroad 0-10-2 No. 604. Built in 1936, it is the largest steam switcher ever built. Several railcars are also on display. Museum exhibits highlight a CTC panel from Bessemer Railroad, Empire cars, and the invention of the parachute. It is open weekends during May, September, and October. During summer months, the museum is open Tuesday through Sunday.

LOCATION: 314 Main Street, Greenville
PHONE: 724-588-4009
WEBSITE: greenvilletrainmuseum.org
E-MAIL: greenvillerailroadpark@gmail.com

## Harris Tower Museum

Visitors to the switch tower can operate an actual interlocking machine and model board that controls virtual trains from the 1940s. Throw any of the 113 levers on the interlocking machine, which controlled track switches and signals, and watch the model board light up to show what would happen. The tower is next to operating tracks, so railfans can watch Norfolk Southern and Amtrak trains go by. It is open Saturdays June through October.

LOCATION: 637 Walnut Street, Harrisburg
PHONE: 717-232-6221
WEBSITE: harristower.org
E-MAIL: harristower@verizon.net

## Kiski Junction Railroad

This freight-hauling railroad also hauls passengers. From June to October, on Tuesdays, Fridays, and Saturdays, it offers train rides along the scenic Kiski River to Bagdad and back. You can ride aboard a caboose, coach, or open-air car. Special Christmas trains also run.

LOCATION: 130 Railroad Street, Schenley
PHONE: 724-295-5577
WEBSITE: kiskijunction.com
E-MAIL: info@kiskijunction.com

## Ligonier Valley Rail Road Museum

The Ligonier Valley Rail Road Museum is housed in the restored Darlington station, and its exhibits show the history of the Ligonier Valley Rail Road. It is open Wednesday through Saturday and then just Saturdays during winter. It displays a 1905 caboose and has 3,000 items in its collection.

LOCATION: 3032 Idlewild Hill Lane, Ligonier
PHONE: 724-238-7819
WEBSITE: lvrra.org
E-MAIL: info@lvrra.org

## Ma & Pa Railroad Heritage Village

The village has been preserved as a rural commerce crossroads circa 1915, with a general store, post office, and mill. Several pieces of rolling stock are on site, and motor car rides are offered. The village is open on summer Sundays and for several additional special events. Fall foliage excursions take place in October, and the Christmas City Express runs in December.

LOCATION: 1258 Muddy Creek Forks Road, Muddy Creek Forks
PHONE: 717-927-9565
WEBSITE: maandparailroad.com
E-MAIL: info@maandparailroad.com

## Pioneer Tunnel Coal Mine & Steam Train

Take a scenic ride along Mahanoy Mountain as you hear stories about mining, bootlegging, and the Centralia Mine fire. A 1927 narrow gauge 0-4-0 steam locomotive takes you around the mountain. You can also tour a real anthracite coal mine in open mine cars. It is open April through October.

LOCATION: 19th Street and Oak Street, Ashland
PHONE: 570-875-3850
WEBSITE: pioneertunnel.com

## Portage Station Museum

The museum is located in a restored Pennsylvania Railroad train station, originally built in 1926. The first floor contains a stationmaster's office and items from the Pennsylvania Railroad, and on the second floor, there is a display of mining artifacts and a large model train that depicts railroading of the area. It is open Wednesday through Saturday.

LOCATION: 400 Lee Street, Portage
PHONE: 814-736-9223
WEBSITE: portagepa.us
E-MAIL: ihuschak@comcast.net

## Reading Railroad Heritage Museum

You can't take a ride on the Reading Railroad, but you can discover its heritage in this museum. You can tour the museum's large outdoor collection of vintage Reading Railroad cars and locomotives. Inside, you can view a 1930s station agent's office, photographs, and artifacts. The museum is open weekends.

LOCATION: 500 S. Third Street, Hamburg
PHONE: 610-562-5513
WEBSITE: readingrailroad.org
E-MAIL: info@readingrailroad.org

## The Stourbridge Line

The Stourbridge Line offers a scenic train ride that winds along 25 miles of historic railroad tracks in the Lackawaxen River Valley. Seasonal rides take place on weekends Memorial Day through fall, and special trains also operate.

LOCATION: 812 Main Street, Honesdale
PHONE: 570-470-2697
WEBSITE: thestourbridgeline.net
E-MAIL: info@thestourbridgeline.net

## Tunnels Park & Museum

From the nearby Jackson Street Bridge, you get a great view of the twin tunnels, which are 3,605 feet long. The site also features a museum and a restored 1942 Pennsylvania Railroad caboose. The museum includes railroad artifacts and photos. It is open Monday through Friday May through October.

LOCATION: 411 Convent Street, Gallitzin
PHONE: 814-886-8871
WEBSITE: gallitzin.info
E-MAIL: info@gallitzin.info

## Williams Grove Railroad

Operating as part of the Williams Grove Historical Steam Engine Association, the railroad operates steam or diesel train rides on select weekends May into October and during the annual fall steam show at the end of August. Steam power is provided by PRR No. 643. At times during the season, the Run-a-Locomotive program allows you to run one the association's engines.

LOCATION: 1 Steam Engine Hill, Mechanicsburg
PHONE: 717-766-4001
WEBSITE: wgrailroad.com or wghsea.org
E-MAIL: form on wghsea.org

# Colebrookdale Railroad

Colebrookdale Railroad

The Colebrookdale Railroad, once a branch line of the Reading Railroad, winds through deep woods along the Manatawny and Ironstone creeks. The 8.6-mile route traveled on its 2-hour excursions features high trestles and deep rock cuts.

**CHOICES:** Both coach and first-class seating is available, and to take in the panoramic views, all passengers have access to the Secret Valley Explorer open observation car. Locomotive cab and caboose rides also available. The railroad offers many themed rides, including Sunday brunch, wine tasting, and murder mystery trains.

**WHEN TO GO:** Excursions run Saturdays Sundays, and select weekdays, beginning in spring and running through December. Fall foliage can be enjoyed from the Hayride-on-Rails, and autumn evening mini-excursions include a bonfire with music, s'mores, and cider. Daytime Christmas trains include a stop at Santa's Secret Forest, where passengers can select Christmas trees.

**GOOD TO KNOW:** Fine china, silver service, and white jacketed-waiters highlight the Garden Café car, whose décor is inspired by the garden scene in *The Great Gatsby*. Try the Pennsylvania Dutch Pot Pie.

**WORTH DOING:** The Boyertown Museum of Historic Vehicles is located adjacent to the railroad's station. Several rail museums and tourist railroads are located within 45 minutes of the Colebrookdale. Also nearby are Valley Forge and Hopewell Furnace National Historic Sites.

**DON'T MISS:** Along Milepost 6, look for the Devil's Claw, one of the closest rock cuts on a railroad.

**GETTING THERE:** From Highway 100, head west on Route 73 into Boyertown, turn left onto Washington Street, and travel one block.

**LOCATION:** 100 S. Washington Street, Boyertown
**PHONE:** 866-289-4021 or 610-367-0200
**WEBSITE:** colebrookdalerailroad.com
**E-MAIL:** info@colebrookdalerailroad.com

## Pennsylvania
# Electric City Trolley Museum

Dave Crosby

The Electric City Trolley Museum features both static and operating exhibits. The main museum building is located in a former silk mill on the grounds of Steamtown National Historic Site. A 9-mile round-trip excursion takes passengers along the former Lackawanna & Wyoming Valley Railroad to Montage Mountain.

CHOICES: In the museum, visitors are introduced to the history and significance of electric traction with hands-on exhibits, a short film, and several streetcars and interurbans on display. An optional hour-long trolley ride takes passengers to the restoration shop at Montage Mountain, where they are given a walking tour of the facility. Trolley excursions leave from the Steamtown depot. There is also a playroom for children.

WHEN TO GO: The museum is open year-round, with the exception of Thanksgiving, Christmas, and New Year's Day. The excursion season typically runs from late April through October, with cars operating Thursday through Sunday. Additional dates in November and December are often added when Santa Claus pays a visit to the museum. During the baseball season, trolleys take spectators to select home games of the Scranton/Wilkes Barre Yankees AAA baseball team.

GOOD TO KNOW: The trolley operates over a portion of the former Lackawanna & Wyoming Valley Railroad line, commonly known as the Laurel Line, which connected Scranton and Wilkes Barre. The current route features several bridges and a nearly mile-long tunnel under Scranton's South Side neighborhood.

WORTH DOING: The museum is adjacent to Steamtown National Historic Site, where you can explore a number of railroad history exhibits. The Scranton Iron Furnaces, Lackawanna Coal Mine Tour, and Everhart Museum (a natural history, science and art museum) are nearby.

DON'T MISS: Be sure to check the museum's website for updates on the restoration of Scranton Transit car 505, one of only three remaining cars from the city.

GETTING THERE: Take Exit 185 off I-81 to downtown Scranton and then follow the signs to the Steamtown grounds.

**LOCATION:** 300 Cliff Street, Scranton
**PHONE:** 570-963-6590
**WEBSITE:** ectma.org
**E-MAIL:** trolley@lackawannacounty.org

# Everett Railroad

Everett Railroad

Located in south central Pennsylvania, the Everett Railroad provides a 1-hour (or longer) scenic train ride through green farmlands and along the banks of the Juniata River. You'll take it all in aboard open-window coaches pulled by a vintage steam locomotive for an authentic 1940s experience.

**CHOICES:** On this regional railroad, trains operate on many weekends during the year, from March through December. A variety of excursions and special events are offered including ice cream socials, holiday-themed rides, and even trips to a nearby annual agricultural parade. Steam locomotive No. 11, a 1920 Alco-Cooke 2-6-0, powers most trains. Excursions run to Brookes Mills, Roaring Spring, or Kladder.

**WHEN TO GO:** The fall foliage season from late September through October is a favorite time to ride the train, since the hills and mountains surrounding the railroad are prime areas for "leaf-peeping." The Pumpkin Patch and Santa trains have quickly become favorites of many area families.

**GOOD TO KNOW:** The Everett Railroad is also a freight hauler, serving a variety of area industries daily. Restored by Everett, No. 11 returned to service in 2015 for the first time since the 1970s. It was constructed in 1920 and put to work in 1923 by Rhode Island's Narragansett Pier Railroad.

**WORTH DOING:** From the Hollidaysburg station, which is a combination of architectural styles, you'll see Chimney Rocks, an interesting geological feature. Now developed into a park, the limestone pillars offer a scenic overlook of the area. The park includes picnic sites and makes for a relaxing place to visit.

**DON'T MISS:** Not far from the great railroad hub of Altoona, nearby attractions include the world-famous Horseshoe Curve and the Railroaders Memorial Museum, as well as the Allegheny Portage Railroad National Historic Site in Cresson.

**GETTING THERE:** Located about 10 miles south of Altoona, Hollidaysburg is a short distance from I-99. The station is on the south side of the town, where you can take Route 36 (Penn Street) to Loop Road and loop around the road to the station.

**LOCATION:** 244 Loop Road, Hollidaysburg
**PHONE:** 814-696-3877
**WEBSITE:** everettrailroad.com
**E-MAIL:** excursions@everettrailroad.com

# Horseshoe Curve National Historic Landmark

Samuel Phillips

Horseshoe Curve is an engineering marvel completed in 1854 as part of the Pennsylvania Railroad's main line over the Allegheny Mountains. By curving the track across the face of a mountain, builders were able to gain elevation without making the grade too steep for trains to climb. Today, the curve is as vital as ever, serving as a key link in the Norfolk Southern system, with more than 50 trains passing over its three tracks each day.

**CHOICES:** Attractions at Horseshoe Curve consist of a visitor center at ground level and the trackside park, which is accessible by a 194-step walkway or by a funicular railway. First-timers will want to tour the visitor center, ride the funicular up to track level for some train-watching, and perhaps take the stairway back down. The best show at the curve is the passage of a heavy westbound train, laboring up the grade with helper engines on the front and/or rear. Try to stay long enough to catch this spectacle. Recent brush-clearing has greatly enhanced the view of the tracks from the park.

**WHEN TO GO:** The visitor center and funicular are open from early April through late November. In October, the fall colors can be brilliant. Freight traffic tends to build toward the end of each week, so there may be more trains to see on Thursday, Friday, and Saturday.

**GOOD TO KNOW:** The site is managed by the Altoona Railroaders Memorial Museum in downtown Altoona. Combined admission tickets are available.

**WORTH DOING:** Continue west on Kittanning Point Road to Gallitzin and visit the small park at the west portal of one of the tunnels the railroad uses to pierce the spine of the Alleghenies. Cresson, a little further west is also a good place to watch trains, and the Station Inn railfan hostelry faces the tracks.

**DON'T MISS:** The longer you stay at Horseshoe Curve, the greater the chances of seeing two or even three trains rounding the curve simultaneously, a thrilling occurrence.

**GETTING THERE:** Horseshoe Curve is located 5 miles west of Altoona. Altoona is on I-99, 33 miles north of I-70/76. Amtrak's New York-Philadelphia-Pittsburgh *Pennsylvanian* stops at Altoona daily.

**LOCATION:** Veterans Memorial Highway, Altoona
**PHONE:** 888-425-8666 or 814-946-0834
**WEBSITE:** railroadcity.com
**E-MAIL:** info@railroadcity.com

# Lake Shore Railway Museum

Lake Shore Railway Museum

**On the grounds of a former New York Central passenger depot, you'll find a museum that maintains a collection focused on General Electric, Heisler, and Pullman equipment as well as on local railroads.**

CHOICES: The restored New York Central passenger station houses numerous artifacts, and 24 pieces of rolling stock are displayed outdoors. A freight station built in 1869 by the Lake Shore & Michigan Southern also sits on the grounds. View fireless 0-6-0 No. 6, one of 29 such Heisler locomotives built between 1934 and 1941. Recent additions to the museum are a 1939 General Electric 23-ton diesel-electric boxcab, an 18-ton Plymouth model JHG locomotive, and Norfolk Southern GE Dash 8-32B, which is the first Dash-8 to be preserved in a museum.

WHEN TO GO: From Memorial Day through Labor Day, the museum is open Wednesdays through Sundays. It is open weekends in April, May, September, and October. January through March, it is open on Saturdays.

GOOD TO KNOW: Enjoy Christmas at the Station on weekends following Thanksgiving with caboose rides and other activities.

WORTH DOING: Time your visit with the cherry festival in July or the wine festival in September. There are more than five wineries in or near North East. You can also drive along Lake Erie and stop at one of the local beaches. Also, in December, look for the town's Sugar Plum Weekend.

DON'T MISS: CSX's Chicago-New York main line and Norfolk Southern's line to Buffalo run beside the museum. You can watch 60–80 trains each day from the platform, including Amtrak's *Lake Shore Limited* passenger train.

GETTING THERE: The museum is located about 15 miles east of Erie, Pa., near the New York state border. From Erie, take Route 20 to North East, where it becomes Main Street. Turn right on Clinton, right on Mill Street, and then left on Wall Street.

**LOCATION:** 31 Wall Street, North East
**PHONE:** 814-725-1911
**WEBSITE:** lakeshorerailway.com
**E-MAIL:** form on website

# Lehigh Gorge Scenic Railway

Dave Crosby

This 16-mile round trip into the Lehigh Gorge is among the most beautiful in Pennsylvania, a state blessed with numerous great tourist railroads and museums. Trains run on the tracks of the Reading & Northern regional railroad, paralleling a bike path into an isolated, narrow chasm.

**CHOICES:** The 1-hour, narrated excursion follows the winding Lehigh River, curve after curve, and crosses it in several places, until it reaches Old Penn Haven. Leaving from the renovated, distinct Central Railroad of New Jersey depot, you can ride behind a diesel locomotive in a vintage 1920s coach or an open-air car.

**WHEN TO GO:** The railway operates on Saturdays and Sundays May through December. The mountains present a new look for each season, but fall offers beautiful foliage and an extended schedule in October. Santa trains run in December.

**GOOD TO KNOW:** In 1953, the towns of Mauch Chunk and East Mauch Chunk merged into one town with the name of Jim Thorpe when that famous athlete was buried there. Looking for a place that would help develop a memorial for her husband, who had no previous ties to the area, Thorpe's widow found assistance from the two towns.

**WORTH DOING:** Explore the town of Jim Thorpe, a charming village of shops, stores, and B&Bs, many featuring Victorian architecture. The town was once known as the Switzerland of America for its steep hillsides, narrow streets, and terraced gardens.

**DON'T MISS:** On the bike train to White Haven, you ride the train up Lehigh Gorge and pedal your bike back the 25 miles to Jim Thorpe along a scenic bike trail.

**GETTING THERE:** Located in the heart of the Poconos, Jim Thorpe is approximately 90 miles from Philadelphia. From there, take I-476 to Exit 74. Then take Route 209 south into Jim Thorpe, where it becomes Susquehanna Street, and follow it to the railway.

**LOCATION:** 1 Susquehanna Street, Jim Thorpe
**PHONE:** 610-562-2102
**WEBSITE:** lgsry.com
**E-MAIL:** form on website

# Middletown & Hummelstown Railroad

Dave Crosby

**If you're looking for a relaxing train ride in central Pennsylvania, here's your ride. The M&H provides a trip along the Swatara Creek that travels past the ruins of a canal and makes a dramatic bridge crossing of a creek on an 10-mile round trip.**

CHOICES: The M&H offers plenty of different trips, from scenic outings to murder mystery dinner trains. Trains depart from the 1891 freight station in Middletown. Most trains are powered by a 65-ton GE diesel-electric center-cab locomotive. Aboard the train's Delaware, Lackawanna & Western coaches, you'll hear informative narration about the area.

WHEN TO GO: Excursions begin Memorial Day weekend and end in October. They run Thursdays, Saturdays, and Sundays during summer and weekends during the remaining schedule. There are numerous special events during the year, including Easter Bunny and Santa trains. Ice cream sundae trains run most Sunday afternoons.

GOOD TO KNOW: Formerly part of the Reading Railroad, the M&H also provides freight service using Alco diesel switchers. At the Middletown yard, the railroad displays a collection of rolling stock that includes antique freight equipment, streetcars, and passenger cars.

WORTH DOING: Nothing finer than breakfast or lunch at Kuppy's Diner, a short walk from the boarding station. In Hershey, you can hop on more than 60 rides, including roller coasters and water rides, at Hersheypark amusement park.

DON'T MISS: Tour nearby Indian Echo Caves for an interesting underground outing.

GETTING THERE: Middletown is situated between Harrisburg and Hershey, both 10 miles away, and 100 miles from Philadelphia. From Philadelphia, take I-76 to Route 283. Exit at Middletown and from Main Street, turn left on Pine Street, and then left on Brown Street to get to the station.

**LOCATION:** 136 Brown Street, Middletown
**PHONE:** 877-987-2469 or 717-944-4435
**WEBSITE:** mhrailroad.com
**E-MAIL:** form on website

# New Hope & Ivyland Railroad

New Hope & Ivyland Railroad

**The New Hope & Ivyland Railroad provides a scenic, 45-minute trip through the rolling hills and valleys of Bucks County, leaving from the quaint resort village of New Hope on the Delaware River.**

**CHOICES:** In addition to the traditional excursion to Lahaska, New Hope also offers a 90-minute Buckingham Valley evening ride. The 1920s vintage passenger coaches are pulled by steam engine No. 40, a 1925 Baldwin type 2-8-0, or a diesel locomotive. Coach class, first-class, and open-air seating is available. Coach class provides standard seating and heating in winter, while first-class offers climate-control year-round and a full-service bar.

**WHEN TO GO:** The New Hope & Ivyland operates year-round. From January through March, excursions run on Saturdays and Sundays. In April, May, and November, Friday runs are added to the weekend schedule. And beginning Memorial Day weekend, excursions operate daily through the end of October. Special trains operate throughout the year, and December is filled with holiday trains.

**GOOD TO KNOW:** The restored Victorian station at New Hope has been in operation since 1891. An original "witch's hat" station, it once housed the railroad's telegraph operator.

**WORTH DOING:** While in New Hope, you can take a mule-drawn boat ride in the Delaware Division of the Pennsylvania Canal or stroll along the Delaware River. History buffs can visit Valley Forge National Historical Park, which is about 40 miles from New Hope.

**DON'T MISS:** Try out open-air car No. 1525 and enjoy the breeze—and unobstructed views. The former Reading car was built in 1925.

**GETTING THERE:** New Hope is 45 miles northeast of Philadelphia. From Philadelphia, take the Pennsylvania Turnpike east to the Willow Grove exit. Then take Route 611 to Route 202. Turn north on Route 202 and go 10 miles to Route 179, which leads you into New Hope.

**LOCATION:** 32 W. Bridge Street, New Hope
**PHONE:** 215-862-2332
**WEBSITE:** newhoperailroad.com
**E-MAIL:** on website

# Oil Creek & Titusville Railroad

Oil Creek & Titusville Railroad

The Oil Creek & Titusville Railroad follows Oil Creek through the nation's first oil patch, where oil was discovered by Colonel Edwin L. Drake in 1859. Along the way, the train passes a number of ghost towns that sprang up during the oil boom and just as quickly disappeared when the rush faded.

CHOICES: Much of the route along the 3-hour excursion runs through Oil Creek State Park, a popular venue for camping, fishing, and kayaking. Along the way, tour guides tell stories about Oil Country. One choice is to ride one way and then bike, hike canoe, or kayak back to your vehicle. For a more comfortable rider, try first-class seating in the Wabash Cannonball.

WHEN TO GO: The Oil Creek & Titusville operates weekends June through October, with select Wednesdays and Thursdays added in July and August, and October sees trains running Wednesday through Sunday. The fall foliage season is spectacular in the area and is a favored time to visit.

GOOD TO KNOW: At various times throughout the year, murder mystery dinner trains, Peter Cottontail trains, and Santa trains operate. A highlight is Speeder Day, when visitors have an opportunity to ride small railway maintenance cars along part of the line. A World War II reenactment also takes place.

WORTH DOING: Stopping at Drake Well Park gives you a chance to see a replica of the very first oil well in the United States, from which oil still flows today. The park also displays a large collection of machinery and equipment used to produce oil.

DON'T MISS: The OC&TR operates the only Railway Post Office in regular service in the United States. Postcards mailed on the train will receive the official "Oil Creek & Titusville R.P.O." cancellation.

GETTING THERE: Titusville is in the forested mountains of northwestern Pennsylvania. From I-80, take Exit 29 and then Route 8 north through Oil City to Titusville. From Erie and I-90, take Route 97 south to its junction with Route 8 and then follow Route 8 to Titusville.

LOCATION: 409 S. Perry Street, Titusville
PHONE: 814-676-1733
WEBSITE: octrr.org
E-MAIL: ocandt@usachoice.net

# Pennsylvania Trolley Museum

Jeff terry

Starting operations in 1963, the Pennsylvania Trolley Museum is the oldest trolley museum in Pennsylvania. It offers a short trolley ride on which you can enjoy the clang of the gong and the rumble of steel wheels on the rails as the surge of electricity speeds an historic trolley along the line. Part of the 4-mile round trip is over track of the original interurban route to Pittsburgh.

**CHOICES:** The museum has an extensive collection (almost 50) of restored and operational trolleys, several of which are used on operating days. Your admission includes a short guided tour and unlimited trolley rides. On weekends, for an extra nominal fee, you can take an extended behind-the-scenes tour in the Trolley Display Building, where you can see many of the museum's restored trolleys.

**WHEN TO GO:** The museum is open daily in June, July, and August; however, with a few exceptions, there no trolleys or tours on Mondays. It is also open weekends during April and May and then September through December. Special events, many aimed at children, take place throughout the year.

**GOOD TO KNOW:** One of the museum's restored structures is the Richfol shelter, where you can board the trolley. It was a stop in Canonsburg on the original Washington interurban trolley line. It was then moved to a farm, where it became a school bus stop, before being brought to the museum in 1982 and restored.

**WORTH DOING:** Washington is home to a craft distillery, the Washington Winery, and Meadows Racetrack and Casino, which conducts harness racing year-round. You can also take in a Washington Wild Things game at CONSOL Energy Park, when the independent minor league baseball is at home.

**DON'T MISS:** Be sure to view the 12-minute introductory video that presents an overview of the trolley era and the museum. The visitor center includes a pictorial exhibit about trolleys and interactive activities for kids including a small trolley to play on.

**GETTING THERE:** About 30 miles south of Pittsburgh, the museum is a short distance from I-79. You can reach it by taking either Exit 40 or Exit 41. From either exit, follow North Main Street to Museum Road, turn left and go a half-mile to the museum. It's very close to I-70 and Highway 19 as well.

**LOCATION:** 1 Museum Road, Washington
**PHONE:** 724-228-9256
**WEBSITE:** pa-trolley.org
**E-MAIL:** ptm@pa-trolley.org

# Railroad Museum of Pennsylvania

Rob McGonigal

The Railroad Museum of Pennsylvania boasts one of the top rolling stock collections in the United States. The highlight is a dozen steam locomotives preserved by the Pennsylvania Railroad in the 1950s; very few PRR engines exist elsewhere. The collection also includes about 100 other locomotives and cars from the PRR and other railroads serving the state, many displayed in a 100,000-square-foot exhibition hall.

**CHOICES:** Go up, down, and out: an elevated walkway gives a fine view of the Rolling Stock Hall, a pit between the rails allows inspection of the underside of one of the locomotives, and tours of the rolling stock yard are sometimes available. Be sure to see recently restored PRR 4-4-2 No. 460, the engine that sped newsreel films to New York of Charles Lindbergh's arrival in Washington after his famous flight; PRR GG1 No. 4935, the best-preserved example of the most famous class of electric locomotives; and PRR E7 No. 5901, the only surviving example of General Motors' top-selling passenger diesel.

**WHEN TO GO:** The museum is open every day except for certain major holidays and most Mondays November through March. A variety of special events are scheduled throughout the year.

**GOOD TO KNOW:** Part of the exhibition hall is patterned after an early 20th century, glass-roofed train shed. The hall contains about 50 locomotives and railcars on five tracks.

**WORTH DOING:** Spend part of the day at the museum and then take a ride on a steam train on the Strasburg Rail Road, located right across the road.

**DON'T MISS:** Take the controls of a diesel locomotive with the museum's cab simulator and feel the thrill of operating a locomotive on a trip from Lancaster to Harrisburg.

**GETTING THERE:** The museum is on Route 741 (Gap Road) 1 mile east of Strasburg, which is about 15 minutes from Lancaster, 1 hour from Harrisburg or Reading, and 90 minutes from Philadelphia. Most folks take Route 30 to Route 896 south to Route 741.

**LOCATION:** 300 Gap Road, Strasburg
**PHONE:** 717-687-8628
**WEBSITE:** rrmuseumpa.org
**E-MAIL:** info@rrmuseumpa.org

# Pennsylvania
# Railroaders Memorial Museum

Jeff Terry

Of all the places in the United States deserving a first-rate railroad museum, Altoona is certainly at the top of the list. The museum here is among the best when it comes to providing an interactive experience and telling the story of this shop town that in the 1920s employed more than 15,000 Pennsylvania Railroad workers. Today, Altoona is still a shop city for Norfolk Southern, and the museum tells the story of how it became so important and the people who made it so.

**CHOICES:** Be sure to step into the re-created community bar to hear all about the lives of railroaders as they sit and sip a cold one. Also look at the exhibit on the PPR's testing and research lab. Their efforts were astounding.

**WHEN TO GO:** The museum is open daily May through October and Friday through Sunday in November and April. It closes December through March.

**GOOD TO KNOW:** The museum is housed in the Pennsylvania Railroad's former master mechanic's building, which was built in 1882. It features three floors of exhibits.

**WORTH DOING:** The Allegheny Portage Railroad National Historic Site and Staple Bend Tunnel are both within 25 miles of Altoona.

**DON'T MISS:** Take a day and spend half of it in the museum and the other half watching trains at Horseshoe Curve. Combined admission tickets are available.

**GETTING THERE:** Altoona is about 95 miles east of Pittsburgh. From Pittsburgh, take Route 22 to I-99 north. Take Exit 33, 17th Street, and a right turn on Ninth Avenue takes you to the museum.

**LOCATION:** 1300 Ninth Avenue, Altoona
**PHONE:** 888-425-8666 or 814-946-0834
**WEBSITE:** railroadcity.com
**E-MAIL:** info@railroadcity.com

# Rockhill Trolley Museum

Rockhill Trolley, Joel Salomon

Established on the right of way of the former Shade Gap branch of the East Broad Top Railroad, the Rockhill Trolley Museum includes one of the nation's most diverse collection of historic trolleys, interurbans, and subway cars. Admission includes a 3-mile ride that takes you past two carbarns, through pleasant woodlands and meadows, and near Blacklog Creek.

**CHOICES:** The museum's 23-piece collection ranges from wooden streetcars to an articulated Liberty Liner interurban train to one of the first modern "light rail" vehicles. Trolley rides depart from the Meadow Street platform, travel to Blacklog Narrows, and reverse for the return trip. You can arrange to disembark anywhere along the trolley line to take photographs and be picked up later by another car.

**WHEN TO GO:** The museum is open Saturdays and Sundays Memorial Day weekend through October, with additional special events in November and December. Special weekends for particular cars in the fleet are also scheduled through the year.

**WORTH DOING:** The annual Fall Spectacular occurs Columbus Day weekend, with extra runs and equipment on display.

**DON'T MISS:** Immediately adjacent to the museum is the historic, narrow gauge East Broad Top Railroad. It is mostly extant (albeit overgrown in places) and can be followed and explored from Mount Union to Robertsdale and Woodvale over back country roads.

**GOOD TO KNOW:** Raystown Lake area is about an hour away. There, you can explore caves such as Indian Caverns, Lincoln Caverns, and Penn's Cave. You can also hike, bike, and take part in various water sports.

**GETTING THERE:** Rockhill Furnace is in south-central Pennsylvania between Harrisburg and Altoona on Highway 522 between the Fort Littleton exit of the Pennsylvania Turnpike and Mount Union (junction with Highway 22). To get to the museum from Highway 522, turn left on Highway 994. Cross the bridge over Blacklog Creek and go just past the post office.

**LOCATION:** 430 Meadow Street, Rockhill Furnace
**PHONE:** 610-428-7200 (weekdays) or 814-447-9576 (weekends)
**WEBSITE:** rockhilltrolley.org
**E-MAIL:** form on website

# Steam Into History

Karl Zimmermann

With the mission of re-creating Civil War railroad history, Steam Into History operates over 10 miles of the former Northern Central Railway, the line that Abraham Lincoln rode on the way to deliver his Gettysburg Address. This history is brought to life by a narrator, along with reenactors and musicians. Motive power is most often 4-4-0 No. 17, an accurate replica of an 1869 Rodgers Locomotive Works engine. An ex-Pennsylvania Railroad GP10 sometime fills in.

**CHOICES:** Steam Into History offers a 1-hour round-trip excursion to Glen Rock and a 2.5-hour round trip to Hanover Junction. The Hanover Junction Limited provides passengers a layover of roughly 30 minutes for exploring the original Hanover Junction station, which was completed in 1852 and contains a small museum.

**WHEN TO GO:** Trains operate on weekends from April through December, with the schedule expanding to five days a week in summer and in October for fall foliage. The railroad offers holiday-themed events, including Christmas tree trains that allow passengers to harvest their own trees.

**GOOD TO KNOW:** York County abounds in Civil War history, with Gettysburg and Gettysburg National Military Park only 35 miles from New Freedom.

**WORTH DOING:** Those wishing to explore more of the Northern Central, on foot or bicycle, can walk or ride the 21-mile Heritage Rail Trail, which extends from the Mason-Dixon Line (just south of New Freedom) north to York.

**DON'T MISS:** During one weekend in mid-November the railroad recreates President Lincoln's 1863 journey over the Northern Central on his way to deliver the Gettysburg Address.

**GETTING THERE:** New Freedom is located 18 miles south of York. Steam Into History is 4 miles from the Shrewsbury exit on I-83. From there, take 851 west into Shrewsbury, turn left on Main Street, follow it for several miles, and turn right in New Freedom on Constitution Avenue. Then turn right on Main Street and go just past the tracks.

**LOCATION:** 2 W. Main Street, New Freedom
**PHONE:** 717-942-2370
**WEBSITE:** steamintohistory.com
**E-MAIL:** form on website

# Steamtown National Historic Site

NPS

The former Delaware Lackawanna & Western railroad shop complex is home to one of the East's most complete railroad history exhibits. Located on 66 acres, including the preserved Lackawanna's roundhouse, Steamtown provides a shrine to steam-era railroading in the northeastern United States. It also offers both short and long train rides. The real treat is a walk through the active portion of the roundhouse, where steam locomotives are still maintained.

**CHOICES:** The site includes both a steam history museum as well as a technology museum. The orientation movie, archeology exhibit, and equipment displays offer hands-on experiences. For a brief visit, you can walk through the museums and take the Scranton Limited, a half-hour ride on vintage commuter coaches. If you have time, schedule your visit when you can spend a day with the exhibits and then ride a longer steam excursion train to Moscow, or other locations in the Pocono Mountain region.

**WHEN TO GO:** Steamtown is open daily year-round with the exception of Thanksgiving, Christmas, and New Year's Day. The Scranton Limited runs on select days mid-April through November. On some Sundays, the Scranton Limited transforms into the Nay Aug Limited, an expanded ride that travels to the Ice Age era Nay Aug Gorge Natural Landmark. Most Moscow excursions operate on weekends beginning in May.

**GOOD TO KNOW:** Monthly tour and Scranton Limited schedules are posted online about a week before the beginning of each month. The 45-minute shop tour, offered daily, provides a good behind-the-scenes look at heavy-duty restoration work underway on several locomotives.

**WORTH DOING:** Nearby, you can view the Scranton Iron Furnaces or tour a coal mine.

**DON'T MISS:** Union Pacific No. 4012 is one of the largest steam locomotives ever built. The Big Boy is the only one of its type on exhibit in the eastern United States.

**GETTING THERE:** From I-81, take Exit 185. At the first traffic light, turn left on Lackawanna Avenue. Pass the mall and turn left on Cliff Street. GPS: 350 Cliff St., Scranton, PA 18503

**LOCATION:** 350 Cliff Street, Scranton
**PHONE:** 888-693-9391 or 570-340-5200
**WEBSITE:** nps.gov/stea
**E-MAIL:** form on website

# Strasburg Rail Road

Strasburg Rail Road

The 9-mile, 45-minute round trip from Strasburg to Paradise through Amish farmland, aboard authentic 19th century wooden coaches being pulled by a steam locomotive, recalls travel before automobiles. Narration provides an entertaining and educational ride.

**CHOICES:** Different types of service are available on regular excursions, and you can ride in a coach, open-air car, dining car, or first-class car. Get off the train at Groffs Grove for a picnic or to just watch the action. Lunch, dinner, wine and cheese, train robberies, and other special trains are also offered. Tours of the shop and engine house are available.

**WHEN TO GO:** Steam trains are scheduled to run every day April through October and on weekends and for special events during March, November, and December. A rare, wooden self-propelled doodlebug from a long-abandoned Lancaster County short line runs several days in March and in November. Strasburg's Thomas the Tank Engine events draw big crowds three times a year.

**GOOD TO KNOW:** Locomotives pull trains tender-first on the outbound trips and engine-first on the return. Sit on the right-hand side of the train out of Strasburg for the best view of the locomotive changing ends at Paradise. For an interesting overnight experience, you can stay in one of 38 cabooses at the nearby Red Caboose Motel.

**WORTH DOING:** Take a drive through the heart of scenic Pennsylvania Dutch Country, one of the largest Amish communities in America. Buggy rides are offered by various enterprises.

**DON'T MISS:** View the Railroad Museum of Pennsylvania's world-class collection, which is right across the road or take in the nearby Toy Train Museum.

**GETTING THERE:** The railroad is on Gap Road (Route 741) 1 mile east of Strasburg.

**LOCATION:** 301 Gap Road, Strasburg
**PHONE:** 866-725-9666
**WEBSITE:** strasburgrailroad.com
**E-MAIL:** srrtrain@strasburgrailroad.com

# Tioga Central Railroad

Sam Botts

Tioga Central operates over a right-of-way that in part dates to 1840. The ride takes you along Crooked Creek, through forests, and to Lake Hammond, a large reservoir. It's a good trip at a brisk pace behind rare Alco diesels.

**CHOICES:** The Tioga Central, in addition to operating its regular, 24-mile, 90-minute excursions, offers a dinner train. Ride the train's open-air car and keep a lookout for wildlife such as osprey, blue heron, deer, and even bald eagles.

**WHEN TO GO:** The railroad offers regular excursions Thursdays through Sundays from Memorial Day weekend into September. In fall, additional excursions operate to view the spectacular foliage.

**GOOD TO KNOW:** The railroad owes its good views of Lake Hammond, which it parallels for much of its journey, to a dam project that almost resulted in the railroad's abandonment. Fortunately, the railroad was relocated to the side of the reservoir.

**WORTH DOING:** Explore the nearby Pine Creek Gorge however you like. You can take a hike, ride a bike, or raft a river. Called the Grand Canyon of Pennsylvania, the 1,000-foot-deep gorge winds its way through acres of scenic landscape. Various parks provide breathtaking views of the canyon from hiking trails. You can also bike the Pine Creek Trail, a former rail line, through the canyon. Rafting is best in spring.

**DON'T MISS:** At the station, take a look at the railroad's oldest piece of rolling stock. Now an office, Car 54 was originally a double-ended, open-platform paymaster car built in 1894 for the Grand Trunk Western.

**GETTING THERE:** Wellsboro is in north-central Pennsylvania, 50 miles north of Williamsport. Trains leave from Wellsboro Junction, which is about 3 miles north of Wellsboro on Route 287.

**LOCATION:** 7 Muck Road, Wellsboro
**PHONE:** 570-724-0990
**WEBSITE:** tiogacentral.com

# Wanamaker, Kempton & Southern Railroad

Jeff Terry

While it's short on mileage, the Wanamaker Kempton & Southern, known as the Hawk Mountain Line, is long on atmosphere. For more than 50 years, this friendly little line has operated in the relaxed style of a country branch line railroad, with authentically painted and lettered equipment.

**CHOICES:** Diesel locomotives power trains on the 40-minute round trip, with hourly departures on operating days. In addition to scheduled trains, a variety of special events take place throughout the season, including Easter Bunny, Harvest Moon, Halloween and Santa specials, as well as murder mystery, wine and cheese, and fall foliage trains.

**WHEN TO GO:** WK&S operates trains on Sundays May through October. As it passes farms and orchards and crosses Ontelaunee Creek, the excursion takes riders through beautiful scenery at any time of year. The fall colors in late September and early October on the surrounding mountains are breathtaking.

**GOOD TO KNOW:** Every train includes an open-air car and a caboose as well as a standard, open-window coach.

**WORTH DOING:** A visit to WK&S can easily be combined with a trip to other rail attractions such as Steamtown National Historic Site and the Pioneer Tunnel Coal Mine. Also close by are the Mid-Atlantic Air Museum, Crystal Cave, Hawk Mountain Raptor Sanctuary, and Roadside America, where you can see 200 years of American life depicted in miniature.

**DON'T MISS:** Ride the left side of the train for the best views of Ontelaunee Creek and vistas of the nearby mountains, orchards, and farms. Be sure to leave the train during the layover at Wanamaker for a quick look at the original station and the old-fashioned general store just a few steps away.

**GETTING THERE:** WK&S is located in east-central Pennsylvania, 5 miles north of I-78, just off Route 737 in Kempton. Follow signs to the station, which is a short distance north of the village.

**LOCATION:** 42 Community Center Drive, Kempton
**PHONE:** 610-756-6469
**WEBSITE:** kemptontrain.com
**E-MAIL:** allaboard@kemptontrain.com

# West Chester Railroad

West Chester Railroad, Derek Slifer

The West Chester Railroad operates 90-minute round-trip excursions over a historic route through the Chester Creek Valley on a former Pennsylvania Railroad branch line. The nostalgic train rides travel from West Chester to Glen Mills. Along the way, you'll see several historic railroad stations.

**CHOICES:** Ride through the scenic woods in comfortable and heated remodeled coaches that were built in 1931 and 1932 for the Reading Railroad. All trains stop for 20 minutes to allow passengers to explore the Glen Mills station. Pack a lunch and enjoy the picnic trains that run on summer Sundays. A history train provides a look at the area's history and what it was like to ride a train in past centuries.

**WHEN TO GO:** Trains operate most Sundays June through December. In addition to the regular trains, the schedule expands with Saturday rides for a number of special events including for Easter, Mother's Day, Father's Day, Memorial Day, Halloween, and Christmas. Fall foliage trains offer a look at the area's color.

**GOOD TO KNOW:** West Chester is the county seat of historic Chester County. The downtown district is listed on the National Register of Historic Places, and the town features more than 3,000 structures that date back to the colonial period.

**WORTH DOING:** Visit the nearby Brandywine River Museum, which features works of art by three generations of the Wyeth family. Also nearby is Longwood Gardens, a world-famous botanical garden and arboretum, the American Helicopter Museum, and the Brandywine Battlefield state historic site.

**DON'T MISS:** The West Chester's Christmas tree train allows passengers to ride the train to a Christmas tree farm and select their trees, which are then cut and loaded on the train for the return trip.

**GETTING THERE:** West Chester is in southeastern Pennsylvania, about 25 miles west of Philadelphia. Once in downtown West Chester, drive south on High Street and then east on Market Street. Parking is on the right, just past the bright yellow locomotive.

**LOCATION:** 230 E. Market Street, West Chester
**PHONE:** 610-430-2233
**WEBSITE:** westchesterrr.com
**E-MAIL:** info@westchesterrr.com

# VIRGINIA

## C&O Railway Heritage Center

A restored 1895 C&O freight depot exhibits the history of the Chesapeake & Ohio Railway. The center also displays a restored 1949 C&O caboose, dining car, and combination car. You can also climb into a replica signal tower and watch trains roll by. It is open Friday through Monday.

LOCATION: 705 Main Street, Clifton Forge
PHONE: 540 862 8653 or 540-862-2210
WEBSITE: candoheritage.org
E-MAIL: cohs@cohs.org

## Crewe Railroad Museum

Housed in a rail station, the museum features memorabilia from the Norfolk & Western Railroad and a display of the Crewe roundhouse. The yard contains a steam locomotive, diesel engine, caboose, and several boxcars. The museum is open Friday through Sunday year-round.

LOCATION: 100 E. Virginia Avenue, Crewe
PHONE: 434-645-9868
WEBSITE: townofcrewe.com

## Eastern Shore Railway Museum

The museum is housed in a restored 1906 Pennsylvania Railroad passenger station. On the siding are two cabooses, a baggage car, a Pullman sleeper, a Budd dining car, and a touring car. The museum also includes an 1890s maintenance-of-way tool shed, a crossing guard shanty, and various railroad artifacts. It is open Wednesday through Saturday March through October.

LOCATION: 18468 Dunne Avenue, Parksley
PHONE: 757-665-7245
WEBSITE: easternshorerailwaymuseum.com

## Fairfax Station Railroad Museum

At the Fairfax museum, visitors can learn about the Orange & Alexandria Railroad and Civil War history. Stations on the site played a role in several Civil War battles, and Clara Barton tended to wounded soldiers here. The current building is a restored 1903 station, and a Norfolk Southern caboose is also on display. The museum is open Sunday afternoons.

LOCATION: 11200 Fairfax Station Road, Fairfax
PHONE: 703-425-9225
WEBSITE: fairfax-station.org
E-MAIL: information@fairfax-station.org

## Rappahannock Railway Workers Museum

Only at this museum can you ride the Little Yellow Train, a maintenance train composed of a speeder and various track cars, and learn more about working on the railroad. The museum contains dining car china, uniforms, lanterns, and other items. Also on display are several cabooses, a Pennsylvania baggage car, and a boxcar. It is open Saturdays mid-March through October.

LOCATION: 11700 Main Street, Fredericksburg
WEBSITE: rcnrhs.com
E-MAIL: form on website

## Richmond Railroad Museum

With its exhibits, the museum highlights the railroads that served central Virginia. The restored Southern Railway passenger station includes a stationmaster's office and a freight room containing artifacts. Guided tours are available, and excursions are offered several times a year. On display outside are a steam saddle locomotive, baggage car, and caboose. It is open Saturdays and Sundays year-round.

LOCATION: 102 Hull Street, Richmond
PHONE: 804-233-6237
WEBSITE: richmondrailroadmuseum.org

## Suffolk Seaboard Station Railroad Museum

The restored Victorian Seaboard Air Line passenger station features items from Seaboard, Virginian, Norfolk & Western, and Atlantic & Danville railroads. It is also home to a two-room HO scale model of Suffolk in 1907 and a caboose originally built for the Nickel Plate Line. It is open Wednesday through Sunday.

LOCATION: 326 N. Main Street, Suffolk
PHONE: 757-923-4750
WEBSITE: suffolktrainstation.org
E-MAIL: info@suffolktrainstation.org

# O. Winston Link Museum

O. Winston Link Museum

Only two photographers in the United States have their own museums. One belongs to noted landscape photographer Ansel Adams. The other is O. Winston Link. A commercial photographer, Link was fascinated with steam locomotives and made a pilgrimage to record the last of these on the Norfolk & Western in the late 1950s.

**CHOICES:** The museum is housed in the former Norfolk & Western passenger station in downtown Roanoke. The station was the departure point for many of the trains Link photographed, making it an excellent departure point for a world of Link's photography. More than 300 of Link's photographs are on display. The museum includes interactive exhibits, Link's photography equipment, and his railroad sound recordings. Be sure to watch the documentary film on Link's life. It's an excellent look at the man and his work through his voice and those of many others.

**WHEN TO GO:** The museum is open Tuesdays through Saturdays. Fall and spring in the Blue Ridge Mountains are magnificent and wonderful times to explore the area.

**GOOD TO KNOW:** Famous for his nighttime scenes that record the passing railroad as well as slices of rural life, Link took many photos of the region in the late '50s and early '60s. For years, Link's work languished, but in the 1980s, his career rebounded as the art world discovered his genius of capturing steam at night in (mostly) black and white.

**WORTH DOING:** The museum offers guided tours to groups of all ages in which docents discuss the historic passenger station, the history of the N&W and Link's photography. Call ahead to book a tour.

**DON'T MISS:** The former station is a Virginia Historic Landmark and is listed on the National Register of Historic Places. It is one of several renovated railroad buildings in the area. Another is the Virginia Museum of Transportation, which is a short walk away. The two museums offer a combined admission.

**GETTING THERE:** Roanoke is about 190 miles west of Richmond and near West Virginia and North Carolina. To reach the museum from I-81, take I-581 south and exit at Williamson Road and turn right on Shenandoah Avenue.

**LOCATION:** 101 Shenandoah Avenue NE, Roanoke
**PHONE:** 540-982-5465
**WEBSITE:** linkmuseum.org
**E-MAIL:** info@vahistorymuseum.org

# Virginia Museum of Transportation

Jim Wrinn

Roanoke was once synonymous with the best steam locomotives in the land. The Norfolk & Western built many of them right here, just a few blocks away. While the museum's scope is the broad subject of transportation, with more than 50 pieces of rolling stock, its heart is and always will be railroading.

**CHOICES:** The museum is housed in a historic rail setting, the former N&W freight station. Through exhibits and rolling stock displays, you'll learn about how people got around in the Old Dominion State. It displays steam and diesel locomotives, antique automobiles, trucks, wagons, tractors, and even a post office bus.

**WHEN TO GO:** The museum is open daily throughout the year, except for some holidays and during inclement weather.

**GOOD TO KNOW:** Joint admissions are available with the O. Winston Link Museum. Discounts are available for members of several other rail-heritage organizations in western Virginia.

**WORTH DOING:** Stroll along the rail walk that connects the museum with the O. Winston Link Museum and Hotel Roanoke. The walk parallels the Norfolk Southern's mainline track and features displays and interactive exhibits along the way.

**DON'T MISS:** One of the museum's prize exhibits, Norfolk & Western 4-8-4 No. 611, has been restored and is in operation on mainline excursions. Known as the Spirit of Roanoke, it is the last of its kind, one of 13 Class J locomotives that pulled the N&W's named trains. Capable of sprinting faster than 100 mph or climbing the mountains of West Virginia, these locomotives were considered to be among the best and most powerful of their kind. Also note Norfolk & Western Y6a, No. 2156, on loan from the Museum of Transportation in St. Louis.

**GETTING THERE:** Roanoke is situated in Roanoke Valley in Virginia's Blue Ridge Mountains. The museum can be easily reached from I-81 via I-581/220 South. It is located downtown on Norfolk Avenue between Second and Fifth Streets. Look for the long building with the Jupiter rocket next to it.

**LOCATION:** 303 Norfolk Avenue SW, Roanoke
**PHONE:** 540-342-5670
**WEBSITE:** vmt.org
**E-MAIL:** info@vmt.org

# WEST VIRGINIA

## Princeton Railroad Museum

The museum is a replica of the Virginian Railway station that stood in Princeton for 70 years. It features exhibits devoted to the Virginian and Norfolk & Western Railways. It contains art, more than 100 lanterns, and other artifacts. A Virginian caboose is also on display. The museum is open Tuesday through Sunday May through September and Thursday through Sunday October through April.

**LOCATION:** 99 Mercer Street, Princeton
**PHONE:** 304-487-5060
**WEBSITE:** princetonrailroadmuseum.com
**E-MAIL:** princetonrailroadmuseum@aol.com

# Cass Scenic Railroad

Chase Gunoe

**The Cass Scenic Railroad is as close as you'll ever come to experiencing a mountain logging railroad—because it once was one. Leaving from the mill town of Cass along the beautiful Greenbrier River, trains climb steep grades out of the Leatherbark Creek area, negotiate two switchbacks, and hug hillsides to gain elevation.**

CHOICES: For a shorter ride, you can take a 2-hour trip to Whitaker Station and back. For a longer ride, you can enjoy a half-day trip to Bald Knob and back. At Whittaker, trains pause for servicing, and there you can inspect a re-created railroad logging camp. Continuing on, trains powered by unusual geared steam locomotives work their way to Bald Knob, which is 4,880 feet high. The view is spectacular, and the trains climb an 11 percent grade. Other trips include a murder mystery train, and the Wild Heart of West Virginia package offers an excursion to Old Spruce with an option to transfer to a vintage, diesel-powered locomotive that continues to Elkins.

WHEN TO GO: The railroad runs late May through October, with heavy passenger counts during the colorful autumn. It schedules several special events during the season.

GOOD TO KNOW: The Cass Scenic Railroad regularly operates, in conjunction with preservation and railfan partners, special photo trips featuring Shay geared locomotives and authentic log and freight consists.

WORTH DOING: Near Cass, there are several state parks and forests, including Droop Mountain Battlefield State Park, the site of the state's last major battle during the Civil War. The Greenbrier River Trail is a biking and hiking trail that runs along the river for many of its 78 miles.

DON'T MISS: The state park features a logging museum, Cass Showcase diorama, logging camp tour, and shop tour (when available).

GETTING THERE: Cass Scenic Railroad is located in eastern West Virginia. Once off the Interstate, two-lane state and county roads are the rule. Route 66 becomes Main Street in Cass.

LOCATION: 242 Main Street, Cass (Cass Scenic Railroad State Park)
PHONE: 877-686-7245
WEBSITE: mountainrailwv.com

# Durbin & Greenbrier Valley Railroad

Durbin & Greenbrier Valley Railroad

The Durbin & Greenbrier Valley Railroad operates several separate and distinct railways in the Mountain State. The Cheat Mountain Salamander offers a ride into the high country of Cheat Mountain, the Durbin Rocket operates a 1910 Climax locomotive, and the New Tygart Flyer is a diesel-powered train that pulls coaches and first-class cars through the wilderness. It also now operates the Cass Scenic Railroad.

**CHOICES:** This railroad is all about choices. The Cheat Mountain Salamander offers an 8-hour round trip through remote high mountain country to Old Spruce where passengers can transfer to or from the Cass Scenic Railroad. The Durbin Rocket is a 2-hour ride aboard a caboose, coach, or open gondola behind a Climax or Heisler geared steam locomotive traveling along the unspoiled Greenbrier River. The New Tygart Flyer provides a dramatic 4-hour round trip through a curved tunnel, across a deep canyon, and over a rushing river to an impressive waterfall that puts an exclamation point on the journey. A Mountain Explorer dinner train also operates.

**WHEN TO GO:** Trains operate April through December. Murder mystery, Polar Express, Elf Unlimited, and other special trains are scheduled throughout the season.

**GOOD TO KNOW:** To get closer to nature, you can stay overnight along the Greenbrier River in a Castaway Caboose, a restored Wabash caboose, on the Durbin Rocket.

**WORTH DOING:** In the surrounding Monongahela National Forest, you can mountain bike, view waterfalls, and see trees that are more than 300 years old.

**DON'T MISS:** All Durbin & Greenbrier Valley railways are located close to each other, enabling multiple train excursions in one impressive mountain setting.

**GETTING THERE:** Route 250 connects Elkins and Durbin, which is 35 miles south. The Elkins station, where the New Tygart Flyer and the Cheat Mountain Salamander board, is downtown near the river. The Durbin Rocket takes off from the restored C&O Railway depot in Durbin. Cass is 19 miles south of Durbin via Routes 92 and 66.

**LOCATION:** 315 Railroad Avenue, Elkins; 4759 Staunton Parkersburg Turnpike, Durbin
**PHONE:** 877-686-7245
**WEBSITE:** mountainrailwv.com

# New River Train

Chase Gunoe

The Collis P. Huntington Railroad Historical Society sponsors the New River Train, which runs all-day excursions during October to view autumn foliage. The society also maintains an outdoor museum and sponsors trips to other locations, such as New York City and Washington, D.C., during the year.

**CHOICES:** The New River Train travels over the former C&O main line from Huntington to Hinton. You'll go under the New River Gorge Bridge, the largest arch bridge in the country, and enjoy a spectacular view of it. Other sights along the way include Kanawha Falls, Hawks Nest Dam, and Stretcher Neck Tunnel. You'll also roll past ghost towns and old mining sites. Seating choices are coach, premium coach, and dome. You can board the Amtrak-powered train at Huntington or St. Albans. The outdoor museum displays ex-Chesapeake & Ohio Class H-6 articulated No. 1308, a saddle-tank switcher, a restored B&O section house, and other items.

**WHEN TO GO:** The New River Train runs two October weekends during the peak fall foliage season. The museum is open Sundays Memorial Day to Labor Day.

**GOOD TO KNOW:** The town and society were named for Collis P. Huntington, who helped develop the transcontinental railroad and the Chesapeake & Ohio.

**WORTH DOING:** While in Huntington, stop by the Cabell-Huntington Convention & Visitors Bureau. The bureau is housed in a former B&O passenger station, where the former Elk River Coal & Lumber Co. locomotive No 10 is displayed.

**DON'T MISS:** Huntington is 2 hours away from the New River Gorge National Park, which contains the bridge. You can plan a trip to the park by driving or by Amtrak's *Cardinal*. The third Saturday of October is Bridge Day, the only day you are allowed to walk across the bridge—or parachute from it.

**GETTING THERE:** To reach the outdoor museum, take I-64 to Exit 6. Follow Highway 52 north toward the Ohio River and get off at the first exit, Madison Avenue. Go east on Madison Avenue about 3 blocks to 14th Street West, turn right, and go south three more blocks and through the CSX underpass. The museum is on the right.

**LOCATION:** Memorial Boulevard and 14th Street West, Huntington (outdoor museum)
**PHONE:** 866-639-7487 or 304-523-0364
**WEBSITE:** newrivertrain.com
**E-MAIL:** info@newrivertrain.com

# Potomac Eagle Scenic Railroad

Mark Perri

**Here's a 3-hour train ride that goes in search of bald eagles down a remote stretch of the Potomac River just inside West Virginia.**

**CHOICES:** Most trains depart from the Wappocomo station, just north of Romney. The 40-mile excursion travels along the South Branch of the Potomac River and through the 6-mile Trough, a narrow mountain valley where eagles are often seen. You can ride in open-air coaches or first-class cars. Historic narration adds extra insight into the journey. EMD F units in striking C&O and B&O heritage schemes provide power for most of the trains.

**WHEN TO GO:** Trains run Memorial Day weekend into November. Departures are on Saturdays with a few Sundays sprinkled in. Autumn makes an especially great time to visit this railroad, and it offers trips almost daily during October.

**GOOD TO KNOW:** The railroad says eagles are spotted on 90 percent of its trains. As it enters the most remote and steepest portion of the valley, the train pauses, so you can find a seat in the open gondola for the best views.

**WORTH DOING:** Explore Romney, which includes numerous historic homes and buildings. Possibly the oldest town in West Virginia, it is said to have changed hands 56 times during the Civil War.

**DON'T MISS:** The railroad runs all-day trips the length of the railroad on the last Saturday of each month, and on special occasions, runs short trips from Petersburg, at the south end of the railroad.

**GETTING THERE:** Romney is located on Route 50 in the northeast corner of the state. It is about 25 miles south of Cumberland, Md. Route 28 takes you to the station, which is 1.5 miles north of Romney on Eagle Drive.

**LOCATION:** 149 Eagle Drive, Romney
**PHONE:** 304-424-0736
**WEBSITE:** potomaceagle.info
**E-MAIL:** potomaceaglewv@gmail.com

# REGION 3

Tweetsie Railroad, page 120

## ALABAMA

1 Foley Railroad Museum
2 Fort Payne Depot Museum
3 Huntsville Depot & Museum
4 Leeds Historic Depot
5 Heart of Dixie Railroad Museum
6 North Alabama Railroad Museum
7 Stevenson Railroad Depot Museum
8 Tuscumbia Railway Museum

## FLORIDA

9 Boca Express Train Museum
10 Central Florida Railroad Museum
11 Flagler Museum
12 Florida Railroad Museum
13 Gold Coast Railroad Museum
14 Henry B. Plant Museum
15 Naples Depot Museum
16 Seminole Gulf Railway
17 Tampa Union Station
18 TECO Line Streetcar System
19 West Florida Railroad Museum

## GEORGIA

20 Atlanta History Center
21 Blue Ridge Scenic Railway
22 Georgia Museum of Agriculture and Historic Village
23 Georgia State Railroad Museum
24 Okefenokee Heritage Center
25 St. Marys Railroad
26 SAM Shortline
27 Southeastern Railway Museum
28 Southern Museum of Civil War & Locomotive History
29 Stone Mountain Scenic Railroad
30 Thronateeska Heritage Center

## MISSISSIPPI

31 Canton Train Museum
32 McComb Railroad Museum
33 Water Valley Casey Jones Railroad Museum

## NORTH CAROLINA

34 Craggy Mountain Line
35 Great Smoky Mountains Railroad
36 New Hope Valley Railway
37 North Carolina Transportation Museum
38 Tweetsie Railroad
39 Wilmington Railroad Museum

## SOUTH CAROLINA

40 Best Friend of Charleston Railway Museum
41 Railroad Historical Center
42 South Carolina Railroad Museum

### TENNESSEE

**43** Anqui Station & Visitor Center

**44** Casey Jones Railroad Museum

**45** Cookeville Depot Museum

**46** Cowan Railroad Museum

**47** Dollywood

**48** The Incline Railway

**49** Little River Railroad Museum

**50** Memphis Railroad & Trolley Museum

**51** Monterey Depot Transportation Museum

**52** Nashville, Chattanooga & St. Louis Depot and Railroad Museum

**53** Tennessee Central Railway Museum

**54** Tennessee Valley Railroad Museum

**55** Three Rivers Rambler

# ALABAMA

## Foley Railroad Museum

Housed in a former Louisville & Nashville depot, the museum contains photos and artifacts relating to railroads, the City of Foley, and Baldwin County history. It displays an L&N diesel switch engine, several boxcars, and a caboose, plus a 24' x 60' model train layout. The museum is open Monday through Friday.

LOCATION: 125 E. Laurel Avenue, Foley
PHONE: 251-943-1818
WEBSITE: foleyrailroadmuseum.com
E-MAIL: foleymuseum@gulftel.com

## Fort Payne Depot Museum

Located in northeast Alabama, the museum is a former passenger station built in the late 1800s of pink sandstone, and it displays railroad artifacts in a caboose. It also includes local historical, military, and Native American items. The museum is open Wednesdays, Thursdays, and Fridays.

LOCATION: 105 Fifth Street NE, Fort Payne
PHONE: 256-845-5714
WEBSITE: fortpaynedepotmuseum.com
E-MAIL: depotmuseum@bellsouth.net

## Huntsville Depot & Museum

Built in 1860, the depot is the oldest in Alabama and is listed on the National Register of Historic Places. You can read graffiti left by Civil War soldiers and climb aboard several steam locomotives for an up-close look. The museum is open Wednesday through Saturday March through December. The annual WhistleStop festival takes place in early May.

LOCATION: 320 Church Street NW, Huntsville
PHONE: 256-564-8100
WEBSITE: earlyworks.com
E-MAIL: form on website

## Leeds Historic Depot

3uilt in 1884 by the Georgia Pacific Railway, the Leeds depot was restored in 1984. It serves as headquarters for the Mid-South Chapter of the Railway & Locomotive Historical Society. The agent-operator's office has been authentically restored, and a former waiting room houses the Frank E. Ardrey Jr. Photographic Exhibit.

LOCATION: 933 Thornton Ave NE, Leeds
PHONE: 205-405-1623
WEBSITE: midsouth.rlhs.org

## Stevenson Railroad Depot Museum

Situated at an important Civil War railroad junction on the Tennessee River, the depot, which is listed in the National Register of Historic Places, now houses a collection of railroad, military, agricultural, and other local artifacts and memorabilia. It is open Monday through Friday.

LOCATION: 207 W. Main Street, Stevenson
PHONE: 256-437-3012
WEBSITE: cityofstevensonalabama.com

## Tuscumbia Railway Museum

Housed in a restored depot, the museum features rail and train memorabilia, interactive train simulators, telegraph demonstrations, and information about Tuscumbia's history. The depot was used frequently by Helen Keller, who lived in nearby Muscle Shoals. It is open Tuesday through Friday.

LOCATION: 204 W. Fifth Street, Tuscumbia
PHONE: 256-389-1357
WEBSITE: facebook.com/tuscumbia-depot-and-roundhouse-175461209295798
E-MAIL: tuscumbiadepot@comcast.net

# Heart of Dixie Railroad Museum

Heart of Dixie Railroad Museum, Alan Dismukes

The museum features exhibits housed in a restored depot from Wilton, Ala. It operates two trains and displays a variety of locomotives and rolling stock. The Heart of Dixie has been designated as the official railroad museum for the state of Alabama.

**CHOICES:** The museum's Calera & Shelby Railroad operates over 5.5 miles of the Louisville & Nashville's former Alabama Mineral branch line through the forested countryside. One-hour, diesel-powered excursions run every Saturday. The museum is open Tuesdays through Saturdays mid-March through mid-December. Admission to the depot museum and outdoor exhibits is free (donations are welcome). A pavilion is available for picnics.

**WHEN TO GO:** With comfortable temperatures and lower humidity, spring and autumn are ideal seasons for a visit, as well as the best times to enjoy the colorful foliage along the heavily wooded Calera & Shelby right-of-way. For family outings, the museum regularly operates a number of theme-related excursions including the Cottontail Express, Day Out with Thomas, Pumpkin Patch Express, Santa Special, and the ever-popular North Pole Express.

**GOOD TO KNOW:** The Ozan Winery offers wine tasting and a train ride on Saturday afternoons. Trains board at the winery, where tickets are available.

**WORTH DOING:** Located only a 15-minute drive from the museum, the American Village provides a delightful setting for a Revolutionary-era village, complete with special events and tours.

**DON'T MISS:** Housed in an early 20th century L&N freight house, the museum's Boone Library contains an extensive archive of books, periodicals, maps, and other local railroadiana. It is open on Saturdays.

**GETTING THERE:** The museum is located 30 miles south of Birmingham, just 1 mile off I-65 at Exit 228. Drive towards Calera and turn left onto Ninth Street to the museum.

**LOCATION:** 1919 Ninth Street, Calera
**PHONE:** 205-757-8383 or 205-668-3435
**WEBSITE:** hodrrm.org
**E-MAIL:** info@hodrrm.org

# North Alabama Railroad Museum

Bryan Turner

Combining a nicely restored country depot with a surprising variety of early diesel motive power and vintage rolling stock, the North Alabama Railroad Museum is a hidden jewel tucked away in the scenic Tennessee Valley.

**CHOICES:** The museum's depot and collection of rolling stock with more than 30 pieces is open for self-guided tours Wednesdays and Saturdays April through October. The museum also runs a diesel-powered, 10-mile round-trip excursion over its Mercury & Chase Railroad. Trains are air-conditioned, and all seats are reserved.

**WHEN TO GO:** Excursions operate primarily on select Saturdays April through December. Many trips have a special theme, such as the Punkin' Pickin' run and Santa rides. Regular excursions last an hour, while other rides can last 35 or 45 minutes. North Alabama's Tennessee Valley is at its scenic best in the early spring and late fall when the weather is typically ideal for taking a train ride.

**GOOD TO KNOW:** The centerpiece of the museum is the Chase depot built by the Chase family in 1937 to serve its nursery business and the community that grew around it. The depot served the Southern Railway and the Nashville, Chattanooga & St. Louis.

**WORTH DOING:** No trip to the Huntsville area is complete without a visit to the U.S. Space & Rocket Center, a 10-minute drive from the museum. Other area attractions include the EarlyWorks Children's Museum, the Museum of Art, and Monte Sano State Park.

**DON'T MISS:** The historic Huntsville Depot is located downtown. Built in the 1860s by the Memphis & Charleston Railroad, this building is steeped in Civil War history. It features exhibits on Alabama railroads, with displays of rolling stock, locomotives, and Civil War artifacts.

**GETTING THERE:** The museum is located a few minutes east of Huntsville. Take Highway 72 to Moores Mill Road for about a mile and then turn left onto Chase Road for a half mile. The museum grounds are on the left.

**LOCATION:** 694 Chase Road, Huntsville
**PHONE:** 256-851-6276
**WEBSITE:** northalabamarailroadmuseum.com
**E-MAIL:** narm-mail@comcast.net

# FLORIDA

## Boca Express Train Museum

Guided tours take you through two restored 1947 Seaboard Air Line streamlined rail cars, both of which are listed on the National Register of Historic Places. The museum also includes a 1930 restored Florida East Coast depot, a 1940s Atlantic Coast Line caboose, and a Baldwin steam engine. It operates the first and third Fridays January through April.

LOCATION: 747 S. Dixie Highway, Boca Raton
PHONE: 561-395-6766
WEBSITE: bocahistory.org
E-MAIL: tours@bocahistory.org

## Central Florida Railroad Museum

Located in a former 1913 Tavares & Gulf Railroad station, the museum features a Clinchfield caboose and a 1938 Fairmont motor car. Exhibits focus on central Florida railroads. The museum is operated by the Winter Garden Heritage Foundation, which also operates the nearby Heritage Museum. That museum is housed in a 1918 Atlantic Coast Line depot and exhibits some railroad memorabilia, a Chessie caboose, and local historical items. Both museums are open daily.

LOCATION: 101 S. Boyd Street, Winter Garden
PHONE: 407-656-0559
WEBSITE: cfrhs.org
E-MAIL: info@cfrhs.org

## Flagler Museum

The home of Henry Flagler, who developed the Florida East Coast Railway, is now a museum of the Gilded Age. Docent-led tours are offered, or you can tour the 55-room Whitehall on your own. The Flagler Kenan Pavilion, designed in the style of a 19th century Beaux Arts railway palace, houses Henry Flagler's private railcar. It is closed Mondays.

LOCATION: 1 Whitehall Way, Palm Beach
PHONE: 561-655-2833
WEBSITE: flaglermuseum.us
E-MAIL: form on website

# Henry B. Plant Museum

You'll find the Henry B. Plant Museum on the University of Tampa campus in the Tampa Bay Hotel, a listed National Historic Landmark that features Moorish architecture. The building now contains exhibits on Plant and his network of Southeastern railroads. You can also view restored period rooms from America's Gilded Age. The museum is open Tuesdays through Sundays January through November and daily during the Victorian Christmas Stroll (which features period holiday decorations and events) throughout much of December.

LOCATION: 401 W. Kennedy Boulevard, Tampa
PHONE: 813-254-1891
WEBSITE: plantmuseum.com
E-MAIL: info@plantmuseum.com

# Naples Depot Museum

Recently renovated, the museum is housed in a former Seaboard Air Line passenger station and listed on the National Register of Historic Places. It features restored railcars, interactive exhibits, and a model railroad. Miniature train rides are also offered. It is open Monday through Saturday.

LOCATION: 1051 Fifth Avenue South, Naples
PHONE: 239-262-6525
WEBSITE: colliermuseums.com
E-MAIL: museums@colliergov.net

# Tampa Union Station

Tampa Union Station was opened in 1912 by the Atlantic Coast Line, Seaboard Air Line, and Tampa Northern Railroads and is listed on the National Register of Historic Places. The Italian Renaissance Revival-style building was restored in 1998. Displays in the ornate waiting room of the station chronicle the history of the station and the story of railroading on the west coast of Florida.

LOCATION: 601 N. Nebraska Avenue, Tampa
PHONE: 813-445-3493
WEBSITE: tampaunionstation.com
E-MAIL: friends@tampaunionstation.com

# West Florida Railroad Museum

The museum is located in the 1909 L&N depot and exhibits a variety of memorabilia from the L&N, Frisco, and other railroads. On display are various railcars including an L&N dining car, boxcar, flatcar, and caboose. You can also see a bridge tender's house from the Escambia Bay trestle and a section shed with a motor car.

LOCATION: 5003 Henry Street, Milton
PHONE: 850-623-3645
WEBSITE: wfrm.org
E-MAIL: conductor@wfrm.org

# Florida Railroad Museum

Florida Railroad Museum

The Florida Railroad Museum operates diesel-powered trains on a 13-mile round trip in southwest Florida. Leisurely rides in air-conditioned and open-air coaches through farmland, piney woods, and palmetto flats give riders a glimpse of Florida before Disney and interstate highways.

**CHOICES:** Diesel-powered trains pull a variety of air-conditioned and open-air coaches on museum excursions, with coaches from railroads as diverse as the Atlantic Coast Line, Union Pacific, and Lackawanna. The air-conditioned cars are recommended. Get there well before train time to get a cool seat. The museum has added numerous displays in recent years, including static displays of steam and diesel locomotives and a variety of other historic equipment. Special events include a World War II reenactment, a train robbery, and Halloween and Christmas trains.

**WHEN TO GO:** The Florida Railroad Museum is open Wednesdays through Sundays year-round, with train rides operating weekends year-round. Mid-December through Easter is Florida's high season. The Florida Railroad Museum is busiest then, but this season also boasts Florida's mildest weather, making it the perfect time to combine a ride on the railroad with a canoe trip or a picnic at nearby Little Manatee River State Park.

**GOOD TO KNOW:** The Florida Railroad Museum's locomotive rental program allows you to learn the operation of a locomotive and then take the controls for an hour.

**WORTH DOING:** Other area attractions include Manatee Village Historical Park, which displays a variety of historic buildings and a steam locomotive, the South Florida Museum that also includes an aquarium and planetarium, and the Gamble Plantation Historic State Park.

**DON'T MISS:** The museum's static exhibits at Parrish are worth taking in. Included among them is the *Bradenton* sleeping car built in 1949 for service on New York-Florida streamliners and named for the Florida city located near the museum.

**GETTING THERE:** Amtrak serves Tampa by train and Sarasota and Bradenton by dedicated connecting motor coach. By car, take I-75 for speed or Highway 301 to see more of the real Florida.

**LOCATION:** 12210 83rd Street East, Parrish
**PHONE:** 941-776-0906
**WEBSITE:** frrm.org
**E-MAIL:** form on website

# Gold Coast Railroad Museum

Gold Coast Railroad Museum

With its impressive collection of rolling stock and locomotives—featuring the *Ferdinand Magellan*, a Pullman office car used by Presidents Roosevelt, Truman, Eisenhower, and Reagan—and its historic location on the site of a World War II airship base, the Gold Coast Railroad Museum is a fascinating place to visit.

**CHOICES:** Interested in former Florida East Coast Railway or *California Zephyr* passenger equipment? You'll find it here, along with diesels and steam locomotives from other railroads. On most weekends, the Gold Coast offers a 25-minute standard gauge train ride using a diesel-electric (usually an EMD E9 or GP7) and a former Florida East Coast open-air coach, often an air-conditioned coach, and a caboose. In addition to the more than 40 pieces of historic railroad equipment on display, guided tours are available.

**WHEN TO GO:** The Gold Coast Railroad Museum is open daily year-round, except for some holidays. The museum offers special events throughout the year, including a Polar Express train ride.

**GOOD TO KNOW:** Currently, restoration of the *Ferdinand Magellan*'s interior is taking place. The museum is home to Florida East Coast caboose No. 715, which is also being restored. Florida East Coast Railway 4-6-2 steam locomotive No. 153, like the *Ferdinand Magellan*, is a National Historic Landmark. Used on "the railroad that died at sea," No. 153 pulled a rescue train that delivered evacuees safely to Miami just before a hurricane destroyed the Key West line in 1935.

**WORTH DOING:** Consider combining your trip to the Gold Coast with a visit to Zoo Miami, which is located next to the railroad museum.

**DON'T MISS:** The Gold Coast offers cab rides on its weekend diesel-hauled passenger trains for an additional fee. Make sure, however, you call ahead for reservations.

**GETTING THERE:** The museum is located between Miami and Homestead, just off the Florida Turnpike. Use the Zoo Miami's main entrance to enter the museum.

**LOCATION:** 12450 SW 152nd Street, Miami
**PHONE:** 305-253-0063
**WEBSITE:** gcrm.org
**E-MAIL:** webmaster@gcrm.org

# Seminole Gulf Railway

Scott Hartley

**Seminole Gulf is a regional railroad with about 118 miles of track that operates a murder mystery dinner train, as well as providing freight service to Gulf communities in the Fort Myers and Sarasota areas.**

**CHOICES:** Throughout the year, the railroad offers a variety of themed murder mysteries aboard a dinner train. Along the 3.5-hour entertaining journey, the train takes you across the Caloosahatchee River over a railroad drawbridge. The views from this and other numerous bridges you cross are especially scenic, not that you'll be able to watch the scenery. You will be busy enjoying a five-course meal and trying to solve a mystery. If you do and are a super sleuth, you may even win a prize.

**WHEN TO GO:** The mystery dinner train operates Wednesday through Sunday evenings year-round, but of course, Florida is always best enjoyed in winter! Several specials take place around various holidays. People who want to see scenery in daylight may wish to ride during the spring and summer periods with their later sunsets.

**GOOD TO KNOW:** The railroad operates on the tracks of the former Atlantic Coast Line and Seaboard Air Line, which joined in 1967 to become Seaboard Coast Line.

**WORTH DOING:** Southwest Florida is home to some of the world's best beaches and golf courses, and Lee County is home to both the Boston Red Sox and the Minnesota Twins spring training centers. For the adventurer, the region boasts miles of rivers and estuaries for canoeing and kayaking, and Everglades National Park is about a 2-hour drive from Fort Myers.

**DON'T MISS:** Several Christmastime rail-boat events combine a longer train trip to Punta Gorda with dinner and a boat ride through Punta Gorda Isles' lighted holiday festivities.

**GETTING THERE:** The railway is located in Fort Myers, which is on the southwestern Florida coast 40 miles north of Naples. The depot is located 1.5 miles from Route 41 and 3 miles from I-75.

**LOCATION:** 2805 Colonial Boulevard, Fort Myers
**PHONE:** 800-736-4853 or 239-275-8487
**WEBSITE:** semgulf.com

# TECO Line Streetcar System

Scott Hartley

Replica streetcars take passengers along a 2.7-mile route that connects downtown Tampa, Channelside, and the Ybor City entertainment district.

**CHOICES:** You can ride a streetcar to Whiting Station in the heart of downtown Tampa. You can also board anywhere along the line's other 10 stops. Get off, enjoy the neighborhood, and catch a later car. Five stops are located in Tampa's Channelside District, four are in historic Ybor City section, and another is downtown at the Dick Greco Plaza. The TECO fleet includes a restored original Birney streetcar, replicas of Birney safety streetcars, and an open-air streetcar. Fares are charged per person per trip, but one-day unlimited, three-day, and family ride cards are also available. The streetcar system also offers guided group tours.

**WHEN TO GO:** Cars operate daily on 20- or 30-minute intervals. There are extended evening hours on Fridays and Saturdays.

**GOOD TO KNOW:** Tampa's streetcar system dates back to 1892 when it carried local residents to and from work, and families to recreational destinations on weekends. At its peak, it operated 11 lines totaling 53 miles. All streetcar lines were shut down by 1946, with the current route opening in 2002.

**WORTH DOING:** The Florida Aquarium, the Tampa Convention Center, the Tampa Bay History Center, the Ybor City Museum, and cruise ship terminals are accessible from the line.

**DON'T MISS:** Public art at some stations reflects historical and contemporary designs. In Ybor City, bronze chair sculptures duplicate the lectern chairs used by the readers in cigar factories at the turn of the century. Another bronze sculpture of Dick Greco (a four-term mayor of Tampa) was installed at Greco Plaza.

**GETTING THERE:** From I-4, follow the signs to Ybor City on the east side of Tampa. At the Dick Greco Plaza downtown, you can connect to trolleys, buses, and taxis.

**LOCATION:** St. Pete Times Forum Drive, Tampa
**PHONE:** 813-254-4278
**WEBSITE:** tecolinestreetcar.org
**E-MAIL:** customerservice@gohart.org

# GEORGIA

## Atlanta History Center

The Atlanta History Center's exhibits touch upon nearly every aspect of the city's past. The Western & Atlantic steam locomotive *Texas*, which gained fame during the Civil War's Great Locomotive Chase, recently moved to the center, where it is displayed with the Battle of Atlanta Cyclorama painting.

LOCATION: 130 West Paces Ferry Road NW, Atlanta
PHONE: 404-814-4000
WEBSITE: atlantahistorycenter.com
E-MAIL: form on website

## Georgia Museum of Agriculture & Historic Village

On the 95-acre site, you can tour 35 buildings from the state's past including a railroad depot, sawmill, and steam-powered woodworking shop. Costumed interpreters explain the lifestyle found in late 19th century. On Saturdays and during special events, you can ride aboard a narrow gauge steam train that takes you around the site. The Agriculture Center contains exhibits related to Georgia's farming history. The site is open Tuesday through Saturday year-round.

LOCATION: 1392 Whiddon Mill Road, Tifton
PHONE: 229-391-5205
WEBSITE: abac.edu/museum
E-MAIL: abacinfo@abac.edu

## Okefenokee Heritage Center

This regional art and history museum displays Old Nine, a restored 1912 Baldwin 2-8-2 steam locomotive. The rail exhibit also includes a baggage car, REA Express car, passenger coach, caboose, and an early Waycross depot that describes regional rail history. Music fans may be interested in the exhibit of Waycross native Gram Parsons. It is open Tuesday through Saturday year-round.

LOCATION: 1460 N. Augusta Avenue, Waycross
PHONE: 912-285-4260
WEBSITE: okefenokeeheritagecenter.org
E-MAIL: okeheritage@gmail.com

# St. Marys Railroad

St. Marys Express is powered by a 1952 diesel locomotive, or sometimes a steam engine, as it travels through the surrounding woods and marshes and across picturesque Borrell Creek. Along the way, narrators give you a glimpse into the past, and you may encounter live scarecrows, superheroes, cowboys, zombies, or Santa, depending on the excursion.

LOCATION: 1000 Osborne Street, St. Marys
PHONE: 912-200-5235
WEBSITE: stmarysrailroad.com
E-MAIL: barbara@stmarysmagazine.com

# Stone Mountain Scenic Railroad

A 1940s locomotive with open-air cars takes you on a 5-mile, 30-minute excursion around Stone Mountain. Narration offers a look at rail history and provides interesting facts about the mountain. The train can be boarded from the marketplace depot in the Crossroads area. The park has plenty of other fun events and attractions including a mini golf course themed around the Great Locomotive Chase. In December, the train ride becomes a Christmas sing-along.

LOCATION: 1000 Robert E. Lee Boulevard, Stone Mountain
PHONE: 800-401-2407
WEBSITE: stonemountainpark.com
E-MAIL: form on website

# Thronateeska Heritage Center

The Thronateeska Heritage Center contains several historic railroad structures including an original 1857 freight depot and Railway Express Agency building, and its history museum is located in the 1912 Union Depot. Its transportation annex displays a variety of railcars and Georgia Northern Railway steam locomotive No. 107. The complex also includes a planetarium and science center. It is open Thursday through Saturday.

LOCATION: 100 W. Roosevelt Avenue, Albany
PHONE: 229-432-6955
WEBSITE: heritagecenter.org
E-MAIL: ayoung@heritagecenter.org

# Blue Ridge Scenic Railway

The Louisville & Nashville's original route from Knoxville to Atlanta covered some rugged territory, and today it makes for a scenic ride into the wilderness. Following the unspoiled Toccoa River, this 26-mile round trip takes riders between the depot at Blue Ridge and McCaysville on the Tennessee border.

**CHOICES:** Trains depart downtown Blue Ridge from the depot, which was constructed in 1906 and is listed on the National Register of Historical Places. You can ride in either a closed-window car or an open-air car. As the diesel-powered train climbs through the north Georgia mountains, commentary is piped into the cars, and a conductor may add his own perspective to the trip. Premier class gives you first-class service.

**WHEN TO GO:** Trains run mid-March through December, and spring and fall are great seasons for travel in the Southeast. The region's lush vegetation has a tendency to create a tunnel effect. During spring and fall, you have the chance to see into the forest as well as take in the scenery. Santa trains offer family fun.

**GOOD TO KNOW:** This railroad started out as a narrow gauge line in the late 1880s with the tracks being 3 feet wide. Later investors changed it to standard gauge. The railway is the only mainline railroad excursion service based in Georgia.

**WORTH DOING:** For a wet and wild adventure, you can raft the nearby Oconee River or tube down the Toccoa River.

**DON'T MISS:** On the 2-hour layover in McCaysville, you can actually explore two towns in one. It is split by the state line with Tennessee, where it is called Copperhill. You will have time to eat lunch, poke around craft stores and antique shops, and walk across an old bridge to view the river.

**GETTING THERE:** Blue Ridge is about 90 miles north of Atlanta and about 80 miles from Chattanooga, Tenn. From Atlanta, take I-75 north to I-575, which turns into Highway 515, and continue on Highway 515 to Blue Ridge. The depot is on the left side of Depot Street.

**LOCATION:** 241 Depot Street, Blue Ridge
**PHONE:** 877-413-8724
**WEBSITE:** brscenic.com
**E-MAIL:** info@brscenic.com

# Georgia State Railroad Museum

Jim Wrinn

Part of the multi-site Coastal Heritage Society museum complex, Georgia State Railroad Museum is a destination for those interested in early American railroading technology. Located on the edge of Savannah's renowned historic district, the museum encompasses 13 structures from the original Central of Georgia shops site, several of which date back to the early 1850s.

**CHOICES:** The 1926 roundhouse contains a collection of Georgia steam locomotives, passenger cars, and freight cars, including the 1886 0-6-0 shop switcher No. 8 and a rare 1878 wooden business car. A self-guided tour provides information about the history and technology of the site. The operating turntable in the roundhouse is a must-see. Every month, the museum offers train rides powered by a diesel or steam locomotive. April through July offers the most opportunities with rides offered five days a week.

**WHEN TO GO:** The museum is open year-round. Savannah's near-tropical climate offers a welcome relief from northern cold throughout the winter months.

**GOOD TO KNOW:** Georgia State Railroad Museum is built on the site of the Battle of Savannah, which was fought in 1779. It is the largest pre-Civil War era railroad complex of it's size still operating.

**WORTH DOING:** The Savannah Historic District, a National Historic Landmark, is one of America's premier urban historic neighborhoods. You'll find fine examples of buildings in Georgian, Greek Revival, and Gothic styles.

**DON'T MISS:** Expand your tour with a visit to the other sites in the complex. The Savannah History Museum is housed in the 1850s Central of Georgia passenger station and train shed 1 block north of the roundhouse. Old Fort Jackson, a brick fort built before the War of 1812, presents cannon-firing demonstrations. Battlefield Park commemorates a Revolutionary War battle fought in Savannah.

**GETTING THERE:** Amtrak's station is 3 miles away. By car, Highways 16 and 17 lead to Martin Luther King Jr. Boulevard, which takes you to the museum.

**LOCATION:** 655 Louisville Road, Savannah
**PHONE:** 912-651-6823
**WEBSITE:** chsgeorgia.org
**E-MAIL:** info@chsgeorgia.org

# SAM Shortline

SAM Shortline

The SAM Shortline offers a relaxing trip through the small towns of southwest Georgia. The train leaves from Cordele, and along the way, you travel through the towns of Leslie, Americus, Archery, and Plains, the home of President Jimmy Carter.

**CHOICES:** There are several different excursion trains, and each one stops for a layover in a different town along the route. Trains leave from either the depot in Cordele or from Georgia Veterans State Park. You can also board at several depots along the route. SAM offers coach, premium, and VIP lounge seating. Coach class provides bench seating. Premium seating is in the Americus car and features tables and chairs. Lounge seating is in the Samuel H. Hawkins car, and it offers lounges, booths, tables, and an observation area. All the cars are climate-controlled.

**WHEN TO GO:** Most trains run on Saturdays as well as on many Fridays February through December. Candy cane and other Christmas specials operate in December.

**GOOD TO KNOW:** Why SAM? The original railroad was the Savannah, Americus & Montgomery Railroad built during the 1880s and headed by Colonel Samuel Hugh Hawkins of Americus.

**WORTH DOING:** In Americus, you can visit Habitat for Humanity's Global Village, and if you want to make a longer trip, the Andersonville National Historic Site and National POW Museum is 11 miles northeast.

**DON'T MISS:** The Peanut Express stops in Plains, and the Presidential Flyer goes to Archery, where you can visit Jimmy Carter's childhood farm. In Plains, the Seaboard Coast Line depot was his campaign headquarters during the 1976 election.

**GETTING THERE:** Cordele is about 140 miles south of Atlanta. To reach the Coldele depot, from I-75, take Exit 101 and go west on Highway 280 for 1 mile. Turn right and head north on Highway 41 for another mile and turn right after the first set of railroad tracks. Georgia Veterans State Park is west on Highway 280 about 8 miles past Cordele.

**LOCATION:** 105 E. Ninth Avenue or 2459 Highway 280 West, Cordele
**PHONE:** 229-276-0755
**WEBSITE:** samshortline.com

# Southeastern Railway Museum

Jeff Terry

This museum showcases railroading in Georgia and the Southeast with exhibits and more than 90 pieces of rolling stock. Among the highlights are a business car used to help convince leaders to bring the 1996 Olympics to Atlanta, a private car once used by President Warren G. Harding, and one of the famous green and gold *Southern Crescent* passenger diesels. It also offers short train rides.

CHOICES: The 35-acre museum features a variety of buildings and displays. Building 1, the main exhibit hall, contains excursion queen Savannah & Atlanta 750 and the 1911 Pullman private car *Superb*, which was used by President Harding and is on the National Register of Historic Places. The museum's collection includes passenger coaches, private cars, baggage cars, freight cars, cabooses, and maintenance-of-way equipment. In Building 2, you'll find a collection of stainless steel passenger equipment as well as a MARTA historic diesel bus collection. A diesel-powered train ride takes you around the museum's site aboard vintage cabooses, including the recently restored N&W 500837.

WHEN TO GO: The museum is open Wednesday through Saturday March through December. In June and July, it is also open on Tuesdays. During January and February it is Thursday through Saturday. Train rides are offered in season, and special days take place during the year including those with Santa. Second Thursdays at the museum are geared towards preschool children and features a different program each month.

GOOD TO KNOW: The museum also operates a miniature train ride on the grounds.

WORTH DOING: From professional sports to botanical gardens and the zoo, take a few days and see all that the Atlanta area has to offer.

DON'T MISS: View famous excursion engines Savannah & Atlanta Pacific type No. 750, known for appearing in the film *Biloxi Blues*. Also look for *General II,* which was rebuilt to resemble the *General* of Civil War fame.

GETTING THERE: The museum is located in Duluth, a northeast suburb of Atlanta. It is just south of downtown Duluth. From Atlanta, take I-85 to Exit 104 and take Pleasant Hill Road to Buford Highway. Turn right on Buford Highway and then left onto Peachtree Road to the museum.

**LOCATION:** 3595 Buford Highway, Duluth
**PHONE:** 770-476-2013
**WEBSITE:** train-museum.org
**E-MAIL:** form on website

# Southern Museum of Civil War & Locomotive History

Southern Museum of Civil War & Locomotive History

A museum of high-caliber exhibits and static displays, the Southern Museum of Civil War & Locomotive History displays the famed steam locomotive *General*. The *General*, a Western & Atlantic Railroad 4-4-0 built in 1855, was the star in one of the Civil War's greatest acts of intrigue—the Great Locomotive Chase. The museum, part of which is located in a former cotton gin, is a must-see attraction.

**CHOICES:** While the story of the Andrews Raid and the *General* is still the biggest offering at the museum, additional railroading and Civil War displays are featured. It also chronicles the story of Georgia locomotive manufacturer Glover Machine Works, which manufactured steam locomotives, locomotive parts, and other industrial products from 1902 until the 1930s. Patterns from the casting shop are artfully displayed, and extensive exhibits cover the story of the locomotive manufacturer.

**WHEN TO GO:** The museum is open daily year-round, except for major holidays, and the weather is generally mild. The museum also offers a variety of special events throughout the year, including a narrated bus tour that follows the route of the Great Locomotive Chase.

**GOOD TO KNOW:** The story of the Andrews Raid was thrilling and unique enough to attract the attention of the Walt Disney Company, which released the film *The Great Locomotive Chase* in 1956.

**WORTH DOING:** Take a walking tour of historic Kennesaw (once known as Big Shanty) after exiting the front door of the museum and view a 1908 Western & Atlantic Railroad depot, numerous 19th century residences, and an 1887 grocery store.

**DON'T MISS:** The Atlanta History Center in Buckhead houses the *Texas*, the Western & Atlantic locomotive used by Confederates to hunt down Andrews Raiders.

**GETTING THERE:** Kennesaw is located between I-75 and Highway 41, about 30 miles from Atlanta. From I-75, take Exit 273 and go west on Wade Green Road, which becomes Cherokee Street. The museum is on the right.

**LOCATION:** 2829 Cherokee Street, Kennesaw
**PHONE:** 770-427-2117
**WEBSITE:** southernmuseum.org
**E-MAIL:** events@southernmuseum.org

# MISSISSIPPI

## Canton Train Museum

Canton's depot served Illinois Central freight and passenger trains such as the *Green Diamond, Panama Limited,* and *City of New Orleans*. Built in 1890, the depot has been restored as a museum that showcases the rail history of Canton and the surrounding area. While in town, you can also visit several movie museums, which are dedicated to films such as *O Brother, Where Art Thou* that were filmed in Canton.

**LOCATION:** 108 Depot Drive, Canton
**PHONE:** 601-859-4733
**WEBSITE:** cantontourism.com
**E-MAIL:** trains@canton-mississippi.com

## McComb City Railroad Depot Museum

Housed in an Illinois Central passenger terminal, the museum contains almost 1,500 artifacts related to railroading in southwest Mississippi. Outside, you can view a restored Illinois Central steam locomotive, aluminum refrigerator car, and caboose. The museum is open Mondays through Saturdays.

**LOCATION:** 108 N. Railroad Boulevard, McComb
**PHONE:** 601-684-2291
**WEBSITE:** mcrrmuseum.com
**E-MAIL:** trainmaster@mcrrmuseum.com

## Water Valley Casey Jones Railroad Museum

The restored Water Valley depot contains Illinois Central and local railroad items, photographs, and documents. It also displays an Illinois Central caboose and a banana car. It is open Thurday through Saturday.

**LOCATION:** 105 Railroad Avenue, Water Valley
**PHONE:** 662-473-1154
**WEBSITE:** caseyjonesmuseum.com
**E-MAIL:** jackgurner@yahoo.com

# NORTH CAROLINA

## Craggy Mountain Line

This operation offers a trolley ride over 3 miles of historic track from Asheville to Craggy Branch. Its collection of equipment includes several restored Southern Railway cabooses, an original 1925 Asheville trolley car, and a Tweetsie gas-powered motor car.

LOCATION: 111 N. Woodfin Avenue, Asheville
PHONE: 828-808-4877
WEBSITE: craggymountainline.com
E-MAIL: rocky@craggymountainline.com

## Wilmington Railroad Museum

The museum is housed in an 1880s railroad freight warehouse, where you can view Atlantic Coast Line artifacts and a re-creation of a country station. Outside, you can inspect a 1910 Baldwin steam locomotive, a hobo display in a boxcar, and an Atlantic Coast Line caboose. The museum is open daily year-round, except for Sundays mid-October through mid-April.

LOCATION: 505 Nutt Street, Wilmington
PHONE: 910-763-2634
WEBSITE: wrrm.org
E-MAIL: wrrmnc@bellsouth.net

# Great Smoky Mountains Railroad

Joshua Scott

Few mountain railroads in the southeastern United States traverse such splendid scenery as this line does. Created from a portion of Southern Railway's Murphy Branch, the GSMR hugs the rushing Tuckaseegee and Nantahala rivers and rolls out over a 700-foot-long trestle at Fontana Lake.

**CHOICES:** GSMR offers a variety of accommodations on two different train rides. The train features open-air cars, traditional sealed-window coaches, and air-conditioned lounge cars. A 4.5-hour excursion travels to Nantahala Gorge and back and includes a layover at the Nantahala Outdoor Center. The other ride is a 32-mile round trip along the Tuckasegee River to Dillsboro. Seating options include coach class, crown class, open-air, and first class. First-class service includes lunch options.

**WHEN TO GO:** The railroad runs year-round. Beginning in April, there is a train running five days a week and the every day during summer and fall. Spring and fall offer mild weather best suited to open cars and the chance to see beyond the trees and into the forest. Summer can be humid, and the tremendous foliage of the Southeast can restrict the views. The autumn color show in the Smokies is long and gorgeous.

**GOOD TO KNOW:** The railroad offers several special events throughout the year, including some that are ideal for kids (Pumpkin Patch Express and the Polar Express).

**WORTH DOING:** Steam locomotive No. 1702, a Consolidation built for the U.S. Army in World War II, has returned to service and pulls select excursions.

**DON'T MISS:** Try an adventurous combination package in which you ride the train from Bryson City into the Nantahala Gorge and then raft the river for 3 hours. There are also packages that include ziplining and Jeep tours to the Appalachian Trail.

**GETTING THERE:** The railroad is about 3 hours north of Atlanta and 1 hour west of Asheville. Major highways to the area include I-40, Route 19/23, and Route 441. The station in Bryson City is downtown.

**LOCATION:** 45 Mitchell Street, Bryson City
**PHONE:** 800-872-4681
**WEBSITE:** gsmr.com
**E-MAIL:** form on website

## North Carolina
# New Hope Valley Railway

New Hope Valley Railway

Operating from the North Carolina Railroad Museum, the New Hope Valley Railway provides an hour-long trip through the scenic pine forests situated south of Raleigh and Durham in central North Carolina.

**CHOICES:** The railway offers 60-minute round trips between Bonsal and New Hill in covered, open-air railcars. The museum features an outdoor exhibit of railroad equipment as well as displays of local rail artifacts. It includes a variety of industrial and shortline diesel locomotives.

**WHEN TO GO:** Trains operate from April to December. Typically, weekend rides take place the second Sunday and last Saturday of each month. Weekday rides for tour groups and others are held the second Wednesday and fourth Friday. Monthly events include a strawberry festival, ice cream social, Brew 'n' Choo, and beach party and luau days.

**GOOD TO KNOW:** In 2017, the railway is moving the 1884 Goldston Train Depot 25 miles from Goldston to its site for renovation and display.

**WORTH DOING:** Built over part of an old rail line that carried tobacco, the American Tobacco Trail runs near the railway. You can hike, bike, and ride horses along the trail.

**DON'T MISS:** Kids will especially enjoy the G scale garden railroad that operates on the grounds. It features more than 1,000 feet of track, tunnels, bridges, trees, houses, and its own engine house.

**GETTING THERE:** Located between Bonsal and New Hill, the railroad is a 30-minute drive from Raleigh along Route 1. Take Exit 89, turn right on New Hill Holleman Road, and then turn left onto old Route 1 for 2.5 miles. The museum is on the right on Daisey Street, and parking for the train rides is on the left on Bonsal Road.

**LOCATION:** 3900 Bonsal Road, New Hill
**PHONE:** 919-362-5416
**WEBSITE:** triangletrain.com
**E-MAIL:** info@triangletrain.com

# North Carolina Transportation Museum

North Carolina Transportation Museum

The state's transportation museum is housed in buildings from Southern Railway's largest steam locomotive repair shop that date from before 1900 to 1924. But this is no static museum. Trains run on 2.5 miles of track, giving visitors the chance to experience a 25-minute train ride that covers most of the 60-acre site.

**CHOICES:** Among the giant structures you'll see are the nation's largest preserved roundhouse, the 37-stall Bob Julian Roundhouse, which houses railroad displays, a restoration shop, active locomotives, and rolling stock. You will also see the Back Shop, a 600-foot-long, 80-foot-tall building once used to overhaul steam locomotives. The narrated train rides take place daily during summer, Saturdays during January and February, and Thursday through Sunday the rest of the year. You can ride in the locomotive cab for an extra fare. You'll get a unique view and a personalized tour. You might even get to blow the horn.

**WHEN TO GO:** The museum is open Wednesday through Sunday in winter (November through February) and Tuesday through Sunday March through October. Any time of the year is enjoyable for a visit. An annual railfan event typically takes place in summer. Summer can be sweltering, but fall is long and mild.

**GOOD TO KNOW:** The museum offers guided tours of the roundhouse Friday through Sunday for no extra charge, as well as other seasonal tours, like Legends by Lantern, or restoration tours.

**WORTH DOING:** There are plenty of pork barbecue places in the region if you want to sample real local food, and a diner is right across the street.

**DON'T MISS:** Take a 5-minute ride on the museum's turntable. The 100-foot-long lazy Susan is used to turn locomotives at the roundhouse, and it helps define the term *in the round.*

**GETTING THERE:** About an hour's drive from Charlotte or Winston-Salem, the museum is a few minutes off I-85. Take Exit 79 and then follow the signs to the museum in Spencer.

**LOCATION:** 411 S. Salisbury Avenue, Spencer
**PHONE:** 704-636-2889
**WEBSITE:** nctrans.org
**E-MAIL:** form on website

# Tweetsie Railroad

Tweetsie Railroad

One of the original Wild West theme parks of the 1950s, when TV cowboys were popular, Tweetsie has roots in one of the most famous Southeastern narrow gauge railroads, the East Tennessee & Western North Carolina. The 3-mile train ride gives the historic, coal-fired engines a chance to work and show that they are still the real thing.

**CHOICES:** The train is pulled by original ET&WNC steam locomotive No. 12 or No. 190, *Yukon Queen*, which came from Alaska's White Pass & Yukon Railway. No. 12 is listed on the National Register of Historic Places. Ride in a coach close to the engine, so you can hear it work up grade and listen to the whistle echo about the mountains.

**WHEN TO GO:** The park is open April through October. From Memorial Day weekend through mid-August, it is open daily. Otherwise, it is open Friday through Sunday. An rail heritage weekend is held in August, and a ghost train runs in fall.

**GOOD TO KNOW:** The East Tennessee & Western North Carolina ran from Johnson City, Tenn., to Boone, N.C., for many years. Its whistle sounded a "tweet," and from that, locals nicknamed the railroad *Tweetsie*.

**WORTH DOING:** Visit the Blowing Rock and learn its legend. Hike or drive through the scenic Blue Ridge Mountains. At Grandfather Mountain, you can cross the Mile High Swinging Bridge, a 228-foot long suspension bridge that spans an 80-foot chasm.

**DON'T MISS:** Bring the entire family along—there's lots to see and do for kids in the park. Admission to the railroad includes amusement rides, live shows, and other attractions.

**GETTING THERE:** The railroad is west of Winston-Salem in the Blue Ridge Mountains near the Tennessee border. It is located off Route 321 between Boone and Blowing Rock.

**LOCATION:** 300 Tweetsie Railroad Lane, Blowing Rock
**PHONE:** 800-526-5740 or 828-264-9061
**WEBSITE:** tweetsie.com
**E-MAIL:** info@tweetsie.com

# SOUTH CAROLINA

## Best Friend of Charleston Railway Museum

Built in 1830, the *Best Friend of Charleston* was an early steam locomotive used for passenger service. A full-size replica of the engine was built, and is now on display in the museum along with Southern Railway artifacts. The museum is open daily.

LOCATION: 23 Ann Street, Charleston
WEBSITE: bestfriendofcharleston.org
E-MAIL: bfoc1830@gmail.com

## Hub City Railroad Museum

Located in a former Southern Railway depot, the museum highlights the history of Spartanburg's railroads, including the Southern Railway, Clinchfield, and Piedmont & Northern, as well as two major industries of the area, textiles and peaches. A Southern Railway caboose is on display. It is open Wednesdays and Saturdays.

LOCATION: 298 Magnolia Street, Spartanburg
WEBSITE: hubcityrrmuseum.org
E-MAIL: form on website

## Railroad Historical Center

A walk-through display of rolling stock includes a 1906 2-8-2 steam engine, Pullman cars, and Piedmont & Northern cars. It is operated in partnership with The Museum in Greenwood, located 4 blocks north, which features a wide range of historical exhibits and educational programs. The Railroad Historical Center is open Fridays and Saturdays May through September.

LOCATION: 908 S. Main Street, Greenwood
PHONE: 864-229-7093
WEBSITE: emeraldtriangle.us
E-MAIL: greenwoodmuseumdirector@gmail.com

# South Carolina Railroad Museum

South Carolina Railroad Museum, Vince LiBrizzi

The South Carolina Railroad Museum's Rockton, Rion & Western Railroad offers visitors a slice of Southeastern shortline history. A former granite-hauling freight line, the RR&W brings the experience of a casual Southeastern short line to life on a scenic 10-mile, 1-hour round trip excursion. It is the only tourist railroad in the state.

**CHOICES:** The railroad runs past antebellum plantation remains and through pine forests and a hand-hewn rock cut on the way to Rion. On most excursions, passengers have the choice of riding in a historic Southern Railway dining car, coach, open-air car, or caboose. The museum's collection showcases South Carolina's railroad heritage through track tools, artifacts, and photographs. Rolling stock includes passenger cars, freight cars, cabooses, and other equipment from the Lancaster & Chester, Southern, Seaboard, and other railroads.

**WHEN TO GO:** The museum is open Wednesdays through Saturdays June through December, with most train rides scheduled on Saturdays. It also hosts a variety of special events throughout the year, including Easter, barbecue, twilight, and Santa trains.

**GOOD TO KNOW:** The railroad is more than a hundred years old and is listed on the National Register of Historic Places. Its two 100-ton SW8 diesels saw action for the U.S. Army during the Korean War.

**WORTH DOING:** Wet a fishing line in one of the state's top fishing lakes. Lake Wateree has more than 13,700 acres and contains bream, catfish, crappie, and bass. Lake Wateree State Recreation Area also features a nature trail for a short hike.

**DON'T MISS:** Take a look at steam locomotive 4-6-0 No. 44 from the Hampton & Branchville. It is one of the few steam locomotives on display in South Carolina. The gallery and display train contain bells, whistles, and other railroad artifacts.

**GETTING THERE:** About 70 minutes from Charlotte, N.C., Winnsboro is between Columbia and Rock Hill, just off I-77. Take Exit 34 and follow Route 34 about 5 miles and turn left before the museum sign and railroad crossing. The entrance and parking lot is on the right.

**LOCATION:** 110 Industrial Park Road, Winnsboro
**PHONE:** 803-635-9893
**WEBSITE:** scrm.org
**E-MAIL:** info@scrm.org

# TENNESSEE

## Amqui Station & Visitor Center

A former Louisville & Nashville Railroad combination depot and tower once owned by singer Johnny Cash is now restored, serving as a historic museum and a part of the Madison Visitor Center. This unique structure contains railroad memorabilia and exhibits related to country music. The center is open Mondays through Fridays.

LOCATION: 303 Madison Street, Madison
PHONE: 615-891-1154
WEBSITE: amquistation.org
E-MAIL: execdirector@amquistation.org

## Casey Jones Railroad Museum

At Casey Jones Village, you can learn about the life and legend of this famous engineer by touring his family home and a replica of No. 382, Casey's engine. The museum contains related displays and artifacts as well as those of Jackson's railroad history. It is open daily. Be sure to walk through the *Judge Milton Brown* Pullman railcar.

LOCATION: 30 Casey Jones Lane, Jackson
PHONE: 731-668-1222
WEBSITE: caseyjones.com
E-MAIL: caseyjonesmuseum@gmail.com

## Cookeville Depot Museum

The railroad museum is housed in a 1909 Tennessee Central Railway depot. It contains changing displays of railway artifacts and photos highlighting local railroad history. A renovated L&N caboose contains additional exhibits, and a Tennessee Central locomotive, tender, and caboose are on display. It is open year-round Tuesday through Saturday.

LOCATION: 116 W. Broad Street, Cookeville
PHONE: 931-528-8570
WEBSITE: cookevilledepot.com
E-MAIL: depot@cookeville-tn.org

# Cowan Railroad Museum

Featured in this century-old depot are displays, photographs, and artifacts relating to Cowan and the railroads around the city. Led by a 1920 Porter locomotive, a complete train is displayed next to the museum. Also on display are a GE diesel switcher and several motor cars. It is open Thursday through Saturday May through October.

LOCATION: 108 Front Street, Cowan
PHONE: 931-967-3078
WEBSITE: cowanrailroadmuseum.org
E-MAIL: secretary@cowanrailroadmuseum.org

# Dollywood

Two former White Pass & Yukon 2-8-2 locomotives alternate pulling the Dollywood Express through the mountains surrounding the Dollywood theme park. The 3-foot gauge railroad totals just under 3 miles in length and has grades topping 6 percent. The park's season runs from late April through December.

LOCATION: 2700 Dollywood Parks Boulevard, Pigeon Forge
PHONE: 800-365-5996
WEBSITE: dollywood.com
E-MAIL: form on website

# Little River Railroad Museum

The museum holds a number of tools, artifacts, and photographs dedicated to the Little River Railroad and the lumber company it served. It displays a restored 1909 Shay locomotive, several pieces of rolling stock, logging equipment, and a water tower. It is open April through November.

LOCATION: 7747 E. Lamar Alexander Parkway, Townsend
PHONE: 865-661-0170
WEBSITE: littleriverrailroad.org
E-MAIL: president@littleriverrailroad.org

## Memphis Railroad & Trolley Museum

The museum is located on the first floor of Central Station, which is being developed into an hotel. During construction, the museum will be renovated and is scheduled to reopen fall 2017. It contains artifacts and memorabilia from the eight railroads that once served Memphis and on the history of the city's trolleys.

LOCATION: 545 S. Main Street, Suite 121, Memphis
PHONE: 901-590-3099
WEBSITE: mrtm.org
E-MAIL: form on website

## Monterey Depot Museum

The museum, a replica of the town's earlier Tennessee Central depot, preserves transportation-related items, which include artifacts from the Tennessee Central and other railroads that operated in the area, and features other exhibits. The museum is open daily.

LOCATION: 1 E. Depot Street, Monterey
PHONE: 931-839-2111
WEBSITE: montereytn.com
E-MAIL: depotadm@frontier.com

## Nashville, Chattanooga & St. Louis Depot and Railroad Museum

The museum houses a collection of artifacts, photographs, and memorabilia associated with railroad and local history. The grounds feature a dining car and two cabooses. Built in 1907, the depot is listed on the National Register of Historic Places. It is open year-round, Monday through Saturday.

LOCATION: 582 S. Royal Street, Jackson
PHONE: 731-425-8223
WEBSITE: jacksonrecandparks.com
E-MAIL: thedepot@cityofjackson.net

# The Incline Railway

Incline Railway

This is not a trip for the faint of heart. Lasting only 15 minutes, the 1-mile journey from the base of Lookout Mountain to the top is one of the steepest rides around, with grades of up to 72.7 percent.

**CHOICES:** A trolley-style railcar takes you slowly up and back down the mountain. You'll pass the houses of many people living on the side of the mountain. The best place to ride is at the end of the car—you can't beat the view from there. From the observation decks at the top of the mountain, you can watch the cars ascend and descend, as well as view the Tennessee Valley.

**WHEN TO GO:** You can ride the railway any day of the year except Thanksgiving and Christmas.

**GOOD TO KNOW:** Designated as both a National Historic Site and a National Historic Mechanical Engineering Landmark, the Incline Railway has been carrying people up the mountain since 1895. Heavy-duty cables handle the duties today, but when the railroad was originally in service, steam locomotives were the power. They were replaced in 1911.

**WORTH DOING:** Combo tickets are available that allow you to see Rock City Gardens and Ruby Falls, as well as ride the Incline Railway. Rock City Gardens is a walking trail that showcases rock formations, caves, and gardens. At Ruby Falls, you can take a guided cave tour to see a 145-foot underground waterfall.

**DON'T MISS:** At the top of the mountain, you can walk to Point Park Battlefield, which is a unit of Chickamauga and Chattanooga National Military Park. The visitor center contains a mural and videos about the battle of Chattanooga.

**GETTING THERE:** Many highways can take you to the St. Elmo base station including I-24, Highway 17, and Highway 58.

**LOCATION:** 3917 St. Elmo Avenue, Chattanooga
**PHONE:** 423-821-4224
**WEBSITE:** ridetheincline.com
**E-MAIL:** pettman2001@yahoo.com

# Tennessee Central Railway Museum

Scott Hartley

The museum, operating excursions for over 25 years, offers day trips on a streamlined passenger train through scenic middle Tennessee over the tracks of the Nashville & Eastern Railroad to various locations. Duration of excursions vary from 2 to 12 hours, depending on the destination.

**CHOICES:** Excursions run throughout the year to Watertown, Baxter, Lebanon, Cookeville, Monterey, and other destinations. Dome seating is limited and sells out early on most trips. All excursion seats are reserved and offer large windows with great views. Trains are air-conditioned, and refreshments and snacks are available. All trains have a special theme: from on-board train robberies, murder mysteries and winery trains to seasonal Easter Bunny or North Pole trips during the holidays. During each September, TCRM offers rides behind Thomas the Tank Engine.

**WHEN TO GO:** Excursions run on select Saturdays throughout the year. The longer trips to Cookeville or Monterey take place in the fall when the foliage is most brilliant. Tours of the museum grounds and equipment are available on select days.

**GOOD TO KNOW:** The museum is housed in the former Tennessee Central Railway's master mechanic's office, and it includes a large collection of Tennessee Central artifacts and memorabilia.

**WORTH DOING:** Only minutes away are numerous downtown attractions that will appeal to the entire family. These include the Country Music Hall of Fame and Museum, Music City Center, Ascend Amphitheater, Frist Center for the Visual Arts, Tennessee State Capitol building, and Riverfront Park.

**DON'T MISS:** Tour Nashville's historic 117-year-old restored Union Station, which is now a hotel. Ride Nashville's *Music City Star* commuter train from downtown's Riverfront Station. Both are a short drive from the museum.

**GETTING THERE:** The museum is located a mile east of downtown Nashville. From I-40, take Exit 212 and turn left. Go a block to Hermitage Avenue (Highway 70) and turn left. Turn right at Fairfield Avenue which becomes Willow Street. Follow signs to the museum, which is located at bottom of the hill on the left.

**LOCATION:** 220 Willow Street, Nashville
**PHONE:** 615-244-9001
**WEBSITE:** tcry.org

# Tennessee Valley Railroad Museum

Dave Crosby

If you were to take a major steam railroad from the 1920s, shrink it, and preserve it, you'd have the Tennessee Valley Railroad. It offers a variety of steam- or diesel-powered excursions that depart from its magnificent Chattanooga station or from its satellite operation in Etowah.

**CHOICES:** The Missionary Ridge Local takes you on a 6-mile, 60-minute round trip between Grand Junction and East Chattanooga. It crosses a high trestle and other bridges and passes through a pre-Civil War horseshoe tunnel. The Chickamauga Turn, a 6-hour ride, takes you to Chickamauga and back. It includes a 90-minute layover in Chickamauga and a shorter layover at Wilder Tower in Chickamauga & Chattanooga National Military Park on the return trip. Departing out of Etowah, the railroad offers trips through Cherokee National Forest, along the scenic Hiwassee River, and through the secluded Hiwassee River Gorge. At the Great Hiwassee Loop, you pass over a bridge 62 feet above the tracks you just rode on.

**WHEN TO GO:** Excursions run every month, and except for some weekdays, there is a train running almost every day March through October. Dinner trains and other specials are scheduled throughout the year. In fall, the Summerville Steam Special takes you on an all-day trip to Summerville, Ga., for a look at the area's foliage.

**GOOD TO KNOW:** Railfest takes place in September and features various train rides, live music, family activities, special displays, and food.

**WORTH DOING:** In Chattanooga, activities include visiting the Tennessee Aquarium and taking a riverboat cruise on the Tennessee River. History buffs can explore both the Lookout Mountain and Chickamauga battlefields.

**DON'T MISS:** At East Chattanooga, a guided tour of the shop and turntable is included with the Missionary Ridge Local.

**GETTING THERE:** The railroad is in the northeast section of Chattanooga. To get there, take Route 153 to Exit 3. At the end of the exit ramp, turn left over Route 153 and turn right onto Cromwell Road.

**LOCATION:** 4119 Cromwell Road, Chattanooga
**PHONE:** 423-894-8028
**WEBSITE:** tvrail.com

# Three Rivers Rambler

Jim Wrinn

There are few perfect chances to ride a steam train in a beautiful part of the Appalachians, leaving from one of the more pleasant areas of a small city like Knoxville. But the Three Rivers Rambler offers just such an outing. From its departure point on the Tennessee River, it makes its way into the country to its namesake point: the confluence of the Holston and French Broad Rivers that creates the mighty Tennessee. The train bridges this point on a magnificent trestle that puts an exclamation point on the trip.

**CHOICES:** On the 90-minute round trip, you'll ride in a coach or an open-air car. A steam engine and various diesel locomotives provide the power. The premier locomotive is No. 154, an 1890 steam engine.

**WHEN TO GO:** Excursions operate around holidays and special events during the year, with an extended schedule for Christmas trains. Since the Rambler hauls freight Monday through Friday, most passenger trains run on Saturdays and Sundays.

**GOOD TO KNOW:** Before its return to the rails, former Southern Railway steam engine No. 154, a 2-8-0 Consolidation built by Schenectady Locomotive Works, had been on display since 1953 in Knoxville's Chilhowee Park. It is the oldest Southern Railway locomotive in operation.

**WORTH DOING:** The departure point is near the University of Tennessee in an area with several good restaurants within walking distance. Sports fans could try and catch a Volunteers football or basketball game or visit the Women's Basketball Hall of Fame.

**DON'T MISS:** Along the way, feel free to ask the conductor or volunteer staff questions about the train or local history.

**GETTING THERE:** From I-40, take Exit 386B to U.S. 129 (Alcoa Highway). Drive a half mile to the off-ramp for Kingston Pike. Keeping to the outer lane, turn left onto Kingston Pike. In less than a quarter of a mile, turn right into the University Commons Plaza. The depot and parking lot are located on the left. Cross the tracks to reach the parking lot.

**LOCATION:** 2560 University Commons Way, Knoxville
**PHONE:** 865-524-9411
**WEBSITE:** threeriversrambler.com
**E-MAIL:** form on website

# REGION 4

## ILLINOIS

1 Amboy Depot Museum
2 Chicago Great Western Railway Depot Museum
3 Chicago History Museum
4 Fox River Trolley Museum
5 Galesburg Railroad Museum
6 Greenup Depot
7 Historic Pullman Foundation
8 Illinois Railway Museum
9 Kankakee Railroad Museum
10 Monticello Railway Museum
11 Museum of Science and Industry
12 Silver Creek & Stephenson Railroad
13 Trolley Car 36
14 Union Depot Railroad Museum
15 Wheels O' Time Museum

## INDIANA

16 The Depot
17 Fort Wayne Railroad Historical Society
18 French Lick Scenic Railway
19 Hesston Steam Museum
20 Hoosier Valley Railroad Museum
21 Indiana Transportation Museum
22 Linden Depot Museum
23 Madison Railroad Station
24 Monon Connection Museum
25 National New York Central Railroad Museum
26 Princeton Depot Museum
27 Spirit of Jasper
28 Wabash Valley Railroaders Museum
29 Whitewater Valley Railroad

## MICHIGAN

30 Clinton Northern Railway Museum
31 Coopersville & Marne Railway
32 Durand Union Station
33 Flushing Area Museum
34 Greenfield Village at the Henry Ford
35 Houghton County Historical Museum
36 Huckleberry Railroad
37 Little River Railroad
38 Michigan Transit Museum
39 New Buffalo Railroad Museum
40 Old Road Dinner Train
41 Saginaw Railway Museum
42 Southern Michigan Railroad
43 SS City of Milwaukee
44 Steam Railroading Institute
45 Tri-Cities Historical Museum
46 Wheels of History

## OHIO

47 Bradord Railroad Museum
48 Carillon Historical Park
49 Cedar Point
50 Cincinnati Dinner Train
51 Conneaut Railroad Museum
52 Cuyahoga Valley Scenic Railroad
53 Dennison Railroad Depot Museum
54 Hocking Valley Scenic Railway
55 Jefferson Depot Village
56 Lebanon Mason Monroe Railroad
57 Mad River & NKP Railroad Museum
58 Marion Union Station
59 Northern Ohio Railway Museum
60 Ohio Railway Museum
61 Orrville Railroad Heritage Society

## WISCONSIN

62 Brodhead Historical Society Depot Museum
63 Camp Five
64 Colfax Railroad Museum
65 East Troy Electric Railroad
66 Frederic Historical Society Museum
67 Historical Village
68 Mid-Continent Railway Museum
69 Mineral Point Railroad Museum
70 National Railroad Museum
71 Osceola & St. Croix Valley Railway
72 Railroad Memories Museum
73 Wisconsin Great Northern Railroad

Houghton

Marquette

Sault Ste. Marie

Superior

73

66 72

71

94 64

Escanaba

63

Menominee

Alpena

Traverse City

WISCONSIN

67 70

75

Oshkosh

Fond Du Lac

Manitowoc

Sheboygan

43

MICHIGAN

41

68

30 44 33

36

94

Madison

Milwaukee

45 31 96

32

38

69

62

65

Lansing

42 34

Detroit

2 12 13

Rockford

Waukegan

94

40

51

55

8 4

3

Chicago

39

37

80

Toledo

Cleveland

88

1

7

11

25

49

52

Youngstown

14

Gary

19

57

Akron

77

80

20

Fort Wayne

17

59 61

5

9

OHIO

58 Marion

73

15

24

INDIANA

75

53

74

Peoria

57

65

69

47

Columbus

60

70

Zanesville

10

Urbana

74 22 21

70

Dayton

48

71

54

55

6

28

29

56

Quincy

Indianapolis

65

Cincinnati

50

70

18 16

23

St. Louis

64

26 27

Louisville

64

64

Evansville

Marion

Paducah

# ILLINOIS

## Amboy Depot Museum

Built in 1876, this former Illinois Central division headquarters building has been restored, inside and out. It is now a museum that presents the history of Amboy and features artifacts of the Illinois Central Railroad. The museum also contains a freight house with additional artifacts, a 0-8-0 Baldwin steam engine, a wooden caboose, and a schoolhouse. It is open Thursday through Sunday April through October. The Depot Days festival takes place in August.

LOCATION: 99 E. Main Street, Amboy
PHONE: 815-857-4700
WEBSITE: amboydepotmuseum.org
E-MAIL: information@amboydepotmuseum.org

## Chicago Great Western Railway Depot Museum

This depot museum displays artifacts of the Chicago Great Western Railway. The depot serviced the nearby Winston Tunnel, the longest railroad tunnel in Illinois. The museum features a Milwaukee Road caboose, a working telegraph, and operating model railroads. It is open weekends May through October.

LOCATION: 111 E. Myrtle Street, Elizabeth
PHONE: 815-858-2343
WEBSITE: elizabethhistoricalsociety.com
E-MAIL: elizabethhistoricalsociety@gmail.com

## Chicago History Museum

This museum traces the development of railroads in Chicago through exhibits that include the first L car, the Pioneer locomotive, and the history of the Union Stock Yard. You can explore other elements of the city's history in additional galleries. The museum is open daily.

LOCATION: 1601 N. Clark Street, Chicago
PHONE: 312-642-4600
WEBSITE: chicagohistory.org
E-MAIL: form on website

## Galesburg Railroad Museum

The Galesburg Railroad Museum displays a Chicago, Burlington & Quincy Hudson steam locomotive, a Railway Post Office car, a 1930 caboose, a Pullman parlor car, and various pieces of rail equipment and artifacts. The museum is open April through September, and Railroad Days take place in June. It is closed Mondays.

LOCATION: 211 S. Seminary Street, Galesburg
PHONE: 309-342-9400
WEBSITE: galesburgrailroadmuseum.org
E-MAIL: form on website

## Greenup Depot

The historic Greenup depot is a museum that displays artifacts of railroad and telegraph history. The preserved 1870 Vandalia Line depot also maintains a collection of audio, visual, and written materials related to these subjects. It is open Thursday through Sunday year-round. Just west of the town is a 200-foot reconstructed covered bridge; Abraham Lincoln helped construct the original bridge.

LOCATION: 216 Cumberland Street, Greenup
PHONE: 217-923-9306
WEBSITE: cumberlandcountyhistory.org
E-MAIL: historic@rr1.net

## Historic Pullman Foundation

Now a National Monument, the Pullman Visitor Center features artifacts, photos, and a video that informs visitors about George Pullman, the Pullman Company, and Pullman's 1880s model industrial town. You can take a self-guided tour of the historic area or a guided walking tour, which are offered the first Sunday of the month from May through October. The visitor center is closed Mondays.

LOCATION: 11141 S. Cottage Grove Avenue, Chicago
PHONE: 773-785-8901
WEBSITE: pullmanil.org
E-MAIL: foundation@pullmanil.org

# Kankakee Railroad Museum

Kankakee's restored train depot displays railroad memorabilia and a model train layout of Kankakee in the 1950s. Also on display are a 1947 Pullman coach, a caboose, and a trolley that ran in Kankakee from 1916 until 1932. The museum is open Friday through Sunday.

LOCATION: 197 S. East Avenue, Kankakee
PHONE: 815-929-9320
WEBSITE: kankakeerrmuseum.com

# Trolley Car 36

Departing from downtown's Riverview Park, a 45-minute trolley ride transports you along Rockford's historic riverfront, with a 10-minute stopover at Sinnissippi Rose Garden and Eclipse Lagoon. Excursions on the trolley take place Thursday through Sunday during the summer, and on weekends in fall. Riverboat cruises are also available.

LOCATION: 324 N. Madison Street, Rockford
PHONE: 815-987-8894
WEBSITE: rockfordparkdistrict.org
E-MAIL: rpdmail@rockfordparkdistrict.org

# Union Depot Railroad Museum

The railroad museum is housed in an 1888 depot building. It contains displays related to the Chicago, Burlington & Quincy, Illinois Central, and Milwaukee Road. You can tour a 1923 Mikado type 2-8-2 steam locomotive, a Milwaukee Road combine car, and a 1911 caboose. You can also ride on the Gandy Dancer Express, a motorized inspection car. It is open Saturdays and Sundays March through mid-December.

LOCATION: 783 Main Street, Mendota
PHONE: 815-539-3373
WEBSITE: mendotamuseums.org
E-MAIL: mmhsmuseum@yahoo.com

# Wheels O' Time Museum

Started by two guys looking for a place to store some collector cars, the museum now includes planes, trains, tractors, trucks, and smaller artifacts. Displayed outdoors are a Rock Island steam locomotive, Milwaukee Road combine car, Plymouth switch engine, and caboose. The museum is open Wednesday through Sunday May through September.

LOCATION: 1710 W. Woodside Drive, Dunlap
PHONE: 309-243-9020
WEBSITE: wheelsotime.org
E-MAIL: wotmuseum@aol.com

# Fox River Trolley Museum

Fox River Trolley Museum

**Tucked away in the western suburbs of Chicago is the Fox River Trolley Museum, where young and old can take a nostalgic trolley ride along the scenic Fox River.**

CHOICES: The museum operates a 4-mile round trip over the last remaining section of the original Aurora, Elgin & Fox River electric line that once linked Carpentersville, Elgin, Aurora, and Yorkville. The trolley ride travels from South Elgin to the Jon J. Duerr Forest Preserve just north of St. Charles. A variety of trolleys run including Car 20, which could be the oldest operating interurban trolley in the country. It entered service in 1902. Also look for Car 304, which is one of the last cars to operate on the Aurora, Elgin & Fox River electric line back in 1935. The trolleys board at the Castlemuir depot. A caboose and occasionally some of the museum's other cars are on display. And when the carbarn doors are open, you can sneak a peek at the cars inside.

WHEN TO GO: The museum is open on weekends and summer holidays as well as for several special events. It is open on Sundays from Mother's Day through October and on summer Saturdays through Labor Day weekend. Trolleys depart every 30 minutes. On October weekends, families can enjoy the Pumpkin Trolley or Halloween ghost trains.

GOOD TO KNOW: Picnic tables are available around the depot, and in the Jon J. Duerr Forest Preserve, there are covered shelters with grills that can be reserved.

WORTH DOING: For a unique look at the trolleys in action, hike or bike along the Fox River Bike Trail, which parallels the trolley line and crosses the Fox River on a bridge built on old railway piers and abutments.

DON'T MISS: The Village of South Elgin celebrates Riverfest in August with live entertainment, carnival rides, food, fireworks, a craft show, and a car show. In conjunction, the museum runs Trolleyfest with trolley rides and railcar displays.

GETTING THERE: The museum is 40 miles west of Chicago. From Chicago, take I-90 or Highway 20 west to Elgin. Exit on Highway 31 (State Street which becomes LaFox Street) and go south 2 miles to the museum.

**LOCATION:** 365 S. LaFox Street, South Elgin
**PHONE:** 847-697-4676
**WEBSITE:** foxtrolley.org
**E-MAIL:** info@foxtrolley.org

# Illinois Railway Museum

Jim Wrinn

Just 90 minutes northwest from downtown Chicago, and about half an hour from Union Pacific's Geneva Subdivision, lies the Illinois Railway Museum. It operates both diesel and steam trains. The museum also pays homage to its beginnings as an electric railway museum by operating streetcars and interurban cars.

**CHOICES:** As an operating museum, there are a variety of trains to ride. You can even ride a trolley or electric bus from one equipment barn to another. When you're not riding trains, explore the 80 acres of land and 400 pieces of equipment, including almost 90 freight cars, plus signals, tools, signage, and other artifacts. Six barns contain rail equipment, and another has bus equipment. Admission includes unlimited rides.

**WHEN TO GO:** The museum is open daily Memorial Day through Labor Day and weekends in April, September, and October. If visiting in July or August, remember that not all the cars and none of the barns are air-conditioned. The museum operates numerous special events including Happy Holiday Railway, Vintage Transport Extravaganza, and two Day Out with Thomas weekends.

**GOOD TO KNOW:** IRM's signature piece, the Chicago, Burlington & Quincy *Nebraska Zephyr*, runs on Diesel Days, Museum Showcase Weekend, and several other days.

**WORTH DOING:** Union is centrally located between Rockford and suburban Chicago. It also offers tourists Donley's Wild West Town with gunslinger shows, pony rides, and gold panning.

**DON'T MISS:** Diesel Days in July and Museum Showcase Weekend in September are great times to see a lot of equipment running. Typically, a variety of vintage locomotives are put to work pulling freight and commuter trains on Diesel Days. On Museum Showcase Weekend, the staff operates less-frequently run equipment.

**GETTING THERE:** If driving from Chicago, take I-90 to Highway 20, the Marengo exit. Drive northwest about 4.5 miles to Union Road and then take Union Road to Coral Road. Turn right on Coral Road and then left on Olson Road.

**LOCATION:** 7000 Olson Road, Union
**PHONE:** 800-244-7247 or 815-923-4000
**WEBSITE:** irm.org

# Monticello Railway Museum

Dave Crosby

In the midsection of Illinois, this museum offers one of the best collections of rolling stock and a good train ride to boot. All decked out in their original attire, two streamlined diesel locomotives of the 1950s, one from Canadian National and the other from the Wabash Railroad, are among the most popular locomotives.

**CHOICES:** Although the museum runs an operable steam engine, it has one of the Midwest's premier diesel locomotive collections. The collection includes a Milwaukee Road NW2, a Wabash F7-A, a Canadian National FPA-4, as well as more than 80 pieces of rolling stock. You board the 8-mile round trip over former Illinois Central and Illinois Terminal trackage from the museum grounds. You can make a layover for additional exploration or lunch and then catch a later return trip back to the museum.

**WHEN TO GO:** The museum is open on weekends May through October. Special events, including Railroad Days in September, are scheduled throughout the year for train buffs and families alike.

**GOOD TO KNOW:** Southern Railway steam engine No. 401 pulls excursions one weekend each month for the museum. On an average excursion day, No. 401 goes through about 300 gallons of oil and 5,000 gallons of water. The Baldwin engine was built in 1907.

**WORTH DOING:** Just a short drive away, on Allerton Road, is one of the Seven Wonders of Illinois. The Allerton Park and Retreat Center was once a private mansion. And you can now walk through its 14 miles of wooded trails and gardens, which contain 100 sculptures.

**DON'T MISS:** For a fee, you can operate a diese locomotive for 30 minutes under the supervision of a regular member of the train crew during spring and fall throttle times.

**GETTING THERE:** The museum is located between Champaign and Decatur, just off I-72. At Exit 166, take Market Street to Iron Horse Place and follow the frontage road to the end. The town of Monticello is 2 miles away via Highway 105.

**LOCATION:** 992 Iron Horse Place, Monticello
**PHONE:** 877-762-9011 or 217-762-9011
**WEBSITE:** mrym.org
**E-MAIL:** info@mrym.org

137

# Museum of Science and Industry

One of the Windy City's premier attractions, the Museum of Science and Industry provides an enjoyable, interactive, and educational experience for everyone. You can "ride" the famous *Pioneer Zephyr*, take a coal mine adventure, and view a railroad journey from Chicago to Seattle in miniature.

**CHOICES:** The museum has many railroad-themed exhibits, highlighted by the *Pioneer Zephyr*, which completed a record-setting 13-hour run from Denver to Chicago in 1934. You can tour the locomotive cab, and a tour guide takes you through an observation car, a baggage car, and several other cars. You'll also want to take the coal mine tour, where you can see coal loaded onto a train, and then board a work train.

**WHEN TO GO:** The museum is open daily with extended hours on select days. Special exhibits, including the coal mine and submarine, cost extra.

**GOOD TO KNOW:** There's a lot to see, so it's best to plan your day around the coal mine tour and the *Pioneer Zephyr* experience. You can bring your lunch or grab sandwiches at the museum's Brain Food Court. (The museum is not within walking distance of restaurants.) When exiting the food court, watch the Swiss Jolly Ball, where a metal ball rides a locomotive while navigating around a pinball-type contraption.

**WORTH DOING:** The museum is home to the only German submarine in the United States, which is a popular tour. Also, there are many other interesting permanent and changing exhibits to take in.

**DON'T MISS:** The world's largest model railroad, called The Great Train Story, runs on 1,425 feet of track with 30 trains making their way through Midwest farm fields, around mountains, and over 28 bridges.

**GETTING THERE:** Take a train. Amtrak offers free rides to kids on the *Hiawatha* on summer weekends. Chicago's Metra Electric Line and Indiana's South Shore Line trains stop two blocks from the museum's north entrance (the 57th Street Station).

**LOCATION:** 5700 S. Lake Shore Drive, Chicago
**PHONE:** 773-684-1414
**WEBSITE:** msichicago.org
**E-MAIL:** form on website

# Silver Creek & Stephenson Railroad

Jim Wrinn

This railroad offers a 4-mile ride behind a 1912 geared Heisler steam engine. Trains leave from a reproduction of the original Illinois Central depot in Elroy, and the building houses a large collection of railroad memorabilia.

**CHOICES:** A Heisler steam locomotive pulls several cabooses and an open-air car through farmlands and across Yellow Creek on a 30-foot-high cement and stone pier bridge. The Silver Creek depot houses the ticket office and railroad displays.

**WHEN TO GO:** The train ride operates on various weekends and holidays between Memorial Day and the end of October. The Train of Terror operates in October.

**GOOD TO KNOW:** Volunteers created this railroad on the abandoned right-of-way of the Chicago, Milwaukee, St. Paul & Pacific Railroad. Because rails and ties were removed prior to purchase, members had to haul rail in from as far away as Minnesota, and ties were salvaged from across Illinois.

**WORTH DOING:** While in Freeport, visit the Silver Creek Museum. It contains 28 rooms of historical displays. It is open the same days as the railroad.

**DON'T MISS:** Give the 36-ton Heisler a close inspection. Unlike most steam locomotives, it is driven with a V-2 arrangement of the cylinders on either side of the boiler; they run a crankshaft that moves a gearbox and wheels. Fewer than 1,200 of these locomotives were built, and only a handful remain in operation today.

**GETTING THERE:** Freeport is about 20 miles west of Rockford on Highway 20, and the museum is on the corner of Walnut and Lamm Roads.

**LOCATION:** 2954 S. Walnut Road, Freeport
**PHONE:** 815-232-2306 or 815-235-2198
**WEBSITE:** thefreeportshow.com
**E-MAIL:** thefreeportshow@thefreeportshow.com

# INDIANA

## The Depot

A replica of Salem's former Monon depot, this museum was built by high school students. It features a Monon caboose, various artifacts, and a model railroad. The museum is open Tuesdays through Saturdays April through December and Saturdays only the rest of the year. The depot is part of the John Hay Center museum complex, which also contains a pioneer village and the Stevens Memorial Museum.

LOCATION: 206 S. College Avenue, Salem
PHONE: 812-883-1884
WEBSITE: salemdepot.com
E-MAIL: cecil38@gmail.com

## Hoosier Valley Railroad Museum

The museum sits in an area rich in railroad history. HVRM brings the past back to life with historic equipment that served not only North Judson, but northern Indiana, Illinois, and Michigan. Open Saturdays year-round, the museum has more than 30 pieces of rolling stock. It also offers 45-minute train rides every Saturday May through October and for special events.

LOCATION: 507 Mulberry Street, North Judson
PHONE: 574-896-3950
WEBSITE: hoosiervalley.org
E-MAIL: questions@hoosiervalley.org

## Indiana Transportation Museum

Located in picturesque Forest Park in Noblesville, the Indiana Transportation Museum offers visitors an excellent way to learn about the history of railroads in Indiana through static displays and tours of the facilities. Forest Park offers a full day of activities for a family, including an aquatic center, carousel, miniature golf, and a playground area. Trains are currently not operating.

LOCATION: Forest Park Drive, Noblesville
PHONE: 317-773-6000
WEBSITE: itm.org
E-MAIL: info@itm.org

# Linden Depot Museum

The Linden Depot Museum contains memorabilia from the two railroads it served, the Nickel Plate Road and the Monon Railroad. It displays a caboose from the NKP, several railcars, and other pieces of equipment. Built in 1907, it is listed on the National Register of Historic Places. It is open Fridays through Sundays April through October with special hours for winter holidays.

LOCATION: 520 N. Main Street, Linden
PHONE: 765-427-3630
WEBSITE: lindendepotmuseum.org
E-MAIL: lindendepotmuseum@gmail.com

# Madison Railroad Station

This restored 1895 Pennsylvania Railroad station is known for its unique octagon waiting room with stained glass windows. Exhibits describe the railroad station and Madison's railroad incline. You can visit an agent's office, try the functional telegraph key, and walk through a restored, wooden caboose. It is open Tuesday through Saturday.

LOCATION: 615 W. First Street, Madison
PHONE: 812-265-2335
WEBSITE: jchshc.net
E-MAIL: form on website

# Monon Connection Museum

The museum features a completely furnished, full-size replica of an Illinois Central depot and outdoor displays. Exhibits include a large collection of dining car china, hundreds of hand-held lanterns, and restored brass steam locomotive bells and whistles. It is open Tuesday through Sunday. The Whistle Stop restaurant adjoins the museum.

LOCATION: 10012 N. Highway 421, Monon
PHONE: 219-253-4101
WEBSITE: mononconnection.com
E-MAIL: form on website

# National New York Central Railroad Museum

You begin your journey through the history of the New York Central by entering through a 1915 passenger coach. In the main gallery, which is a 100-year-old freight house, hands-on exhibits let you construct track and operate a steam locomotive. Outside, the museum's collection of locomotives and rolling stock includes an NYC Mohawk 4-8-2 and a Pennsylvania Railroad GG1. It is closed Mondays.

LOCATION: 721 S. Main Street, Elkhart
PHONE: 574-294-3001
WEBSITE: nycrrmuseum.org
E-MAIL: info@nycrrmuseum.org

# Princeton Train Depot

The Princeton depot features artifacts of the railroads that served the area and displays a caboose. The restored Chicago & Eastern Illinois passenger depot was built in 1875. The Gibson County Visitors Bureau is also housed in the depot. It is open Monday through Friday.

LOCATION: 702 W. Broadway Street, Princeton
PHONE: 812-385-0999
WEBSITE: gibsoncountyin.org
E-MAIL: info@gibsoncountyin.org

# Spirit of Jasper

Owned by the city, the Spirit of Jasper operates an excursion to French Lick as well as a dinner train. The excursion allows you to explore the Indiana Railway Museum, French Lick Springs Resort & Casino, and the West Baden Springs Hotel. Aboard the dinner train, you can partake in a meal provided by a local German restaurant. Fall foliage, Strassenfest, and other dinner excursions also run.

LOCATION: 201 Mill Street, Jasper
PHONE: 812-482-5959 or 812-482-9229
WEBSITE: spiritofjasper.com
E-MAIL: form on website

# Wabash Valley Railroaders Museum

The museum features two interlocking towers with operating machines, a depot, a PRR caboose, and a viewing platform adjacent to CSXT main lines. Haley Tower was one of the last manned interlocking towers in the Midwest, and the 1910 Spring Hill Tower was the last lever interlocking machine on the Canadian Pacific. It is open weekends May through October.

LOCATION: 1316 Plum Street, Terre Haute
PHONE: 812-238-9958
WEBSITE: wvrrm.org
E-MAIL: wvrrminfo@gmail.com

# Fort Wayne Railroad Historical Society

Samuel Phillips

The Fort Wayne Railroad Historical Society operates one of the nation's largest operational, mainline steam locomotives, Nickel Plate Road 2-8-4 No. 765, which runs on excursions in the Northeast, Midwest, and Chicago areas.

**CHOICES:** On weekends when the locomotive is not on tour, you can tour the shop and check out the 400-ton No. 765 and other pieces of historic rail equipment. Make sure to talk with volunteers who restore everything from baggage carts to locomotives.

**WHEN TO GO:** During the society's annual open house, you can view No. 765 and ride aboard a vintage caboose. Santa trains run in December. The locomotive typically visits the Cuyahoga Valley Scenic Railroad between Cleveland, Ohio, and Akron, Ohio, each September. Check the website for current details.

**GOOD TO KNOW:** No. 765, a 1944 Berkshire type and a product of the Lima (Ohio) Locomotive Works, is one of the most modern and powerful steam locomotives still capable of operation. It was restored to operation in 1979 after years of work and, before that, display in Fort Wayne.

**WORTH DOING:** Excursions typically offer coach, lounge, and first-class seating. A ride in a dome car is an exceptional experience that provides a unique vantage point.

**DON'T MISS:** You can track No. 765 using a GPS app available from the society's website.

**GETTING THERE:** The restoration shop is just east of Fort Wayne in the village of New Haven. From Fort Wayne, take I-469 to Exit 21. Turn right on Harper Road, then right on Ryan Road, and left on Edgerton Road.

**LOCATION:** 15808 Edgerton Road, New Haven
**PHONE:** 260-493-0765
**WEBSITE:** fortwaynerailroad.org
**E-MAIL:** contact@fwrhs.org

# French Lick Scenic Railway

Steve Patterson

For many years, the Southern Railway and the Monon Railroad brought scores of vacationers to the mineral spring baths in the southern Indiana hill country. Today, the museum offers a 18-mile diesel-powered round trip that leaves from the historic 1907 depot that served both railroads and travels through beautiful forested country and the 2,200-foot Burton tunnel.

**CHOICES:** Located in a historic passenger depot, the Indiana Railway Museum operates the French Lick Scenic Railway. Two-hour excursions through the Hoosier National Forest travel along lakes and limestone cuts. The museum also features an impressive collection of equipment that includes more that 65 pieces of rolling stock, including steam and diesel locomotives.

**WHEN TO GO:** The museum is open year-round. Trains begin operating in March with special trains running throughout the year including train robberies and the popular Polar Express in November and December. Trips in October feature beautiful fall colors of the scenic Hoosier National Forest.

**GOOD TO KNOW:** French Lick is on Eastern Standard Time, which is good to remember when visiting from the Central time zone. You are still able to soak in the sulfur-rich spring water with 25-minute baths at the spas of the French Lick Springs Hotel and the West Baden Springs Hotel.

**WORTH DOING:** Southern Indiana is home to a variety of caves ready for exploring, such as Squire Boone Caverns, Wyandotte Caves, and Marengo Cave.

**DON'T MISS:** Be sure to check out the former Louisville, New Albany & Corydon Railroad boxcar No. 14023 repainted as a Pluto water car that shipped Pluto mineral water, which was bottled by the French Lick Springs Hotel.

**GETTING THERE:** French Lick is in southern Indiana, easily accessible from Bloomington (60 miles), Columbus (90 miles), and Indianapolis (110 miles). From Indianapolis or Bloomington, take Highway 37 to Highway 56. Take Highway 56 west to French Lick and the museum. From Columbus, take I-65 to Highway 56.

**LOCATION:** 8594 W. State Road 56, French Lick
**PHONE:** 800-748-7246
**WEBSITE:** frenchlickscenicrailway.org
**E-MAIL:** form on website

# Hesston Steam Museum

Hesston Steam Museum, Gary Babcoke III

**This museum runs steam trains of two narrow gauges, 2-foot and 3-foot, in a parklike setting. It also offers miniature live steam operations and other steam-powered attractions including a sawmill and a steam crane.**

**CHOICES:** Ride a steam locomotive, in your choice of gauges, through the museum's 155-acre site. Each train travels over a different route. Wander through a unique collection of steam equipment. Be sure to look for a 1929 Shay logging locomotive and a Czech 0-4-0 built in 1940. On special days, watch the 92-ton, steam-powered log crane feed logs to the steam-powered lumber mill.

**WHEN TO GO:** Trains run weekends and holidays Memorial Day through Labor Day and then on several Sundays in October. On Memorial Day weekend and over the July 4th holiday, additional steam equipment runs, the sawmill operates, and other activities take place. In fall, ride the ghost train if you dare, and in December, try the Candy Cane Express. Several other special days take place during the season.

**GOOD TO KNOW:** Keep an eye out for a Kiddieland train ride. The museum operates two of the locomotives from the former suburban Chicago amusement park. The locomotives are coal-powered steam engines.

**WORTH DOING:** You can visit the La Porte County Historical Society Museum, which contains 80,000 artifacts. Among them are more than 800 antique firearms and weapons.

**DON'T MISS:** At the steam museum, Doc's 1930's vintage soda fountain serves up ice cream treats in a historic setting. The annual Hesston Steam & Power Show takes place over Labor Day weekend. In addition to train rides, the event features the operation of antique farm equipment, tractors, and other machinery.

**GETTING THERE:** The museum is in northern Indiana near the Michigan border and is about a 90-minute drive from Chicago. It is easily accessible from either I-94 (Exit 1) or the Indiana toll road (Exit 49) on County Road 1000.

**LOCATION:** 1201 E. County Road 1000 North, La Porte
**PHONE:** 219-778-2783 or 219-872-5055
**WEBSITE:** hesston.org
**E-MAIL:** ted.rita@hesston.org

# Whitewater Valley Railroad

WVRR Collection/Thomas Bookout

This surprising 19-mile line travels from Connersville to Metamora with much of the trip near the Whitewater Canal. The scenic route features excellent views of area forests and farms.

**CHOICES:** The railroad offers standard, open-window coaches as well as caboose rides on its 32-mile, 5-hour round trip. A 2-hour layover gives you a chance to tour Metamora, a restored canal town.

**WHEN TO GO:** Regular excursion trains operate on Saturdays and Sundays from May through October. During the year, watch for special event trains, such as the Metamora Canal Days Limited, the Wild West Train, a dinner train, and fall foliage trains. Other events are themed around holidays and children's activities.

**GOOD TO KNOW:** Look for New York Central transfer caboose No. 18278 and try to ride aboard this unique railcar.

**WORTH DOING:** Metamora is a popular getaway spot with plenty of art galleries, shops, and restaurants. Take time to explore the city's historic buildings. You can also watch its water-powered grist mill in action and take a boat ride along the canal. Enjoy Canal Days in early October with a train ride, shopping, food, and arts and crafts.

**DON'T MISS:** Inspect the operating diesel built by the Lima-Hamilton Locomotive Works. Believed to be the last of its kind in operation today, locomotive No. 25 was one of only 174 diesels built by this company. The museum also owns three others from this builder, making this the largest collection of Lima-built diesel locomotives in existence.

**GETTING THERE:** Connersville is about 65 miles southeast of Indianapolis and is accessible from all directions. If coming from the north, take Highway 1 off I-70 into Connersville. The depot is on your left between Fourth and Fifth Streets.

**LOCATION:** 455 Market Street, Connersville
**PHONE:** 765-825-2054
**WEBSITE:** whitewatervalleyrr.org
**E-MAIL:** publicity@whitewatervalleyrr.org

# MICHIGAN

## Clinton Northern Railway Museum

Housed in a historic Grand Trunk depot, the museum's artifacts include tools, signs, and station agent items. A 1902 Barney & Smith sleeper car, a 1903 post office-baggage car, a 1926 Ann Arbor maintenance-of-way crew car, and a 1927 wooden caboose are also on display. It is open Sundays May through October.

LOCATION: 107 E. Railroad Street, St. Johns
PHONE: 989-224-6134
WEBSITE: clintonnorthernrailway.org
E-MAIL: mccampbell60@gmail.com

## Coopersville & Marne Railway

Powered by an EMD SW9 diesel locomotive, this railway's 14-mile, 90-minute round-trip excursion travels through farmland and over an open-deck girder bridge. At Marne, you can watch the engine uncouple, run along a passing siding, and couple to the other end. Excursions run Wednesdays and Saturdays May through September with special theme trains in other months. Look for a new station at 306 E. Main Street in fall 2017.

LOCATION: 311 Danforth Street, Coopersville
PHONE: 616-997-7000
WEBSITE: coopersvilleandmarne.org
E-MAIL: info@mitrain.net

## Durand Union Station

This 100-year-old depot museum was the second busiest depot in Michigan, and its lower level has been restored to its former glory with terrazzo floors and oak trim. Still functioning as a depot, the building also houses the Michigan Railroad History Museum. Open Tuesday through Sunday, the museum contains changing exhibits on state and local railroading.

LOCATION: 200 Railroad Street, Durand
PHONE: 989-288-3561
WEBSITE: durandstation.org
E-MAIL: form on website

# Flushing Area Museum

The museum's collection includes permanent displays of railroad artifacts as well as local historical exhibits. It is housed in the Flushing depot, which was built in 1888 and provided passenger service until 1971. The building was restored to its former appearance by the Flushing Area Historical Society. It is open Tuesdays all year and Sundays May to December.

LOCATION: 431 W. Main Street, Flushing
PHONE: 810-487-0814
WEBSITE: flushinghistorical.org
E-MAIL: fahs@att.net

# Houghton County Historical Museum

The museum includes the restored Mineral Range depot, which contains a collection of Copper County railroad artifacts, and other historic buildings. The museum operates the Lake Linden & Torch Lake Railroad. A narrow gauge 0-4-0 Porter steam locomotive or a diesel engine takes you on a half-mile ride. The museum is open June through September.

LOCATION: 53102 Highway M-26, Lake Linden
PHONE: 906-296-4121
WEBSITE: houghtonhistory.org
E-MAIL: info@houghtonhistory.org

# Michigan Transit Museum

The Michigan Transit Museum is housed in a depot restored to its 1900 appearance and includes railroading exhibits from that time. The transit museum displays several locomotives and railcars. It also offers a 30-minute, round-trip train ride that departs from Joy Park. Located near the Selfridge Military Air Museum, the transit museum is open weekends year-round, and trains run Sundays June through October.

LOCATION: 200 Grand Avenue, Mount Clemens
PHONE: 586-463-1863
WEBSITE: michigantransitmuseum.org
E-MAIL: webmaster@michigantransitmuseum.org

## New Buffalo Railroad Museum

The museum is housed in a replica of a Pere Marquette depot that stood nearby. It features artifacts from the Pere Marquette, Chesapeake & Ohio, and CSX. Pullman Company memorabilia is also on display. You can walk through a restored Chessie boxcar and a Pullman troop sleeper, which contains WWII artifacts. It is open daily April through December.

LOCATION: 530 S. Whittaker Street, New Buffalo
PHONE: 269 469-8010
WEBSITE: newbuffalorailroadmuseum.org
E-MAIL: ask@newbuffalorailroadmuseum.org

## Old Road Dinner Train

Aboard dining cars from the 1930s, the train provides dining and entertainment from two locations, Blissfield and Charlotte. The murder mystery dinner trains provide a five-course dinner as you participate in a comical, interactive mystery show.

LOCATION: 301 E. Adrian Street, Blissfield
PHONE: 888-467-2451
WEBSITE: murdermysterydinnertrain.com
E-MAIL: form on website

## Saginaw Railway Museum

Located in a restored 1907 Pere Marquette depot, this museum displays an RS1 locomotive, several cabooses, a combine coach, and various boxcars. It includes an 1898 armstrong interlocking tower as well as a variety of smaller artifacts. It is open the first and third Saturdays May through November.

LOCATION: 900 Maple Street, Saginaw
PHONE: 989-790-7994
WEBSITE: facebook.com/saginawrailwaymuseum
E-MAIL: info@saginawrailwaymuseum.org

# Southern Michigan Railroad

The railroad offers passenger excursions between Clinton and Tecumseh. Along the 2-hour round trip, the train crosses River Raisin and the Red Mill Pond on a trestle. The railroad also operates a museum. Rides begin in May and go into December with Santa specials. In fall, you can see the colors or travel to the Clinton Fall Festival and Appleumpkin Festival. Some rides leave from Tecumseh.

LOCATION: 320 S. Division Street, Clinton
PHONE: 517-456-7677
WEBSITE: southernmichiganrailroad.com
E-MAIL: ridesmr@gmail.com

**150**

# SS City of Milwaukee

The SS *City of Milwaukee*, a national historic landmark, is the last surviving traditional Great Lakes railroad car ferry. Built in 1931, the *City of Milwaukee* served the Grand Trunk Western and Ann Arbor Railroads. The car deck houses five Ann Arbor boxcars that serve as exhibit spaces and a theater. The Coast Guard cutter *Acacia* is docked on site, and tours of both ships are offered. In summer, the car ferry provides bed & breakfast service, and in fall, it becomes a ghost ship.

LOCATION: 99 Arthur Street, Manistee
PHONE: 231-723-3587
WEBSITE: carferry.com

# Tri-Cities Historical Museum

The Tri-Cities Historical Museum operates out of two buildings including a former Grand Trunk Western depot that was built in 1870. Located on the banks of the Grand River, the Depot Museum of Transportation contains exhibits related to railroad, maritime, and other forms of transportation. On display is a Pere Marquette Railway steam locomotive. The Depot Museum of Transportation closes during winter.

LOCATION: 1 North Harbor Drive, Grand Haven
PHONE: 616-842-0700
WEBSITE: tri-citiesmuseum.org

# Wheels of History

This history museum is housed in a pre-1905 wooden railroad passenger car and a caboose. Exhibits include photographs and artifacts of area railroads, logging, Lake Superior fishing boats, and everyday life in early Brimley. It is open weekends mid-May to mid-October, with an expanded schedule (Wednesday through Sunday) during summer.

LOCATION: Depot Street and M-221, Brimley
PHONE: 906-248-3665
WEBSITE: baymillsbrimleyhistory.org
E-MAIL: euprussell@yahoo.com

# Greenfield Village at The Henry Ford

The Henry Ford

The Henry Ford claims to be America's greatest history attraction, and even though it's in the capital of—and shrine to—the automobile, railroads are well represented here. The centerpiece for this is the Detroit, Toledo & Milwaukee roundhouse, a reconstruction of the original in Marshall, Mich., believed to be one of only seven 19th century roundhouses remaining. A steam railroad encircles the historic 90-acre village.

**CHOICES:** You can ride the train around the village in open-air cars on a 30-minute narrated trip. Departing from the 1859 Smiths Creek depot, the train also makes stops at strategic locations throughout the village. The roundhouse includes hands-on railroading displays and a 1902 Atlantic engine. A mezzanine provides an excellent vantage point from where you can see work going on. Also, be sure to go inside the Henry Ford museum to view railroad cars and locomotives, including a Chesapeake & Ohio 2-6-6-6 Allegheny type, one of the largest steam locomotives ever built.

**WHEN TO GO:** Greenfield Village is open daily mid-April until early November. In mid-November, it is open Friday through Sunday, and in December, it is open select evenings for Holiday Nights. It is closed the remainder of the year.

**GOOD TO KNOW:** Railroad Junction, where the roundhouse and depot are located, is one of seven different historic districts in Greenfield Village. In Henry Ford's Model T District, you can tour a replica of Ford's first factory and ride in a Model T.

**WORTH DOING:** On December nights, celebrate the holidays in Greenfield Village. The Holiday Nights event features entertainment, carriage and Model T rides, Santa and his reindeer, ice skating, and fireworks.

**DON'T MISS:** Get to the roundhouse early in the day to help the crew turn the steam engine on the turntable. It's so well balanced that two people can do it, but it's more fun when you get to push a giant engine around.

**GETTING THERE:** Just west of Detroit, the Henry Ford is located in Dearborn on the corner of Village Road and Oakwood Boulevard, just west of the Southfield Freeway and south of Michigan Avenue (Highway 12). There is easy access from I-94 or I-75.

**LOCATION:** 20900 Oakwood Boulevard, Dearborn
**PHONE:** 800-835-5237 or 313-982-6001
**WEBSITE:** thehenryford.org
**E-MAIL:** form on website

# Huckleberry Railroad

Huckleberry Railroad

The Huckleberry Railroad is part of a historical village that is operated by Genesee County Parks in Flint. The narrow gauge railroad is built on an abandoned Pere Marquette Railway right-of-way. An 8-mile, 40-minute ride carries passengers through neighborhoods, by a lake, and into wooded areas.

**CHOICES:** Ride in one of the railroad's historic coaches or cabooses pulled by a Baldwin 4-6-0 or a Baldwin 2-8-2.

**WHEN TO GO:** Trains run Memorial Day weekend through Labor Day, with special events held throughout the year, including days out with Thomas the Tank Engine and Halloween and Christmas trains. During the railroad's railfan weekend, usually held in August, you can see all the trains, take photos, and talk with the train crews.

**GOOD TO KNOW:** The Huckleberry Railroad was named because it ran so slow that a person could jump off the train, pick some huckleberries, and jump back on the train without breaking a sweat.

**WORTH DOING:** Take a stroll through Crossroads Village, which has 34 historic structures on 51 acres. Costumed interpreters welcome you to the homes, mills, and shops that date back to the 1800s. Special events are scheduled throughout the summer, and you can take a ride on a paddle-wheel riverboat.

**DON'T MISS:** Take a close look at Rio Grande 2-8-2 No. 464, which is one of a rare class of narrow gauge Mikado type steam locomotives on the Colorado railroad. Built in 1903 and restored in 2005, it was nicknamed *Mudhen* because it waddled like a chicken as it went down the tracks.

**GETTING THERE:** The railroad is located just north of Flint, about an hour from Detroit. From Detroit, take I-75 to I-475. Follow I-475 north to Saginaw Street (Exit 13). Take Saginaw Street north to Stanley Road, turn east on Stanley Road, and then turn south on Bray Road to the village and railroad.

**LOCATION:** 6140 Bray Road, Flint
**PHONE:** 800-648-7275 or 810-736-7100
**WEBSITE:** geneseecountyparks.org
**E-MAIL:** parkswebteam@gcparks.org

# Little River Railroad

Dave Crosby

Whoever said bigger is better never visited the Little River Railroad. This railroad is home to one of the smallest standard gauge steam locomotives of its type ever built. No. 110 is a 57-ton Pacific that has all the charm of a ballerina, and the railroad offers trips behind it from Coldwater to nearby Quincy.

CHOICES: Ride in a coach or open-air car. During the 30-minute layover in Quincy, be sure to exit the train and watch as the locomotive is switched to the other end of the train. At times, a second locomotive, 0-4-0T No. 1, is in service. The railroad offers a variety of special events throughout the year including fall color trains, Christmas trains, and Easter trains. Length of trips range between 45 and 90 minutes.

WHEN TO GO: Regular excursions run weekends Memorial Day through September.

GOOD TO KNOW: Engine No. 110 started out on the Little River Railroad in east Tennessee. An Indiana family, the Blooms, rescued her and rebuilt it for excursion work in the 1970s, and members of that same family continue this tradition of preservation.

WORTH DOING: The area features many antique shops and preserved buildings. In Coldwater, take in a film at the Capri Drive-in, one of the last of its kind.

DON'T MISS: Take time to look over the exhibits in the Coldwater depot, an 1883 Lake Shore & Michigan Southern depot.

GETTING THERE: Coldwater is in south-central Michigan. Take I-69 to Exit 13 for Coldwater. Follow Highway 12 west, turn left onto Division Street, and then turn right onto Park Avenue to the depot.

**LOCATION:** 29 W. Park Avenue, Coldwater
**PHONE:** 574-215-0751
**WEBSITE:** littleriverrailroad.com
**E-MAIL:** customerservice@
littleriverrailroad.com

# Steam Railroading Institute

Jim Wrinn

The Steam Railroading Institute is all about preserving steam locomotives, and there is always restoration work going on. The institute displays equipment and offers some all-day train rides.

**CHOICES:** Both steam- and diesel-powered excursions are offered. Steam power is provided by Pere Marquette 2-8-4 No. 1225. The 7-acre site includes a roundhouse, a turntable, and a variety of railcars. Look around the museum, which is housed in a renovated freight warehouse that was also a creamery. It now contains exhibits, artifacts, and a model train layout.

**WHEN TO GO:** The museum is open Wednesday through Sunday Memorial Day to Labor Day, and special events are scheduled as well. It closes in January and February and then reopens Fridays to Sundays. In November and December, the North Pole Express is the big event as a diesel locomotive takes visitors on a 24-mile round trip to the North Pole, where kids can enjoy hot cocoa, activities, and visiting Santa. Reserve early, as this event sells out fast.

**GOOD TO KNOW:** No. 1225 was the model and sound effects source for the steam train in the popular movie, *The Polar Express*.

**WORTH DOING:** If you like to watch things go fast, the Owosso Speedway offers short track racing on Saturday, Saturday, Saturday.

**DON'T MISS:** The Michigan Railroad History Museum is housed in historic Durand Union Station, 20 minutes away in Durand.

**GETTING THERE:** Owosso is about 30 miles northeast of Lansing and 30 miles west of Flint. From Flint, take Highway 21 west to Owosso. From Lansing, take I-69 to Highway 52 north to Owosso. In Owosso, the Steam Railroading Institute is on south Washington Street.

**LOCATION:** 405 S. Washington Street, Owosso
**PHONE:** 989-725-9464
**WEBSITE:** michigansteamtrain.com
**E-MAIL:** info@mstrp.com

# OHIO

## Bradford Railroad Museum

Located in a former bank building, the museum contains photos and displays that allow you to journey through Bradford's railroad history. The museum has also restored Bradford's former PRR interlocking tower. It is open Saturdays April through September.

LOCATION: 200 N. Miami Avenue, Bradford
PHONE: 937-552-2196
WEBSITE: bradfordrrmuseum.org
E-MAIL: bormrr@yahoo.com

## Carillon Historical Park

Resembling a train station, as well as a roundhouse, the park's transportation center houses the 1835 B&O *John Quincy Adams* (the oldest existing American-built locomotive), a Barney & Smith parlor car, and other rail and transportation exhibits. It is open daily.

LOCATION: 1000 Carillon Boulevard, Dayton
PHONE: 937-293-2841
WEBSITE: daytonhistory.org
E-MAIL: info@ daytonhistory.org

## Cedar Point

Several coal-fired steam locomotives operate on the 3-foot gauge Cedar Point & Lake Erie Railroad, located within the Cedar Point Amusement Park. Trains operate on a 1.5-mile loop continuously throughout the day at the park known as the "Roller Coaster Capital of the World." The park's season runs from May through October.

LOCATION: 1 Cedar Point Drive, Sandusky
PHONE: 419-627-2350
WEBSITE: cedarpoint.com
E-MAIL: form on website

# Cincinnati Dinner Train

Operating every Saturday throughout the year except during January and February, the dinner train travels east from Madisonville to downtown Cincinnati, along the riverfront, and back. You'll enjoy the scenery and a four-course meal during a leisurely 3-hour excursion aboard two restored 1940s dining cars or the Silver Sword, which was originally a Chicago, Burlington & Quincy coach.

LOCATION: 4725 Madison Road, Cincinnati
PHONE: 513-791-7245
WEBSITE: cincinnatirailway.com/dinnertrain
E-MAIL: form on website

# Conneaut Railroad Museum

Located in a Lake Shore & Michigan Southern depot, which was built in 1900, this museum displays railroad memorabilia, photos, and artifacts such as lanterns and timetables. Be sure to climb aboard and inspect the cab of Nickel Plate Berkshire No. 755 displayed outside. It is open Memorial Day weekend through Labor Day.

LOCATION: 363 Depot Street, Conneaut
PHONE: 440-599-7878
WEBSITE: facebook.com/chrrm

# Jefferson Depot Village

The Jefferson Depot is more than a depot. It is a small village. In addition to the restored 1872 Lake Shore & Michigan Southern Railroad station, the site features a 1918 caboose and several 19th century buildings including a one-room schoolhouse, a post office, and a church. It is open Saturdays, Sundays, Mondays, and Thursdays June through mid-October.

LOCATION: 147 E. Jefferson Street, Jefferson
PHONE: 614-507-5246 or 440-576-0496
WEBSITE: jeffersondepotvillage.org
E-MAIL: duttonjg@hotmail.com

## Marion Union Station

The station contains a museum, and a fully restored Erie Railroad tower is also on site. Located between two diamond crossings, the station is also a great place to watch trains from. More than 100 go by daily. The museum is open Tuesdays and Thursdays.

LOCATION: 532 W. Center Street, Marion
PHONE: 740-383-3768
WEBSITE: mariononline.com

## Northern Ohio Railway Museum

Numbering more than 40, the museum's collection of streetcars, interurbans, and other railcars continues to grow. It features streetcars and equipment that operated in Cleveland, Shaker Heights, and other cities. You can stop in and take a guided walking tour on Saturdays mid-May through October.

LOCATION: 5515 Buffham Road, Seville
PHONE: 330-769-5501
WEBSITE: northernohiorailwaymuseum.org
E-MAIL: wstoner001@neo.rr.com

## Ohio Railway Museum

This museum displays more than 30 pieces of equipment, including locomotives, passenger cars, and streetcars, with a focus on the Ohio Railway. It offers 2-mile streetcar rides as well as some rides in its diesel-pulled passenger car. The museum is open Sunday afternoons.

LOCATION: 990 Proprietors Road, Worthington
PHONE: 614-885-7345
WEBSITE: ohiorailwaymuseum.org
E-MAIL: info@ohiorailwaymuseum.net

## Orrville Railroad Heritage Society

The society offers a variety of excursions, including trips on the Wheeling & Lake Erie Railway, fall rides, and holiday trains. Railroad Days in August and other special events take place at the restored Orrville depot.

LOCATION: 145 Depot Street, Orrville
PHONE: 330-683-2426
WEBSITE: orrvillerailroad.com
E-MAIL: form on website

# Cuyahoga Valley Scenic Railroad

Mark Perri

The Cuyahoga Valley Scenic Railroad regularly operates 25 miles of track through northeastern Ohio, from Independence (near Cleveland) through Peninsula to downtown Akron. Much of the railroad is in the picturesque Cuyahoga Valley National Park, along the Cuyahoga River and the route of the abandoned Ohio & Erie Canal.

**CHOICES:** The CVSR runs an extensive schedule of regular trains, beginning in late January, from various boarding stations. In addition, special events run February through November. They include a variety of wine trains, educational trains, and a premier Polar Express train. There are several seating options including those in an elevated dome section that offer a panoramic view of the park. For 2017, the railroad has debuted a new version of its striking paint scheme on its classic FPA4 locomotives.

**WHEN TO GO:** The summer months offer the most extensive schedule of regular trains. Mid-October offers extra trains for viewing the beautiful fall foliage. Trains are less crowded yet still offer spectacular scenery in April and September.

**GOOD TO KNOW:** The Cuyahoga Valley National Park features the Towpath Trail, which was built along much of the Ohio and Erie Canal Towpath. It is excellent for hiking and biking, and the railroad has an extensive schedule of heavily discounted Bike Aboard fares that cater to bicyclists.

**WORTH DOING:** Explore many of the restored historical buildings in the national park, including the Canal Visitor Center (accessible by train) that details the canal's history and includes an operating canal lock.

**DON'T MISS:** The east side of the train generally includes the best views of the Cuyahoga River, which parallels the railroad, especially on the north end from Peninsula up to Independence. Many photo opportunities abound, and the park has re-created the feel of the early 1900s by building many of the railroad's depots and shelters in a style modeled after the railroad's original structures.

**GETTING THERE:** The Ohio Turnpike crosses the CVSR near Peninsula, and I-77 generally parallels the railroad from Cleveland to Canton.

**LOCATION:** 1630 W. Mill Street, Peninsula
**PHONE:** 800-468-4070 or 330-439-5708
**WEBSITE:** cvsr.com
**E-MAIL:** form on website

# Dennison Railroad Depot Museum

Mark Perri

This meticulously restored ex-Pennsylvania Railroad depot, built in 1873, houses a comprehensive collection of exhibits highlighting the depot's significance as a World War II serviceman's canteen. It was awarded National Historic Landmark status.

**CHOICES:** Dennison Railroad Depot Museum offers both guided and self-guided tours. Take time to explore a recent addition, the Times Square, an ex-Pennsy business car that is now an exhibit and meeting space. A variety of interactive exhibits, many designed for children, allows visitors to climb in a caboose, sleep in a Pullman bunk, and send a message by telegraph. The museum also contains local history exhibits, houses a research library, and features a collection of railcars.

**WHEN TO GO:** The museum is open year-round but is closed on Mondays. It hosts numerous special events including an annual three-day Soldiers Homecoming Festival, complete with reenactors that celebrates the museum's wartime heritage.

**GOOD TO KNOW:** If you are hungry, a diner-style restaurant, the Canteen Grill, is located in the depot and offers excellent meals. Across the street, Dennison Yard, a local bar and grill, features a wonderful home-cooked Italian menu. There is also a picnic area on the museum's platform.

**WORTH DOING:** Dennison is close to Ohio's Amish Country in the east-central part of the state. The Pro Football Hall of Fame is 45 minutes north in Canton. The museum offers a Golden Triple Ticket, which provides discounted admission to its nearby affiliated museum partners, the Uhrichsville Clay Museum and Historic Schoenbrunn Village.

**DON'T MISS:** If you would like to see a hand-carved wooden locomotive, Warther Carvings Museum, 15 minutes away near Dover, features an extensive collection of carved railroad pieces in walnut, ebony, and ivory.

**GETTING THERE:** By car, Dennison is easily reached from I-77 via Route 250 (from the north) or Route 36 (from the south). Once in Dennison, take Second Street past the tracks and then turn left on Center Street.

**LOCATION:** 400 Center Street, Dennison
**PHONE:** 740-922-6776
**WEBSITE:** dennisondepot.org
**E-MAIL:** director@dennisondepot.org

# Hocking Valley Scenic Railway

Hocking Valley, Scenic Railway, T.L. Warren

The Hocking Valley Scenic Railway offers diesel-powered excursions with vintage open-window coaches between Nelsonville and East Logan, over part of the original Hocking Valley Railway's Athens branch. The train takes you through Wayne National Forest, in the foothills of the Appalachians, and along the Hocking River.

**CHOICES:** The railroad's basic excursions are a 14-mile trip to Haydenville and a 22-mile trip to East Logan. The trips are narrated, and you can ride in a 1920s coach, a 1930s heavyweight passenger car, or an open-air car. Along the way, besides enjoying the scenery, you'll see a canal lock, take in historical landmarks, and stop at Robbins Crossing, an 1850s-era log village. The railroad has returned 1920 Baldwin 0-6-0 No. 3 to service for steam power.

**WHEN TO GO:** Regular excursions begin Memorial Day weekend and end in October. To view the stunning fall foliage, Friday trains are added in October. Various holiday and theme trips are offered throughout the year, and include Easter, Halloween, Christmas and train robbery excursions.

**GOOD TO KNOW:** Once a year, the HVR runs a special caboose train that railfans and photographers will especially enjoy.

**WORTH DOING:** There is something to do for everyone in Wayne National Forest. It has more than 300 miles of trails for hiking and riding bikes, horses, and ATVs. In Nelsonville, you can explore the Public Square, which contains Stuart's Opera House, the Dew House, and other historic buildings.

**DON'T MISS:** On your visit to Robbins Crossing, you'll see a group of original log cabins arranged into a historical village. They include a schoolhouse, blacksmith shop, general store, and several homes. Costumed guides offer commentary and demonstrate crafts.

**GETTING THERE:** Nelsonville is approximately 56 miles from Columbus and about 200 miles from Cleveland. From Columbus, take Route 33 to Nelsonville. In downtown Nelsonville, take Hocking Parkway south to the depot.

**LOCATION:** 33 W. Canal Street, Nelsonville
**PHONE:** 740-249-1452
**WEBSITE:** hvsry.org

# Lebanon Mason Monroe Railroad

Lebanon Mason Monroe Railroad

The Lebanon Mason Monroe Railroad offers a relaxed, 9-mile round-trip through the rural scenery of Warren County and features vintage open-window Lackawanna coaches.

**CHOICES:** The railroad's 1-hour excursions offer seating in open-window coaches, or weather permitting, in an open-air gondola. On the trip, conductors provide narration that describes the railroad's history and operation. In addition to their basic excursions, the LM&M offers many seasonal and theme trains, such as a pizza train, Easter Bunny Express, Day Out with Thomas, and murder mystery trains.

**WHEN TO GO:** Weekend trains begin in April, with occasional weekday trips added in the summer months. October offers the most options, as riders can take in the stunning fall foliage, as well as view fireworks and attend Applefest. The season concludes in December with North Pole Express trains.

**GOOD TO KNOW:** The LM&M partners with the Cincinnati Dinner Train, which runs on Saturdays from Madisonville, about 30 miles away. Dinner train schedules are posted on the LM&M website's calendar.

**WORTH DOING:** Kings Island, one of Ohio's premier roller-coaster amusement parks, is about 20 minutes away, and provides family entertainment and many dining and hotel options.

**DON"T MISS:** Plan on spending time in historic downtown Lebanon, with its classic small town charm. Shopping, arts, antique stores, and restaurants are all within walking distance of the station.

**GETTING THERE:** Lebanon is north of Cincinnati and south of Dayton between I-71 and I-75.

**LOCATION:** 127 S. Mechanic Street, Lebanon
**PHONE:** 513-933-8022
**WEBSITE:** lebanonrr.com
**EMAIL:** info@lebanonrr.com

# Mad River & NKP Railroad Museum

Mad River & NKP Railroad Museum, Brandon Townley

The Mad River & NKP Railroad Museum opened on our nation's bicentennial in 1976 as a lasting tribute to the transportation industry. The museum has a widely varied collection of railroad locomotives, coaches, freight cars, equipment, and structures.

**CHOICES:** While the museum focuses on the Nickel Plate Road and its successors, and includes a substantial collection of diesel locomotives, many unique pieces of equipment, such as CB&Q Silver Dome No. 4714 (the first dome car built in the United States) are present. The museum is comprised of static exhibits. However, many pieces, especially the passenger equipment, have interiors that are open for inspection. In addition, some cars are outfitted with museum displays.

**WHEN TO GO:** The museum is open afternoons daily Memorial Day through Labor Day. In addition, the museum is open weekends in May, September, and October.

**GOOD TO KNOW:** Bellevue is a thriving, quaint rural Ohio town, with ample amenities for food and lodging, and many other options for tourists such as antique shops and flea markets.

**WORTH DOING:** Bellevue is a 30-minute drive from Sandusky and the Cedar Point amusement park, which is known for its roller coasters and its steam-powered, narrow gauge railroad.

**DON'T MISS:** Many opportunities exist for watching and photographing trains from public property around town. Mainline tracks bisect the museum, where you can see Norfolk Southern Heritage units or regional Wheeling & Lake Erie Railway trains. The new Kemper Railroad Park pavilion, located a short walk from the museum, provides a safe vantage point for railfans.

**GETTING THERE:** Bellevue is 20 minutes from the Ohio Turnpike. From the east, take Exit 110, Route 4 south to Route 113, and west to Route 20. From the west, use Exit 91, Route 53 south, and Route 20 east to Bellevue.

**LOCATION:** 253 Southwest Street, Bellevue
**PHONE:** 419-483-2222
**WEBSITE:** madrivermuseum.org
**E-MAIL:** madriver@onebellevue.com

# WISCONSIN

## Brodhead Historical Society Depot Museum

This restored Chicago, Milwaukee & St. Paul depot, built in 1881, houses a permanent railroad display with rotating historical displays. Milwaukee Road Fairbanks-Morse switch engine No. 781 and caboose No. 01900 stand alongside the depot. It is open on Wednesdays, Saturdays, and Sundays between Memorial Day and Labor Day.

LOCATION: 1108 First Center Avenue, Brodhead
PHONE: 608-897-4150
WEBSITE: brodheadhistory.org
E-MAIL: info@brodheadhistory.org

## Colfax Railroad Museum

This museum includes a large collection of railroad memorabilia and an outdoor display of locomotives and rolling stock that features a Porter steam locomotive, Soo Line GP30 diesel engine, a wooden Soo caboose, a heavyweight coach, and other pieces of rolling stock. It is open Wednesday through Sunday May through October.

LOCATION: 500 E. Railroad Avenue, Colfax
PHONE: 715-962-2076
WEBSITE: colfaxrrmuseum.org
E-MAIL: form on website

## Frederic Historical Society Museum

This museum is housed in a restored 1901 Soo Line depot. It features railroad memorabilia as well as displays of the area's history. Also on display is a 1963 Soo Line caboose. It is open weekends Memorial Day into fall.

LOCATION: 210 W. Oak Street, Frederic
PHONE: 715-327-4158
WEBSITE: fredericwi.com

# Historical Village

The village features a restored C&NW depot and several other historical structures, including an octagon house. Built in 1923, the depot is authentically furnished and contains railroad artifacts. It also displays a 1941 diesel engine, a Soo caboose, and a C&NW caboose. The museum is open the first and third Sundays during summer and Heritage Days & Rail Fest in August.

LOCATION: 900 Montgomery Street, New London
PHONE: 920-982-8557 or 920-982-5186
WEBSITE: historicalvillage.org

# Mineral Point Railroad Museum

The museum is housed in a stone Milwaukee Road depot, which is the oldest depot building in the state. It contains exhibits on the two Mineral Point railroads as well as others. A interactive diorama of the area around 1920 is a popular attraction. The museum is open Thursdays through Sundays May through October.

LOCATION: 11 Commerce Street, Mineral Point
PHONE: 608-987-2695
WEBSITE: mineralpointrailroads.com
E-MAIL: form on website

# Railroad Memories Museum

This museum contains 12 rooms filled with railroad memories. Artifacts include lanterns, track equipment, photos, and other items. Housed in a former C&NW depot, it is located next to the Wisconsin Great Northern Railroad. The museum is open Memorial Day weekend through Labor Day.

LOCATION: 424 N. Front Street, Spooner
PHONE: 715-635-3325
WEBSITE: facebook.com/railroadmemoriesmuseumspooner
E-MAIL: rrmuseumspoonx@gmail.com

# Camp Five

Jeff Terry

Camp Five offers a steam train powered by a vintage 2-6-2 type logging locomotive. It takes you to the site of a timber company's 1914 farm camp, where you can tour a logging museum and other buildings.

**CHOICES:** After boarding at an 1880s Soo Line depot, you ride the steam train 2.5 miles to the museum. You can ride in a passenger coach, an open-air car made from a boxcar, or a caboose. Your admission includes a 30-minute narrated tour about forestry techniques on a motorized surrey through a forest of indigenous trees.

**WHEN TO GO:** Camp Five has a short season. It is open Monday through Saturday, starting in June and running through August. It is also open Saturdays in September.

**GOOD TO KNOW:** At the farm camp, the lumber company raised meat, produce, and horses to supply other camps as they set up in the forest. The camp's 4-Spot locomotive was built in 1916 and is the only Prairie-style steam locomotive operating in the state.

**WORTH DOING:** Forest County is filled with lakes and covered by the Nicolet National Forest, so there are many opportunities for fishing, hiking, and other recreational activities.

**DON'T MISS:** There is plenty to do at Camp Five. You can view exhibits on forestry, examine logging equipment, visit a nature center, feed farm animals, and take an ecology walking tour. At the logging camp's blacksmith shop, watch a smithy pound and shape horseshoes over the original forge. You can even find your way through a 7-acre corn maze.

**GETTING THERE:** Camp Five is located off Highway 8 west of Laona, about 2 hours north of Green Bay. From Green Bay, take Highway 141 north to Highway 64. Follow Highway 64 west to Highway 32. Continue on Highway 32 and turn left on Highway 8.

**LOCATION:** 5064 Highway 8, Laona
**PHONE:** 715-674-3414
**WEBSITE:** camp5museum.org
**E-MAIL:** info@lumberjacksteamtrain.com

# East Troy Electric Railroad

East Troy Electric Railroad, Larry Pearlman

Interurban railroads once plied much of the Midwest, moving passengers easily from farm to city and vice versa. Today, a sprig of that heritage remains at the East Troy Electric Railroad, where electric trains run through the scenic countryside.

**CHOICES:** On a 10-mile round trip, the railroad offers a variety of cars to ride that includes trolleys, electric freight motors pulling a caboose, and electrically powered traditional coaches from the famous South Shore Line. Trains depart from both East Troy and Mukwonago. The railroad also offers pizza trains and dinner trains that run to Phantom Lake and back. After viewing the exhibits in the depot, you can walk 2 blocks to the shops and look at the equipment being refurbished.

**WHEN TO GO:** Regular weekend excursions run May through October. From mid-June through August, trains also operate on Fridays. There are several special events during the year including a Christmas Express that runs in November and December.

**GOOD TO KNOW:** Sheboygan car No. 26 is a 1908 interurban built by the Cincinnati Car Company for Sheboygan Light, Power and Railway. No 26 later became a summer cottage until it was restored.

**WORTH DOING:** Regular excursions operate from East Troy to the Elegant Farmer near Mukwonago. What's an Elegant Farmer? It makes a great destination as the Farmer provides a deli, greenhouse, and market all in one. Be sure and try the award-winning apple pie baked in a bag.

**DON'T MISS:** You can explore the substation in East Troy, which is the heart of the operating gear for the electric railroad.

**GETTING THERE:** East Troy is located in southeastern Wisconsin, about 35 miles from Milwaukee and 15 miles from Lake Geneva. From Milwaukee, take I-43 south to Exit 38. Take Highway 20 to Main Street. Follow Main Street to Church Street and turn right to the museum.

**LOCATION:** 1992 Church Street, East Troy
**PHONE:** 262-642-3263
**WEBSITE:** easttroyrr.org
**E-MAIL:** form on website

# Mid-Continent Railway Museum

Jim Wrinn

One of the best museums for the preservation of wooden railroad cars, Mid-Continent features numerous exhibits and a large collection of rolling stock, much of it kept indoors. The museum also offers a diesel train ride. It's all aimed at re-creating the experience of a branch line or short line between 1885 and 1915.

**CHOICES:** Leaving from a restored 1894 C&NW depot, the 7-mile, 55-minute ride takes you through the rolling countryside. You can ride the restored 1915 steel coaches, but you can also get a ticket for a caboose.

**WHEN TO GO:** The railway operates from May into October and also includes a variety of special events. From June until Labor Day, it is open daily; otherwise, on weekends only. Fall color, pumpkin, and Santa specials operate, as does a snow train and a variety of food and dinner trains.

**GOOD TO KNOW:** More than 100 pieces of equipment are on display. One is an office car of Great Northern Railway founder James J. Hill's son that included space for hauling an automobile. Structures include a water tower, a crossing shanty, a section shed, a crossing tower, and a freight house.

**WORTH DOING:** Explore Devil's Lake State Park near Baraboo. This large park features 500-foot cliffs, hiking trails, and kayaking.

**DON'T MISS:** Make sure you go into the coach shed to see some of the finest wood craftsmanship around when it comes to railroad cars. On one September weekend, you can view the cars' interiors on a guided tour.

**GETTING THERE:** The scenic route from Madison is along Highway 12 going north. Turn left on Highway 36 and then left again on Highway PF to North Freedom. In North Freedom, follow Walnut Street west to the museum.

**LOCATION:** E8948 Museum Road, North Freedom
**PHONE:** 800-930-1385 or 608-522-4261
**WEBSITE:** midcontinent.org
**E-MAIL:** inquiries@midcontinent.org

# National Railroad Museum

National Railroad Museum

Begun in 1956 by a group wishing to preserve a steam locomotive, the only congressionally designated national railroad museum has grown to encompass more than 70 pieces of rolling stock, 100,000 objects, a seasonal train ride, and an unmatched collection of drumheads—the illuminated signs seen on the rear of many passenger trains.

**CHOICES:** Explore the museum on your own and then take a train ride. During the 25-minute train ride, the conductor provides information about railroad history and museum exhibits. Highlights include a Union Pacific Big Boy, a 1950s Aerotrain, and a Pennsylvania Railroad GG1 electric locomotive. The command train for General Dwight D. Eisenhower is also located at the museum. Guided group tours are available.

**WHEN TO GO:** The museum is open daily year-round, except for Mondays January through March and several holidays. Train rides operate May through October, and numerous special events are scheduled during the year.

**GOOD TO KNOW:** The museum features exhibits on Pullman porters and rotating exhibits. In the museum's theater, you can view *Last of the Giants*, a 25-minute documentary chronicling the Union Pacific's Big Boys.

**WORTH DOING:** Take the kids to Bay Beach Amusement Park for some old-fashioned fun on classic midway rides. Football fans can visit the Green Bay Packers Hall of Fame and tour historic Lambeau Field.

**DON'T MISS:** Climb to the top of the 85-foot-tall observation tower for a bird's-eye view of the museum and its extensive rolling stock collection.

**GETTING THERE:** Green Bay is 2 hours north of Milwaukee. From Milwaukee, take I-43 to Exit 180. Take Highway 172 west and exit at Ashland Avenue. Bear right on Pilgrim Way and then turn left on Broadway Street.

**LOCATION:** 2285 S. Broadway Street, Green Bay
**PHONE:** 920-437-7623
**WEBSITE:** nationalrrmuseum.org
**E-MAIL:** form on website

# Osceola & St. Croix Valley Railway

Steve Glischinski

The Minnesota Transportation Museum's Osceola & St. Croix Valley Railway offers diesel-powered train rides through the scenic St. Croix River Valley along the Wisconsin–Minnesota border over the former Soo Line route that was part of the original Minneapolis, St. Paul & Sault Ste. Marie main line.

**CHOICES:** The railway offers two regular excursions from Osceola. One heads west 10 miles to Marine on St. Croix, Minn. This trip follows the beautiful St. Croix Valley for its entire length. The other trip goes east to Dresser, Wis., a former Soo Line junction town. A variety of special trips take place including dinner, brunch, pizza, and fall color trains. You can ride aboard either air-conditioned or open-window coaches.

**WHEN TO GO:** Trains operate weekends and holidays from May to October. For the best views of the St. Croix River, May is the time to ride before the leaves begin to obstruct views of the river. Early October provides the chance to view the autumn colors before the long northern winter begins. There's nothing like experiencing a crisp, blue-sky autumn day while rolling through the St. Croix Valley in an open-window coach.

**GOOD TO KNOW:** Osceola's downtown contains many examples of late 19th and early 20th century architecture. The St. Croix National Scenic Riverway includes 154 miles of the river and offers recreational opportunities on and off the river.

**WORTH DOING:** Take the 90-minute train ride to Marine and ride over the Cedar Bend swing bridge across the St. Croix River from Wisconsin into Minnesota. Although the bridge doesn't swing open any more, the classic steel structure, built in 1916, is worth seeing.

**DON'T MISS:** The museum occasionally picks up mail on the fly with ex-Northern Pacific Railway Post Office car No. 1102 from a mail crane at Osceola's restored passenger depot.

**GETTING THERE:** Osceola is about an hour's drive from Minneapolis. For a scenic drive, follow Highway 95 along the east bank of the St. Croix from Stillwater north to Osceola. Once in Osceola, you'll come to Highway 35. Turn right and proceed under the railroad bridge and immediately turn right again onto Depot Road.

**LOCATION:** 114 Depot Road, Osceola
**PHONE:** 715-294-2890 or 651-228-0263
**WEBSITE:** transportationmuseum.org
**E-MAIL:** form on website

# Wisconsin Great Northern Railroad

Jim Wrinn

The Wisconsin Great Northern Railroad operates excursion and dinner trains on approximately 9 miles of former Chicago & North Western track between Spooner and Veazie Springs, just east of Trego, Wis.

CHOICES: In addition to 90-minute sightseeing excursions, the Wisconsin Great Northern offers a variety of regularly scheduled dinner trains that include elegant dining, pizza, and Sunday brunches. The railroad also offers 45-minute rides in a former Texas Electric motor car built in 1913.

WHEN TO GO: Sightseeing excursions run Fridays, Saturdays, and Sundays May through October. Summer and early fall are great times to ride. The cars are ex-Duluth, Missabe & Iron Range Railway heavyweights with windows that can be opened, and it's a delight to take in the sights and sounds during these times.

GOOD TO KNOW: The railroad also operates a bed & breakfast train. Passengers board a sleeping car, which is coupled to the dinner train. You can enjoy drinks, dinner, and dessert and then settle in your private bedroom for the night. The next morning, a hot breakfast is served.

WORTH DOING: While Spooner is off the beaten path, there is much to do in the area, such as fishing, hiking, biking, camping, and tubing. You can also take a drive 30 miles to Hayward, which is the site of the annual Lumberjack World Championships and the Chequamegon Fat Tire Festival, the largest mass start mountain bike race in the United States.

DON'T MISS: In Spooner, you'll find the Railroad Memories Museum. Housed in the former Chicago & North Western Spooner depot, the museum contains lanterns, track equipment, photos, and other railroad memorabilia.

GETTING THERE: The Wisconsin Great Northern is about 90 minutes from Eau Claire and 2 hours from Minneapolis and St. Paul. To get to the depot, from Spooner take Highway 63 north, which joins with Highway 53. After about 5 miles from Spooner, turn on Dilly Lake Road and continue to the depot.

**LOCATION:** N6639 Dilly Lake Road, Trego
**PHONE:** 715-635-3200
**WEBSITE:** spoonertrainride.com
**E-MAIL:** info@spoonertrainride.com

Boone & Scenic Valley Railroad, page 176

# REGION 5

**IOWA**

1  Boone & Scenic Valley Railroad
2  Hub City Railroad Museum
3  Marquette Depot Museum
4  Minneapolis & St. Louis No. 457
5  Midwest Central Railroad
6  RailsWest Railroad Museum
7  Sioux City Railroad Museum
8  Union Pacific Railroad Museum

**MINNESOTA**

9  Depot Museum
10 End-O-Line Railroad Park & Museum
11 Jackson Street Roundhouse
12 Kandiyohi County Historical Museum
13 Lake Superior & Mississippi Railroad
14 Lake Superior Railroad Museum
15 Milwaukee Road 261
16 Minnehaha Depot
17 Minnesota Discovery Center
18 Minnesota Museum of Mining
19 Minnesota Streetcar Museum
20 Western Minnesota Steam Threshers Reunion

**NEBRASKA**

21 Cody Park Railroad Museum
22 Durham Museum
23 Golden Spike Tower
24 Lauritzen Gardens
25 Rock Island Depot Railroad Museum
26 Stuhr Museum of the Prairie Pioneer
27 Trails & Rails Museum

**NORTH DAKOTA**

28 Bonanzaville USA
29 Fort Lincoln Trolley
30 Midland Continental Depot Transportation Museum
31 North Dakota State Railroad Museum
32 Old Soo Depot Transportation Museum
33 Railroad Museum of Minot

**SOUTH DAKOTA**

34 Black Hills Central Railroad
35 Prairie Village
36 South Dakota State Railroad Museum

172

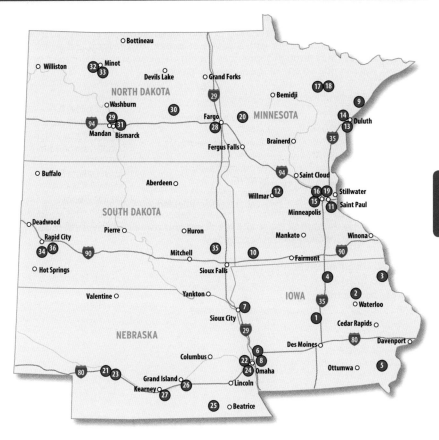

# IOWA

## Hub City Railway Museum

This museum consists of a former Railway Express Agency building, a Chicago Great Western yard office, and a tower, with a display of locomotives, railcars, and artifacts. It is open Sundays May through September. During Oelwein's annual Heritage Days weekend, you can ride on one of the museum's handcars.

**LOCATION:** 26 Second Avenue SW, Oelwein
**PHONE:** 319-283-1939
**WEBSITE:** cgwoelwein.com
**E-MAIL:** info@cgwoelwein.org

## Marquette Depot Museum

Housed in a renovated Milwaukee Road depot, the museum contains Milwaukee Road exhibits and general railroad artifacts. A restored caboose is on display. The museum is open daily May through October, and the depot also contains a travel information center. Railroad Days take place in September.

**LOCATION:** 216 Edgar Street, Marquette
**PHONE:** 563-873-1200
**WEBSITE:** mcgreg-marq.org
**E-MAIL:** marquettedepotmuseum@alpinecom.net

## Minneapolis & St. Louis No. 457

Get an up-close look at M&StL No. 457, a Consolidation type steam locomotive built in 1912, which has been in East Park since 1959. Fog machines provide smoke and steam, and a sound system provides an engine's whistle. It is open to the public on weekend afternoons mid-May through October.

LOCATION: East Park, Mason City
WEBSITE: friendsofthe457.org
E-MAIL: form on website

## RailsWest Railroad Museum

This former Chicago, Rock Island & Pacific passenger depot was built in 1899. The museum displays a Lincoln, Neb.-built Chicago, Burlington & Quincy 4-6-0 locomotive, Union Pacific 4-8-4 (Northern) locomotive, Plymouth locomotive, and Rock Island caboose. A large HO scale model railroad is also part of the museum and worth seeing. Check the museum website for days and hours.

LOCATION: 16th Avenue and South Main Street, Council Bluffs
PHONE: 712-323-2509
WEBSITE: thehistoricalsociety.org
E-MAIL: form on website

## Sioux City Railroad Museum

Located in a former Milwaukee Road roundhouse and shop complex, this 30-acre museum encompasses several buildings including a turntable and six stalls of a one-time 30-stall roundhouse. Great Northern 4-6-2 No. 1355 is displayed inside the roundhouse. The museum is open March through December.

LOCATION: 3400 Sioux River Road, Sioux City
PHONE: 712-233-6996
WEBSITE: siouxcityrailroadmuseum.org
E-MAIL: contact@milwaukeerailroadshops.org

# Boone & Scenic Valley Railroad

Jeff Terry

Iowa isn't known for rolling terrain, but this fascinating railroad provides a scenic ride with interesting landscape through the Des Moines River Valley. The railroad runs across two impressive bridges, with the 156-foot-tall Bass Point Creek High Bridge being the highlight of a 15-mile round trip. The railroad's dinner, dessert, and picnic trains run on a slightly longer route.

**CHOICES:** The railroad is one of the few in the country that offers steam-, diesel-, and electric-powered trains. You can ride a 1920s excursion in coach, opt for the Valley View open-air car, or ride in an air-conditioned first-class car. There is also limited seating in the train's caboose. Hop the restored 1915 Charles City & Western electric trolley for an interurban run through downtown Boone. Picnic trains travel the same route as the dinner or dessert trains, you just have to supply the lunch.

**WHEN TO GO:** Between Memorial Day and the end of October, excursion trains run daily, with steam locomotives on Saturdays. Dinner trains are scheduled on Fridays and Saturdays. Dessert trains run on Saturdays and picnic trains on Sundays. Trolleys operate on Saturdays. The museum is open Monday through Saturday.

**GOOD TO KNOW:** The James H. Andrew Railroad Museum & History Center is a 9,000-square-foot facility that includes displays and memorabilia about railroading in Iowa.

**WORTH DOING:** The city of Boone celebrates its railroad heritage during Pufferbilly Days, an annual September event with train rides, a model train display, a parade, and a spike-driving contest.

**DON'T MISS:** On the dinner, dessert, and picnic trains, step outside on the City of San Francisco's rear observation deck for a unique experience.

**GETTING THERE:** The railroad is in central Iowa, an hour's drive northwest of Des Moines. Take I-35 to Ames and travel west on Highway 30 to Boone. Go north on Story Street through the business district to 10th Street and then go west 6 blocks to the depot.

**LOCATION:** 225 10th Street, Boone
**PHONE:** 800-626-0319 or 515-432-4249
**WEBSITE:** scenic-valleyrr.com
**E-MAIL:** info@bsvrr.com

# Midwest Central Railroad

Steve Glischinski

The Midwest Central Railroad was established when volunteers built a 1.25-mile loop of track around the Midwest Old Threshers Reunion site and acquired several steam locomotives and cars. Later, to bring visitors and exhibitors into the grounds, a counter-clockwise trolley loop line was built, dubbed the Midwest Electric Railway.

**CHOICES:** Both the railroad and the electric railway are in full operation during the Old Threshers Reunion. During the reunion, the trains haul approximately 35,000 to 40,000 passengers. The railroad operates Baldwin 2-6-2 locomotive No. 12, which was built for Hawaii's Kahului Railroad in 1929.

**WHEN TO GO:** The Midwest Old Threshers Reunion begins the Thursday before Labor Day and ends on Labor Day. In addition, both the railway and the electric line operate trips over haunted rails each October, and the railroad runs a train for the 4th of July as well as a North Pole Express.

**GOOD TO KNOW:** The Old Threshers Reunion is the largest of its kind in the United States. Farmers and tractor enthusiasts gather for fun and demonstrations of steam tractors, early gas tractors, and other period farm implements. There are tractor pulls, a steam-powered merry-go-round, and much more. It's like an old-fashioned state fair, but its emphasis is on living agricultural history.

**WORTH DOING:** If you're a camper, stay at the Old Threshers campground and take the trolley into the grounds and then ride the train. You can take in the whole show without the hassle of parking and enjoy the sights and sounds of steam as you camp.

**DON'T MISS:** On the grounds, two museums operate during the year. Open year-round, the Heritage Museum focuses on agriculture, and in summer, you can visit the Theatre Museum, which preserves artifacts from early repertoire theater, and even take in a live performance.

**GETTING THERE:** Probably the best way to visit Mount Pleasant is by driving. Located in southeastern Iowa, Mount Pleasant is south of Iowa City on Highway 218. The city is also served daily by Amtrak trains 5 and 6, the *California Zephyr*.

**LOCATION:** 405 E. Threshers Road, Mount Pleasant
**PHONE:** 319-385-2912 or 319-385-8937
**WEBSITE:** oldthreshers.org or mcrr.org
**E-MAIL:** info@oldthreshers.org

# Union Pacific Railroad Museum

Jim Wrinn

Few railroads have gone to the great lengths of the Union Pacific to preserve and document their past. The Union Pacific Railroad Museum houses one of the oldest corporation collections of any kind in the country. Visitors will not find lines of steam locomotives, diesels, or rolling stock. Rather, they will be inundated with a tasteful display of artifacts, photographs, and documents that trace the development of the UP and the role it played in American West.

**CHOICES:** The museum can be taken in whole or digested by specific eras depending on your interests. The Union Pacific's history is a history of the American West. The collection dates from the mid-1800s and features materials highlighting the building of the transcontinental railroad. Surveying equipment, early rail equipment, firearms, and other artifacts fill the building.

**WHEN TO GO:** With the exception of a raging snowstorm, even winter is a good time to visit the museum. It is open Thursdays through Saturdays. Exhibits are changed and special events occur periodically during the year.

**GOOD TO KNOW:** One of the museum's permanent exhibits is devoted to passenger service. It features a cutaway coach, lounge, and dining cars as well as multimedia exhibits and thousands of artifacts.

**WORTH DOING:** Take time to tour both Council Bluffs and Omaha. Both are culturally rich cities with much to offer visitors. Council Bluffs has several casinos and is Iowa's leading gaming spot. The Henry Doorly Zoo in Omaha is a world-class zoo that appeals to adults and children alike.

**DON'T MISS:** The museum has a combination of static and interactive displays. The working locomotive simulator is educational as well as a lot of fun.

**GETTING THERE:** Located on the east side of Council Bluffs, the museum is easily accessible for motorists from I-80 or I-29. It is near Bayliss Park with its lighted water fountain, monuments, and sculptures.

**LOCATION:** 200 Pearl Street, Council Bluffs
**PHONE:** 712-329-8307
**WEBSITE:** uprrmuseum.org
**E-MAIL:** form on website

# MINNESOTA

## Depot Museum
Located in the 1907 headquarters of the Duluth & Iron Range Railroad, this museum highlights the timber industry, iron mining, and the railroad. It displays a Mallet steam locomotive and a Baldwin 3-Spot. The Lake County Historical Society operates this museum and two others including an 1892 lighthouse. They are open daily Memorial Day weekend into October, and the Depot Museum is open Saturdays in winter.

LOCATION: 520 South Avenue, Two Harbors
PHONE: 218-834-4898
WEBSITE: lakecountyhistoricalsociety.org
E-MAIL: lakehist@lakeconnections.net

## End-O-Line Railroad Park & Museum
End-O-Line Railroad Park includes a 1901 manually operated turntable, a rebuilt engine house, an original four-room depot, a water tower, an 1899 section foreman's house, a Grand Trunk Western caboose, and two steam locomotives. Open Wednesdays through Sundays Memorial Day weekend to Labor Day weekend, the site also includes other buildings of local historical interest.

LOCATION: 440 N. Mill Street, Currie
PHONE: 507-763-3708
WEBSITE: endoline.com
E-MAIL: endoline@co.murray.mn.us

## Kandiyohi County Historical Museum
The museum complex consists of several buildings including a one-room schoolhouse and the former Kandiyohi railroad station depot, which is the entrance to the main museum. Great Northern No. 2523, a Baldwin P-2 class steam locomotive, is also on display. It is open daily Memorial Day through Labor Day.

LOCATION: 610 NE Highway 71, Willmar
PHONE: 320-235-1881
WEBSITE: kandiyohicountyhistory.com
E-MAIL: kandhist@msn.com

## Minnehaha Depot
Located in Minnehaha Park, the tiny depot's architecture features delicate gingerbread details. Built in 1875, the building replaced an earlier Milwaukee Road depot on the first line into the Twin Cities from Chicago. Managed by the Minnesota Transportation Museum, the depot is open Sundays Memorial Day weekend through Labor Day.

LOCATION: Highway 55 and Minnehaha Parkway, Minneapolis
PHONE: 651-228-0263
WEBSITE: transportationmuseum.org
E-MAIL: form on website

# Minnesota Discovery Center

The center offers a 2.5-mile trolley ride to a re-created mining community. The 40-minute trip, aboard a 1928 Melbourne trolley, offers views of the Pillsbury mine. Preserving Iron Range history, the center includes a museum, hall of geology, and mini golf course. It is open year-round, but closed Mondays all year and Sundays during winter. Trolleys operate late May to October.

LOCATION: 1005 Discovery Drive, Chisholm
PHONE: 218-254-7959
WEBSITE: mndiscoverycenter.com
E-MAIL: info@mndiscoverycenter.com

# Minnesota Museum of Mining

The museum tells the story of iron ore mining in the state. Along with mining equipment and vehicles, a 1907 Alco steam locomotive is on display with ore cars and a caboose. Inside, you'll find a re-created mining town, a building-filling train layout, and a simulated underground mine. It is open Memorial Day to Labor Day, and picnicking is encouraged.

LOCATION: 701 West Lake Street, Chisholm
PHONE: 218-254-5543
WEBSITE: mnmuseumofmining.org
E-MAIL: info@mnmuseumofmining.org

# Minnesota Streetcar Museum

This museum operates two different streetcar lines from May into fall, with a variety of special events. Located southwest of downtown Minneapolis, the Como-Harriet Line runs between Lake Harriet and Lake Calhoun. The Excelsior Line is about 15 miles west of downtown Minneapolis. The museum exhibits electric streetcars, railcars, and a steamboat.

LOCATION: 2330 W. 42nd Street, Minneapolis
PHONE: 952-922-1096
WEBSITE: trolleyride.org
E-MAIL: mnscmuseum@gmail.com

# Western Minnesota Steam Threshers Reunion

This event has been a Labor Day tradition since 1954. The grounds cover 210 acres filled with steam-powered equipment, historic buildings, tractor pulls, and a steam-powered earth mover, among other items. The star of the show is 1920-built Alco 0-6-0 No. 353, an ex-Soo Line steam locomotive that pulls passengers in modified (and cleaned!) stockcars around a 2-mile loop of track.

LOCATION: 27488 102nd Avenue South, Hawley
PHONE: 701-212-2034
WEBSITE: rollag.com
E-MAIL: secretary@rollag.com

# Jackson Street Roundhouse

Jeff Terry

The former Great Northern Jackson Street Roundhouse was built in 1907 to service passenger locomotives. Closed in 1959, the roundhouse was converted to nonrailroad use and the tracks were removed. The Minnesota Transportation Museum purchased it in 1985 and reinstalled the turntable and added roundhouse doors built to 1906 blueprints. It sits on 9 acres less than a mile north of downtown St. Paul and houses museum space, a restoration shop, blacksmith shop, the Northern Pacific depot from Rutledge, Minn., and a train yard filled with historic railroad equipment and vintage buses. Included in the collection are three Northern Pacific steam locomotives and a variety of passenger and freight cars, including a former Burlington dome car.

**CHOICES:** Visitors can roam the roundhouse and the outdoor grounds, take a short caboose ride pulled by a switch engine on Saturdays (heated ones in winter), and participate in interactive exhibits. Visitors can also ride one of the classic buses.

**WHEN TO GO:** The museum is open Wednesdays and Saturdays year-round, but no train or bus rides are offered on Wednesdays. Summer or early fall are the best times to visit, as it can be chilly inside the roundhouse in the winter and downright cold outside.

**GOOD TO KNOW:** After taking in the roundhouse, you can visit the St. Paul home of James J. Hill, the Great Northern's founder. Completed in 1891, the 36,000-square-foot mansion was the largest and most expensive home in Minnesota at the time.

**WORTH DOING:** Make sure to inquire about seeing the Northern Pacific steam locomotives undergoing restoration in the roundhouse. The area is not open to the public, but museum personnel offer guided tours to see the two Pacifics.

**DON'T MISS:** Walk inside the cab of Dan Patch Lines No. 100, built in 1913 by General Electric, and you've walked into history. One of the first locomotives to use an internal combustion engine, it is the granddaddy of today's diesel locomotives.

**GETTING THERE:** The roundhouse is located north of the Minnesota State Capitol. Take the Pennsylvania Avenue exit off I-35E and drive west 2 blocks to the roundhouse.

**LOCATION:** 193 E. Pennsylvania Avenue, St. Paul
**PHONE:** 651-228-0263
**WEBSITE:** transportationmuseum.org
**E-MAIL:** form on website

# Lake Superior & Mississippi Railroad

Jeff Terry

Here's a laid-back operation that is a great complement to the marshlands near Duluth. A 90-minute ride on this railroad is a great way to relax and enjoy nature along the St. Louis River estuary, Spirit Lake, and Mud Lake. Keep your eyes on the marshes for egrets!

**CHOICES:** While taking in the scenery and wildlife when riding in a restored, open-window coach, you can listen to narration of the area's rich history. The coaches, built in 1912, operated between the Iron Range and Duluth. For a truly outdoor experience, ride the Safari Car, a converted flatcar. Power is provided by a General Electric industrial switcher built in 1946.

**WHEN TO GO:** Excursions operate on Saturdays and Sundays, beginning in June and running into October.

**GOOD TO KNOW:** The railroad takes its name from the first line built between the Twin Cities and Duluth, and it uses some of that line's original track.

**WORTH DOING:** Duluth and the Lake Superior area offer much to do. There are historic ships to see (SS *William A. Irvin* and SS *Meteor*), museums to tour, and parks to explore.

**DON'T MISS:** The railroad offers a kayak/canoe option. You can rent or bring your own kayak or canoe, ride the train to the start and then paddle back.

**GETTING THERE:** Duluth is on Lake Superior, about 150 miles from the Twin Cities. In Duluth, go south on I-35, take Exit 251B onto Grand Avenue. The boarding location is across from the Lake Superior Zoo.

**LOCATION:** 7100 Grand Avenue, Duluth
**PHONE:** 218-624-7549
**WEBSITE:** lsmrr.org
**E-MAIL:** lsmrr46@hotmail.com

# Lake Superior Railroad Museum

Jeff Terry

This is a combination of a great railroad museum and a great train ride. The Lake Superior Railroad Museum is located in a historic depot in downtown Duluth. Its extensive rolling stock collection rests in the train shed, and just outside, excursion trains ply the route to Two Harbors, with outstanding views along the way.

**CHOICES:** The Lake Superior Railroad Museum has a large collection of steam, diesel, and electric locomotives as well as passenger coaches, freight cars, and cabooses. Much of the equipment was used on Minnesota railroads, including the first locomotive operated in the state. The museum also operates the North Shore Scenic Railroad, which conducts two regular excursions. A 6-hour round trip takes you through the countryside into Two Harbors. A shorter (90-minute) excursion runs along the shores of Lake Superior to Lester River. Also operating are a pizza train and a variety of specials.

**WHEN TO GO:** The museum is open daily year-round, with extended summer hours. Regular excursions are offered late May through mid-October.

**GOOD TO KNOW:** Take a close look at the *William Crooks*, the first locomotive operated in Minnesota. Built in 1861, it is one of a handful of engines remaining from the Civil War era. Duluth & Northeastern 2-8-0 No. 28 pulls steam excursions.

**WORTH DOING:** The Duluth depot (St. Louis County Heritage and Arts Center) is also home to the Duluth Art Institute, St. Louis County Historical Society museum, and several arts groups.

**DON'T MISS:** Watch the massive Duluth, Missabe & Iron Range Railroad Yellowstone type locomotive come to life. Clever museum folks have set it up so that every 30 minutes an electric motor sets the drivers in motion, rotating the running gear, and operates lights and sounds.

**GETTING THERE:** Situated on Lake Superior, Duluth is 150 miles from the Twin Cities. To reach the museum, take Exit 256 off I-35 and follow Michigan Street to the depot.

**LOCATION:** 506 W. Michigan Street, Duluth
**PHONE:** 218-727-8025 (museum) or
218-722-1273 (train)
**WEBSITE:** lsrm.org or northshorescenicrailroad.org
**E-MAIL:** forms on websites

# Milwaukee Road 261

Steve Glischinski

Railroading Heritage of Midwest America and its operating arm, The Friends of the 261, operate main line excursion trips around the Midwest pulled by former Milwaukee Road steam locomotive No. 261, a 4-8-4 built by American Locomotive Company in 1944. The group also operates historic passenger cars on Amtrak trains, most frequently on the *Empire Builder* between the Twin Cities and Chicago. These trips are usually open to the public.

**CHOICES:** Friends of the 261 offers several options for passengers. All trips include coach, first-class, and premium-class services. Premium class includes hors d'oeuvres and gourmet meals prepared onboard and a ride in one of two former Milwaukee Road *Hiawatha* cars: Skytop lounge observation *Cedar Rapids* or full-length Super Dome No. 53. First class includes an upscale meal plan with hors d'oeuvres and a ride in parlor or lounge cars. Both first and premium class include complimentary beverages.

**WHEN TO GO:** Generally, the Friends operate trips beginning in May and running as late as October.

**GOOD TO KNOW:** For a complete Milwaukee Road experience, stay in one of the two hotels at the former Milwaukee Road Minneapolis passenger depot, built in 1898 and beautifully restored. Rail memorabilia and photographs can be found throughout the building.

**WORTH DOING:** Trains usually leave from the 261 facility in northeast Minneapolis. Head down to the shop in Minneapolis the evening before a trip just to take in the sights and sounds of a large steam engine at night. Usually the crew has a donation box out, and for a small price, you can have a look in the cab.

**DON'T MISS:** Get a close look at Skytop lounge observation car *Cedar Rapids*. Built by the Milwaukee Road in 1948, with their large glass area, the Skytops were unlike any other rail passenger car. The *Cedar Rapids* is the only Skytop still in operation.

**GETTING THERE:** A short walk from the Metro Transit bus stop at Central Avenue and Broadway will get you to the shop, or you can take a taxi. Ample parking is available at the shop on excursion days.

**LOCATION:** 401 Harrison Street NE, Minneapolis
**WEBSITE:** 261.com
**E-MAIL:** form on website

# NEBRASKA

## Cody Park Railroad Museum

The Cody Park Railroad Museum displays one of the two remaining Challenger class locomotives. Also displayed are a UP diesel engine, baggage car, mail car, and caboose. The restored Hershey depot contains Union Pacific items, telegraph equipment, and other exhibits. It is open May through September.

LOCATION: 1400 N. Jeffers Street, North Platte
PHONE: 308-532-4729
WEBSITE: visitnorthplatte.com
E-MAIL: info@visitnorthplatte.com

## Durham Museum

Built in 1931, Omaha's Union Station is a beautiful example of Art Deco style. This historic railroad station now houses both permanent and temporary historical exhibits. Rail displays include Union Pacific 4-6-0 No. 1243 steam locomotive, which was built in the 1890s, a streetcar, caboose 25559, and several passenger cars. Be sure to have a malt, ice cream soda, or phosphate at the restored soda fountain as travelers did in 1931. Railroad Days take place during the summer.

LOCATION: 801 S. 10th Street, Omaha
PHONE: 402-444-5071
WEBSITE: durhammuseum.org
E-MAIL: info@durhammuseum.org

## Golden Spike Tower

Golden Spike Tower is an observation tower that overlooks the world's largest railroad yard. The visitor center includes artifacts of the Union Pacific. The lobby features equipment exhibits and a model train. The enclosed 8th floor includes informational kiosks with children's activities.

LOCATION: 1249 N. Homestead Road, North Platte
PHONE: 308-532-9920
WEBSITE: goldenspiketower.com
E-MAIL: form on website

# Lauritzen Gardens

What does a botanical garden have to do with railroad history? Plenty, since it exhibits two of the largest locomotives ever built, Union Pacific DDA40X diesel locomotive No. 6900 and Big Boy steam locomotive No. 4023. Viewing platforms allow a peek inside the cabs of both locomotives. The gardens are open daily, with extended evening hours on Mondays and Tuesday mid-May through mid-September.

**LOCATION:** 100 Bancroft Street, Omaha
**PHONE:** 402-346-4002
**WEBSITE:** lauritzengardens.org
**E-MAIL:** form on website

# Rock Island Depot Railroad Museum

The museum is located in one of the state's only remaining Rock Island depots. Built in 1914, the brick building also housed the railroad's Western Division Headquarters. The collection features Rock Island artifacts and a restored baggage room, lobby, and ticket office. The site also includes restored gardens. Rock Island Rail Days take place in June. It is open Wednesday through Sunday.

**LOCATION:** 910 Second Street, Fairbury
**PHONE:** 402-729-5131
**WEBSITE:** fairbury.com
**E-MAIL:** fairburyridepot@windstream.net

# Stuhr Museum of the Prairie Pioneer

This interactive museum takes you back to an 1890s railroad town with more than 60 restored buildings. During the summer, townspeople dressed in period clothing demonstrate daily life on the Plains. A 1901 steam locomotive, a 1912 caboose, an 1871 coach, and other railcars are on display. It is open daily except for Mondays in January, February, and March.

**LOCATION:** 3133 W. Highway 34, Grand Island
**PHONE:** 308-385-5316
**WEBSITE:** stuhrmuseum.org
**E-MAIL:** info@sturhmuseum.org

# Trails & Rails Museum

The Rails portion of the museum includes an 1898 Union Pacific depot. The depot houses transportation exhibits, and its waiting room and ticket office have been restored. On display are a 2-8-0 Baldwin steam engine, a UP flatcar, a caboose, and other equipment. The museum contains other historic buildings including the distinctive Freighters Hotel. It is open year-round, except for weekends September through May.

**LOCATION:** 710 W. 11th Street, Kearney
**PHONE:** 308-234-3041
**WEBSITE:** bchs.us
**E-MAIL:** bchs.us@hotmail.com

# NORTH DAKOTA

## Bonanzaville USA

The museum features more than 40 historic buildings and 400,000 artifacts that depict life when bonanza homes dotted the Plains. Rail structures include a vintage Northern Pacific train depot, a water tower, and a train shed. The train shed displays an 1883 NP 4-4-0 steam locomotive, a caboose, and a 1930s Pullman car. It is open May through September.

LOCATION: 1351 W. Main Avenue, West Fargo
PHONE: 701-282-2822
WEBSITE: bonanzaville.org
E-MAIL: form on website

## Fort Lincoln Trolley

The trolley car takes you on a 9-mile excursion along the Heart River from Mandan to Fort Abraham Lincoln State Park and back. The park features several reconstructed buildings that would have been found in the original fort.

LOCATION: 2000 Third Street SE, Mandan
PHONE: 701-663-9018
WEBSITE: ndtourism.com/mandan/forts/fort-lincoln-trolley

## Midland Continental Depot Transportation Museum

The restored depot is the only surviving Midland Continental station and is on the National Register of Historic Places. The first floor houses railroad exhibits and the upper floor, once the agent's living quarters, has exhibits honoring singer Peggy Lee, who lived in the depot when her father was the agent. It is open from Memorial Day to Labor Day.

LOCATION: 401 Railway Street, Wimbledon
PHONE: 701-320-1020 or 701-435-2875
WEBSITE: midlandcontinentaldepot.com
E-MAIL: midlandcontinentaldepot@gmail.com

# North Dakota State Railroad Museum

New exhibits to the 5-acre museum include an 1890 depot moved from Steele and a 1953 diesel switcher. The main museum building, a former BN yard office, houses artifacts from several railroads. Rolling stock includes cabooses, boxcars, and a tank car. It is open daily Memorial Day through Labor Day, with special events, such as Watermelon Days, scheduled during the summer.

LOCATION: 3102 37th Street NW, Mandan
PHONE: 701-663-9322
WEBSITE: ndsrm.org
E-MAIL: ndstaterrmuseum@gmail.com

# Old Soo Depot Transportation Museum

This museum focuses on the transportation history of the American West and includes materials on trains, planes, and automobiles. Located in a completely restored 1912 Soo Line depot, it also offers an excellent location for train-watching. The museum is open Monday through Friday.

LOCATION: 15 N. Main Street, Minot
PHONE: 701-852-2234
WEBSITE: visitminot.org
E-MAIL: soodepot@srt.com

# Railroad Museum of Minot

The Railroad Museum of Minot contains artifacts relating to the Great Northern Railway and other railroads of the area. A Great Northern Railway caboose and a snowplow car are also on display. The museum is open 10-2 on Saturdays.

LOCATION: 19 First Street NE, Minot
PHONE: 701-852-7091
WEBSITE: facebook.com/pages/RailRoad-Museum-of-Minot/276975999071833
E-MAIL: railroadmuseum@srt.com

# SOUTH DAKOTA

## Prairie Village

Prairie Village is a collection of restored buildings, rail equipment, and farm machinery that preserves the past. Rail structures include several historical depots, a roundhouse, and an operating turntable. The museum is open daily mid-May until Labor Day. On Saturdays, you can take a 2-mile train ride around the village. Several steam and diesel locomotives, various cabooses, and a unique chapel car are featured. Railroad Days take place in July, and a pumpkin train runs in October.

LOCATION: 45205 Highway 34, Madison
PHONE: 800-693-3644 or 605-256-3644
WEBSITE: prairievillage.org
E-MAIL: info@prairievillage.org

## South Dakota State Railroad Museum

The museum contains artifacts and rolling stock related to the railroads that have served South Dakota since 1872. It also features additional displays and seasonal activities including the annual Trees and Trains exhibit. The museum is located next to the Black Hills Central Railroad. It is open daily May into October.

LOCATION: 222 Railroad Avenue, Hill City
PHONE: 605-574-9000
WEBSITE: sdsrm.org
E-MAIL: sdsrrm@gmail.com

# Black Hills Central Railroad

Timothy Tonge

This railroad gives you a chance to ride on a real mountain railroad with its steep grades, mines, and scenic hills. Situated close to Mount Rushmore, the Black Hills Central, also known as the 1880s Train, carries riders between Keystone and Hill City.

**CHOICES:** The 2-hour, 20-mile round trip is a beautiful journey through the historic, rugged landscape of the Black Hills. Both steam and diesel locomotives power the train, with steam engines being more prevalent. You can ride in a coach or climb into the drover's car, believed to be one of only two left from the Chicago & North Western Railroad and the only one in use. Cattlemen lived in these cars while following their herds to market. Fitting for the area, Wild West shootouts take place several times during the season. Other special events also take place.

**WHEN TO GO:** With a few exceptions, trains operate daily between mid-May and mid-October, departing from both Keystone and Hill City. Trains make several trips a day on most days. Some last-train departures from Keystone are one-way trips only. Holiday trains run in November and December.

**GOOD TO KNOW:** Keystone is rich in tourist offerings including restaurants, shows, and shops. Hill City has amenities but without the tourist hubbub.

**WORTH DOING:** The Black Hills area is filled with must-see activities, including a trip to Mount Rushmore. You can experience the rugged beauty of the Badlands, see bison in Custer State Park, and visit the Wild West town of Deadwood. The South Dakota State Railroad Museum is right next to the Black Hills Central's depot in Hill City.

**DON'T MISS:** Try to ride behind steam locomotive No. 110, one of only three operating Mallet locomotives. The locomotive is impressive as it tackles grades as steep as 5 percent for almost a mile but never breaks a sweat.

**GETTING THERE:** Whether traveling east or west, I-90 gets you to the train. To reach Keystone from Rapid City, take Highway 16 to Highway 244. To reach Hill City from Deadwood, take Highway 385.

**LOCATION:** 222 Railroad Avenue, Hill City
**PHONE:** 605-574-2222
**WEBSITE:** 1880train.com
**E-MAIL:** form on website

Branson Scenic Railway, page 206

# REGION 6

# ARKANSAS

## Fort Smith Trolley Museum

Visit this museum and you can see its collection of railroad, streetcar, and transportation exhibits, including Frisco steam locomotive 4003. Board No. 224, a restored Fort Smith streetcar at the Fort Smith Museum of History on Rogers Avenue for an enjoyable trolley ride. The museum is open Saturdays year-round, and trolleys run daily May through October and Friday through Sunday the rest of the year.

LOCATION: 100 S. Fourth Street, Fort Smith
PHONE: 479-783-0205
WEBSITE: fstm.org
E-MAIL: info@fstm.org

## Frisco Depot Museum

This restored Victorian depot was built in 1886 and operated by the Frisco Railroad. Take a self-guided tour and hear the stories of 14 figures representing passengers, station workers, and a train crew. You can also examine a Frisco caboose. Located in Mammoth Spring State Park, the depot is closed on Mondays.

LOCATION: Highway 9 and Highway 63, Mammoth Spring
PHONE: 870-625-7364
WEBSITE: arkansasstateparks.com/mammothspring
E-MAIL: mammothspring@arkansas.com

# Arkansas & Missouri Railroad

David Hoge

From the highest point to down in the hollers, the Arkansas & Missouri operates excursion trains powered by its all-Alco roster of diesels. Rebuilt air-conditioned coaches transport riders through some of the most rugged terrain between the Appalachians and the Rockies. The A&M operates 139 miles of former St. Louis-San Francisco trackage from Monett, Mo., to Fort Smith, Ark., through the Boston Mountains of northwest Arkansas.

**CHOICES:** The longest ride is a 134-mile round trip from Springdale to Van Buren with a 3-hour stop in Van Buren, where passengers can shop or dine near the 1901 Frisco depot. Another ride is a 70-mile round trip from Van Buren to Winslow with a ride over 100-foot trestles and through the 1,700-foot-long Winslow tunnel. A winter excursion takes you from Fort Smith over the Arkansas River to Winslow.

**WHEN TO GO:** With its schedule of special events, trains run all year. Fall offers the best scenery, and fall trips sell out quickly, but spring is also popular because everything is blooming.

**GOOD TO KNOW:** Three classes—first class, club, and coach—are offered on all trips, with lunch or snacks provided for first class and club class. Fares increase for trips during the fall foliage season.

**WORTH DOING:** The A&M excursion fits in nicely with a trip to Branson or to the William J. Clinton Presidential Library in Little Rock. Eureka Springs offers shopping, and the nearby Buffalo and Mulberry Rivers provide camping, canoeing, and hiking opportunities. Two Civil War battlefields are nearby.

**DON'T MISS:** For an old-time railroading experience, you can purchase a ticket for the restored B&O cupola caboose, which holds about a dozen passengers.

**GETTING THERE:** Traveling over I-540, I-49, and I-40 gives the area quick access, making the A&M easily accessible for a day of fun.

**LOCATION:** 306 E. Emma Avenue, Springdale
**PHONE:** 800-687-8600 or 479-751-8600
**WEBSITE:** amrailroad.com
**E-MAIL:** brenda@amrailroad.com

# Arkansas Railroad Museum

David Hoge

The Arkansas Railroad Museum is the state's largest railroad museum. The museum is located in the machine shop built in the later part of the 19th century for the St. Louis Southwestern Railway, or Cotton Belt. The machine shop was part of a large complex of buildings and shops once located at Pine Bluff.

**CHOICES:** The museum's most famous tenant is the last steam locomotive built for the St. Louis Southwestern. No. 819 was assembled in the building that now houses the museum and was placed in service in early 1943. Along with No. 819, SSW No. 336 is also housed at the museum. Several diesel Alcos are also on display along with some passenger cars, a complete SSW work train, cabooses, and a Jordan snowplow. The museum features a large collection of memorabilia from the Cotton Belt and other Arkansas and east Texas railroads.

**WHEN TO GO:** The museum is open Monday through Saturday. Most exhibits are located inside, but much of the museum is not climate-controlled and therefore subject to the heat and cold. Operating hours can be affected by extreme temperatures.

**GOOD TO KNOW:** Engines 819 and 336 are the only surviving Cotton Belt steam locomotives, and both are on the National Register of Historic Places.

**WORTH DOING:** While in Pine Bluff, you can take in the historical museum, which is located in a restored union station that is also listed on the National Register of Historic Places.

**DON'T MISS:** The museum holds an annual railroadiana show in April.

**GETTING THERE:** The museum is easily accessible from Little Rock, which has a daily Amtrak stop. The museum lies just a short distance off I-530, which connects Little Rock and Pine Bluff.

**LOCATION:** 1700 Port Road, Pine Bluff
**PHONE:** 870-535-8819
**WEBSITE:** arkansasrailroadmuseum.org
**E-MAIL:** info@arkansasrailroadmuseum.org

# Eureka Springs & North Arkansas Railway

Patrick Hiatte

Spend a pleasant hour on one of the last remnants of the Missouri & North Arkansas Railroad, from Eureka Springs north to Junction and back. Along the way, enjoy the natural beauty of the hills of the Ozarks and Leatherwood Valley.

**CHOICES:** For the 4.5-mile, round-trip excursion, you can ride an ex-Rock Island commuter coach (complete with straps for standees) to Junction, where the locomotive turns and runs around the train for the return trip to Eureka Springs. You can also enjoy the noon lunch train or the evening dinner train. The train is powered by a 1942 vintage diesel locomotive.

**WHEN TO GO:** From mid-May through October, there are multiple daily departures Tuesday through Saturday. Excursions also operate Saturdays in April and into May. Eureka Springs is a year-round resort area, but most visitors arrive during the summer months or autumn, when the surrounding wooded hills are ablaze with color. The tourist tide ebbs briefly in late August.

**GOOD TO KNOW:** The Eurekan dining car is climate-controlled, but the coaches are not, except for the pot-bellied stove and ceiling fans. Coach windows can be opened to catch the Ozarks breeze on warm days.

**WORTH DOING:** Explore Eureka Springs, as the entire city was designated as a historic district. In about 2 square miles, almost 500 buildings have historic significance. Wander the steep, winding streets and browse the art galleries and boutiques. Visit the many springs that were promoted because of their healing powers. View classic Victorian hotels, including The Crescent and the Basin Park, which has ground-level access to each of its eight stories (the hillside on which it's built is that steep).

**DON'T MISS:** Look through the Eureka Springs depot, which was built in 1913, and the rail equipment displayed outside. Gems include steam locomotive 201, built for service in Panama, and a station wagon equipped to run on rails as an inspection car. On the train ride, keep an eye out for the cut-stone bridge abutments built in 1883.

**GETTING THERE:** Eureka Springs is about an hour northeast of Fayetteville along Highway 62 or an hour southwest of Branson, Mo., via Highways 65, 86, and 23.

**LOCATION:** 299 N. Main Street, Eureka Springs
**PHONE:** 479-253-9623
**WEBSITE:** esnarailway.com
**E-MAIL:** form on website

197

# METRO Streetcar

Ralcon Wagner

METRO Streetcar is a heritage trolley line operated by the Rock Region METRO between Little Rock and North Little Rock using replica vintage electric cars. The 3.4-mile route connects historical districts and tourist attractions in both cities.

**CHOICES:** METRO Streetcar operators provide information on historic sites and attractions during the leisurely ride through a variety of unique neighborhoods. Trolleys only stop at the 15 designated stations along the route. All cars are climate-controlled and handicap accessible. Fares are reasonable; however, exact fare is required. If you intend on riding more than once, a one- or three-day pass is your best bet. Passes are available from car operators and at select locations.

**WHEN TO GO:** The streetcars operate year-round except on major holidays. Service from North Little Rock to downtown Little Rock and the Clinton Presidential Center (Blue Line) operates daily from morning until evening with extended hours Thursday through Saturday. Additional service is provided over the downtown loop (Green Line), Monday through Saturday until early evening.

**GOOD TO KNOW:** The current roster of replica trolleys was built specifically for METRO Streetcar. All of the cars were designed to resemble the Birney-type streetcars that were once used in Little Rock until the late 1940s.

**WORTH DOING:** Little Rock has many attractions that appeal to the entire family. You can tour the State Capitol Building or the Clinton Presidential Center, shop and enjoy a meal in the River Market District, watch boats cruise down the Arkansas River as you stroll through Riverfront Park, or visit the kid-friendly Museum of Discovery.

**DON'T MISS:** Take time to walk or bike across the former railroad vertical lift bridges spanning the Arkansas River. Both have been converted to pedestrian use as part of the impressive River Trail network. You can view the ornate 1899 Choctaw & Memphis depot, now restored as part of the Clinton Presidential Center campus.

**GETTING THERE:** Follow I-30 into downtown Little Rock, take Exit 141A (Second Street), and proceed west. There is ample parking (free and paid) adjacent to the trolley along both Second Street and President Clinton Avenue around the River Market District.

**LOCATION:** President Clinton Avenue and Third Street, Little Rock
**PHONE:** 501-375-6717
**WEBSITE:** rrmetro.org/services/streetcar
**E-MAIL:** info@rrmetro.org

# KANSAS

## Atchison Rail Museum

The Atchison Rail Museum features an outdoor collection of railcars. On summer weekends, the cars are open for viewing and a miniature railroad operates. It is adjacent to a restored 1880 Santa Fe depot that now houses the county's historical society museum. In summer, trolleys leave from the depot on 45-minute, narrated historical tours.

LOCATION: 200 S. 10th Street, Atchison
PHONE: 913-367-2427
WEBSITE: atchisonkansas.net

## Great Plains Transportation Museum

The museum features an outdoor display of locomotives, cabooses, and cars, including Santa Fe steam locomotive No. 3768 and Santa Fe FP45 diesel No. 93. Indoor exhibits feature railroad signs, lanterns, tools, and other artifacts. It is open year-round on Saturdays and also on Sundays from April to October. On the museum's website, you can view historical railroad documents such as timetables, train orders, and waybills.

LOCATION: 700 E. Douglas Avenue, Wichita
PHONE: 316-263-0944
WEBSITE: gptm.us
E-MAIL: info@gptm.us

## Heart of the Heartlands Museum

The museum complex includes a building of rail exhibits, two Missouri Pacific depots, and a collection of locomotives and railcars. The museum offers several short train excursions and motor car rides. The buildings are open the first and third weekends June through August.

LOCATION: 6769 NW 20th Street, Scammon
PHONE: 620-396-8594
WEBSITE: heartlandstrainclub.org
E-MAIL: heartlands@cox.net

## Kansas Belle Dinner Train

The Kansas Belle Dinner Train operates 3-hour Saturday evening runs using 1940s-themed cars, more formal and romantic, with an optional murder mystery play, WWII USO show, or melodrama. Sunday afternoon dinner trips offer a more casual setting, better suited for families, with a slightly shorter run time. The trips operate over Midland Railway track between Baldwin City and Ottawa using Midland's locomotives.

LOCATION: 1515 High Street, Baldwin City
PHONE: 785-594-8505
WEBSITE: kansasbelle.com
E-MAIL: form on website

# Abilene & Smoky Valley Railroad

Patrick Hiatte

**A 90-minute, 9-mile round trip takes you through the Smoky Hill River Valley from historic Abilene to Enterprise. Along the way, you'll cross the Smoky Hill River on an early steel truss bridge, see stone houses and barns built by German settlers, and enjoy America's agricultural heartland.**

**CHOICES:** Ride behind a Santa Fe Pacific or an Alco S1 in a restored Katy railroad coach, a pair of open-air (but shaded) gondola cars, or an ex-Union Pacific caboose. An extra fare gets you on board the caboose or in the locomotive cab. On some Saturdays, you can extend your trip on the Silver Flyer railbus, which meets the train in Enterprise and runs on rails to the German/Swedish community of Woodbine, where lunch is included.

**WHEN TO GO:** Trains run Wednesday through Sunday from Memorial Day to Labor Day and on weekends in May, September, and October. The steam engine typically operates on Memorial Day, Independence Day, and Labor Day weekends and for the National Day of the Cowboy, the fourth weekend in July, and Chisholm Trail Day, the first weekend in October. Dinner trains catered by local restaurants run on select Saturday evenings.

**GOOD TO KNOW:** The Dwight D. Eisenhower Presidential Library and Museum complex, including Ike's boyhood home, is across the tracks from the ASV depot.

**WORTH DOING:** Just south of the depot, you can wander through Old Abilene Town, which features replica 19th century buildings, gunfights, and dancing girls. In 2017, look for special events that celebrate the 150th anniversary of the first cattle being driven on the Chisolm Trail to Abilene.

**DON'T MISS:** In addition to the ASV's restored Rock Island depot, the Santa Fe (now BNSF) combination depot and the Union Pacific depot and freight house are still standing. The UP depot is open to the public and houses the Abilene Visitor Center, where you can enjoy a sugar cookie made from Mamie Eisenhower's recipe.

**GETTING THERE:** Abilene is on I-70 about 150 miles west of Kansas City and about 90 miles north of Wichita. The ASV depot is about 2 miles south of I-70 off Highway 15 (Buckeye Avenue), just south of the Eisenhower complex.

**LOCATION:** 200 SE Fifth Street, Abilene
**PHONE:** 888-426-6687 or 785-263-1077
**WEBSITE:** asvrr.org
**E-MAIL:** asvrail@gmail.com

# Midland Railway

Ralcon Wagner

The Midland Railway offers 20-mile round trips in the pleasant Kansas countryside between Baldwin City and Ottawa. The museum has a roster of first-generation diesels that includes an ex-Missouri-Kansas-Texas Alco RS3 and a former Chicago, Burlington & Quincy EMD NW2. The Midland uses passenger coaches, cabooses, and a transfer caboose on its excursions.

**CHOICES:** Regular service includes 1-hour excursions from Baldwin City to Norwood that cross two 200-foot trestles and 2-hour trips to the end of the line at Ottawa Junction, where the line meets BNSF's Transcon. Midland also offers Thomas the Tank Engine, Halloween Night Trains of Terror, Santa trains, an Ice Cream Express, and other special excursions.

**WHEN TO GO:** The Midland operates primarily on weekends from June to October, with Thursday trains added for summer. The Midland also participates in various community festivals including the Maple Leaf Festival, which takes place the third weekend in October.

**GOOD TO KNOW:** The Kansas Belle Dinner Train operates over the Midland Railway's route from Baldwin City to Ottawa on many weekends.

**WORTH DOING:** Journey south to Ottawa and visit the Old Depot Museum, housed in an old 1888 Santa Fe depot or stroll down the Prairie Spirit Trail (the trailhead is behind the Old Depot Museum), a converted rail trail.

**DON'T MISS:** Look through the Midland's 1906 Baldwin City depot, which is listed on the National Register of Historic Places.

**GETTING THERE:** Baldwin City is 45 miles southwest of Kansas City on Highway 56. The Midland depot is on High Street, just west of the town square.

**LOCATION:** 1515 W. High Street, Baldwin City
**PHONE:** 913-721-1211 or 785-594-6982 (depot)
**WEBSITE:** midlandrailway.org
**E-MAIL:** form on website

# LOUISIANA

## DeQuincy Railroad Museum

Home to the DeQuincy Railroad Museum, the former Kansas City Southern depot is an outstanding example of Mission Revival architecture and is on the National Register of Historic Places. It displays a 1913 Alco steam locomotive, a caboose, and a passenger coach as well as artifacts and memorabilia. It is open Tuesdays through Saturdays. The annual Louisiana Railroad Days Festival is held here in April.

LOCATION: 400 Lake Charles Avenue, DeQuincy
PHONE: 337-786-2823
WEBSITE: dequincyrailroadmuseum.com
E-MAIL: form on website

## Southern Forest Heritage Museum

At this museum, a guided tour takes you around a 57-acre historic sawmill complex, where you'll see a roundhouse and other industrial structures, three early logging locomotives, two McGiffert loaders, a Clyde skidder, and other steam equipment. Railbus rides on original Red River & Gulf Railroad track are available. An exhibit also highlights the history of the railroad. It is open Tuesdays through Sundays but closes during winter.

LOCATION: 77 Longleaf Road, Longleaf
PHONE: 318-748-8404
WEBSITE: forestheritagemuseum.org
E-MAIL: sfhmwebadmin@cox.net

# New Orleans Streetcars

Elrond Lawrence

Streetcars are a great way to see New Orleans, and if you have the desire, you can ride several different streetcar lines, operated today by the city's transit agency. While all of them make it simple to get around the Big Easy, each has its own character and charm that truly offers a fascinating view of this diverse city.

**CHOICES:** The St. Charles Line features the oldest continuously operating street railway system in the world. Named as a National Historic Landmark, it passes antebellum mansions, historic monuments, universities, and other sights. The Canal Street Line, which has two branches, takes passengers from the French Market through the central business district to City Park Avenue or to an area of historic cemeteries. The Riverfront Line travels the downtown area along the Mississippi River. The Rampart-St. Claude Streetcar Line runs down Loyola from New Orleans Union Passenger Terminal to Elysian Fields.

**WHEN TO GO:** All lines run every day of the year. As with most coastal cities, expect humidity and high temperatures in summer; this is especially noticeable on the St. Charles Line as its historic Perley Thomas cars lack air-conditioning.

**GOOD TO KNOW:** Despite fewer amenities, fans of history and interurbans alike will enjoy the trip along St. Charles Avenue. The line was built in 1835, and since it's on the National Register of Historic Places, the cars must remain as they were back in 1923.

**WORTH DOING:** It's hard to think of New Orleans and not associate Mardi Gras with it. The parties and parades actually begin the weekend before, and as the city's population explodes during this time, consider that when making travel plans.

**DON'T MISS:** Sure, there's the French Quarter, but outside this half-square-mile box, you'll find a Mississippi River cruise aboard an authentic steamboat, the National World War II Museum, the Audubon Nature Institute, plus music festivals and restaurants featuring notable indigenous cuisine.

**GETTING THERE:** Thanks to the line's sprawling routes, there are many places to catch a New Orleans streetcar. One of the best is via the Canal Street Line connection at the New Orleans Union Passenger Terminal.

**LOCATION:** Carrolton Avenue, Claiborne Avenue, Canal Street, New Orleans
**PHONE:** 504-248-3900
**WEBSITE:** norta.com
**E-MAIL:** comments@norta.com

# MISSOURI

## Belton, Grandview & Kansas City Railroad

At this laid-back railroad, you can walk around the yard, look at displayed equipment, and talk to the crew before boarding a 5-mile excursion. The 45-minute round trip runs south from Belton. Rides in the locomotive with the engineer are also available. Trains run May through October with additional Santa trains.

LOCATION: 502 E. Walnut Street, Belton
PHONE: 816-331-0630
WEBSITE: beltonrailroad.org
E-MAIL: info@beltonrailroad.org

## Chicago & Alton Railroad Depot

Built in 1879, the two-story Chicago & Alton depot features a restored four-room stationmaster's residence on the second floor. The first floor contains a waiting room, baggage room, and stationmaster's room. The depot contains hundreds of C&A artifacts. It is open daily (but closed on Tuesdays) April through October.

LOCATION: 318 W. Pacific Avenue, Independence
PHONE: 816-325-7955
WEBSITE: chicagoalton1879depot.com
E-MAIL: chicagoaltondepot@gmail.com

# KC Rail Experience

Located in historic Union Station, the KC Rail Experience features a vintage railcar, a diesel engine, artifacts, and a locomotive simulator. Admission is included with a ticket to Science City, an interactive science center. You can also view trains of all sizes, from a model railroad exhibit to actual operating trains that you can see from a footbridge over the tracks.

LOCATION: 30 W. Pershing Road, Kansas City
PHONE: 816-460-2020
WEBSITE: unionstation.org
E-MAIL: visitor@unionstation.org

# Railroad Historical Museum

Located in Grant Beach Park, this train museum is an actual train. A locomotive, baggage car, commuter car, and caboose contain artifacts from the St. Louis-San Francisco and other railroads. After touring the museum, you can enjoy the park's pool, playground, and picnic area. It is open Saturdays May through October.

LOCATION: 1300 N. Grant Street, Springfield
PHONE: 417-833-0994
WEBSITE: rrhistoricalmuseum.zoomshare.com
E-MAIL: railroadhistoricalmuseum@yahoo.com

# St. Louis Iron Mountain & Southern Railway

From April through December, this railway offers a large variety of trips including sightseeing excursions, murder mysteries, train robberies, and holiday-themed rides. Trains are pulled by Pennsylvania Railroad No. 5898, a 1950 E unit.

LOCATION: 225 E. Jackson Boulevard, Jackson
PHONE: 573-243-1688
WEBSITE: slimrr.com
E-MAIL: slimrr1@gmail.com

# Branson Scenic Railway

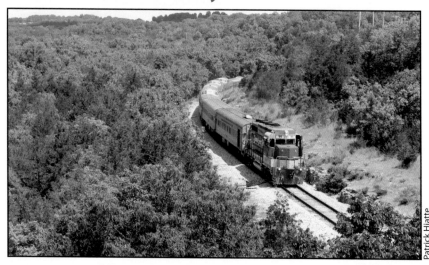

Patrick Hiatte

Enjoy a 40-mile round trip through the Ozarks on the former Missouri Pacific Railroad White River Line, which was built more than a century ago. View historic towns and town sites as you pass through tunnels and over high bridges along the banks of the White River and its tributaries.

**CHOICES:** The train usually runs south from Branson but may run north, depending on freight traffic and track work on the host Missouri & North Arkansas Railroad. There is open seating on the dome cars, 60-seat deluxe coach, and lounge car that comprise the regular train. A dinner train, serving a candlelit, four-course meal, operates on Saturday evenings April through October. Beginning in late November and continuing into December, the Polar Express begins its holiday run.

**WHEN TO GO:** The Ozarks are scenic any time of the year, but especially in the fall, when the oaks and other hardwoods turn red, yellow, and orange in a display that rivals any fall foliage in the country. BSR operates four trains a day during the two weeks in October when the colors are usually at their height, as well as during the peak months of June and July. At least two trains a day operate from mid-March through mid-December.

**GOOD TO KNOW:** Seating is open and boarding is by group based on ticket number— the sooner you buy your ticket, the more likely you are to get a seat in one of the three domes.

**WORTH DOING:** Branson offers more than 100 shows, including musical tributes, comedy headliners, and dozens of country music shows. For a quiet (and free) getaway, walk the boardwalk along the shore of Lake Taneycomo and enjoy the fire and water fountain show at Branson Landing.

**DON'T MISS:** At Silver Dollar City theme park, you can ride the Frisco Silver Dollar steam train, named for the Frisco Railway, which had its operating headquarters just up the road in Springfield.

**GETTING THERE:** Branson is in southwest Missouri about 45 miles south of Springfield on Highway 65. The depot is downtown on Main Street (Highway 76).

**LOCATION:** 206 E. Main Street, Branson
**PHONE:** 800-287-2462 or 417-334-6110
**WEBSITE:** bransontrain.com
**E-MAIL:** form on website

# Museum of Transportation

Jeff Terry

If you want to be surrounded by trains, this is the place. A visit here brings you in touch with more than 70 locomotives of steam, diesel, and electric power. You'll see scores of railcars and even one of the first railroad tunnels west of the Mississippi. The 150-acre site also houses airplanes, cars, and riverboats.

**CHOICES:** The museum features a visitor center, 10 other buildings, and almost 200 pieces of rail equipment. Its collection has more than 30 steam locomotives, and stairs let you climb into the cabs of many of them. Many rare and unusual items grace the site, including the world's largest tank car, an Aerotrain, and even a cast-iron turntable.

**WHEN TO GO:** The museum is open year-round with variable hours. It is open daily during its summer schedule and open Thursday through Sunday during January and February. Trolley rides are offered April through October.

**GOOD TO KNOW:** At the visitor center, you can board the miniature train that runs through the site. The Creation Station is a hands-on learning center for children 5 and under. It is open weekday mornings and first and third Sundays. It has an extra fee.

**WORTH DOING:** Of course, if you haven't already done so, enjoy the view from the top of Gateway Arch. You can also take a riverboat cruise, play some ragtime at Scott Joplin's home, enjoy the Missouri Botanical Garden, or view the mosaics at Cathedral Basilica.

**DON'T MISS:** Climb into the cab of the Union Pacific Big Boy No. 4006 and see what it felt like to be the engineer on one of the world's largest steam locomotives. And climb aboard Santa Fe No. 5011 and ring the engine's bell.

**GETTING THERE:** The museum is about 12 miles west of downtown St. Louis. When driving from I-270, either north or south, exit at Dougherty Ferry Road (Exit 8), go west about 1 mile to Barrett Station Road, and turn left. The museum is on the right.

**LOCATION:** 3015 Barrett Station Road, St. Louis
**PHONE:** 314-965-6212
**WEBSITE:** transportmuseumassociation.org
**E-MAIL:** museum@transportmuseumassociation.org

# OKLAHOMA

## Frisco Depot Museum

Once a main hub for the Frisco, the depot in Hugo is now a museum. Listed on the National Register of Historic Places, the museum features preserved Harvey Girl rooms, railroad artifacts, and displays on local history. It also includes a restored and operational Harvey House restaurant. Outside the museum, the depot park contains a narrow gauge steam locomotive and picnic areas. It is open Tuesday through Saturday.

LOCATION: 307 N. B Street, Hugo
PHONE: 580-326-6630
WEBSITE: friscodepot.org
E-MAIL: friscodepot@live.com

## Heritage Express Trolley

This 25-minute trolley ride is the only rail-based trolley in operation in Oklahoma. It runs from Heritage Park to downtown El Reno. Heritage Park is also home of the Canadian County Museum, which is based in a historical Rock Island train depot. A Rock Island caboose, coal car, and various historic buildings are located on the museum grounds. The trolley runs and the museum is open Wednesdays through Sundays.

LOCATION: 300 S. Grand Avenue, El Reno
PHONE: 405-262-5121
WEBSITE: elrenotourism.org

## Railroad Museum of Oklahoma

Located in a former Santa Fe freight house, this museum houses a large collection of railroad artifacts and memorabilia including a replica Pullman car interior. In the yard, you can climb aboard a 1925 Baldwin 4-8-2 steam locomotive, wander through cabooses from nine different railroads, and view an assortment of freight cars. The museum also sponsors several all-caboose excursions. It is open Tuesdays through Saturdays year-round.

LOCATION: 702 N. Washington Street, Enid
PHONE: 580-233-3051
WEBSITE: railroadmuseumofoklahoma.com
E-MAIL: railroad_museum@att.net

## Route 66 Historical Village

In the village, you'll see the restored Frisco 4500 *Meteor* steam engine along with a passenger coach, tank car, caboose, and trolley car. A 154-foot oil derrick stands next to the railcars. It also features indoor historical exhibits related to Route 66 and Tulsa.

LOCATION: 3770 Southwest Boulevard, Tulsa
PHONE: 918-609-0405
WEBSITE: facebook.com/route66village

## Santa Fe Depot Museum

This 1905 Santa Fe depot has been restored and now contains a collection of railroad photos and other local historical artifacts. On display are 1907 Baldwin steam locomotive Santa Fe No. 1951, a coal tender, and a caboose. The museum is open Tuesday through Saturday, and it features a convenient picnic area. A toy and action figure museum is also located in Pauls Valley.

LOCATION: 204 S. Santa Fe Street, Pauls Valley
PHONE: 405-238-2244
WEBSITE: facebook.com/paulsvalleysantafedepot

## Waynoka Air-Rail Museum

The Waynoka Station complex includes a restored 1910 Santa Fe depot and Harvey House, 1918 section foreman's house, water tower, and diesel locomotive. The museum contains displays on Fred Harvey, the Santa Fe Railroad, Waynoka transportation history, and other subjects. The museum is open Tuesday through Saturday.

LOCATION: 1386 S. Cleveland Street, Waynoka
PHONE: 580-824-1886
WEBSITE: waynoka.org
E-MAIL: waynokahs@hotmail.com

# Oklahoma Railway Museum

Jeff Terry

The Oklahoma Railway Museum boasts an impressive collection of vintage railroad equipment with ties to the Sooner State. The museum is best known for its collection of working first-generation diesel locomotives, which includes a former Rock Island Alco RS-1, a Santa Fe CF7, and an EMD F7A painted in Frisco colors. On the spacious grounds are more than a dozen freight cars, cabooses, and passenger cars from Oklahoma railroads. Work equipment on exhibit includes a 1954 rail crane and a unique inspection car that was home-built by the Missouri-Kansas-Texas in 1973.

**CHOICES:** On the first and third Saturday of each month, from April through August, museum visitors are offered a 40-minute train ride over an original MKT line. Passengers may choose to ride in an open-air excursion car or aboard one of three 1940s-era streamlined cars that were used on Santa Fe trains such as the *Texas Chief* and *El Capitan*. The train is often pulled by an 1952 SW8 diesel locomotive that's been painted in MKT's classic green and yellow livery.

**WHEN TO GO:** Besides the regular Saturday excursions, special train rides are scheduled throughout the year, including an Easter Bunny Express, Halloween and Christmas trains, and Day Out with Thomas events.

**GOOD TO KNOW:** Start your visit at the Oakwood depot, a traditional small-town station built in 1905 to serve the Kansas City, Mexico & Orient Railway. Unused after 1958, the wooden depot was moved to its present location in 2000 and restored.

**WORTH DOING:** Two miles north of the museum is Oklahoma City's Adventure District, which is home to many of the city's most visited attractions. These include the Oklahoma City Zoo and Botanical Garden, which features 1,900 animals, and Science Museum Oklahoma, where visitors can inspect a full-size replica of Nasa's Apollo lunar lander. And lovers of western history, art, and culture will enjoy the National Cowboy & Western Heritage Museum.

**DON'T MISS:** Santa Fe 2-8-0 steam locomotive No. 643 is one of the oldest AT&SF steam locomotives in existence, having been constructed as an American-type in 1879 and rebuilt into its present configuration in 1897.

**GETTING THERE:** The museum is located a half-mile west of I-35 off Exit 131 (NE 36th Street) on historic Grand Boulevard.

**LOCATION:** 3400 NE Grand Boulevard, Oklahoma City
**PHONE:** 405-424-8222
**WEBSITE:** oklahomarailwaymuseum.org
**E-MAIL:** form on website

# TEXAS

## B-RI Railroad Museum

Constructed in 1906, the two-story depot served the Burlington Route and Rock Island Railroads until becoming a museum in 1970. The first floor is home to numerous vintage rail artifacts, while the upstairs is devoted to local history. A 1926 Baldwin 2-8-2 locomotive and BN caboose are also on display. It is open on weekends.

LOCATION: 208 S. Third Avenue, Teague
PHONE: 254-739-2061 or 254-359-4100 (evenings)
WEBSITE: therailroadmuseum.com
E-MAIL: adladyginny@gmail.com

## Eagle Lake Depot Museum

The museum showcases varied artifacts from dozens of area railroads. Inside the 1911 Santa Fe depot, the agent's office includes an operating telegraph and authentic equipment. The freight room houses an assortment of vintage equipment, tools, signals, signs, and lanterns. It is open the second and fourth Saturdays of each month.

LOCATION: 322 E. Main Street, Eagle Lake
WEBSITE: eaglelakedepot.org

## Ennis Railroad and Cultural Heritage Museum

Housed in a 1915 building, the museum contains railroad memorabilia, dioramas, depot replicas, and china, as well as a variety of cultural exhibits. It is open daily, and a MKT caboose is displayed outside. Nearby, the city's visitor center is located in a former Wells Fargo freight office. It is open Tuesdays through Sundays.

LOCATION: 105 NE Main Street, Ennis
PHONE: 972-875-1901 or 972-878-4748
WEBSITE: visitennis.org

# History Center

The History Center features indoor and outdoor interpretive exhibits. Permanent displays include a 1920 Baldwin 4-6-0 from Texas Southeastern Railroad, on which you can ring its bell and blow its whistle, a log car, and a caboose. The center contains many photos on east Texas railroading and logging operations. It is closed Sundays.

LOCATION: 102 N. Temple Drive, Diboll
PHONE: 936-829-3543
WEBSITE: thehistorycenteronline.com
E-MAIL: info@thehistorycenteronline.com

## Interurban Railway Museum

Located in downtown Plano, the Interurban Railway Museum is housed in a building that served as a primary stop on the Texas Electric Railway that ran from Denison to Dallas beginning in 1908. The museum contains artifacts associated with the interurban line and the history of Plano. Open Monday through Saturday, it also offers guided tours through restored trolley car 360.

LOCATION: 901 E. 15th Street, Plano
PHONE: 972-941-2117
WEBSITE: interurbanrailwaymuseum.org
E-MAIL: info@interurbanrailwaymuseum.org

## Lehnis Railroad Museum

This railroad museum displays an AT&SF steam locomotive, a business car, and a caboose. It includes a collection of railroad china, lanterns, equipment, and photos. From the train-watching platform, you can look for passing BNSF trains. Located next to a Harvey House and Santa Fe depot, the museum is open Tuesdays through Saturdays.

LOCATION: 700 E. Adams Street, Brownwood
PHONE: 325-643-6376
WEBSITE: brownwoodtexas.gov
E-MAIL: bnorris@brownwoodtexas.gov

# New Braunfels Railroad Museum

Housed in the restored 1907 International & Great Northern depot, the museum displays a 0-6-0T Porter oil-fired steam locomotive, a Missouri Pacific caboose, and numerous railroad artifacts. It is open Thursday through Monday.

LOCATION: 302 W. San Antonio Street, New Braunfels
PHONE: 830-627-2447
WEBSITE: newbraunfelsrailroadmuseum.org
E-MAIL: info@newbraunfelsrailroadmuseum.org

# Railway Museum of San Angelo

Located in a historic Kansas City, Mexico & Orient depot, which was completed in 1910, the museum highlights local railroad history. It features a large collection of railroad photos by Allen Johnson. Static displays include two diesel locomotives and a Santa Fe boxcar and caboose. It is open on Saturdays. For a unique special event for kids, try Hobo Day in August and try to fry an egg on the track.

LOCATION: 703 S. Chadbourne Street, San Angelo
PHONE: 325-486-2140
WEBSITE: railwaymuseumsanangelo.homestead.com
E-MAIL: form on website

# Rosenberg Railroad Museum

The museum features Tower 17, the last manned interlocking tower in Texas. Inside the fully restored tower, you can work the interlocking machine. Also on display are the *Quebec*, an 1879 business car, diesel switcher No. 2350, and a Missouri Pacific caboose. The museum building, modeled after the city's original depot, contains signaling, station agent, and telegraph artifacts. It is open Wednesdays through Sundays.

LOCATION: 1921 Avenue F, Rosenberg
PHONE: 281-633-2846
WEBSITE: rosenbergrrmuseum.org
E-MAIL: info@rosenbergrrmuseum.org

# Temple Railroad and Heritage Museum

Housed in a 1910 Santa Fe depot, the museum features exhibits related to the Santa Fe Railway and the city of Temple including those on Harvey Houses, the Santa Fe Hospital, and railroad lanterns. Outdoor displays feature a variety of cars, including a troop sleeper, a 1921 Pacific type Baldwin steam locomotive, and a 1937 diesel engine. The museum is open Tuesday through Saturday.

LOCATION: 315 W. Avenue B, Temple
PHONE: 254-298-5172
WEBSITE: templerrhm.org
E-MAIL: rrhm@templetx.gov

# Texas & Pacific Railway Museum

Located in the Ginocchio National Historic District, the restored 1912 depot still operates as a passenger station, now for Amtrak. The T&P museum is on the second floor, and T&P 2-8-2 Mikado No. 400 and a Union Pacific caboose are displayed on the grounds. It is open Tuesday through Saturday.

LOCATION: 800 N. Washington Avenue, Marshall
PHONE: 903-938-9495
WEBSITE: facebook.com/marshall.depot

# Texas Transportation Museum

The museum displays automobiles, fire trucks, and carriages, as well as a variety of railroad structures and equipment including two steam locomotives, two diesel engines, and rolling stock. It features a Southern Pacific depot built in 1913 that was moved from Converse. The two-room building contains memorabilia from the railroads that served San Antonio. The museum operates a short train ride on weekends. It is open Friday through Sunday.

LOCATION: 11731 Wetmore Road, San Antonio
PHONE: 210-490-3554
WEBSITE: txtransportationmuseum.org
E-MAIL: form on website

# Wichita Falls Railroad Museum

The museum's collection includes a Fort Worth & Denver steam locomotive, a Missouri-Kansas-Texas switch engine, a 1913 Pullman all-steel sleeper, troop sleepers, cabooses, and other cars. Artifacts center on the railroads that served Wichita Falls. The museum is open Saturdays year-round.

LOCATION: 500 Ninth Street, Wichita Falls
PHONE: 940-723-2661
WEBSITE: wfrrm.com
E-MAIL: susieacain@sbcglobal.net

# Austin Steam Train

Mike Harbour

This tourist line was formed in 1989 to provide weekend service over a portion of a 167-mile route purchased from Southern Pacific. The train operates out of Cedar Park and rolls through the scenic Texas hill country.

**CHOICES:** The railroad offers two regular excursions. The Hill Country Flyer makes a 66-mile, 6-hour round trip between Cedar Park and Burnet. The trip includes a leisurely layover, allowing you to enjoy lunch, explore the town, and watch a Wild West gunfight. On the 44-mile round trip aboard the Bertram Flyer, you'll leave Cedar Park, cross the South San Gabriel River, and arrive in Bertram. Rolling stock consists of vintage coach and lounge cars. You have a choice of riding excursion coach or first class (coach or lounge). The cars are climate-controlled.

**WHEN TO GO:** Excursions run weekends all year. Many visitors choose to ride during the spring and fall and bypass the summer heat. Some midweek and evening trains run. A variety of specials operate including Day Out with Thomas, murder mysteries, and the North Pole Flyer.

**GOOD TO KNOW:** Trains are pulled by an Alco RSD15, a unit originally built for Santa Fe, that's been repainted in an SP-inspired "black widow" scheme. Namesake motive power No. 786, an ex-SP Mikado, is undergoing restoration.

**WORTH DOING:** Both Cedar Park and Burnet have numerous lodging and dining options for visitors, while Austin is famous for its museums, entertainment, scenic drives, and area lakes.

**DON'T MISS:** Special events for adults usually take place in the Nambe or the Rippling Stream, a 1949 Budd car that served on the New York Central.

**GETTING THERE:** Cedar Park is 20 miles north of Austin. You can reach the station by exiting I-35 at Exit 256. Follow RM 1431, which turns into Whitestone Boulevard, for 8 miles. The station is in the Cedar Park Shopping Center.

**LOCATION:** 401 E. Whitestone Boulevard, Cedar Park
**PHONE:** 512-477-8468
**WEBSITE:** austinsteamtrain.org
**E-MAIL:** info@austinsteamtrain.org

# Galveston Railroad Museum

Galveston Railroad Museum

Housed in the former Santa Fe station on Galveston Island's east end, the museum features a yard full of fascinating rolling stock, including a pair of EMD F7s painted in AT&SF's classic warbonnet scheme.

**CHOICES:** After a tour of the static displays, take a trip on the Harborside Express, a 15-minute excursion aboard a ex-Missouri Pacific caboose that runs several times most Saturdays. The museum features one of the largest collections of railroad china and dinnerware in the United States. In the station's waiting room, you'll see Ghosts of Travelers Past, full-sized plaster figures of people congregating there as it appeared in 1932. With the touch of a button, you can operate a large model train layout.

**WHEN TO GO:** The museum is open daily year-round, but summers on the Texas Gulf Coast tend to be hot and humid. The other three seasons are usually more pleasant when spending time outdoors.

**GOOD TO KNOW:** In fall, the museum hosts a train show weekend, complete with model railroads on display, caboose rides, and other activities.

**WORTH DOING:** Like in New Orleans to the east, Mardi Gras is a big deal on the island. The center of all the activity takes place near the museum on The Strand, Galveston's historic downtown district. Another popular destination is Moody Gardens, which contains a rain forest pyramid, aquarium, and other attractions.

**DON'T MISS:** No trip to the island would be complete without a visit to a beach. Galveston features 32 miles of beaches and most operated by the city. If you want to get away from the crowds but still enjoy the surf, head to the island's west end to Galveston Island State Park, a 2,000-plus-acre site that offers camping, bird-watching, hiking, mountain biking, fishing, and swimming.

**GETTING THERE:** From Houston, take I-45 south to Exit 1C. Turn left onto Harborside Drive, then turn right on 25th Street/Rosenberg Street, turn right on Santa Fe, and then right again to the museum.

**LOCATION:** 2602 Santa Fe Place, Galveston
**PHONE:** 409-765-5700
**WEBSITE:** galvestonrrmuseum.com
**E-MAIL:** form on website

# Grapevine Vintage Railroad

Grapevine Convention & Visitors Bureau

Grapevine operates the only 19th century steam locomotive in Texas. Based at the restored 1888 Cotton Belt depot in downtown Grapevine, the railroad runs over 21 miles of ex-Cotton Belt track into the famous Fort Worth Stockyards Mall. It also includes a 6-mile branch line running south from the mall across the Trinity River.

**CHOICES:** A 75-minute ride takes you from Grapevine to the Stockyards, and the 2-hour layover allows ample time for exploring the mall's many offerings. The Trinity River run passes through Trinity Park and the Fort Worth Zoo along a segment of the famous Chisholm Trail. Vinny, a former AT&SF Electro-Motive GP7, provides the motive power for the train. Trains carry four 1925-era day coaches (19th century décor) plus a pair of open-air excursion coaches.

**WHEN TO GO:** Regular excursions run February through November. From Memorial Day weekend through Labor Day weekend, they operate Friday through Sunday. Frequency is reduced to two days (Saturday and Sunday) during the rest of the season. One-hour fun trains operate on Saturdays. The line offers numerous special events including train robberies and wine tastings, as well as holiday trains.

**GOOD TO KNOW:** The Grapevine to the stockyards round-trip excursion has assigned seating. It is anticipated that Puffy, an 1896 Cooke 4-6-0 steam locomotive, will return to service in 2017.

**WORTH DOING:** True to its name, Grapevine is home to numerous wineries with regular tours and a special Grapefest celebration in September.

**DON'T MISS:** During the Trinity River trip, the train crosses both channels of the river, goes through Trinity Park, and stops in a switchyard before returning to the Stockyards. During the trip, a narrative of the history of Fort Worth and the railroad is provided.

**GETTING THERE:** The city of Grapevine is adjacent to the northwest corner of DFW Airport. Three highways (114, 121, and 360) intersect at Grapevine, with I-30 being a few miles south of the airport and I-35E a few miles east.

**LOCATION:** 705 S. Main Street, Grapevine
**PHONE:** 817-410-3185
**WEBSITE:** grapevinetexasusa.com
**E-MAIL:** form on website

# McKinney Avenue Trolley

Ralcon Wagner

**Vintage electric trolley cars take riders back in time during a leisurely 4.6-mile ride down McKinney Avenue and other streets in Dallas' historic Uptown neighborhood.**

**CHOICES:** The heritage trolley route, referred to locally as the M-Line, has become increasingly popular with tourists and as a transportation option for commuters. To board a trolley, just locate an M-Line street sign and wait for a trolley car. A new extension down Olive Street opened in 2015. Most of the cars are air-conditioned and stop only at designated stations. Because of the historical nature of the trolleys, cars are not equipped for handicapped boarding. Since the trolley line is operated as a nonprofit organization, there is no fare, except for charter runs.

**WHEN TO GO:** Trolleys operate year-round and run every 15 to 25 minutes from morning through evening with extended hours on Fridays and Saturdays.

**GOOD TO KNOW:** Most of the cars trundling down the M-Line were built between 1909 and 1925 by a variety of builders. As a result, each car is unique in appearance and design, sporting names such as *Rosie*, *Petunia*, and *Betty*.

**WORTH DOING:** There are a variety of things to do along the McKinney Avenue corridor, such as dining at one of the many restaurants and sidewalk cafes and browsing through art galleries, boutiques, and antique shops. The Dallas World Aquarium and Museum of Art are a short walk from the trolley line.

**DON'T MISS:** Only minutes away, Dallas Union Station is an architectural gem that serves as a transportation hub for DART light rail, Trinity Railway Express commuter trains, and Amtrak. Just across the street is the new Dallas Streetcar, a 2.45-mile modern streetcar line running to the Bishop Arts District.

**GETTING THERE:** You can park on Cityplace West Boulevard or any cross street and board the trolley at the waiting shelter or the Uptown Station. If using public transit, ride any DART light rail Blue, Red, or Orange Line train to the Cityplace/Uptown subway station. Take the west exit to the surface to board the trolley.

**LOCATION:** McKinney Avenue, Dallas
**PHONE:** 214-855-0006
**WEBSITE:** mata.org
**E-MAIL:** form on website

# Museum of the American Railroad

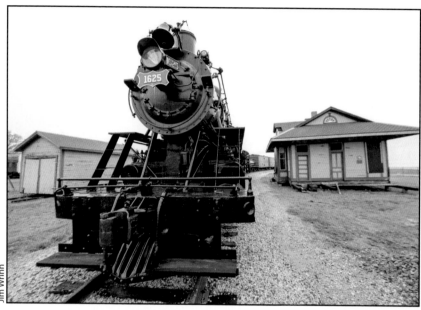

Jim Wrinn

The museum features more than 40 pieces of vintage equipment. It is still in the process of constructing its site in Frisco, after moving from Dallas, and is not yet open on a regular schedule. Currently, it has some small exhibits on display at the nearby Frisco Heritage Museum that include photos on local railroad history, Pullman car artifacts, china, a wig-wag signal, and a handcar.

**CHOICES:** Guided tours of the site take place on Thursdays and Saturdays. The 45-minute tours begin at the Frisco Heritage Museum. The Frisco Heritage Museum features a village of historic buildings that includes a replicated Frisco railroad depot. Frisco steam locomotive No. 19 is also on display.

**WHEN TO GO:** The Frisco Heritage Museum is open Wednesdays through Sundays.

**GOOD TO KNOW:** The museum's collection contains an eclectic mix of all types of locomotives including Union Pacific steam locomotive Big Boy No. 4018, a Santa Fe FP45 warbonnet diesel, and a Pennsylvania GG1 electric. It features one of the nation's largest collections of pre-World War II heavyweight passenger equipment. It also has a variety of lightweight passenger cars, freight cars, and cabooses. Historic structures include a Santa Fe interlocking tower and a Houston & Texas Central depot.

**WORTH DOING:** While Dallas and all its attractions are a half hour away, Frisco has activities and attractions as well, such as the Texas Sculpture Garden and the Sci-Tech Discovery Center.

**DON'T MISS:** For a ride on a vintage train, the Grapevine Vintage Railroad is 30 miles southwest of Frisco.

**GETTING THERE:** The easiest route to Frisco from Dallas is on the Dallas North Tollway. Although when traffic is bad, the 30-mile drive may take an hour.

**LOCATION:** 6455 Page Street (Heritage Museum), Frisco
**PHONE:** 214-428-0101
**WEBSITE:** museumoftheamericanrailroad.org
**E-MAIL:** form on website

# Texas State Railroad

Tom Kline

Built by prison inmates in 1896 and operating excursions behind steam since 1976, the Texas State Railroad offers a relaxing ride through the piney woods region of east Texas between the towns of Rusk and Palestine. A collection of various steam and diesel locomotives with regional history pulls trains at a leisurely pace through tall stands of timber in the I.D. Fairchild National Forest, giving riders a glimpse into the railroad's history of hauling agricultural and timber products.

**CHOICES:** A 25-mile round trip lasts about 4 hours, including a 90-minute lunch layover at the opposite end of the line while the train is turned for its return. Trains departing Rusk use vintage steam power, while Palestine departures are pulled by diesel engines. Standard seating offers cushioned seats in enclosed coaches with opening windows or bench-style seats in open-air coaches. Premium class offers climate-controlled seating at tables with beverage and snack service.

**WHEN TO GO:** Round trip and one-way excursions depart from Rusk between March and November, while Palestine departures begin in early July and run until early November. Texas summers can be hot so book early for air-conditioned premium seating. Spring and fall are generally mild, and open-air seating is very enjoyable at those times. Numerous special events also occur throughout the year.

**GOOD TO KNOW:** Both stations contain historical exhibits and displays, some that highlight the railroad's role in various movie and TV productions. You can picnic on the grounds at both depots, and full service RV hookups and camping sites are offered at Rusk.

**WORTH DOING:** Palestine features many restored Victorian homes, historic buildings from the early 1800s, and the Dogwood Trails Festival in late March into April.

**DON'T MISS:** For the more adventurous, you can upgrade to a one-way or round-trip cab ride in the engine.

**GETTING THERE:** From Dallas or Houston, it is a leisurely 3-hour drive to either east Texas town. Both depots are located off Highway 84, about 30 miles apart.

**LOCATION:** 535 Park Road 76, Rusk;
789 Park Road 70, Palestine
**PHONE:** 877-726-7245
**WEBSITE:** texasstaterr.com
**E-MAIL:** customerservice@premierrails.com

220

# REGION 7

Chehalis-Centralia Railroad, page 234

**IDAHO**

1 Nampa Train Depot Museum

2 Northern Pacific Depot Railroad Museum

3 Silverwood Central Railroad

4 Washington, Idaho & Montana Railway Depot

**MONTANA**

5 Alder Gulch Short Line

6 Charlie Russell Chew-Choo Dinner Train

7 Heritage Museum

8 Historical Museum at Fort Missoula

9 Livingston Depot Center

10 Old prison Museum

11 Upper Musselshell Museum

**OREGON**

12 Canby Depot Museum

13 Eagle Cap Excursion Train

14 Mount Hood Railroad

15 Oregon Coast Scenic Railroad

16 Oregon Electric Railway Museum

17 Oregon Rail Heritage Center

18 Sumpter Valley Railroad

19 Wilamette Shore Trolley

223

**WASHINGTON**

20 Cashmere Museum & Pioneer Village

21 Chehalis-Centralia Railroad

22 Chelatchie Prairie Railroad

23 Dayton Historic Depot

24 Issaquah Depot Museum and Trolley

25 Lake Whatcom Railway

26 Mt. Rainier Scenic Railroad & Museum

27 Northern Pacific Railway Museum

28 Northwest Railway Museum

29 Ritzville Railroad Depot History Museum

30 Yakima Valley Trolleys

**WYOMING**

31 Cheyenne Depot Museum

32 Douglas Railroad Interpretive Center

33 Union Pacific Railroad

34 Union Pacific Roundhouse and Turntable

# IDAHO

## Nampa Train Depot Museum

Built in 1903, the building served as the Oregon Short Line depot and was then used as offices for the Union Pacific. The building now houses artifacts relating to local history. Outside, a 1942 UP caboose is available for viewing. The museum is open Thursdays through Saturdays year-round.

LOCATION: 1200 Front Street, Nampa
PHONE: 208-467-7611
WEBSITE: canyoncountyhistory.com
E-MAIL: info@canyoncountyhistory.com

## Northern Pacific Depot Railroad Museum

Listed on the National Register of Historic Places, this building served as a station until the 1980s. The elegant chateau-style depot was built at the turn of the 20th century from brick transported from China and concrete panels made from mine tailings. It now serves as a museum that features exhibits on the depot and railroading in the area's mining district. It is open April through October, and Depot Day takes place in May.

LOCATION: 219 Sixth Street, Wallace
PHONE: 208-752-0111
WEBSITE: npdepot.org
E-MAIL: npdepot@gmail.com

## Silverwood Central Railroad

What started out as a small transportation museum turned into a large theme park with roller coasters and water slides. Silverwood's steam train is pulled by a 1915 Porter narrow gauge locomotive. The 30-minute ride through the park and surrounding woods includes surprise appearances by train robbers. The train runs May through September.

LOCATION: 27843 N. Highway 95, Athol
PHONE: 208-683-3400
WEBSITE: silverwoodthemepark.com
E-MAIL: info@silverwoodthemepark.com

## Washington, Idaho & Montana Railway Depot

Built in 1906, the restored depot now houses exhibits on the WI&M, logging, and Potlatch area history. It hosts an annual history day and speeder rides in July and other events throughout the year. It is open Wednesdays through Saturdays.

LOCATION: 185 Sixth Street, Potlach
PHONE: 208-875-1357
WEBSITE: wimryhpg.com

# MONTANA

## Alder Gulch Short Line

This narrow gauge railroad connects the former gold-mining towns of Virginia City and Nevada City. The line winds along Alder Creek, where you can view the remains of gold-mining operations, dredge tailings, and a variety of wildlife. Be sure to explore the historic buildings and displays in Nevada City. The railroad's 1910 Baldwin locomotive is stored in the Nevada City train barn, while a gas-powered engine pulls the train. It runs daily between Memorial Day and Labor Day.

LOCATION: Wallace Street, Virginia City
PHONE: 406-843-5247
WEBSITE: virginiacitymt.com
E-MAIL: form on website

## Charlie Russell Chew-Choo Dinner Train

This dinner train takes you on a 3.5-hour excursion over the old Chicago, Milwaukee, St. Paul & Pacific Railroad line. The ride crosses three historic trestles, passes through a 2,000-foot tunnel, and travels through the land that inspired artist Charles Russell. Along the way, you'll enjoy a catered prime rib dinner. Just keep your eyes open for masked bandits! North Pole runs take place in November and December. The train boards about a 15-minute drive from downtown Lewistown. It operates on select Saturdays, and a few other days, June into October.

LOCATION: 7188 Hanover Road, Lewistown
PHONE: 866-912-3980 or 406-535-5436
WEBSITE: montanadinnertrain.com
E-MAIL: lewchamb@midrivers.com

## Heritage Museum

On display is a Shay locomotive that worked for local logging companies in the early 1900s. Other exhibits are devoted to logging and early railroads as well as mining, wildlife, and life in Libby. The museum is open daily June through August and Tuesday, Friday, and Saturday during September.

LOCATION: 34067 Highway 2, Libby
PHONE: 406-293-7521
WEBSITE: libbyheritagemuseum.org
E-MAIL: heritagemuseum@frontier.com

# Historical Museum at Fort Missoula

Located in Fort Missoula, the Historical Museum includes a variety of structures that depict the area's history. One is the Drummond depot, which was constructed by the Chicago, Milwaukee, St. Paul & Pacific Railroad in 1910. When the trolley barn is open, be sure to visit historic streetcar No. 50, a 100-year-old streetcar that was the last streetcar to run in Missoula. It is open daily except Mondays October through May.

LOCATION: 3400 Captain Rawn Way, Missoula
PHONE: 406-728-3476
WEBSITE: fortmissoulamuseum.org
E-MAIL: ftmslamuseum@montana.com

# Livingston Depot Center

The historic, Italianate-style Livingston depot was built in 1902 as the Northern Pacific's original access to Yellowstone National Park. Restored in the 1980s, the depot contains a museum that highlights local and railroading history. The building also hosts concerts, art festivals, and other events. The museum is open daily late May through mid-September.

LOCATION: 200 W. Park Street, Livingston
PHONE: 406-222-2300
WEBSITE: livingstonmuseums.org
E-MAIL: livingstondepot@gmail.com

# Old Prison Museum

226

On display outside the museum complex is Milwaukee Road Little Joe No. E70, E9 locomotive No. 36A, and a caboose containing exhibits about the railroad. In addition to the prison, you'll find an auto museum, a firearms museum, and a collection of historic buildings. The museums is are open daily.

LOCATION: 1106 Main Street, Deer Lodge
PHONE: 406-846-3111
WEBSITE: pcmaf.org
E-MAIL: info@pcmaf.org

# Upper Musselshell Museum

This museum is located in two historic buildings. The Marshall Building contains a large collection of models related to the Milwaukee Road and other railroads. The Times Building contains 13 heritage rooms that are decorated by families who settled in the area. Also in town is a restored depot, Milwaukee Road ES-3 boxcab electric locomotive No. E57B, and several other pieces of equipment. It is open Mondays through Saturdays Memorial Day through Labor Day.

LOCATION: 11 and 36 S. Central Avenue, Harlowton
PHONE: 406-632-5519
WEBSITE: harlowtonmuseum.org
E-MAIL: museum@mtintouch.net

# OREGON

## Canby Depot Museum

The Canby Depot Museum is housed in what could be the oldest railroad station in Oregon, which has been around since at least 1873. The museum's displays provide a look at 19th century life of this historic community and include a Union Pacific caboose and other rail items. It is open Thursday through Sunday March through December.

LOCATION: 888 NE Fourth Avenue, Canby
PHONE: 503-266-6712
WEBSITE: canbyhistoricalsociety.org
E-MAIL: depotmusuem@canby.com

## Oregon Electric Railway Museum

The museum's collection features a variety of trolleys and traction equipment, which you can see during a carbarn tour. It also offers short trolley rides. The museum is open weekends Memorial Day into September.

LOCATION: 3995 Brooklake Road, Brooks
PHONE: 503-393-2424
WEBSITE: museum.oregontrolley.com
E-MAIL: mark@oerhs.org

## Oregon Rail Heritage Center

The Oregon Rail Heritage Center houses three historical steam locomotives: Oregon Railroad & Navigation 197, Southern Pacific 4449, and Spokane, Portland & Seattle 700. On summer Saturdays, you can ride an Oregon Pacific passenger train from the Oregon Rail Heritage Center and back via the Oaks Bottom Wildlife Refuge along the Willamette River. The center is open Thursday through Sunday.

LOCATION: 2250 SE Water Avenue, Portland
PHONE: 503-233-1156
WEBSITE: orhf.org
E-MAIL: form on website

## Willamette Shore Trolley

Willamette Shore Trolley offers 1-mile rides to Riverwood aboard vintage trolley No. 514. The trolley takes you through the 1,400-foot Elk Rock Tunnel. It operates on weekends Memorial Day through September. Lake Oswego is 9 miles south of Portland.

LOCATION: 311 N. State Street, Lake Oswego
PHONE: 503-697-7436
WEBSITE: wst.oregontrolley.com
E-MAIL: mark@oerhs.org

# Eagle Cap Excursion Train

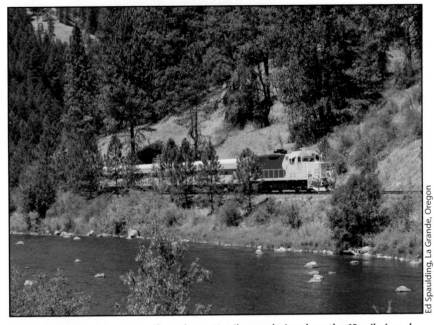

Ed Spaulding, La Grande, Oregon

The Eagle Cap Excursion Train offers 4-hour, 40-mile round trips along the 63-mile Joseph Branch in northeastern Oregon that was first constructed in 1908. The excursion line passes through spectacular rugged and remote areas, most inaccessible to cars, following the Grande Ronde River downstream and then up the wild and scenic Wallowa River.

**CHOICES:** The railroad provides diesel-powered excursion trains with comfortably restored and recently painted coaches. The cars are climate-controlled and have restrooms. Certain excursions feature train robberies. Most trips include lunch.

**WHEN TO GO:** Excursions are available select Saturdays May through October. Fall foliage trips in the heavily wooded forests are offered in October.

**GOOD TO KNOW:** In the remote areas, there is no cell phone coverage, so you'll have to stow away electronic devices and just enjoy the ride. It's all about being close to nature.

**WORTH DOING:** The towns of Elgin, Enterprise, and Joseph all contain historic buildings and quaint shops worth visiting during a trip to northeastern Oregon. Just off the Oregon Trail, the area is also known for outdoor recreation and scenery along the Hells Canyon Scenic Byway.

**DON'T MISS:** Along the ride, you have the opportunity to see bears, eagles, deer, and elk. In 1912, Rocky Mountain elk were transported from Wyoming to Wallowa County via the railroad to reestablish the area's depleted elk herds. These animals are responsible for many of the elk you will see trackside during your excursion.

**GETTING THERE:** Exit I-84 at LaGrande and follow Highway 82 to Elgin. In the center of Elgin, continue past the opera house and city hall to the depot.

**LOCATION:** 300 N. Eighth Street, Elgin
**PHONE:** 800-323-7330 or 541-963-9000
**WEBSITE:** eaglecaptrainrides.com
**E-MAIL:** train@alegretravel.com

# Mount Hood Railroad

Mount Hood Railroad

The Columbia River Gorge is filled with magnificent scenery, and the area around Mount Hood especially so because of its abundant orchards and vineyards. The Mount Hood Railroad offers a 44-mile round trip to Parkdale that features spectacular views of its namesake mountain.

**CHOICES:** The 4-hour excursion departs in the morning and follows the valley between the Columbia River and Mount Hood, providing views of Mount Adams as well. In addition, the railroad schedules brunch trains on Sundays and other special trains. You can choose standard class, first class, or diamond class levels of service.

**WHEN TO GO:** Trains run April through October, operating Wednesday through Saturday during summer (July and August). Otherwise, trains run several times weekly depending on the time of year.

**GOOD TO KNOW:** The railroad still carries a limited amount of freight, so don't be surprised if you see a boxcar somewhere along the line. Not far out of the Mount Hood depot, the train traverses a switchback, where it zigzags up the side of the mountain to gain elevation quickly. The rear of the train becomes the front for the rest of the trip into Parkdale.

**WORTH DOING:** There is much to do in the area. Sample apples and pears from orchards, visit a local winery, or watch wind surfers try to master the winds from the Columbia River Gorge. You can also take a drive on the Mount Hood Loop, which gives you a view of many scenic waterfalls.

**DON'T MISS:** Try first-class seating in the upper level of the dome car and get the same view as the engineer. Premium seating is available in the lower level of the dome car, and regular coach seating is found in other cars.

**GETTING THERE:** The Mount Hood Railroad is located 60 miles east of Portland off I-84. In Hood River, take Exit 63 to reach the depot. If driving from the south, Highway 35 also goes to Hood River.

**LOCATION:** 110 Railroad Street, Hood River
**PHONE:** 800-872-4661
**WEBSITE:** mthoodrr.com
**E-MAIL:** form on website

# Oregon Coast Scenic Railroad

Oregon Coast Scenic Railroad

Experience the Pacific Ocean on a 10-mile, 90-minute excursion along the shores of Tillamook Bay. The train is pulled by a 1910 Heisler or a 1925 Baldwin 2-6-2 and runs between Garibaldi and Rockaway Beach.

**CHOICES:** On your trip along the coast, you can ride in a flatcar, in the restored Southern Pacific 1924 Wilson River coach, or for an extra fee, in the steam locomotive's cab. Wherever you sit, find a seat on the left side of the train. It's on the ocean side, and the views are spectacular. A special fireworks train runs in July, the Candy Cane Express runs in December, and other specials also operate, some departing from Wheeler.

**WHEN TO GO:** Regular excursions operate on weekends from mid-May through September. Daily service begins in June and runs into September.

**GOOD TO KNOW:** Dinner trains operate throughout the year and offer two seating options. Pulled by a diesel locomotive, these trains travel from Garibaldi to Wheeler and back along the coast.

**WORTH DOING:** Oregon's dairy industry is based in Tillamook, and it produces some of the best cheese and ice cream in North America. Be sure to stop at the Tillamook Cheese factory in nearby Tillamook. In addition, the area features an aviation museum housed in a World War II blimp hanger. You can also view numerous lighthouses along the Pacific shore.

**DON'T MISS:** There is a layover between each run that provides the opportunity to explore Garibaldi or Rockaway Beach, get a bite to eat, or just enjoy the oceanside.

**GETTING THERE:** Garibaldi is located 10 miles north of Tillamook, just off Highway 101. At Tillamook, take Highway 101 north to Garibaldi. In Garibaldi, turn left on Third Street to Lumberman's Park, where the train boards.

**LOCATION:** 204 American Way, Garibaldi
**PHONE:** 503-842-7972
**WEBSITE:** oregoncoastscenic.org
**E-MAIL:** info@oregoncoastscenic.org

# Sumpter Valley Railroad

Dave Crosby

A 5-mile portion of one of the most charming narrow gauge lines of the Pacific Northwest has been re-created amid forests and the spoils of a former gold-mining dredge operation. It is a good approximation of a remote steam line in eastern Oregon, where snowcaps rise in the distance even in June.

**CHOICES:** The railway runs between McEwen and Sumpter. Both round-trip and one-way excursions are available at either station. Locomotives currently operating are a wood-burning W. H. Eccles Lumber Co. two-truck Heisler and oil-burning Sumpter Valley Railway 2-8-2 No. 19. Train robberies and special events take place throughout the season.

**WHEN TO GO:** The railway is open on most weekends and holidays, starting with Memorial Day and running through September. A special fall foliage train runs in October, and Christmas trains run in December.

**GOOD TO KNOW:** The Sumpter depot is a replica of the original depot. Located on the Elkhorn Scenic Byway, Sumpter is surrounded by the Elkhorn Mountains. The area is filled with history, and nearby Baker City boasts at least 60 restored buildings.

**WORTH DOING:** Near the Sumpter station, in the Sumpter Valley Dredge State Heritage Area, visit the historic gold dredge that churned up all the rocks the railroad runs through—it's as big as a house and a monster of a machine well worth touring.

**DON'T MISS:** Cab rides aboard the steam locomotive are available.

**GETTING THERE:** The railway is about 330 miles from Portland in northeast Oregon. The McEwen depot is located 23 miles southwest of Baker City on Highway 7. The Sumpter depot is located at the entrance to Dredge State Heritage Area on Austin Street.

**LOCATION:** 211 Austin Street, Sumpter;
12259 Huckleberry Loop, Baker City (McEwen)
**PHONE:** 541-894-2268
**WEBSITE:** sumptervalleyrailroad.org
**E-MAIL:** info@sumptervalleyrailroad.org

# WASHINGTON

## Cashmere Museum & Pioneer Village

The pioneer village features 20 historical structures, dating back to the late 1800s. Railroad displays include a Great Northern section house, a ticket office, a caboose, equipment, and artifacts. The museum also includes exhibits regarding pioneer and Native American history. It is open daily April through October.

LOCATION: 600 Cotlets Way, Cashmere
PHONE: 509-782-3230
WEBSITE: cashmeremuseum.org
E-MAIL: info@cashmeremuseum.org

## Dayton Historic Depot

Built in 1881, this is the oldest surviving railroad station in Washington. The stylish Stick/Eastlake building is now a museum of local history. It includes artifacts from the Union Pacific and the Oregon Railroad & Navigation Company, and a UP caboose is also on display. It is open Wednesday through Saturday year-round.

LOCATION: 222 E. Commercial Street, Dayton
PHONE: 509-382-2026
WEBSITE: daytonhistoricdepot.org
E-MAIL: info@daytonhistoricdepot.org

## Issaquah Depot Museum and Trolley

The museum's display of railcars includes a World War II kitchen car with logging, mining, and railroad artifacts. The depot features a station agent's office with railroad and local history displays. Built in 1925 and powered by a generator car, the Issaquah Valley Trolley runs 1.2 miles to Gilman Boulevard. The museum is open Friday through Sunday with trolley rides on Saturday and Sunday.

LOCATION: 78 First Avenue NE, Issaquah
PHONE: 425-392-3500
WEBSITE: issaquahhistory.org
E-MAIL: info@issaquahhistory.org

# Lake Whatcom Railway

This train ride takes you from the shores of Lake Whatcom into the wooded countryside and back. The vintage coaches and diesel locomotive were all used on the Northern Pacific. Speeder rides are also offered. A 100-year-old steam engine and wooden Great Northern freight cars are also on site. For a good workout, you can try your hand at riding a handcar. Excursions run during summer and for special events.

LOCATION: Highway 9 and NP Road, Wickersham
PHONE: 360-441-0719
WEBSITE: lakewhatcomrailway.com
E-MAIL: info@lakewhatcomrailway.com

# Northern Pacific Railway Museum

The 1911 Northern Pacific Railway depot in Toppenish serves as a museum to that railroad. The site's freight house has been converted to an engine house, where several steam locomotives are being restored. The museum offers caboose rides during special events throughout the year. It is open Tuesday through Sunday May through mid-October.

LOCATION: 10 S. Asotin Avenue, Toppenish
PHONE: 509-865-1911
WEBSITE: nprymuseum.org
E-MAIL: president@nprymuseum.org

# Ritzville Railroad Depot Museum

The brick mission-style depot was built in 1910 and retains many of its original features, including floor scales that you can try out. The museum contains railroad memorabilia, a telegraph machine, and local historical items. Outside the depot, a cupola caboose painted in a yellow and green Northern Pacific scheme is on display. It is open Tuesdays through Saturdays Memorial Day through Labor Day.

233

LOCATION: 201 W. Railroad Avenue, Ritzville
PHONE: 509-659-1656
WEBSITE: museums.goritzville.com
E-MAIL: museums@goritzville.com

# Yakima Valley Trolleys

Yakima Valley trolleys have been operating for more than 100 years. You can ride along the historic line weekends and holidays from Memorial Day through September. Railcars used on the line date between 1910 and 1930. Trolleys leave from the carbarn and museum, which contains various pieces of rolling stock.

LOCATION: South Third Avenue at West Pine Street, Yakima
PHONE: 509-249-5962
WEBSITE: yakimavalleytrolleys.org
E-MAIL: info@yakimavalleytrolleys.org

# Chehalis-Centralia Railroad

Chehalis-Centralia Railroad, Dave LaClair

In the shadow of Mount St. Helens, this relaxing train ride takes you into the forests of western Washington. You'll ride behind a steam locomotive that saw many years of service logging these very forests.

**234**

**CHOICES:** The railroad offers two different excursions. The 12-mile Milburn run takes you through forests and countryside. A longer 18-mile round trip to Ruth extends the ride by following the Chehalis River. The railroad's dinner trains follow the Ruth route and serve meals in a refurbished 1920s dining car.

**WHEN TO GO:** Summer steam train rides begin Memorial Day weekend. The Milburn train operates Saturdays and Sundays through August and Saturdays in September. The Ruth train operates Saturdays through September. Murder mystery trains, holiday trains, and other special events are scheduled throughout the year.

**GOOD TO KNOW:** For an extra fee, you can experience what it is like to ride in the cab of a working steam locomotive with a cab ride in No. 15, a 2-8-2 Mikado type steam engine that was built in 1916.

**WORTH DOING:** Take time to visit Mount St. Helens National Volcanic Monument and view the dramatic changes the area has undergone since the 1980 eruption. The 110,000-acre site contains hiking trails, several visitor centers, and an observatory.

**DON'T MISS:** On clear days, at various spots along the line, you can view Mount Rainier and Mount St. Helens. When you cross the Newaukum River Bridge, you are crossing one of the few laminated wood-beam railroad bridges still in use in the United States.

**GETTING THERE:** The railroad is about a 90-minute drive from either Portland or Seattle. From I-5, take Exit 77 (Main Street) into Chehalis. Turn left on Riverside Drive and then left again on Sylvenus Street. Nearby Centralia is served by Amtrak.

**LOCATION:** 1101 SW Sylvenus Street, Chehalis
**PHONE:** 360-748-9593
**WEBSITE:** steamtrainride.com
**E-MAIL:** info@steamtrainride.com

# Chelatchie Prairie Railroad

Chelatchie Prairie Railroad

The train runs on a remote former logging railroad line in western Washington from Yacolt to Lucia. The 8-mile route includes a 330-foot-long tunnel carved from solid rock, a trestle over the Lewis River, and a half-hour layover at Moulton Falls.

**CHOICES:** You can enjoy the scenic ride by traveling in a coach car, open observation car, circus car, or caboose. Trains are powered by a 1940s Alco diesel or a 1929 Alco 2-8-2T steam locomotive. On the layover in Moulton Falls Park, you can have a picnic and take in two waterfalls and a tall arched bridge.

**WHEN TO GO:** The railroad operates May through December. It runs several weekends each month and offers train robberies, wine trains, and fall color excursions as well as other specials throughout the year, including those for Mother's Day, Father's Day, Halloween, and Christmas.

**GOOD TO KNOW:** The railroad offers a unique Christmas tree and train experience for families. After taking the train to Moulton, you can visit with Santa, enjoy some cookies and hot chocolate, and pick out your Christmas tree. The locally grown tree is loaded into a 1912 heavyweight boxcar for the return trip to Yacolt.

**WORTH DOING:** A half hour may not be enough time to see Moulton Falls Park. The park contains a hiking trail and volcanic rock formations. It also connects to Lucia Falls Park and the Bells Mountain Trail. Mount St. Helens is about an hour's drive north of Yacolt.

**DON'T MISS:** BYCX's coach car No. 60 has seen many changes since being built by the Pullman Company in 1918 as a 12-section sleeping car. It was later converted to a tourist sleeper and then in 1948 remodeled into a baggage car. No. 60 was put in maintenance-of-way service (and first painted mineral red and white) and in 1975, became a kitchen/bunk car. Now it is back in passenger service.

**GETTING THERE:** The railroad is located an hour's drive from Vancouver, Wash., or Portland, Ore. From I-5, take Exit 11 to SR 502, travel to SR 503, turn right on Rock Creek Road for 11 miles to Yacolt. The station is on Railroad Avenue at Yacolt Road.

**LOCATION:** 207 N. Railroad Avenue, Yacolt
**PHONE:** 360-686-3559
**WEBSITE:** bycx.com
**E-MAIL:** admin@bycx.com

# Mt. Rainier Scenic Railroad & Museum

Mt. Rainier Scenic Railroad & Museum

**The Pacific Northwest's logging railroad history comes alive here: the locomotives, the setting, and the route all have the feel of a working railroad. Adjacent to its shop, a museum is home to a comprehensive collection of steam logging locomotives and artifacts.**

**CHOICES:** A pure steam experience, a 2-8-2T logging engine usually pulls the passenger coaches through the foothills of Mount Rainier on a 2-hour round trip. You'll ride over creeks, through forests, and across bridges to Mineral. First-class travel provides table and chair seating. Special trains include the Washington Wine Express, Mother's Day brunch train, Father's Day barbecue train, and Rails & Ales.

**WHEN TO GO:** The railroad operates weekends late May through October, with added weekday excursions during the summer months. Peanuts Great Pumpkin Patch Express runs weekends in October and the Polar Express operates between Thanksgiving and the end of December. The museum is open weekends mid-July through October and Fridays in July and August.

**GOOD TO KNOW:** The railroad operates a rare Willamette type geared steam locomotive. Built in 1929 in Portland, Ore., engine No. 2 was one of only 33 manufactured for use on logging railroads in the Pacific Northwest.

**WORTH DOING:** Mount Rainier National Park offers scenic drives and hikes around the 14,410-foot active volcano. Most roads are open from late May to October.

**DON'T MISS:** In Mineral, the railroad's museum features six logging camp buildings containing displays and artifacts related to logging and railroads. Museum admission is free for train passengers.

**GETTING THERE:** The railroad is located in western Washington near Mount Rainier National Park, approximately 75 miles south of Seattle. To reach Elbe from the Seattle area, take I-5 to Highway 512 and then exit on Highway 7, which is also Mountain Highway. Mineral is 7 miles south of Elbe along Highway 7 and Mineral Road.

**LOCATION:** 54124 Mountain Highway East, Elbe; 349 Mineral Creek Road, Mineral
**PHONE:** 888-783-2611 or 360-569-7959
**WEBSITE:** mtrainierrailroad.com
**E-MAIL:** info@mtrainierrailroad.com

# Northwest Railway Museum

Northwest Railway Museum

The museum is home to more than 70 pieces of rolling stock, most from the Pacific Northwest. The museum also includes a collection of dining car china, tools, signs, and lanterns. It offers a short train ride from either Snoqualmie or North Bend.

CHOICES: The Snoqualmie depot is a restored 1890 Queen Anne-style building listed on the National Register of Historic Places. It features indoor exhibits and outdoor displays of restored equipment including steam locomotives, passenger cars, freight cars, and maintenance equipment. Self-guided and guided tours are available through the exhibit building and education center. Two-hour, 10-mile round trip excursions to North Bend and Snoqualmie Falls are offered in restored heavyweight coaches on weekends April through December.

WHEN TO GO: The museum is open daily year-round except for Thanksgiving, Christmas, and New Year's Day. Day Out with Thomas and other special events are scheduled during the year. Santa trains sell out quickly and run for four weekends.

GOOD TO KNOW: The museum continues its steam locomotive restoration efforts with two locomotives from its collection.

WORTH DOING: View Snoqualmie Falls, one of the state's most popular attractions. The waterfall cascades down 270 feet, which is 100 feet more than Niagara Falls.

DON'T MISS: The museum has restored a unique logging caboose. Built by White River Lumber in 1945, the caboose is just 24 feet long. Because of wartime shortages of raw materials, the caboose was made of wood and recycled parts. The museum is also home to Messenger of Peace, an American Baptist Church chapel car, which was dedicated in 1898 and featured at the 1904 World's Fair in St. Louis.

GETTING THERE: The museum is 30 miles east of Seattle on I-90. From I-90 east, take Exit 25. Heading north, follow Snoqualmie Ridge Parkway for approximately 4 miles to Highway 202. Turn right on Highway 202 and proceed a half mile to the Snoqualmie depot on your right. To get to the North Bend depot, take Exit 31 off I-90. Follow Bendigo Street into North Bend and turn right on North Bend Way.

**LOCATION:** 38625 SE King Street, Snoqualmie
**PHONE:** 425-888-3030
**WEBSITE:** trainmuseum.org
**E-MAIL:** info@trainumseum.org

237

# WYOMING

## Cheyenne Depot Museum

Cheyenne's architectural jewel is a major landmark in the city. Built in 1886, the Union Pacific depot houses a museum that details the history of the building, the operation of the railroad, and founding of the city. It is open daily year-round, and Depot Days take place in May.

LOCATION: 121 W. 15th Street, Cheyenne
PHONE: 307-632-3905
WEBSITE: cheyennedepotmuseum.org
E-MAIL: info@cheyennedepotmuseum.org

## Douglas Railroad Interpretive Center

The Douglas Railroad Interpretive Center is housed in a restored 1886 passenger depot belonging to the Fremont, Elkhorn & Missouri Valley Railroad. It displays a 1940 Chicago, Burlington & Quincy steam locomotive and seven railcars. The building is listed on the National Register of Historic Places, and it is open daily.

LOCATION: 121 Brownfield Road, Douglas
PHONE: 307-358-2950
WEBSITE: facebook.com/douglasvisitorinfocenter

## Union Pacific Roundhouse and Turntable

One section of the 28-bay roundhouse and the machine shop have been restored. (Check with the city for tour information.) In front, the large turntable is still operational. Nearby Railroad Park holds a 1915 steam engine and two boxcars. The Joss House Museum tells the story of the area's Chinese immigrants.

LOCATION: 1440 Main Street, Evanston
PHONE: 307-783-6320
WEBSITE: evanstonwy.org/374/roundhouse
E-MAIL: form on website

# Union Pacific Railroad

John M. Crisanti

This Class I mainline railroad maintains the only steam locomotive never retired, No. 844, a 4-8-4 built in 1944. Rebuilt in 2016, it is used on an annual excursion out of Denver, and on display tours across the Union Pacific system. Big Boy No. 4014 is at the Cheyenne shop undergoing restoration with the aim of having it in steam by 2019. At that time, it will be the world's largest operating steam locomotive.

**CHOICES:** Visit the Cheyenne Depot Museum in the restored UP depot. The museum sponsors occasional tours of the steam shop, including in May during its annual festival. Two historic UP engines are displayed in Cheyenne parks: Big Boy No. 4004 in Holliday Park and the state's oldest steam locomotive, No. 1242, an 1890 4-6-0, in Lions Park.

**WHEN TO GO:** Schedules and routes vary from year to year. The Cheyenne Frontier Days excursion train from Denver to Cheyenne runs the third Saturday of each July, during Cheyenne's 10-day festival featuring rodeo action and western entertainment.

**GOOD TO KNOW:** UP provides a GPS trace system for its steam train at up.com/aboutup/special_trains/steam/trace.cfm. The railroad also sends out updates on Twitter as the locomotive moves.

**WORTH DOING:** Follow I-80 West to Sherman Hill to watch UP freight trains. Then find your way to the site of the pyramid-like Ames Monument, celebrating the railroad's 1860s financiers. There, you can trace the original transcontinental railroad grade.

**DON'T MISS:** Stroll North Greeley Highway bridge for an overhead view of the shop.

**GETTING THERE:** Cheyenne is in southeast Wyoming, about 90 minutes from Denver.

**LOCATION:** UP Steam Shop, Cheyenne
**PHONE:** 307-778-3214
**WEBSITE:** up.com/aboutup

# REGION 8

## ARIZONA
1. Arizona Railway Museum
2. Grand Canyon Railway
3. Scottsdale Railroad Museum
4. Southern Arizona Transportation Museum
5. Tucson Modern Streetcars
6. Verde Canyon Railroad

## COLORADO
7. Boardwalk Park Museum
8. Castle Rock Museum
9. Colorado Railroad Museum
10. Cripple Creek & Victor Narrow Gauge Railroad
11. Cumbres & Toltec Scenic Railroad
12. Durango & Silverton Narrow Gauge Railroad
13. Forney Museum of Transportation
14. Fort Collins Municipal Railway
15. Georgetown Loop Railroad
16. Leadville, Colorado & Southern Railroad
17. Limon Heritage Museum
18. Moffat Railway Car
19. Pikes Peak Cog Railway
20. Platte Valley Trolley
21. Pueblo Railway Museum
22. Ridgway Railroad Museum
23. Rio Grande Scenic Railroad
24. Rio Grande Southern Railroad Museum
25. Royal Gorge Route Railroad

## NEW MEXICO
26. Belen Harvey House Museum
27. Las Cruces Railroad Museum

## UTAH
28. Golden Spike National Historic Site
29. Heber Valley Railroad
30. Ogden Union Station
31. Tooele Valley Railroad Museum
32. Western Mining and Railroad Museum

# ARIZONA

## Arizona Railway Museum

The museum restores and displays railroad equipment of the Southwest and has more than 30 pieces of equipment including locomotives, freight cars, passenger cars, and a PCC trolley. It is open weekends September through May. Several passenger cars and a caboose are usually open for visitors to view. Most cars are open on Arizona Railway Day, which takes place in February.

LOCATION: 330 E. Ryan Road, Chandler
PHONE: 480-821-1108
WEBSITE: azrymuseum.org
E-MAIL: info@azrymuseum.org

## Scottsdale Railroad Museum

Located in McCormick-Stillman Railroad Park, the museum contains the historic *Roald Amundsen* Pullman car, Magma Arizona Railroad locomotive No. 6, a Santa Fe baggage car, and the Peoria Depot, which features other exhibits on railroad history. The park includes other attractions, a carousel, and several train rides. It is open daily.

LOCATION: 7301 E. Indian Bend Road, Scottsdale
PHONE: 480-312-2312
WEBSITE: therailroadpark.com
E-MAIL: therailroadpark@scottsdaleaz.gov

## Southern Arizona Transportation Museum

You can tour the former Southern Pacific Railroad depot Tuesday through Sunday, and take in an exhibit that features oral history accounts of railroaders. The centerpiece of the museum is steam locomotive No. 1673, which was built in 1900. On Saturdays, you can learn more about No. 1673 with a visit to the locomotive's cab.

LOCATION: 414 N. Toole Avenue, Tucson
PHONE: 520-623-2223
WEBSITE: tucsonhistoricdepot.org
E-MAIL: contactus@tucsonhistoricdepot.org

## Tucson Modern Streetcars

Tuscon's streetcar system connects the downtown area with Mercado, the Fourth Avenue Business District, Main Gate Square, and the University of Arizona. The all-electric streetcars operate daily, with expanded schedules Thursday through Saturday.

LOCATION: Convento to Helen Street, Tucson
PHONE: 520-792-9222
WEBSITE: sunlinkstreetcar.com
E-MAIL: sunlinkstreetcarcomments@tucsonaz.gov

# Grand Canyon Railway

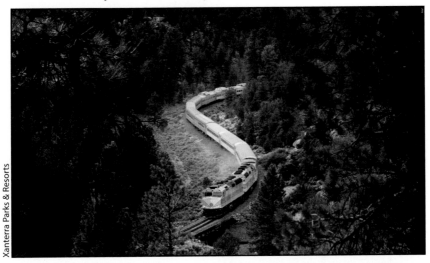

Xanterra Parks & Resorts

This train doesn't take passengers into the canyon, or even along the rim (except for a short distance near the end of the journey), but it offers a unique way to reach one of the great scenic wonders of North America in style. Diesel-powered (and a few steam) trains take riders from Williams on a 65-mile journey to the Grand Canyon's South Rim through high desert and pine forests. An exceptional ride, the trip is also a great value in that it saves you time in trying to find a parking space at the ever-popular South Rim.

**CHOICES:** Grand Canyon Railway offers various levels of service including coach, first class, dome, luxury dome, and luxury parlor. Service and attention are hallmarks of this railroad. Coach passengers won't be disappointed with the strolling musicians and attentive service, while those in cars with higher levels of service will be pampered with extra room, private bars, and fantastic views.

**WHEN TO GO:** Traveling this area any time is fascinating. Christmas Day is the only day the railroad doesn't run. The summer's heat is foiled by air-conditioned cars.

**GOOD TO KNOW:** You can ride from Williams, spend the night at South Rim, and return on the next day's train. The railroad has its own hotel, restaurant, RV park, and pet-sitting service available at Williams, which is a charming western town with plenty of shops and restaurants worth checking out. The Williams depot, built in 1908, was originally home to a Harvey Hotel and is listed on the National Register of Historic Places.

**WORTH DOING:** At South Rim, the train arrives at an old Santa Fe Railway depot. Walk up the hill to El Tovar, the historic railroad hotel, and you'll stand in awe of nature at its finest.

**DON'T MISS:** The railroad offers steam operations on special days during the year behind Burlington Route 2-8-2 No. 4960 and Lake Superior & Ishpeming 2-8-0 No. 29. The engines use recycled vegetable oil. Plan ahead and enjoy a steamy adventure.

**GETTING THERE:** Williams is 32 miles west of Flagstaff. Take I-40 to Exit 163 and follow Grand Canyon Boulevard to the depot.

**LOCATION:** 233 N. Grand Canyon Boulevard, Williams
**PHONE:** 800-843-8724
**WEBSITE:** thetrain.com

# Verde Canyon Railroad

Verde Canyon Railroad

On the Verde Canyon Railroad, you'll travel 42 miles on a former copper mining spur, 1,800 feet below the red rock canyon rim, where eagles often soar. The ride takes you across bridges, around rock formations, and through a 680-foot tunnel.

**CHOICES:** The 4-hour, historic route from Clarkdale to the deserted Perkinsville Ranch travels between two national forests and into Verde Canyon, which is accessible only by rail. Narration describes the history, archaeology, geology, and wildlife of the area. Two levels of service are available. Coach seating features vintage Pullman-style seats, with a snack bar. First-class passage provides plush seating, complimentary appetizers, and a full-service bar. All cars access open-air viewing cars equipped with shaded canopies. A caboose is also available for small private parties, and a cab ride is also offered.

**WHEN TO GO:** Trains run year-round, but summer can be exceptionally hot. In winter, you can view nesting bald eagles in their natural habitat.

**GOOD TO KNOW:** The railroad's pair of streamlined diesel locomotives from the 1950s features a special eagle paint scheme. Located in Clarkdale, the Verde Canyon Railroad depot opened in 1997 on the same site of two previous depots.

**WORTH DOING:** Visit the Tuzigoot National Monument, just outside the railroad's entrance, where an ancient Sinagua pueblo was built. The 42-acre site includes guided tours of the pueblo ruins and hiking trails.

**DON'T MISS:** At the depot, a short walk takes you to the John Bell Museum, a renovated boxcar that contains railroad and mining displays.

**GETTING THERE:** The railroad is about 30 minutes from Sedona and 2 hours from Phoenix. From Sedona, go southwest toward Cottonwood on Highway 89A to Mingus Avenue. Turn right on Mingus Avenue and go 2 miles to Main Street. Turn right on Main Street and travel through Old Town Cottonwood. Look for the sign and turn right on Broadway. From Phoenix, take I-17 north to Exit 287. Go west on Highway 260 and then turn left at Main Street through Old Town Cottonwood. Look for the sign and turn right on Broadway.

**LOCATION:** 300 N. Broadway, Clarkdale
**PHONE:** 800-582-7245
**WEBSITE:** verdecanyonrr.com
**E-MAIL:** info@verdecanyonrr.com

# COLORADO

## Boardwalk Park Museum

Located in Boardwalk Park, a 1880s Colorado & Southern depot houses an exhibit of local steam-era railroading history. You can walk through a freight room, waiting room, and station agent's room. A caboose, schoolhouse, and church are also on site. The museum is open Thursdays through Sundays during summer.

LOCATION: 100 N. Fifth Street, Windsor
PHONE: 970-674-3522
WEBSITE: windsorgov.com
E-MAIL: elucas@windsorgov.com

## Castle Rock Museum

The museum is housed in a restored 1875 Denver & Rio Grande depot built of rhyolite stone. It retains original interior features, such as a ticket window and baggage area, with 125 years of graffiti on its walls. It displays exhibits of the D&RG and Continental Divide Raceways. It is open Wednesdays through Saturdays.

LOCATION: 420 Elbert Street, Castle Rock
PHONE: 303-814-3164
WEBSITE: castlerockhistoricalsociety.org
E-MAIL: museum@castlerockhistoricalsociety.org

## Cripple Creek & Victor Narrow Gauge Railroad

The 4-mile, 45-minute trip takes you through Gold Country over a portion of the old Midland Terminal Railroad. Running south from Cripple Creek, the steam train crosses a reconstructed trestle and passes historic mines near the deserted mining town of Anaconda. The railroad operates three narrow gauge locomotives, and trains operate mid-May to mid-October.

LOCATION: Fifth Street and Bennett Avenue, Cripple Creek
PHONE: 719-689-2640
WEBSITE: cripplecreekrailroad.com
E-MAIL: form on website

## Limon Heritage Museum

This museum focuses on local history and the Union Pacific and Rock Island Railroads. Located in a restored 1910 depot, it features a restored office and rail exhibits. A saddle boxcar, dining car, and UP caboose are on display in the adjacent rail park. It is open Monday through Saturday Memorial Day to Labor Day.

LOCATION: 899 First Street, Limon
PHONE: 719-775-2346
WEBSITE: townoflimon.com

# Moffat Railway Car

Tours of this 1906 Pullman car are available weekdays through the Moffat County Visitor Center, near where it is on display. The car originally belonged to rail magnate David Moffat and was named for his daughter Marcia. The nearby Museum of Northwest Colorado (590 Yampa Avenue) contains a display of Moffat Road memorabilia.

**LOCATION:** 360 E. Victory Way, Craig
**PHONE:** 800-864-4405 or 970-824-5689
**WEBSITE:** craig-chamber.com
**E-MAIL:** form on website

# Pueblo Railway Museum

Concentrating on the golden age of railroading, the museum displays steam engines, diesel locomotives, rolling stock, and unique rocket cars in the yard behind Union Depot. Artifacts and rotating displays are housed in the Southeastern Colorado Heritage Center located across from the depot. Locomotive cab and caboose rides are offered during the year.

**LOCATION:** 201 W. B Street, Pueblo
**PHONE:** 719-251-5024
**WEBSITE:** pueblorailway.org
**E-MAIL:** in_dianajones@earthlink.net

# Ridgway Railroad Museum

The Ridgway Railroad Museum focuses on local railroading history. It displays an assortment of restored railcars, and its indoor collection includes artifacts, photos, and tools. The museum is open daily except during winter months, when it is closed. It holds various special events and monthly work sessions.

246

**LOCATION:** Highway 550 and Highway 62, Ridgway
**WEBSITE:** ridgwayrailroadmuseum.org
**E-MAIL:** ridgwayrailroadmuseum@ouraynet.com

# Rio Grande Southern Railroad Museum

The museum is located in a replica of the original Dolores depot. It is home to the restored Galloping Goose No. 5, which now operates several times during the year on the Cumbres & Toltec Scenic Railroad and the Durango & Silverton Narrow Gauge Railroad. The museum is open Mondays through Saturdays mid-May through mid-October and Tuesdays and Thursdays the rest of the year.

**LOCATION:** 421 Railroad Avenue, Dolores
**PHONE:** 970-882-7082
**WEBSITE:** gallopinggoose5.com
**E-MAIL:** gghs5@centurytel.net

# Colorado Railroad Museum

Steve Sweeney

When you think of Colorado railroading, you think of mountain-climbing, narrow gauge trains of the Denver & Rio Grande Western. And that is exactly what you'll see at this museum just outside Denver in the foothills near Golden. But that's not all—the museum includes 100 pieces of equipment from many other Colorado railroads.

**CHOICES:** The museum features narrow gauge and standard equipment, from a steam locomotive once used on the Pikes Peak Cog Railway to a 317-ton Burlington Route 4-8-4 steam locomotive and even a set of streamlined 1950s passenger diesels from the Rio Grande. You'll see examples of the famous Galloping Goose self-propelled railbuses that ran on the narrow gauge Rio Grande Southern in southwestern Colorado.

**WHEN TO GO:** The museum is open year-round, except for several holidays. On Ride the Rails days, most Saturdays April through October, some Sundays, and daily in July, you can a take a short ride around the 15-acre property. Most passenger trains are powered by a vintage diesel engine. On select days, you can ride aboard a Galloping Goose or behind steam locomotive No. 346.

**GOOD TO KNOW:** No. 687, a 2-8-0 built in 1890 and retired in 1955, is the only preserved standard gauge Rio Grande steam locomotive.

**WORTH DOING:** The MillerCoors Brewery is adjacent to the museum and offers tours on most days throughout the year. You can also explore historic downtown Golden or try tubing nearby Clear Creek.

**DON'T MISS:** Visit the five-stall roundhouse that houses the museum's restoration shop and features an operating turntable. A viewing gallery gives you a peek at the work it takes to maintain the collection.

**GETTING THERE:** The Colorado Railroad Museum is located 12 miles west of downtown Denver and is easily reached from I-70. Take Exit 265 westbound or Exit 266 eastbound, and it is just off Highway 58 between I-70 and Golden.

**LOCATION:** 17155 W. 44th Avenue, Golden
**PHONE:** 800-365-6263 or 303-279-4591
**WEBSITE:** coloradorailroadmuseum.org
**E-MAIL:** form on website

247

# Cumbres & Toltec Scenic Railroad

Jim Wrinn

If you have ever craved going back in time to the 1920s to see what railroading was like, here's your chance. The Cumbres & Toltec operates 64 miles of track through the San Juan Mountains. Steam locomotives still labor up steep grades, cross 100-foot-tall trestles, and hug narrow shelves above yawning gorges. For more than 125 years, passengers have ridden over Cumbres Pass on a 3-foot gauge line that crosses the border between Colorado and New Mexico 11 times.

**CHOICES:** The railroad offers a choice of excursions. From either Antonito or Chama, N.M., you can take a full-day round trip to Osier, Colo., where a buffet lunch is provided. To see this scenic area in two different ways, you can ride the train one way and return by motor coach. Half-day trips take you from Chama to Cumbres with a return by motor coach. Seating options include a parlor car, a tourist car, a coach car, and an open-air gondola car. On many Saturdays, sunset dinner trains operate from Chama to Cumbres. Cinder Bear rides are designed for children.

**WHEN TO GO:** Excursion trains operate daily from the end of May until mid-October, with some special events taking place during the season.

**GOOD TO KNOW:** The Friends of the Cumbres & Toltec Scenic Railroad organization has installed two webcams that allow you to virtually visit the railroad's Chama yard. You can access them at railroad's website or at coloradonewmexicosteamtrain.org.

**WORTH DOING:** Ride Galloping Goose No. 5, which will make several appearances on the railroad in August and September.

**DON'T MISS:** At 10,015 feet elevation, Cumbres Pass is the highest pass reached by rail in the United States. At the summit is an old section house, one of the railroad's many historic buildings. As the train's steep descent begins, you'll see sweeping views of the Chama Valley.

**GETTING THERE:** The railroad is located between Colorado Springs and Santa Fe. Highway 285 takes you to Antonito. To reach Chama from Santa Fe, take Highway 285 to Highway 84.

**LOCATION:** 5234 B Highway 285, Antonito
**PHONE:** 888-286-2737 or 719-376-5483
**WEBSITE:** cumbrestoltec.com
**E-MAIL:** info@cumbrestoltec.com

# Durango & Silverton Narrow Gauge Railroad

Brian Schmidt

The Durango & Silverton is one of the most spectacular narrow gauge steam train rides in North America. Traveling through the Rockies, coal-fired locomotives pull trains 45 miles through the rugged Animas River Gorge on a railroad built in the 1880s to reach silver mines. The destination, Silverton, is a step into the past.

**CHOICES:** The Durango & Silverton offers several options for passengers. During summer, you can live like a railroad executive with Presidential class service on board the Cinco Animas, a private car that features plush seating and observation platforms. For great views, try first-class service on the Silver Vista or Knight Sky, glass-roofed, open-air observation cars with outdoor viewing platforms. First-class service is also available aboard an 1881 parlor car. Deluxe and standard service provide seating in a coach car or a covered gondola. During the winter off-season, the Cascade Canyon train travels 26 miles from Durango to the Cascade station.

**WHEN TO GO:** Winter provides incredible snowy vistas. Summer offers the excitement of up to three trains running each way, but it is also the busy season. September has the best color show when Aspen trees turn a brilliant yellow and quiver in the autumn breeze. Various events take place throughout the year.

**GOOD TO KNOW:** For a fee, yard tours are available to give you a chance to see the inner workings of the railroad.

**WORTH DOING:** Take part in the other activities that abound near Durango, such as whitewater rafting, hiking, and fly fishing. A visit to Mesa Verde National Park is a must.

**DON'T MISS:** There is a 2-hour layover in Silverton, which gives you time to visit the freight yard museum at the depot, which is open May through October and displays many pieces of rolling stock. The Durango museum, part of the roundhouse, is open corresponding to the passenger train schedule. There, a baggage car used in *Butch Cassidy and the Sundance Kid* is now a movie theater.

**GETTING THERE:** The station is located in downtown Durango. The drive to the Four Corners area on Highway 550 is a scenic delight, as long as you don't mind heights.

**LOCATION:** 479 Main Avenue, Durango
**PHONE:** 877-872-4607 or 970-247-2733
**WEBSITE:** durangotrain.com
**E-MAIL:** form on website

# Forney Museum of Transportation

Jeff Terry

**An antique auto collection that began with one Kissel Kar is now a transportation museum with more than 500 items. The museum's showroom contains everything on wheels from buggies and bicycles to fire engines and Denver's only cable car.**

**CHOICES:** In the museum's indoor train pit, you'll find a Big Boy locomotive, cabooses, trolleys, passenger cars, and, of course, a Forney locomotive. While the Big Boy may get the most attention, there are a number of other interesting pieces in the rail collection, including a rotary snow plow, a steam crane, and a 4-6-0 locomotive from the Chicago & North Western.

**WHEN TO GO:** The museum is open daily except major holidays. It features special exhibits, family activities, and events related to different modes of transportation. On Big Boy Weekend in July, you can go inside the cab of the world's largest articulated steam locomotive and walk through a 1920s dining car, 1890s coach, and 1905 caboose.

**GOOD TO KNOW:** One of eight remaining Big Boy locomotives, Union Pacific No. 4005 was wrecked in 1953 and rebuilt.

**WORTH DOING:** There are plenty of things to do in Denver, within 15 minutes of the museum, such as touring the Capitol, the Firefighters Museum, the Botanic Gardens, and the Unsinkable Molly Brown's house.

**DON'T MISS:** Also view highlights of the auto collection such as Amelia Earhart's 1923 Kissel Speedster, a 1967 amphibious car from Germany, a 1911 electric car, a Staver, and a Nyberg.

**GETTING THERE:** The Forney Museum is located northeast of downtown Denver, a short distance off I-70 via Exit 275B. Look for the vintage caboose in the museum's parking lot.

**LOCATION:** 4303 Brighton Boulevard, Denver
**PHONE:** 303-297-1113
**WEBSITE:** forneymuseum.org
**E-MAIL:** customerservice@forneymuseum.org

# Fort Collins Municipal Railway

Bryan Bechtold

Fort Collins was the last city in the United States to operate the tiny four-wheel trolley cars known as Birneys, running its trolley system until 1951. A volunteer group of citizens rebuilt the original Mountain Avenue track and restored Car 21 to like-new condition, returning it to operation on its authentic tree-lined route in 1984.

**CHOICES:** The 3-mile, round-trip trolley ride runs along Mountain Avenue from City Park to Howes Street, 2 blocks west of downtown. A round trip lasts 30 minutes. Other boarding stops are at Shields Street and Loomis Street. There are free rides on special days and for moms on Mother's Day and dads on Father's Day.

**WHEN TO GO:** The trolley operates on weekend afternoons and holidays from May to September.

**GOOD TO KNOW:** The original trolley barn is just 2 blocks north on Howe Street at the downtown end of the line. Inside is Birney Car 25, which is undergoing restoration. Car 25 is one of five remaining cars that ran in Fort Collins.

**WORTH DOING:** Both ends of the route are family friendly. Downtown Fort Collins has an outstanding variety of restaurants and shopping just a short walk from the trolley. You can also pack a picnic and enjoy the City Park end of the line. For outdoor enthusiasts, Rocky Mountain National Park is less than 2 hours away by car.

**DON'T MISS:** For railfans, BNSF freight trains run down the middle of nearby Mason Street for almost a mile providing an opportunity to view mainline action up close.

**GETTING THERE:** Fort Collins is 65 miles north of Denver on I-25. Exit I-25 at Colorado 14 and then drive west through town to City Park. A small depot is next to the tennis courts at Roosevelt and Oak Streets.

**LOCATION:** Roosevelt Street and Oak Street, Fort Collins
**PHONE:** 970-224-5372
**WEBSITE:** fortcollinstrolley.org
**E-MAIL:** fcmrs1919@gmail.com

# Georgetown Loop Railroad

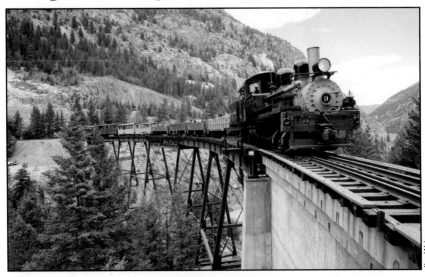

Jim Wrinn

This railroad shows how engineering overcame mountains when it came to reaching precious minerals in the Colorado Rockies. As the name states, the railroad's highlight is a full loop, where the tracks cross over themselves to gain elevation. The reconstructed Devil's Gate viaduct stands no less spectacular than when it was built in the late 1800s.

**CHOICES:** You can board at the Devil's Gate station in Georgetown or at Silver Plume. Either way, you experience the same trip, but riding up grade first is always the better show. As you ride the train, scan the mountain slopes for bighorn sheep. Both diesel and steam locomotives operate. There are three levels of service including open-air coach cars, parlor cars, and a presidential car.

**WHEN TO GO:** The operating season begins in May and continues to November. During much of the season, five trains run on a daily basis. Holiday trains operate in November and December. Beginning in October, the trains are made up of heated coaches pulled by a diesel locomotive.

**GOOD TO KNOW:** Steam locomotive No. 9, built in 1923 by the Lima Locomotive Works, is a rare Shay geared locomotive with three cylinders on one side. New to the loop is a Central American Railways 2-8-0 built in the U.S. and restored in 2016.

**WORTH DOING:** The town of Georgetown is quaint and quiet with little influences of the modern world—with the exception of nearby I-70. Its National Historic Landmark District features unique shops, restaurants, and small museums in restored Victorian buildings.

**DON'T MISS:** After riding the train, travel on I-70 between Georgetown and Silver Plume and watch another train tackle the mountain, with not only the loop but also with a series of zigzags. Accessible only by train, you can take a guided walking tour through the 1870s Lebanon Silver Mine.

**GETTING THERE:** The railroad is about 50 miles west of Denver off I-70. Exit 226 takes you to Silver Plume and, a few miles away, Exit 228 takes you to Georgetown.

**LOCATION:** 646 Loop Drive, Georgetown
**PHONE:** 888-456-6777
**WEBSITE:** georgetownlooprr.com
**E-MAIL:** info@historicrailadventures.com

# Leadville, Colorado & Southern Railroad

Leadville, Colorado & Southern Railroad

In a state with many spectacular scenic railroads, this line doesn't disappoint. Leaving from the charming mining town of Leadville, the LC&S marches up the side of the Rockies near the tree line. Upon departure from the depot, the train leaves the 10,200-foot elevation for a 900-foot climb along the southern side of the upper Arkansas River Valley to a point close to Climax at Fremont Pass. The train passes through forests of lodgepole pine, spruce, and aspen.

**CHOICES:** On the 2.5-hour roundtrip, you can ride in an open car or a car with a roof. Especially for train fans, there are several seats available in the locomotive or in the caboose. If it's a beautiful day in Colorado, as it often is, stick to the open cars for unobstructed views. Stay on the right side of the train for spectacular views of the mountains and the molybdenum mine at the end of the line. Along the way, the conductor provides narration and answers questions.

**WHEN TO GO:** The trains run late May into October, when the aspen trees put on a magnificent show of yellow. In mid-summer, the Wildflower Special lets you view alpine flowers at their peak. Several barbecue specials also run.

**GOOD TO KNOW:** Incorporated in 1878, Leadville is the highest incorporated city in the continental United States at 10,152 feet above sea level. Downtown Leadville is home to many shops, galleries, restaurants, and lodging establishments and makes an easy base camp from which to explore the central Rockies.

**WORTH DOING:** Be sure to explore Leadville's National Historic Landmark District, which includes many buildings built between 1880 and 1905.

**DON'T MISS:** Raft and ride packages are available that combine a half-day rafting trip along Browns Canyon on the Arkansas River with a scenic train ride.

**GETTING THERE:** From Denver, take I-70 west and then Highway 91 south to Leadville. From Vail, take I-70 west to Highway 24 and then Highway 24 south to Leadville.

**LOCATION:** 326 E. Seventh Street, Leadville
**PHONE:** 866-386-3936 or 719-486-3936
**WEBSITE:** leadville-train.com
**E-MAIL:** form on website

253

Colorado

# Pikes Peak Cog Railway

Pikes Peak Cog Railway

The Pikes Peak Cog Railway offers a unique Swiss Alpine experience on rails. Diesel-powered, self-propelled passenger cars navigate unbelievably steep grades with the help of a cog to ascend the 14,110-foot high peak. The view at the top is beautiful, but the journey is awe inspiring as well with trains going beyond the timberline.

**CHOICES:** The railroad offers 3-hour round trips that allow you 30 minutes at the summit. It also provides a one-way trip for anyone who would like to hike up or back down (about 6 hours). During the first part of the trip, the train travels through boulder fields, where you may see some interesting "faces" in the giant boulders. You'll also see wildlife and a bristlecone pine forest with trees believed to be 2,000 years old.

**WHEN TO GO:** The railroad, unbelievably, operates year-round, thanks to a homemade snowplow that operates like a giant snow blower on rails. During summer, the railroad runs up to five trains a day with departures every 80 minutes. During January and February, the train travels to Inspiration Point, which is at 11,500 feet. A Santa train runs halfway up the peak in December.

**GOOD TO KNOW:** The railroad uses modern Swiss-built trains of a type used in the Alps. These units tackle grades of up to 25 percent.

**WORTH DOING:** At the base of Pikes Peak, about an hour's drive away, lie the historic gold-mining towns of Cripple Creek and Victor. You may still find gold in Cripple Creek—at the town's casinos—or ride the Cripple Creek & Victor Narrow Gauge Railroad. In Colorado Springs, explore the many red sandstone formations in the Garden of the Gods or dine in the restaurant in the old Midland Terminal roundhouse.

**DON'T MISS:** At the peak, make sure to walk around the summit and look for Denver. Just be careful. On the north side is a drop-off called the Bottomless Pit.

**GETTING THERE:** Manitou Springs is 6 miles from Colorado Springs. Take Exit 141 off I-25 and go west (toward the mountains) on Highway 24 about 4 miles to the Manitou Avenue (Manitou Springs) exit. Go west on Manitou Avenue for 1.5 miles to Ruxton Avenue. Turn left and go to the top of Ruxton Avenue.

**LOCATION:** 515 Ruxton Avenue, Manitou Springs
**PHONE:** 800-745-3773 or 719-685-5401
**WEBSITE:** cograilway.com
**E-MAIL:** info@cograilway.coma

# Platte Valley Trolley

Platte Valley Trolley, Darrell Arndt

The Platte Valley Trolley is often referred to as one of Denver's best-kept secrets. The trolley runs through the South Platte River Greenway Park linking several of the city's most popular attractions. The trolley is a faithful replica of a turn-of the-century, open-air breezer, which is ideally suited for enjoying the sightseeing trip.

**CHOICES:** The route starts at Confluence Park beside the REI store. The riverfront ride lasts 25 minutes. Stops are made at the Downtown Aquarium, Children's Museum, and Sports Authority Field at Mile High. The trolley only makes intermediate stops southbound, and runs end-to-end northbound.

**WHEN TO GO:** The trolley operates Thursday through Monday Memorial Day weekend to Labor Day. It departs continuously every half hour from REI. For Denver Bronco home games, fans can catch a shuttle to the game.

**GOOD TO KNOW:** Confluence Park is the site of Denver's original settlement and is now a hub for paved bicycle trails that serve the city.

**WORTH DOING:** The Platte River area is a great place to take the family. Combine a trolley ride with nearby attractions, such as the Children's Museum, Elitch Gardens Theme Park, or the aquarium. You can also take a tour of Sports Authority Field and the Colorado Sports Hall of Fame.

**DON'T MISS:** In addition to serving Amtrak, Denver's renovated Union Station is now a hotel and transit hub for commuter rail operations. Shopping and dining options make it an ideal destination for enjoying urban Denver.

**GETTING THERE:** The route is located in downtown Denver. By car, take I-25 to Exit 211 (23rd Street), turn east on Water Street, and follow the signs to the Children's Museum or continue straight to the REI store for your best parking options. RTD buses and light rail operate within a short walk. The trolley is a 15-minute walk from Amtrak at Union Station.

**LOCATION:** 15th Street and Platte Street, Denver
**PHONE:** 303-458-6255
**WEBSITE:** denvertrolley.org
**E-MAIL:** info@denvertrolley.org

# Rio Grande Scenic Railroad

Rio Grande Scenic Railroad

The Denver & Rio Grande built an incredibly scenic route into the San Luis Valley and its biggest city, Alamosa, in the late 1880s. The standard gauge line of today replaced a much more difficult narrow gauge line but lost nothing as far as its engineering marvels or trackside splendor.

**CHOICES:** The railroad offers a variety of train rides. The regular excursion train crosses famous La Veta Pass to let you view the Rockies. On select summer weekdays, a diesel train winds through a variety of scenery, from flat farmland to mountains, on its trip from Alamosa to La Veta. Summer concert trains run to Fir on weekends. Fort Garland is another pick-up location.

**WHEN TO GO:** Regular excursions run late May through September. In addition to the summer concerts, other special events take place.

**GOOD TO KNOW:** Seating choices vary by route and train. They include dome, coach, and open-air cars. Diamond class seating is featured on restored club cars that ran on the fabled *City of New Orleans*.

**WORTH DOING:** Explore the Spanish Peaks country. It is filled with hiking trails, scenic roads, and natural wonders such as the tallest sand dunes in North America, which are found in Great Sand Dunes National Park.

**DON'T MISS:** Between June and August, the railroad presents its summer music festival in a mountain setting that is accessible by excursion trains. You can enjoy music under the stars, surrounded by aspen and pines, in a natural meadow amphitheater.

**GETTING THERE:** Located in south-central Colorado, Alamosa is about 200 miles south of Denver and 90 miles west of Pueblo. Highway 160 is the key route in and out of the San Luis Valley. The highway becomes Main Street in Alamosa, and the depot is just off Main Street on State Avenue.

**LOCATION:** 610 State Avenue, Alamosa
**PHONE:** 877-726-7245
**WEBSITE:** coloradotrain.com
**E-MAIL:** form on website

# Royal Gorge Route Railroad

Royal Gorge Route Railroad

**Nowhere else in America can you ride a train through a narrow mountain gorge with a fast-flowing river and look straight up at one thousand feet of cliff. The railroad offers a range of services on its 24-mile round trip through the Royal Gorge.**

**CHOICES:** Service classes on the 2-hour excursions begin with coach, which seats you in comfortable air-conditioned cars with access to an open-air car. Club class offers unobstructed views out large windows. Vista-dome class provides panoramic views under glass, food service, and a full-service bar. On the gourmet lunch and dinner trains, you can enjoy a three-course meal in a dining car or in the dome car. Cab rides in the railroad's GP40-2 locomotive are also available.

**WHEN TO GO:** Trains begin running daily in March through October, with service expanding during summer. Weekend trips are available during January, February, and November. Murder mystery trains, various specials, and holiday trains also run. Twilight is one of the best times to ride through the gorge.

**GOOD TO KNOW:** After looking up at the world's highest suspension bridge, 1,053 feet above the river, you can go up to Royal Gorge Bridge Park (admission required) and drive, walk, or tram across the gorge.

**WORTH DOING:** Rafting and kayak outfitters in the area offer half- and full-day trips for beginners and experienced paddlers alike. If you make it through Satan's Suckhole, watch out for the deceptively named Puppy Rapids.

**DON'T MISS:** On the popular Santa Express, children of all ages are encouraged to wear jammies and enjoy hot cocoa and a cookie on the way to the North Pole, which is decorated with more than 17,000 lights!

**GETTING THERE:** Cañon City is 115 miles from Denver and 45 minutes from Colorado Springs via Highway 115.

**LOCATION:** 330 Royal Gorge Boulevard, Cañon City
**PHONE:** 888-724-5748 or 719-276-4000
**WEBSITE:** royalgorgeroute.com
**E-MAIL:** info@royalgorgeroute.com

257

# NEW MEXICO

## Belen Harvey House Museum

Adjacent to the BNSF Division yard, the museum contains exhibits on Harvey Houses and the Santa Fe Railroad. Listed on the National Register of Historic Places, the Southwestern-style structure is one of state's few surviving Fred Harvey eating establishments. The museum is open Tuesday through Saturday.

LOCATION: 104 N. First Street, Belen
PHONE: 505-861-0581
WEBSITE: belen-nm.gov

## Las Cruces Railroad Museum

The museum is housed in a 1910 AT&SF depot with a Mission Revival look. Its photographs, artifacts, and displays highlight the depot itself, railroad workers, and railroad communications. It also features a model railroad train room. The museum offers a variety of lectures and programs, including Railroad Days in May. It is open Tuesday through Saturday.

LOCATION: 351 N. Mesilla Street, Las Cruces
PHONE: 575-647-4480
WEBSITE: las-cruces.org
E-MAIL: rrm@las-cruces.org

# UTAH

## Tooele Valley Railroad Museum

Housed in the old Tooele Valley depot, built in 1909, the museum tells the story of the area's colorful mining and smelting years. Tooele Valley Railway steam locomotive No. 11 is the museum's No. 1 attraction. The 1910 Alco 2-8-0 Consolidation type engine is displayed with two wood cabooses and other rolling stock. The museum is open Tuesday through Saturday Memorial Day through September.

**LOCATION:** 35 N. Broadway Street, Tooele
**PHONE:** 435-882-2836 or 435-843-2143
**WEBSITE:** tooelecity.org

## Western Mining and Railroad Museum

Museum exhibits highlight the Denver & Rio Grande Western and other railways. Located in the old Helper Hotel, which was completed in 1914, the museum contains four floors of artifacts. The third floor contains a railroad office and two rooms of railroading artifacts. A 100-year-old caboose is also on display. Other exhibits, including a simulated coal mine, focus on the mining industry and its workers. It is open year-round Monday through Saturday summers and Tuesday through Saturday during winter.

**LOCATION:** 296 S. Main Street, Helper
**PHONE:** 435-472-3009
**WEBSITE:** wmrrm.com
**E-MAIL:** wmrmuseum@helpercity.net

# Golden Spike National Historic Site

Jeff Terry

The construction of the transcontinental railroad is one of the pivotal events in the nation's history. Completed May 10, 1869, at this remote spot northwest of Ogden, the National Park Service does justice to the event by running replica locomotives and conducting reenactments.

**CHOICES:** Reenactments of the Last Spike Ceremony, complete with dignitaries in period dress, take place on Saturdays and holidays May through mid-September. The two steam locomotive replicas, the coal-burning Union Pacific No. 119 and the wood-burning Central Pacific *Jupiter*, are accurate reproductions and fully functional. The visitor center offers informative films and exhibits.

**WHEN TO GO:** The visitor center is open every day, except for Thanksgiving, Christmas, and New Year's Day. Between May and mid-October, the steam locomotives are on display and conduct demonstrations. During winter, when the locomotives are being maintained, engine house tours are available.

**GOOD TO KNOW:** The correct name for the location of Golden Spike National Historic Site is Promontory Summit, not Promontory Point, which is 35 miles to the south. The summit is the highest location on Promontory Pass. For some reason, the wrong location was reported in some records in 1869 and perpetuated throughout history.

**WORTH DOING:** The area is still very rugged. For an even more rugged adventure, go northwest of the park to Devils Playground, which contains granitic rock weathered into fantastic forms and eerie shapes.

**DON'T MISS:** Walk Big Fill Loop Trail (1.5-mile round trip), which takes you out on the original Central Pacific grade and back on the Union Pacific grade. You'll see the site of the Union Pacific's trestle, go through cuts, and see drill marks where workers blasted away rock. West and east auto tours allow you to see interesting elements of the original railroad.

**GETTING THERE:** Golden Spike National Historic Site is in northern Utah, 30 miles west of Brigham City. The site can be accessed from either I-15 or I-84. Highway 83 takes you to the entrance, which is Golden Spike Drive. Road signs help guide you to the park.

**LOCATION:** Golden Spike Drive, Promontory
**PHONE:** 435-471-2209
**WEBSITE:** nps.gov/gosp
**E-MAIL:** form on website

# Heber Valley Railroad

Scott Hartley

This railroad offers a scenic ride beside Deer Creek Reservoir and into Provo Canyon with the Wasatch Mountains as a backdrop over a line that began operating in 1899.

**CHOICES:** Heber Valley offers several regular excursions in the shadow of 12,000-foot Mount Timpanogos aboard vintage coaches. The Provo Canyon Limited is a 3-hour round trip that runs to Vivian Park and back. The 90-minute Deer Creek Express goes to Deer Creek Reservoir and returns. The Lakeside Limited is a scenic 2-hour ride along Deer Creek Reservoir and the base of Mount Timpanogo.

**WHEN TO GO:** The railroad operates year-round. Regular excursions run on a varied schedule, usually four or five days a week. Summer is especially beautiful in Utah, but winter excursions offer a unique look at a snowy wonderland. Summer excursion packages combine river rafting, horseback riding, or ziplining with a train ride. Numerous special events take place, from sunset barbecues to the North Pole Express.

**GOOD TO KNOW:** The railroad's main power are two diesel engines, an ex-Army EMD MRS-1 and a Baldwin switcher. An ex-Union Pacific GP9 is currently being restored and is slated for operation in the 2017 season. Two 2-8-0 steam locomotives, No. 618 and No. 75, are currently undergoing restoration for eventual return to service.

261

**WORTH DOING:** Take a scenic drive along the Provo Canyon Scenic Byway (Highway 189) that runs between Heber Valley and Provo. A short side trip on the Alpine Scenic Loop (Highway 92) takes you past Robert Redford's Sundance Resort.

**DON'T MISS:** For a high-flying adventure, try combining a wilderness zip line with a train ride. The adventure begins with a train ride through Heber Valley, and if you make it through without running into Black Jack Raven and his gang of train robbers, you'll be driven into the Wasatch Mountains to the zip line drop-off, where you'll zip over the scenery.

**GETTING THERE:** The railroad is located between Salt Lake City and Provo. From Salt Lake City, take I-80 east to Exit 148 and then follow Highway 40 into Heber City. Turn right on W. 300 South and then left on S. 600 West to the station.

**LOCATION:** 450 S. 600 West, Heber City
**PHONE:** 435-654-5601
**WEBSITE:** hebervalleyrr.org
**E-MAIL:** info@hebervalleyrr.org

Utah

# Ogden Union Station

Scott Hartley

Built in 1924, Ogden Union Station now houses a variety of museums and galleries, including the Utah State Railroad Museum and Eccles Rail Center. The museum contains artifacts of Utah railroading, and the rail center displays historic pieces of equipment. Other museums in the station focus on history, firearms, gems, classic cars, and the arts.

**CHOICES:** You can browse an extensive collection of rolling stock that is displayed outside the station or go inside. You'll see locomotives and cars from the big Class I railroads that served Utah, including Union Pacific, Southern Pacific, and Rio Grande. Interactive exhibits bring to life the story of the first transcontinental railroad, which was completed nearby at Promontory Summit, just west of Ogden. You'll also pass under timbers used to construct the historic Lucin trestle across the Great Salt Lake. A model railroad depicts scenery from across Utah.

**262**

**WHEN TO GO:** The museum is open Monday through Saturday year-round, but the outdoor railroad exhibits are accessible anytime. Many special events take place at the station, some relating to railroading.

**GOOD TO KNOW:** UP 4-8-4 No. 833, representing the zenith of steam passenger and freight power, was one of the last big steam locomotives built in America.

**WORTH DOING:** There are numerous hiking trails in and around Ogden, on which you can see mountains, waterfalls, forests, and wildlife. In scenic Ogden Valley, you can ski on the same slopes as Olympic skiers did or just enjoy the scenery. In Ogden, you can take in a show or film at Peery's Egyptian Theater, with its restored Egyptian look.

**DON'T MISS:** View the Union Pacific cauldron car, which carried the Olympic flame during the 2002 Winter Olympics that were held in Utah and based in Salt Lake City. The unique car carried the flame more than 3,200 miles across 11 states.

**GETTING THERE:** From Salt Lake City, take I-15 north to Exit 341 and follow Highway 79 east. Turn left onto Wall Avenue. The museum is in downtown Ogden and directions are well marked.

**LOCATION:** 2501 Wall Avenue, Ogden
**PHONE:** 801-393-9886
**WEBSITE:** theunionstation.org
**E-MAIL:** museums@theunionstation.org

# REGION 9

Yosemite Mountain Sugar Pine Railroad, page 290

# REGION 9

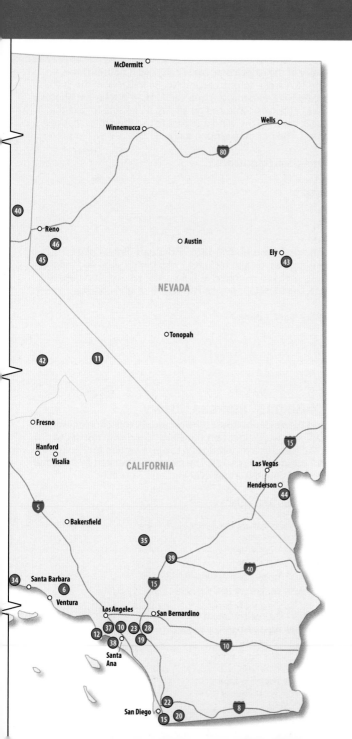

# CALIFORNIA

## Cable Car Museum

This museum tells the history of the city's iconic cable cars, and it houses three antique cable cars from the 1870s: No. 46 grip car and No. 54 trailer from the Sutter Street Railway and Clay Street Hill Railroad No. 8 grip car. Also on display are photos, tools, and models. You'll see cable cars come and go all day. Make sure to take the steps from the museum deck down to the winding room to see the cables that pull the cars along the city streets. The museum is open daily.

LOCATION: 1201 Mason Street, San Francisco
PHONE: 415-474-1887
WEBSITE: cablecarmuseum.org

## Colma Depot

This former Southern Pacific depot was built in 1865 and is part of the Colma Historical Association's museum, which also includes a blacksmith shop and freight shed. The depot was built to shelter passengers at Colma, the second stop between San Francisco and San Jose. The museum is open Tuesday through Sunday.

LOCATION: 1500 Hillside Boulevard, Colma
PHONE: 650-757-1676
WEBSITE: colmahistory.org
E-MAIL: form on website

## Edward Peterman Museum of Railroad History

A restored former Southern Pacific depot houses the museum's collection of artifacts that highlights western railroads with a focus on signaling. Along with the depot, which dates to 1863, the site features a restored 1926 tower, a section tool house, a speeder shed, and OWR&N business car No. 184. The museum, operated by the South Bay Historical Railroad Society, is open Tuesday evenings and Saturdays.

LOCATION: 1005 Railroad Avenue, Santa Clara
PHONE: 408-243-3969
WEBSITE: sbhrs.org
E-MAIL: form on website

## El Dorado Western Railroad

For a different train ride, try the El Dorado Western. The railroad takes you on 35-minute round trips over the Placerville Branch of the Southern Pacific on historic gang cars. Rides leave from El Dorado and Shingle Springs on alternate Sundays. Some special trips last 90 minutes.

LOCATION: 4560 Oriental Street, El Dorado; 4241 Mother Lode Drive, Shingle Springs
PHONE: 503-409-8473
WEBSITE: museum.edcgov.us/el-dorado-western-railroad
E-MAIL: museum@edcgov.us

## Folsom Railroad Museum

Located in a Santa Fe coach, the museum displays railroad artifacts and photographs. It features a reconstructed turntable and a Southern Pacific caboose. A handcar derby takes place in May. It is open Saturdays and Sundays. Johnny Cash fans can visit the nearby Folsom Prison Museum.

LOCATION: 198 Wool Street, Folsom
PHONE: 916-985-6001
WEBSITE: fedshra.org
E-MAIL: feds@fedshra.org

## Fort Humboldt State Historic Park

The park includes a logging museum that displays historic, steam-powered redwood-logging equipment, including two 0-4-0 locomotives and a steam donkey. On select summer Saturdays, the Timber Heritage Association steams up the equipment and provides short train rides. The park also includes a historical museum on the site where Ulysses S. Grant briefly served.

LOCATION: 3431 Fort Avenue, Eureka
PHONE: 707-445-6547
WEBSITE: parks.ca.gov
E-MAIL: info@parks.ca.gov

## History Park

History Park contains 27 original and reconstructed historic buildings including a trolley barn. Operated by the California Trolley & Railroad Corporation, the barn contains trolleys, a horse-drawn streetcar, and other historic vehicles. Buildings are closed during the week, and trolley rides take place on weekends. Southern Pacific steam locomotive No. 1215 and several railcars are also on display.

LOCATION: 635 Phelan Avenue, San Jose
PHONE: 408-287-2290
WEBSITE: historysanjose.org

# Lomita Railroad Museum

This museum is a replica of the Boston & Maine station at Wakefield, Mass. You can climb into the cab of Southern Pacific No. 1765, a 2-6-0 Baldwin built in 1902, and look inside a 1910 UP caboose. Several freight cars and a wooden water tower are also displayed. The museum exhibits lanterns, china, and other artifacts. It is open Thursday through Sunday.

LOCATION: 2137 W. 250th Street, Lomita
PHONE: 310-326-6255
WEBSITE: lomita-rr.org
E-MAIL: lomita.rr.museum@gmail.com

# Millbrae Train Museum

The museum contains photos, artifacts, and documents related to the area's railroad history. Housed in a former Southern Pacific train station, the museum displays a 1941 Pullman sleeper from the *City of San Francisco* streamliner. The museum is one of 10 historical landmarks on a self-guided walking tour. It is open on Saturdays, as is the nearby Millbrae History Museum.

LOCATION: California Drive at Murchison Drive, Millbrae
PHONE: 650-333-1136
WEBSITE: millbraehs.org
E-MAIL: form on website

# National City Depot

Still in its original location, the National City Depot, built in 1882, is the oldest railroad-related structure in San Diego County. Operated by the San Diego Electric Railway Association, it exhibits several trolleys, railroad items, and local historical displays. The depot is open Saturday and Sunday.

LOCATION: 922 W. 23rd Street, National City
PHONE: 619-474-4400
WEBSITE: sdera.org/depot.php
E-MAIL: webmaster@sdera.org

# Nevada County Narrow Gauge Railroad and Transportation Museum

The museum's collection features NCNGRR engine No. 5. The 1875 Baldwin hauled timber, passengers, and freight. Other narrow gauge equipment and wooden railcars are on display as are a 1901 steam-powered automobile and other historic transportation pieces. Docent-led tours of the museum are available. It is open Friday through Tuesday during summer and on weekends in winter.

LOCATION: 5 Kidder Court, Nevada City
PHONE: 530-470-0902
WEBSITE: ncngrrmuseum.org
E-MAIL: form on website

# Niles Depot Museum

The museum focuses on the Southern Pacific and Western Pacific, the early railroads of Fremont, Newark, and Union City. It also includes Union Pacific and Amtrak artifacts. Exhibits include railroad signals, model railroads, and a WP caboose. Housed in a passenger depot and a freight depot, the museum is open on Sundays.

LOCATION: 37592 Niles Boulevard, Fremont
PHONE: 510-797-4449
WEBSITE: nilesdepot.org
E-MAIL: tcsme@nilesdepot.org

# Placerville & Sacramento Valley Railroad

Enjoy the scenery of Gold Country aboard the Placerville & Sacramento Valley Railroad. Rides vary in length and can range from 40-minute to 2-hour excursions aboard motorcars or on railcars pulled by a diesel switcher.

LOCATION: 155 Placerville Road, Folsom
PHONE: 916-708-7368
WEBSITE: psvrr.org
E-MAIL: info@psvrr.org

# Poway-Midland Railroad

You can ride a variety of railroad equipment on this railroad. It operates a 1907 Baldwin 0-4-0 steam locomotive, a trolley car, and a speeder. You'll also see historic buildings, restored rolling stock, and a gallows turntable. Equipment runs on weekends except for the second Sunday of each month.

LOCATION: 14134 Midland Road, Poway
PHONE: 858-486-4063
WEBSITE: powaymidlandrr.org
E-MAIL: info@pmrrv.org

# Roots of Motive Power

Roots of Motive Power collects and restores rail and other equipment used for logging. The organization gets steamed up at various events during the year, both on and off the site, including the Roots of Motive Power Festival at the Roots facility and Frontier Days in Willits. Visitors can also tour the collection during scheduled work days each month.

LOCATION: 400 E. Commercial Street, Willits
WEBSITE: rootsofmotivepower.com
E-MAIL: mail@rootsofmotivepower.com

# San Bernardino History and Railroad Museum

Located in a restored 1918 Santa Fe depot, the museum contains a replicated 1910 railroad station, a variety of railroad inspection and work vehicles, artifacts, and photographs. It also features objects of local historical value including antique vehicles. The museum is open on Saturdays.

LOCATION: 1170 W. Third Street, San Bernardino
PHONE: 909-888-3634
WEBSITE: sbdepotmuseum.squarespace.com
E-MAIL: sbrrdays@me.com

# Santa Cruz & Monterey Bay Railway

The Santa Cruz & Monterey Bay operates over a scenic ex-Union Pacific branch line between the coastal cities of Santa Cruz and Watsonville. SC&MB currently operates a Polar Express holiday train in late November through December, powered by mid-century F9s in dazzling Iowa Pacific colors, boarding at the historic Santa Cruz Boardwalk. Dinner trains are planned now that the railroad has completed bridge repairs along the route.

LOCATION: 400 Beach St. Santa Cruz
PHONE: 888-726-7245
WEBSITE: santacruzrailway.com
E-MAIL: customerservice@premierrails.com

# Society for the Preservation of Carter Railroad Resources

Visit this museum at Ardenwood Historic Farm on a work day and you'll see restoration efforts of wooden cars completed using hand tools and 19th century techniques. Most cars the society preserves were built by Carter Brothers in Newark. For a one-of-a-kind experience, you can ride a train car pulled by Belgian draft horses. Special train rides operate at various times during the year.

LOCATION: 34600 Ardenwood Boulevard, Fremont
WEBSITE: spcrr.org
E-MAIL: publicity@spcrr.org

# South Coast Railroad Museum

The museum's centerpiece is the historic Goleta depot, a Victorian-styled Southern Pacific country station. The museum features hands-on exhibits and a SP bay window caboose. Occasional train rides and special events are scheduled throughout the year, and handcar rides are offered. In the Gandy Dancer Theater, you can view railroading and travel films. It is open Friday through Sunday.

LOCATION: 300 N. Los Carneros Road, Goleta
PHONE: 805-964-3540
WEBSITE: goletadepot.org
E-MAIL: form on website

## Tehachapi Depot Railroad Museum
Built as a Southern Pacific type 23 depot, the building replaced the 1904 depot, which burned down in 2008. Among the museum's artifacts is a collection of working railroad signals. The depot also schedules a variety of events during the year. It is open Thursday through Monday.

LOCATION: 101 W. Tehachapi Boulevard, Tehachapi
PHONE: 661-823-1100
WEBSITE: tehachapidepot.com
E-MAIL: info@tehachapidepot.com

## Timber Heritage Association
Speeder car rides are offered every fourth Saturday June through September. The 4-mile round trip travels from the town of Samoa, along the beautiful Humboldt Bay to Manila. On these Saturdays, the association's shops are open for tours, and you can see its collection of logging artifacts and locomotives. The rides board by the Samoa Cookhouse.

LOCATION: 908 Vance Avenue, Samoa
PHONE: 707-443-2957
WEBSITE: timberheritage.org
E-MAIL: timberheritagebruce@yahoo.com

## Waterfront Red Car Line
The Red Car Line runs along the Port of Los Angeles waterfront as it did in the 1900s. It operates a restored car, No. 1058, as well as several replicas. You can board at World Cruise Center and other stops along the waterfront including the Battleship Iowa Museum. Cars run Friday through Sunday and during some special events.

LOCATION: Sixth Street at Harbor Boulevard, San Pedro
PHONE: 310-732-3473
WEBSITE: portoflosangeles.org/recreation/waterfront_rcl.asp

## Western America Railroad Museum
271
Housed in the restored Casa Del Desierto, a 1911 Harvey House, the museum features railroad art, artifacts, and memorabilia. Its outdoor displays include locomotives, cabooses, and other equipment. Highlights include Santa Fe FP45 No. 95 in classic warbonnet scheme, a 1938 horse car, and an experimental A-frame container car. It is open Fridays, Saturdays, and Sundays.

LOCATION: 685 N. First Street, Barstow
PHONE: 760-256-9276
WEBSITE: barstowrailmuseum.org
E-MAIL: warm95@verizon.net

# California State Railroad Museum

Connecting Cities at 220 miles

Jim Wrinn

This is among the best interpretive museums about railroading. The museum mixes a magnificent large-artifact collection with plenty of details and a sense of drama that brings them to life. Displays, hands-on exhibits, and human interaction all combine to produce an excellent experience for everyone, from those with a passing interest in trains to those with a deep appreciation for railroading. And if you want the real thing, the museum operates its Sacramento Southern Railroad, a short train ride.

**CHOICES:** Made up of several buildings, the museum offers guided tours. The Railroad History Museum, at 100,000 square feet, is the largest exhibit space and contains 21 restored cars and locomotives. Be sure to climb the stairs that take you into the cab of one of the largest preserved steam locomotives, a rare Southern Pacific Cab Forward-type with its crew compartment in front of the boiler.

**WHEN TO GO:** Weekends, April through September, and select Tuesdays are when the museum offers its Sacramento Southern train rides behind Granite Rock No. 10, a rebuilt 1943 tank engine, or a vintage diesel locomotive. The 45-minute, 6-mile round trip travels over the levees of the Sacramento River. The museum also runs special events and excursions throughout the year.

**GOOD TO KNOW:** The museum is situated in the Old Sacramento district of the state capital near where the first transcontinental railroad was launched eastward in the 1800s. The district is a 28-acre National Historic Landmark District and state historic park.

**WORTH DOING:** The Old Sacramento State Historic Park contains a variety of museums, landmarks, and historical buildings.

**DON'T MISS:** When you board the Sacramento Southern, take a look at the reconstructed Central Pacific freight depot, where you'll see displays highlighting the freight transportation industry.

**GETTING THERE:** When driving to Sacramento, take I-80 from San Francisco or I-5 from Reno. If you want the full rail experience, take an Amtrak train. The station is adjacent to Old Sacramento. The museum is at the corner of Second and I Streets.

**LOCATION:** 125 I Street, Sacramento
**PHONE:** 916-323-9280
**WEBSITE:** californiarailroad.museum
**E-MAIL:** form on website

# Fillmore & Western Railway

David Lustig

Operating over a segment of a former Southern Pacific branch line, the Fillmore & Western Railway is a well-run combination of weekend scenic excursion trains, murder mystery dinner trains, and special trains. It is also one of the premier movie location sets. Billing itself as the "Home of the Movie Trains," from wrecks to shootouts, Hollywood has used this scenic little Southern California line to represent Washington D.C., Florida, the Pacific Northwest, and just about every place in between.

CHOICES: On some passenger runs, the F&W operates ex-Duluth & Northeastern 2-8-0 steam engine No. 14. On weekend excursion trains, you can ride in an open-air railcar or in restored vintage passenger coaches. The train stops in downtown Santa Paula for an hour, letting you visit the historic Southern Pacific depot, the amazing rotating water ball in Railroad Plaza Park, the Santa Paula Art Museum, the California Oil Museum, or the Ventura County Agriculture Museum.

WHEN TO GO: Excursions run on Saturdays January through March and on Saturdays and Sundays April through September and in November.

273

GOOD TO KNOW: The railroad hosts several different dinner train options for families including some murder mystery trains.

WORTH DOING: Farther north up the California coast is Santa Barbara, San Luis Obispo, and Hearst Castle, the ultimate in opulence and home of the man who ran the Hearst newspaper and radio empire.

DON'T MISS: Explore the healthy roster of passenger and freight equipment in various states of repair found on the property.

GETTING THERE: Fillmore is about 60 miles northwest of downtown Los Angeles and about 25 miles east of Ventura. From Highway 126 in Fillmore, turn on Central Avenue to Main Street.

**LOCATION:** 364 Main Street, Fillmore
**PHONE:** 805-524-2546
**WEBSITE:** fwry.com
**E-MAIL:** info@fwry.com

# Knott's Berry Farm

Dave Crosby

**Knott's Berry Farm is a Southern California theme park that has morphed from its 1952 western-style operation to a world-class attraction with rides and events designed for every age. Part of the theme park is the original 3-foot-gauge Calico Railroad.**

**CHOICES:** The railroad is just one part of this large theme park operation that rivals any other attraction in the United States. Most trains are powered by one of two Denver & Rio Grande Western 2-8-0s, either No. 41 (former Rio Grande Southern No. 41 and originally Denver & Rio Grande Western No. 409) or No. 340 (also a former D&RGW of the same number). There is also a Rio Grande Southern Galloping Goose and a number of authentic narrow gauge coaches, a parlor car, and a caboose.

**WHEN TO GO:** Southern California is enjoyable almost any time of the year, although summers can get very hot.

**GOOD TO KNOW:** If you're bringing the family, plan to stay all day. Like other theme parks in the area—Universal Studios and Disneyland—this is a kid-friendly destination with everything you need in one giant arena to tucker out even the hardiest person by the end of the day. Look for new twists in the western-themed Ghost Town Alive interactive experience, and try the new Sol Spin thrill ride.

**WORTH DOING:** Southern California abounds in attractions, restaurants, and activities for everyone. Spend a week or a weekend.

**DON'T MISS:** Good news for the railroad fan is that, by carefully selecting your photographic spots, you can come away with images that make it look like you snapped them in Colorado 70 years ago.

**GETTING THERE:** Buena Park is part of the greater Los Angeles area in Orange County. If you have a vehicle, it is accessible by several freeways, and exits are clearly marked. You can also take shuttles, sightseeing tours, and public transportation.

**LOCATION:** 8039 Beach Boulevard, Buena Park
**PHONE:** 714-220-5200
**WEBSITE:** knotts.com
**E-MAIL:** form on website

# Laws Railroad Museum

David Lustig

The 11-acre Laws Railroad Museum is home to the largest collection of equipment that operated on the Southern Pacific's narrow gauge empire, which at one time stretched almost 300 miles from Nevada to the Lone Pine area of Owens Valley.

**CHOICES:** Museum displays include SP 4-6-0 No. 9, one of the last three steam engines to operate on the line, various freight cars, a caboose, a turntable, and the original station. The museum has built a number of structures to show what Laws looked like in its heyday. A former Death Valley Railroad gas-electric doodlebug operates on select summer weekends. New to the museum are replicas of the mule team borax wagons used in Death Valley during the 1880s.

**WHEN TO GO:** The museum is open all year with a few exceptions. It is closed on several major holidays such as New Year's Day, Easter, Thanksgiving, and Christmas. It also may close due to severe weather, and some buildings close during winter.

**GOOD TO KNOW:** The nearest city with restaurants and accommodations is Bishop. If you drive up from the south on Highway 395, there are numerous towns with hotels and eateries, starting with Lone Pine, Independence, and Big Pine. During the ski season, Highway 395 is the main route to and from the various resorts north of Bishop, so you might consider making reservations well in advance.

**WORTH DOING:** Owens Valley is known for the many motion pictures, mostly westerns, that have been filmed there over the years. A number of small nonrail museums dot the area. The remains of the Manzanar Relocation Center, one of the places where Japanese-Americans were interned during World War II, is part of the National Park Service and open to the public.

**DON'T MISS:** The area from Keeler to Laws is littered with narrow gauge artifacts, ranging from the remains of trestles and buildings to 4-6-0 No. 18 in Independence.

**GETTING THERE:** Laws is truly in the middle of nowhere, and the trip to the museum is half the fun. The museum is 4.5 miles north of Bishop on Silver Canyon Road, just off Highway 6.

**LOCATION:** Silver Canyon Road, Bishop
**PHONE:** 760-873-5950
**WEBSITE:** lawsmuseum.org
**E-MAIL:** lawsmuseum@aol.com

# Napa Valley Wine Train

Drew Halverson

When you think of Napa Valley, you think of wine. And if you want a unique wine experience, take this ride through one of the world's most famous grape-growing valleys. You'll ride in elegant style onboard a fashionable train on a 3-hour, 36-mile round trip while enjoying gourmet food and a glass of wine as the vineyards roll by on the way to St. Helena and back.

**CHOICES:** Ride in a heavyweight passenger car or a vista dome, each with a different dining experience. Both lunch and dinner trains operate. You can also take part in many scheduled events such as murder mysteries and sunset trips. Special trains also run around select holidays, and tours at several wineries are available.

**WHEN TO GO:** Any time of the year is good, but the September grape-harvesting season is among the most popular. Daily service begins in March and goes through November, with Friday through Sunday service the rest of the year.

**GOOD TO KNOW:** Attire is generally casual depending on the time of year or type of event. Dinner may be more dressy, and cocktail-party attire is acceptable. As Phil Collins might say, "No jacket required," but they are suggested for cool nights. One bit of advice: no blue jeans.

**WORTH DOING:** Napa Valley is filled with hundreds of wineries to visit as well as having numerous special events.

**DON'T MISS:** Enjoy the wine. The train's wine bar offers a selection of 40–50 wines for tasting. Its wine shop carries almost 300 different wines. All entrees are prepared in the kitchen cars, and you are welcome to sneak a peek inside to watch the action.

**GETTING THERE:** From San Francisco, take I-80 east to Exit 19. Follow Highway 29 north and exit at Napa/Lake Berryessa. Take Highway 221, which becomes Soscol Avenue, into Napa. Turn right on First Street and then turn left on McKinstry Street. Ferry service from San Francisco makes for a fun day.

**LOCATION:** 1275 McKinstry Street, Napa
**PHONE:** 800-427-4124 or 707-253-2111
**WEBSITE:** winetrain.com
**E-MAIL:** form on website

# Niles Canyon Railway

Elrond Lawrence

This museum railroad, a project of the Pacific Locomotive Association, provides a magnificent ride through a dramatic canyon at the edge of the San Francisco Bay area. An outstanding collection of equipment and beautiful scenery make this an excellent day trip in central California.

**CHOICES:** The railway runs 75-minute round trips through scenic Niles Canyon between Sunol and Niles. Departures are scheduled at both stations. On all trains, you can select from open cars, covered cars, or enclosed coaches. Trains are powered by either a diesel or a steam locomotive from the railway's impressive collection that also includes a wide variety of passenger cars, freight cars, and cabooses.

**WHEN TO GO:** The railroad operates Sundays April through August and on the first and third Sundays the remaining months, except November and December, when the holiday schedule for the nighttime Train of Lights offers rides four days a week. Look for special events, such as Steamfest, wine tasting trains, beer tasting trains, and Southern Pacific and Western Pacific days. No trains run in January. Caboose rentals are available for private parties.

**GOOD TO KNOW:** The line was the last completed link of the transcontinental railroad.

**WORTH DOING:** Walk around downtown Niles for specialty and antique stores and restaurants. The Niles depot offers a park and a train-viewing platform.

277

**DON'T MISS:** The restored Sunol depot was originally built in the 1880s, and the Niles depot, which features colonnade-style architecture and houses railroad exhibits, was built in 1901.

**GETTING THERE:** The Niles Canyon Railway is situated between Oakland and San Jose. From San Jose, you can take I-880 to Fremont and exit on Highway 84 east. Turn left onto Mission Boulevard and continue 3 blocks west to Sullivan Street, and the Niles station is on the left. To reach the Sunol depot from San Jose, just take I-680 to Highway 84. Travel west on Highway 84 1 mile and turn right onto Main Street to Kilkare Road. From Oakland, take I-880 to Highway 84 east to get to either location.

**LOCATION:** 6 Kilkare Road, Sunol
**PHONE:** 510-996-8420
**WEBSITE:** ncry.org
**E-MAIL:** form on website

# Orange Empire Railway Museum

Jim Wrinn

The Orange Empire Railway Museum was organized in 1956 by trolley and electric railway enthusiasts to preserve a fast disappearing way of transportation. Visitors can ride on classic trolleys, passenger trains, and other railroad equipment from Southern California's past.

**CHOICES:** Two trolleys run on a half-mile loop line, and one is usually an early Los Angeles streetcar. Another train, pulling freight or passenger cars, operates on the 1.5-mile standard gauge main line. On the freight train, you can ride in either a caboose or open gondola. The cars and locomotives are rotated from the museum's collection, which contains more than 180 vintage pieces. You also have the opportunity to run a locomotive.

**WHEN TO GO:** The museum is open 363 days a year and special events occur during the year. Trains run on weekends and some holidays. The weather is usually bearable during most of the year; however, summertime temperatures can reach triple digits.

**GOOD TO KNOW:** The museum, situated on 100 acres of land, is about 20 miles south of Riverside. It has preserved, and is restoring, an eclectic mix of more than 225 pieces of railroad equipment that includes electric, steam, and diesel power as well as a variety of freight and passenger rolling stock. A Fred Harvey museum is on site.

**WORTH DOING:** The surrounding area, from Riverside to Temecula, is well developed with all the amenities a traveler would expect. For military aircraft fans, the March Field Air Museum has an extensive collection of aircraft adjacent to March Air Reserve Base in Riverside.

**DON'T MISS:** A 1922 oil-burning 2-6-2 steam engine, Ventura County Railway No. 2, operates excursions the third weekend of every month from September to May and during certain special events and major holidays.

**GETTING THERE:** Perris is about an hour's drive from either San Diego or Los Angeles. In Perris, exit at Route 74. Follow Route 74 (Fourth Street) west for 1 mile and turn left onto A Street.

**LOCATION:** 2201 S. A Street, Perris
**PHONE:** 951-943-3020
**WEBSITE:** oerm.org
**E-MAIL:** info@oerm.org

# Pacific Southwest Railway Museum

Pacific Southwest Railway Museum, John Wright

The Pacific Southwest Railway Museum operates in two locations near San Diego. The main collection is at Campo, just north of the U.S.–Mexico border. The other location is at La Mesa, about 10 miles east of downtown San Diego.

**CHOICES:** At Campo, visitors can enjoy several train-riding options, including a 12-mile, diesel-powered trip on a mountain railroad to Tunnel No. 4, and locomotive cab rides are available on the trip. The 40-acre site displays more than 80 pieces of equipment including diesel locomotives (among them, several interesting military switchers), steam locomotives, freight cars, passenger cars, and cabooses. Also featured is a fully restored "Jim Crow" passenger car. The La Mesa site displays railroading exhibits, freight cars, and a steam locomotive.

**WHEN TO GO:** The Campo facility is open most weekends throughout the year. The museum offers a variety of special events, including some tailored to kids, such as pumpkin and North Pole trains. The La Mesa site is open on Saturday afternoons.

**GOOD TO KNOW:** The restored La Mesa depot is the only surviving San Diego & Cuyamaca Railway station.

**WORTH DOING:** The greater San Diego area is brimming with places to visit, including Old Town. Sea World is just north of the city, and the coastline is tourist friendly. If you have always wanted to tour a U.S. Navy aircraft carrier, the decommissioned USS *Midway* is open to the public, with many types of aircraft positioned on its flight deck.

**DON'T MISS:** Now a history museum, the nearby Campo Stone Store was also a military outpost, bank, and post office. Another Campo museum to visit is the Motor Transport Museum with its large collection of vehicles and industrial equipment.

**GETTING THERE:** The Campo site is 50 miles east of San Diego. From San Diego, take Highway 94 to Campo and turn right onto Forrest Gate Road and then left onto Depot Street. Take the Spring Street exit off Highway 94 into La Mesa to reach the La Mesa depot, which is at 4695 Nebo Drive.

**LOCATION:** 750 Depot Street, Campo
**PHONE:** 619-465-7776 or
619-478-9937 (weekends)
**WEBSITE:** psrm.org
**E-MAIL:** form on website

# RailGiants Train Museum

Jim Wrinn

The RailGiants Train Museum houses an outstanding collection of significant locomotives and rolling stock. The site is on the grounds of the Los Angeles County Fairgrounds. The collection includes locomotive No. 9000, the only UP 4-12-2 in existence, locomotive No. 5021, the only Southern Pacific 4-10-2 in existence, rare Santa Fe 4-6-4 No. 3450, and UP Centennial diesel No. 6915. The center of museum activities is the former Santa Fe Depot from Arcadia, Calif., built in 1895 and preserved in 1969.

**CHOICES:** You can wander among the exhibits, various locomotives, a heavyweight Pullman lounge, a Santa Fe wood caboose, a refrigerator car, a Santa Fe horse express car, UP diesel locomotive SD40-2 No. 3105, UP caboose No. 24567, and much more.

**WHEN TO GO:** The exhibit is open one weekend every month and daily during the Los Angles County Fair in September.

**GOOD TO KNOW:** This is one group with roots. A part of the Railway & Locomotive Historical Society, the Southern California Chapter began in 1953 and opened its first exhibit with Climax geared locomotive No. 3, a donation of Sunkist Growers.

**DON'T MISS:** Look for U.S. Potash 2-8-0 No. 3. It is the museum's only 36-inch-gauge locomotive.

**GETTING THERE:** Suburban Los Angeles is the location. The site is easily accessed off Interstate 10. When the fair is open, you can even take a Metrolink commuter train to the grounds.

**LOCATION:** 1101 W. McKinley Avenue, Pomona
**PHONE:** 909-623-0190
**WEBSITE:** railgiants.org
**E-MAIL:** form on website

# Railtown 1897 State Historic Park

Jim Wrinn

Railtown 1897 State Historic Park is considered by many as the premier place for seeing California railroad history. It was originally part of the Sierra Railroad, arguably one of the best-known railroads in the world due to its extensive use in movies and television shows. You can also enjoy a train ride over these historic rails.

**CHOICES:** The historic shops and roundhouse have been operating as a steam locomotive maintenance facility for more than 100 years. One of the highlights of any visit is taking the roundhouse tour and experiencing for yourself what a working facility looks, feels, and smells like. On the 6-mile, 45-minute round trip through California's Gold Country, you can ride in coaches or open-air observation cars. Special theme trains also run during the year.

**WHEN TO GO:** The park is open daily year-round (except Thanksgiving, Christmas, and New Year's Day). Guided roundhouse tours take place each day of the summer schedule but are more limited during the rest of the year. Excursions run every weekend April through October with limited service in November and December. Steam-powered train rides behind Sierra No. 3 usually take place on Saturdays and with diesel locomotives on Sundays.

**GOOD TO KNOW:** The state of California purchased the station, shops, and roundhouse facilities in 1982 to create Railtown 1897. With more than 200 credits, it is one of the most-filmed railroad locations. The first known filming was in 1919 for a silent movie, and scenes for *High Noon, Back to the Future Part III,* and *Unforgiven* were filmed here.

281

**WORTH DOING:** This area, up through Sutter's Mill, is where people settled during the gold strikes, so history abounds. If you like the outdoors and learning western history, this is a great place to explore.

**DON'T MISS:** On the guided tour of the roundhouse, be sure to examine the props that were used in the movies filmed on the railroad.

**GETTING THERE:** From any direction, you have to drive to get to the Jamestown area, but California's Gold Country is almost universally seductive, so you'll enjoy the trip. It is about a 90-minute drive from Stockton.

**LOCATION:** 18115 Fifth Avenue, Jamestown
**PHONE:** 209-984-3953
**WEBSITE:** railtown1897.org
**E-MAIL:** form on website

# Roaring Camp Railroads

Elrond Lawrence

Located in coastal wooded mountains, Roaring Camp runs two unique trains that offer the best of California scenery and vintage railroading. The Roaring Camp & Big Trees operates steam-powered narrow gauge trains through redwood forests, while the Santa Cruz, Big Trees & Pacific runs diesel-powered trips down a scenic river gorge to the ocean.

**CHOICES:** The Roaring Camp & Big Trees operates a fleet of 1880s-era Shay, Heisler, and Climax locomotives on a winding route up Bear Mountain. The route passes through Welch Big Trees Grove. The 75-minute excursions feature open-air coaches, and passengers can detrain at the summit to tour the forest or take a guided walk back. Santa Cruz boardwalk trains employ 1920s-era passenger coaches and open-air cars pulled by ex-Santa Fe CF7 diesels. The 3-hour round trip runs through Henry Cowell Redwoods State Park, down the San Lorenzo River Gorge, and through an 1875 tunnel before arriving at the historic Santa Cruz boardwalk.

**WHEN TO GO:** Despite heavier crowds, summer is a great time to visit as Roaring Camp operates the most daily trains. The higher altitude and marine climate bring moderate temperatures; cool and foggy days are typical in summer. Seasonal trains include moonlight steam trains and dinner parties, days with Thomas and Percy, children's ghost trains in October, and a holiday lights train in November and December.

**GOOD TO KNOW:** In nearby Santa Cruz, the century-old seaside boardwalk is a historic gem and features a 1924 wooden roller coaster. Monterey, Pacific Grove, and Pebble Beach are only a short drive away on California Highway 1.

**WORTH DOING:** Roaring Camp re-creates an 1880s logging town and features historic buildings, a depot, engine house, antique cabooses, and picnic grounds. Access to the grounds is free, and picnicking is encouraged, but there is a charge for parking.

**DON'T MISS:** Seasonal events in Roaring Camp include Civil War reenactments, mountain men gatherings, harvest fairs, and steam festivals.

**GETTING THERE:** Roaring Camp is located 6 miles north of Santa Cruz off Route 17. Take Mount Hermon Road which ends at Graham Hill Road. Turn left on Graham Hill Road and drive a half mile to Roaring Camp.

**LOCATION:** 5401 Graham Hill Road, Felton
**PHONE:** 831-335-4484
**WEBSITE:** roaringcamp.com
**E-MAIL:** form on website

# Sacramento RiverTrain

Sacramento RiverTrain

Just outside of Sacramento, you'll find a uniquely scenic and relaxing train ride through rich farm country and a sprawling wildlife refuge. Operating over a 1911 electric interurban route, the Sacramento RiverTrain rolls between the cities of West Sacramento and Woodland, traveling along the banks of its namesake river and through the Yolo Wildlife Area, which is home to nearly 200 species of birds.

**CHOICES:** The railroad operates dinner, brunch, and lunch trains year-round, mostly on weekends. Passengers can board in either Woodland or West Sacramento for a leisurely 28-mile round trip that lasts up to 3 hours. The recently remodeled train is powered by GP7 No. 136, sporting new blue and gold colors, and includes vintage coaches, diners and open-air cars. Special events include train robberies, wine and beer trains, zombie trains, murder mystery excursions, and sunset dinner trains.

**WHEN TO GO:** Trains run year-round and are climate-controlled. Those who enjoy riding open-air cars might prefer to visit during spring or fall, instead of the sweltering summer months. Seasonal trips include pumpkin trains, valentine specials, a New Year's Eve express, and a popular Christmas train that runs from late November through December.

**GOOD TO KNOW:** The route is rich with history, originally built by the Woodland & Sacramento Railroad and operated by the Northern Electric Railway. Later owners included the Sacramento Northern, Western Pacific, Union Pacific, and Yolo Shortline.

**WORTH DOING:** Woodland features a charming historic downtown, surrounded by museums and wineries. Sacramento, only 15 minutes away, is home to the state capital, the California State Railroad Museum, and many other historic attractions.

**DON'T MISS:** Look for the 8,000-foot Fremont Bridge over the Sacramento River, which the railroad claims is the longest wooden trestle in the western United States.

**GETTING THERE:** From San Francisco, take I-80 East to West Sacramento and continue on I-80 to Reno (right lanes). Go 2 miles north and exit at Reed Avenue. Drive east and turn left on North Harbor Boulevard. The station is almost underneath the I-80 overpass.

**LOCATION:** 400 N. Harbor Boulevard, West Sacramento
**PHONE:** 800-866-1690
**WEBSITE:** sacramentorivertrain.com
**E-MAIL:** form on website

# San Francisco Municipal Railway

Elrond Lawrence

Of all the transportation systems in the United States, one—the cable car—is forever linked to the City by the Bay, San Francisco. The San Francisco Municipal Railway operates the cable cars and historic streetcars as well as light rail and buses. Many of the city's attractions are easily accessible by the cable cars or streetcars.

**CHOICES:** Cable cars run on three lines: Powell-Hyde, Powell-Mason, and California. The Powell-Hyde Line ends near Ghirardelli Square, and the Powell-Mason Line ends at Bay Street in Fisherman's Wharf. The California Street Line runs east-west from Van Ness Avenue to Market Street. To board a cable car along a route, just look for the brown and white signs. Streetcars run regularly along Market Street and the Embarcadero on the F Market & Wharves line that connects the downtown area with Fisherman's Wharf.

**WHEN TO GO:** Cable cars run every day of the year, and there is never a bad time to visit San Francisco. Just be sure to take a jacket—even in summer!

**GOOD TO KNOW:** In San Francisco's diverse and historic streetcar fleet, some of the restored streetcars are more than 100 years old and originally ran in other U.S. cities as well as those in countries such as Italy, Australia, and Switzerland.

**WORTH DOING:** There is always plenty to see and do in San Francisco. You can walk through the Presidio, visit Chinatown, explore Fisherman's Wharf, and take a tour to Alcatraz Island and its prison. Great food and culture abounds.

**DON'T MISS:** The San Francisco Railway Museum, which features a replica of a motorman's platform of a 1911 streetcar and other interactive exhibits, is located at the F Market Steuart Street stop, just across from the Ferry Building.

**GETTING THERE:** Both the Powell-Hyde and Powell-Mason Lines begin at Market Street, and the California Street Line has a terminal at Van Ness Avenue.

**LOCATION:** 1145 Market Street, San Francisco
**PHONE:** 415-701-2311 or 311
**WEBSITE:** sfmta.com or streetcar.org
**E-MAIL:** form on website

# SierraDinner Train

Sierra Railroad

The Sierra Railroad was formed in 1897 to connect the San Joaquin Valley to the Gold Country. Today, the Sierra carries passengers, hauls freight, and makes movies. The Sierra DinnerTrain provides visitors an opportunity to travel on the historic Sierra Railroad while dining and enjoying the passing countryside.

**CHOICES:** There are a variety of trips to choose from, including those featuring dinners, murder mysteries, lunches, Sunday brunches, and Wild West showdowns. Along the route through the scenic Stanislaus River Valley, you'll pass through distinct western scenery and the scenes of various Hollywood westerns including *High Noon, Bad Girls,* and *Pale Rider.*

**WHEN TO GO:** The dinner train runs year-round, and any time is a good time to take a train ride through California's historic and fascinating Gold Country.

**GOOD TO KNOW:** The new signature High Noon Express offers a 2.5-hour trip aboard newly remodeled dining cars or patio cars. Seasonal trips include the popular Christmas train.

**WORTH DOING:** Being way out west, you can visit the Cowboy Museum in Oakdale. The museum is housed in a historic Southern Pacific depot.

**DON'T MISS:** The Sierra Railroad is also a functioning freight operation, so railfans can view more then just passenger cars. To see a historic steam locomotive maintenance facility, you can take in Railtown 1897 Historic Park in nearby Jamestown.

**GETTING THERE:** The Sierra Railroad is located at the junction of Highway 108 and Highway 120 in the city of Oakdale, which is 90 minutes from Sacramento. The train station, which is made of railcars, is on Sierra Avenue.

**LOCATION:** 330 S. Sierra Avenue, Oakdale
**PHONE:** 800-866-1690
**WEBSITE:** sierradinnertrain.com
**E-MAIL:** form on website

# Skunk Train

Sierra Railroad

One of the most amazing attributes of the Skunk Train is its ability to make you feel small. Ride the train from Willits or the coastal town of Fort Bragg and you'll quickly find out why. The route travels through a scenic wilderness filled with towering redwoods. As the train takes you through the mountain scenery, the giant trees will make your neck sore unless you move to an open car, where you can stand in wonder.

**CHOICES:** You can ride from either end of the 40-mile line. You can board at Willits for a scenic 40-mile, half-day round trip. From Fort Bragg, you can catch a short 7-mile excursion known as the Pudding Creek Express. Motor cars operate over the line all year, while diesel-powered trains and steam engine No. 45 run mostly during the summer. The line features 30 trestles, two tunnels, and a route that snakes its way up the redwood-covered mountainside.

**WHEN TO GO:** Trains operate all year, with a variety of special trains scheduled throughout the year.

**GOOD TO KNOW:** The railroad got its nickname from the yellow-painted, self-propelled gas-powered cars of the California Western Railway that provided service starting in 1925 and prompted people to say, "You can smell 'em before you can see 'em."

**WORTH DOING:** Along the coast between December and April, you have a good chance to see a California gray whale as they migrate south from Alaska and then return. For an up-close experience, a whale-watching excursion operates out of Fort Bragg.

**DON'T MISS:** Ride the train on days when steam locomotive No. 45 is running. A 2-8-2 Mikado type built by Philadelphia's famous Baldwin Locomotive Works in 1924, the locomotive is among the largest in regular service today.

**GETTING THERE:** Just over 3 hours north of San Francisco, the scenic drive to Fort Bragg starts on Highway 101. At Cloverdale, exit onto Highway 128 west, which turns into Highway 1, and continue north to Fort Bragg. The depot is at the foot of Laurel Street. Willits is 2.5 hours north of San Francisco on Highway 101. The depot there is at 299 East Commercial Street.

**LOCATION:** 100 W. Laurel Street, Fort Bragg
**PHONE:** 707-964-6371
**WEBSITE:** skunktrain.com
**E-MAIL:** form on website

# Travel Town Museum

David Lustig

Travel Town is a good place to enjoy a couple of hours looking at equipment that has been preserved nowhere else. The museum, part of the Griffith Park complex in Los Angeles County, has a collection of small- to medium-sized steam, diesel, and electric locomotives and a surprisingly diverse roster of rolling stock.

**CHOICES:** Operated by the Department of Recreation and Parks, the museum is free and kid-friendly. Nevertheless, the diversity of the saved equipment makes Travel Town worth stopping at if you're in the area. Steam equipment includes tank locomotives, 0-6-0s, 2-8-0s, a 2-6-2, a 2-8-2, a Shay, and a Heisler. Other equipment to view includes an operating EMD Model 40 diesel, a Baldwin RS-12, a Santa Fe gas-electric, a Pacific Electric freight motor, plus various pieces of rolling stock.

**WHEN TO GO:** The museum is open every day except Christmas. On the second Saturday of each month, docent-led tours through several historic railroad passenger cars take place. In October, Depot Day features special exhibits and activities.

**GOOD TO KNOW:** A food concession is inside, but eating and picnic areas are nearby in other parts of Griffith Park. If you would like to have lunch at a historic eatery, you can grab a chili dog at Pink's, which is 15 minutes away on La Brea Boulevard and has been operating since 1939.

**WORTH DOING:** Explore Griffith Park, a quiet oasis in busy LA, and especially take the time and visit the park's other sites including the famous observatory and world-class Los Angeles Zoo, which is right next to Travel Town.

**DON'T MISS:** If you want to take a break from walking, a rideable scale train encircles the collection.

**GETTING THERE:** Travel Town is near the confluence of I-5 and the 134 Freeway. Freeway exits are clearly marked.

**LOCATION:** 5200 Zoo Drive, Los Angeles
**PHONE:** 323-668-0104
**WEBSITE:** traveltown.org
**E-MAIL:** form on website

# Western Pacific Railroad Museum

Western Pacific Railroad Museum

Here at one of the Western Pacific's last diesel locomotive shops is a great collection of rolling stock. The focus is on one of the West's most beloved railroads, Western Pacific, which traveled through beautiful mountain scenery and hosted the legendary *California Zephyr*. The setting couldn't be more appropriate.

**CHOICES:** This 37-acre site displays more than 100 pieces of equipment. Three former Western Pacific streamlined diesels call the museum home, as do locomotives from the Union Pacific and the Southern Pacific. Western Pacific 0-6-0 No. 165, a steam switcher currently being restored, is the only steam locomotive in the collection. Rolling stock includes passenger cars, boxcars, cabooses, and maintenance-of-way equipment. The museum is hands-on, so you can climb into cabs and hop onto cars.

**WHEN TO GO:** The museum is open daily April into September and select days after that. On summer weekends, caboose rides through a pine forest on a 1-mile loop of track make for a fun train trip. Pumpkin trains run in October and Santa trains in December.

**GOOD TO KNOW:** Visit in August for the annual Portola Railroad Days festival, which includes train rides, food, music, and a parade.

**WORTH DOING:** Close by is Lassen Volcanic National Park, where you can see hydrothermal features such as boiling mud pots, steaming ground, and roaring fumaroles.

**DON'T MISS:** Run a locomotive through the museum's program that puts you in the engineer's seat.

**GETTING THERE:** Portola is located in the Feather River Canyon between Sacramento and Reno. From the west, take I-80 to Highway 89 and go north to Highway 70, which runs into Portola. From the east, take I-80 to Highway 395 to Highway 70.

**LOCATION:** 700 Western Pacific Way, Portola
**PHONE:** 530-832-4131
**WEBSITE:** wplives.org
**E-MAIL:** info@wplives.org

# Western Railway Museum

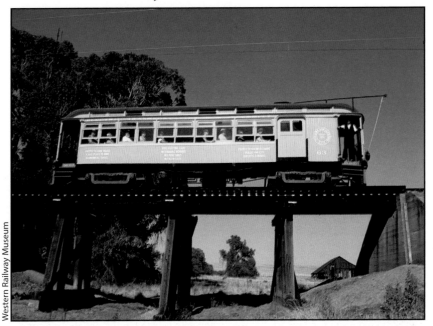

Western Railway Museum

**The Western Railway Museum gives visitors the opportunity to ride historic streetcars and interurban electric trains that once served California and other western states. There are more than 50 cars on display.**

**CHOICES:** A trip to the Western Railway Museum begins in the mission-revival inspired visitor center. After purchasing admission tickets, explore Cameron Hall, a large display and exhibit hall designed in the grand railroad station style. The museum offers 15-minute, 1-mile-long streetcar rides around the grounds. Its interurban ride over the former Sacramento Northern Railway main line runs to Birds Landing Road and features views of Suisun Marsh and Mount Diablo.

**WHEN TO GO:** The Western Railway Museum is open weekends. From Memorial Day through Labor Day, the museum expands its schedule and is open Wednesday through Sunday. It is closed on some holidays.

**GOOD TO KNOW:** You can look through Car House 1, and the museum offers guided tours of Car House 3. It also features a shaded picnic area.

289

**WORTH DOING:** During October, special Pumpkin Patch Trains take visitors on a scenic 5-mile journey to a pumpkin patch, complete with a hay-bale fort, hay rides, live music, animals, and, of course, pumpkins. In April, Scenic Limited wildflower trains and wine-tasting trains also run.

**DON'T MISS:** Visitors can stroll through the museum's large car house or take a guided tour of the building on weekends.

**GETTING THERE:** The museum is about 45 miles northeast of San Francisco, 12 miles east of I-80 on Highway 12. Public transportation is an option in reaching the museum by train and bus service.

**LOCATION:** 5848 Highway 12, Suisun City
**PHONE:** 707-374-2978
**WEBSITE:** wrm.org
**E-MAIL:** form on website

California

# Yosemite Mountain Sugar Pine Railroad

Jim Wrinn

The Yosemite Mountain Sugar Pine Railroad is a 1-hour, 4-mile narrated railroad excursion at Yosemite National Park's south gate. The ride allows you to see what it was like when geared steam locomotives hauled massive log trains through the Sierra Nevadas. It is a restored segment of the old narrow gauge Madera Sugar Pine Lumber Company Railroad, with a portion of the original right-of-way reconstructed using the same techniques as 100 years ago.

**CHOICES:** Two geared Shay steam locomotives, Nos. 10 and 15, formerly used on the West Side Lumber Company, power the excursion trains. A unique experience is riding a Jenny railcar powered by Model A Ford automobile engines, which operate beginning in March. The Moonlight Special, which operates Saturday nights in September and Saturday and Wednesday nights during the summer, begins with a steak dinner and features masked bandits, moonlight, and campfire sing-alongs.

**WHEN TO GO:** The Yosemite Mountain Sugar Pine Railroad operates daily March into October. At close to 5,000 feet elevation, it can get chilly at Fish Camp, even in the summertime. At the height of summer tourist season, Yosemite National Park gets extremely crowded.

**GOOD TO KNOW:** Refurbished railcars, once used to transport logging crews, now carry excursion passengers.

**WORTH DOING:** You can easily spend an entire day or longer in the area. Other activities in the Fish Camp area include fishing, backpacking, hiking, camping, and mountain biking. You can even try your hand at panning for gold.

**DON'T MISS:** For a fun evening, try the moonlight melodrama, which starts with a steak dinner, continues with music and a steam train excursion, and finishes with a play and music in the woods.

**LOCATION:** 56001 Highway 41, Fish Camp
**PHONE:** 559-683-7273
**WEBSITE:** ymsprr.com
**E-MAIL:** info@ymsprr.com

**GETTING THERE:** Fish Camp is 40 miles north of Fresno and 60 miles east of Modesto on Highway 41.

# NEVADA

## Nevada Northern Railway Museum

Dave Crosby

The Nevada Northern is often hailed as the best-preserved standard gauge railroad in the country. The operating railway museum is headquartered on a 56-acre complex with 66 historic buildings, set amid the vastness of the Great Basin. The Nevada Northern was completed in 1906 to haul copper, and most cars and locomotives have been on the railroad since the first day of their service lives.

**CHOICES:** The Nevada Northern offers something for everyone. Its 90-minute excursion goes through two tunnels and up mountain grades on the way to Ruth. Steam locomotives usually run on weekends and vintage diesels on weekdays. The railroad also operates a variety of special and seasonal trains, including Wild West trains, geology trains, and a Halloween ghost train that features stories from the region's colorful past.

**WHEN TO GO:** Regular excursions run mid-April through mid-October. The railway is open daily except for Tuesdays Labor Day through Memorial Day and several holidays. Summer is busy, with trains running daily. Ely is mile-high, so the weather can be unpredictable.

**GOOD TO KNOW:** The Nevada Northern offers guided tours of the shops and grounds after excursions. If you want an even more up-close look at the railway, you can stay overnight in a caboose or a bunkhouse.

**WORTH DOING:** Visit Great Basin National Park, which is 60 miles from Ely. In this diverse environment, you can see 13,000-foot mountains and 5,000-year-old bristlecone pines and explore Lehman Caves.

**DON'T MISS:** At the railway, you can view steam locomotives, wooden passenger cars, and a steam-powered rotary plow. Structures include the original depot, engine house, freight shed, coaling tower, and water tower. Diesels include everything from an SD9 to a Baldwin VO1000 and a trio of Alco RS-model road switchers.

**GETTING THERE:** Ely is in east-central Nevada at the junction of Highways 6, 50, and 93.

**LOCATION:** 1100 Avenue A, Ely
**PHONE:** 866-407-8326 or 775-289-2085
**WEBSITE:** nnry.com
**E-MAIL:** form on website

# Nevada Southern Railway

Nevada Southern Railway

The railway offers a train ride with a historical twist. This was part of the construction railroad from Las Vegas to Hoover Dam, with tracks having been laid in 1931. It's a nice ride in the desert and a break from the hustle of Las Vegas.

**CHOICES:** Along the 35-minute round trip, you get an up-close look at desert plant life, especially when riding in the train's open-air car. The other cars are air-conditioned, restored Pullman coaches dating back to 1911. A generator car behind the locomotive supplies power to the coaches. Operated by the Nevada State Railroad Museum, the railway's outdoor interpretative area displays a variety of equipment, including Union Pacific steam locomotive No. 6264 with its unusual Vanderbilt tender.

**WHEN TO GO:** The railway operates on weekends with four trips each day. Summer in Nevada can be hot, with temperatures hitting triple digits. Santa, train robbery, and other special trains run. It is closed in January. The museum pavilion is open daily.

**GOOD TO KNOW:** A 7.5" gauge steam train operates the second and fourth Saturday each month except for July and August.

**WORTH DOING:** Take a trip to nearby Boulder Dam and tour this technological wonder. Boating on Lake Mead is a popular activity any time of the year.

**DON'T MISS:** Ride a train pulled by a historic diesel. One of the locomotives used, UP No. 844, is one of the last GP30 diesel locomotives—an early 1960s diesel that replaced the first generation of diesel locomotives that had themselves replaced steam power.

**GETTING THERE:** Boulder City is a 30-minute drive from Las Vegas and McCarran International Airport. It is an easy drive from Las Vegas along Highway 93 into Boulder City. Once there, turn left on Yucca Street to the museum and railway.

**LOCATION:** 601 Yucca Street, Boulder City
**PHONE:** 702-486-5933
**WEBSITE:** nevadasouthern.com
**E-MAIL:** webmaster@nevadasouthern.com

# Nevada State Railroad Museum

Joel Kirk

Few states can claim as rich a railroading heritage as Nevada, and this museum does an admirable job of interpreting it. The first transcontinental railroad, the state's many mining railroads, and the historic Virginia & Truckee—which ran right past the museum property—are all represented here. The museum boasts a particularly fine collection of 19th century rolling stock, much of which originally came from the V&T and was used in dozens of Hollywood films and television shows.

**CHOICES:** The museum operates steam train and motor car rides throughout the season. Star of the museum's collection is *Inyo*, a wood-burning 4-4-0 built for the V&T in 1875. When *Inyo* isn't operating, it's on display along with other restored pre-1915 freight and passenger equipment. V&T No. 25 is another operating steam engine. Recently restored, Carson & Tahoe Glenbrook, a 3-foot-gauge 2-6-0 is also operational.

**WHEN TO GO:** The museum is open Thursdays through Mondays. Train rides take place weekends from May until September, with added fall runs and Santa trains.

**GOOD TO KNOW:** Carson City's downtown area is very walkable. The state capitol grounds and surrounding neighborhoods of historic homes are particularly pleasant. A wide variety of hotels, motels, and restaurants can be found nearby.

293

**WORTH DOING:** For those whose interests run toward scholarly pursuits, the museum has impressive static displays exploring such topics as the Central Pacific Railroad in Nevada railroading and the evolution of V&T motive power.

**DON'T MISS:** Ride aboard a national historic landmark. McKeen motor car No. 22 operates several times each year, the only operating McKeen car in the world. The self-propelled railcar was built for the Virginia & Truckee in 1910, and before being restored, it saw time as a restaurant and as a retail store.

**GETTING THERE:** The museum is on Highway 395 (Carson Street) on the south side of Carson City. Carson City is within a day's drive of most major cities on the West Coast.

**LOCATION:** 2180 S. Carson Street, Carson City
**PHONE:** 775-687-6953
**WEBSITE:** museums.nevadaculture.org/nsrmcc
**E-MAIL:** amichalski@nevadaculture.org

# Virginia & Truckee Railroad

Dave Crosby

The famous Comstock Lode yielded more than $400 million of silver and gold during a roughly 30-year period beginning in 1859—and it led to the creation of both Virginia City and the Virginia & Truckee Railroad. The city saw up to 45 arrivals and departures a day. Today's V&T operates a 35-minute, 5-mile round trip from Virginia City to Gold Hill.

**CHOICES:** You can ride the short but historic route from Virginia City to Gold Hill and back, with spectacular views of rugged mountain scenery and mine ruins. For those with the desire for a trip over a longer route, choose the Sisters in History run over the rebuilt track from just outside Carson City into Virginia City. The railroad powers its trains with either a 1916 Baldwin 2-8-0 steam locomotive from the Longview, Portland & Northern or a General Electric 80-ton diesel. Passenger cars include a restored 1914 Pullman coach and a 1907 private car.

**WHEN TO GO:** V&T operates daily from late May to the end of October, when it runs its haunted Halloween train. Civil War, candy cane, and other specials also run. Temperatures are comfortable throughout the operating season. The steam engine operates during summer.

**294**

**GOOD TO KNOW:** Virginia City boasts a variety of restaurants, hotels, and B&Bs that recall the town's frontier heritage. In Gold Hill, you can grab a bite to eat at the Gold Hill Hotel and take a later train back.

**WORTH DOING:** The historic Virginia City walking tour provides a good sense of the Comstock mining boom. It includes historic mansions, churches, the Piper Opera House, and the *Territorial Enterprise* newspaper, where young Mark Twain worked as a reporter.

**DON'T MISS:** The Nevada State Railroad Museum in nearby Carson City displays more than 30 pieces of equipment that operated on the V&T.

**GETTING THERE:** Virginia City is on Highway 341, 25 miles south of Reno and 15 miles north of Carson City.

**LOCATION:** 165 F Street, Virginia City
**PHONE:** 775-847-0380
**WEBSITE:** virginiatruckee.com
**E-MAIL:** info@virginiatruckee.com

# REGION 10

White Pass & Yukon Route, page 300

**ALASKA**

1  Alaska Railroad
2  Museum of Alaska
   Transportation &
   Industry
3  Tanana Valley Railroad
   Museum
4  White Pass & Yukon
   Route

**HAWAII**

# ALASKA

## Museum of Alaska Transportation & Industry

The museum is home to the trains, planes, and other machines that helped develop the state. It features a train yard with locomotives, railcars, and a renovated section house. The museum is open daily mid-May to September.

LOCATION: 3800 W. Museum Drive, Wasilla
PHONE: 907-376-1211
WEBSITE: museumofalaska.org
E-MAIL: form on website

## Tanana Valley Railroad Museum

The museum runs a restored 1899 Porter 0-4-0 steam locomotive around the perimeter of Pioneer Park on select days during the year. The museum is open daily Memorial Day through Labor Day, and visitors may see restoration activity as well as learn about the railroad. Pioneer Park contains several other interesting museums and operates a narrow gauge train through the site.

LOCATION: 2300 Airport Way, Fairbanks
PHONE: 907-459-7421
WEBSITE: facebook.com/tananavalleyrailroad
E-MAIL: ftvrr.inc@gmail.com

# Alaska Railroad

Frank Keller

Completed in 1923, the Alaska Railroad was built to link the Pacific seaport of Seward with the resource-rich interior long before there were highways. Passenger service offers breathtaking excursions into rugged back-country terrain that is often inaccessible by car.

**CHOICES:** The flagship Denali Star operates daily between Anchorage and Fairbanks with stops at Wasilla, Talkeetna, and Denali National Park. A local favorite, the Coastal Classic goes to Seward, where boat tours provide access to Kenai Fjords National Park and Resurrection Bay. Each of these trains includes a refurbished "lower 48" heritage dome car, coach, and bistro car, as well as a GoldStar (first class) dome car sporting open-air viewing decks. Adventure-class (coach) passengers can watch the Alaskan landscape roll by from open Dutch doors. The Hurricane Turn provides flag-stop service for campers and fishermen along the Susitna River. The Glacier Discovery runs from Anchorage to Whittier for glacier cruises and to Spencer Glacier and Grandview whistle-stops for kayaking, rafting, and hiking.

**WHEN TO GO:** Most trains operate mid-May to mid-September when the weather is warm and the days are long. The best time to visit is early in the season, when there is still snow on the mountains and little rain. Winter service is provided by the Aurora winter train operating between Anchorage and Fairbanks on weekends from mid-September to mid-May. The Hurricane Turn runs from Anchorage to Hurricane on the first Thursday of the month beginning in October. Special trains also run during this time of year.

**GOOD TO KNOW:** The railroad works closely with major cruise lines, offering cruise passengers Grandview service to connect the ports of Seward and Whittier with the Anchorage airport. The cruise lines also operate their own train with double-decker domes between Anchorage and Denali Park.

**WORTH DOING:** The Hurricane Turn provides an escape from sightseeing and tourism overload and a chance to visit with friendly Alaskans on their way to remote cabins. It operates Thursday through Monday and features a dome coach.

**DON'T MISS:** Try either the Coastal Classic or Glacier Discovery. The scenery south of Anchorage is more varied and breathtaking than most of the Denali route.

**GETTING THERE:** Airlines fly to both Anchorage and Fairbanks. Cruise ships from Vancouver and Seattle are another option.

**LOCATION:** 411 W. First Avenue, Anchorage
**PHONE:** 800-544-0552 or 907-265-2494
**WEBSITE:** alaskarailroad.com
**E-MAIL:** reservations@akrr.com

**Alaska**

# White Pass & Yukon Route

Karl Zimmermann

The White Pass & Yukon's 67.5 route miles make it the longest operating narrow gauge railroad in North America. More importantly, virtually every one of those miles is knockout beautiful—a potpourri of lakes, rivers, and snow-capped mountains. Completed in 1900, the railroad was built to link the Yukon and other booming gold-mining districts with tidewater at Skagway.

**CHOICES:** The most popular trip is the half-day, 40-mile round trip to White Pass Summit. Other possibilities include going 7 miles farther to Fraser and continuing on to Whitehorse by motor coach. Even better are the five-days-a-week, 8-hour trips along the full length of the line, Skagway to Carcross, riding the train one way and a motor coach the other. Additional train-motor coach combinations are available, and the trains will drop off and pick up hikers at certain locations.

**WHEN TO GO:** The White Pass & Yukon operates from early May to late September, and any time in that window is fine for a visit—though it is likely to be bracingly chilly early and late. As compensation, the snow-capped mountains will be more scenic.

**GOOD TO KNOW:** One of the railroad's two steam locomotives, either Mikado No. 73 or Consolidation No. 69, operates three days a week for much of the season on excursions to Fraser Meadows. Unique and colorful diesels—modernized, shovel-nose General Electric units and newer low-nose road switchers—handle all the other trains.

**WORTH DOING:** The few hotels and handful of B&Bs in Skagway are best booked in advance. You can tour Skagway, the Yukon, and other scenic areas by Jeep, raft, horseback, or dogsled.

**DON'T MISS:** Although the entire line is spectacular, pay particular attention to the first 20 miles to White Pass Summit. Here, the railroad uses grades of up to 3.9 percent to climb 2,865 feet. For the best views, grab seats on the left side of the train.

**GETTING THERE:** Most passengers arrive at Skagway by cruise ship, but you can get to Skagway from Bellingham, Wash., or Prince Rupert aboard the comfortable ferries of the Alaska Marine Highway. For motorists, Skagway is 110 miles south of the Alaska Highway via the South Klondike Highway.

**LOCATION:** 231 Second Avenue, Skagway
**PHONE:** 800-343-7373
**WEBSITE:** wpyr.com
**E-MAIL:** info@wpyr.com

# HAWAII

## Lahaina Kaanapali Railroad
The Sugar Cane Train travels around the historical whaling town of Lahaina on the Hawaiian island of Maui. Narrow gauge steam engines transport visitors in open-air cars through golf courses, along the ocean, and across a scenic railroad trestle.

LOCATION: Pu'ukoli'i Road, Lahaina
PHONE: 808-667-6851
WEBSITE: sugarcanetrain.com
E-MAIL: form on website

## Laupahoehoe Train Museum
The musem is located on the Big Island along the Hamakua Heritage Coast. It is housed in a station agent's home, which has been restored and furnished to its early 1900s appearance. The museum contains photos and artifacts of the Hilo Railroad and displays a standard gauge caboose, narrow gauge boxcar, and diesel switcher.

LOCATION: 36-2377 Mamalahoa Highway, Laupahoehoe
PHONE: 808-962-6300
WEBSITE: thetrainmuseum.com
E-MAIL: laupahoehoetrainmuseum@yahoo.com

# Hawaiian Railway Society

Hawaiian Railway Society

The Hawaiian Railway Society operates the only active train on the island of Oahu. It offers regularly scheduled 90-minute, fully narrated rides over 6.5 miles of track. Along the way, you'll pass a variety of interesting and historical sites, including Fort Barrette. The train stops at Kahe Point, so you can take in the extraordinary ocean views.

**CHOICES:** Regular excursions take place Saturday and twice on Sunday. On the second Sunday of each month, parlor car No. 64 is added to the regular train of open cars, and reservations (and an additional fare) are necessary for riding in this beautifully restored car. Three side-rod diesel locomotives have been restored to operation, and several steam locomotives have been cosmetically restored. The society also has a collection of railcars and other equipment on display.

**WHEN TO GO:** The 3 p.m. Saturday and Sunday rides are ice cream rides on which the train stops at Two Scoops in Ko'Olina, where ice cream can be purchased.

**GOOD TO KNOW:** Parlor car No. 64 is the luxurious parlor car that Benjamin Dillingham, founder of the Oahu Railway & Land Company, had built for his personal use in 1900. Restored by the Hawaiian Railway Society, No. 64 is worth the ride, and the fare for riding the car goes toward its upkeep.

**WORTH DOING:** No trip to Oahu would be complete without a heart-rending visit to Pearl Harbor. You can also wander over Oahu and other islands and literally discover pieces of Hawaii's railroading past, which included sugar plantation, military, and common carrier railways.

**DON'T MISS:** The society's site, which is situated on what was part of the Oahu Railway & Land Company main line, is north of Pearl Harbor. The scenery is incredible. Wear comfortable shoes and wander through the train yard and then relax with lunch in the picnic area.

**GETTING THERE:** The operation is minutes from Honolulu by bus or car. If you drive, take H1 west and exit on 5A Ewa. Then take Highway 76 south for 2.5 miles, turn right at Renton Road, and continue for 1.5 miles to the entrance.

**LOCATION:** 91-1001 Renton Road, Ewa
**PHONE:** 808-681-5461
**WEBSITE:** hawaiianrailway.com
**E-MAIL:** info@hawaiianrailway.com

# Kauai Plantation Railway

David Lustig

The Kauai Plantation Railway operates daily on a genuine Hawaiian plantation. Experience plantation life and learn about Kauai agriculture as the train travels through more than 100 acres of unspoiled Hawaii on a 3-foot-gauge train. Passengers enjoy a 40-minute journey through fields of sugar cane, pineapple, banana, papaya, coffee, tropical flowers, and hardwood trees.

**CHOICES:** Train rides leave from a Hawaiian train depot, and you can ride in a reproduction of a railway car from the time of King Kalakaua or an open-sided excursion car. In addition, there is a ride-hike-lunch-orchard tour. Motive power is a pair of small diesels, including a restored 1939 Whitcomb engine.

**WHEN TO GO:** The train operates daily, and there are up to five runs a day. Hawaii is in the tropics, and any day is a beautiful day.

**GOOD TO KNOW:** The 3-foot-gauge railway was the first railroad built on Kauai in almost 100 years. More than 2.5 miles of roadbed was constructed with rails hand-spiked onto 6,000 wooden ties. More than 50 varieties of fruits and vegetables can be found on the plantation, from avocado and bananas to rambutan and sugar cane. The plantation also features a restaurant and shops as well as a tasting room for Kōloa Rum, which is produced on the island with sugar cane.

**WORTH DOING:** A train and luau package is available for Tuesday and Friday evenings in which you can experience a Hawaiian feast and entertainment.

**DON'T MISS:** On the tour package, after riding the train, you can hike in the rain forest and sample fresh fruit picked right off the tree. You also have the opportunity to feed goats, sheep, and pigs.

303

**GETTING THERE:** The Kauai Plantation is just off Route 50 (Kaumualii Highway) approximately 1 mile south of Lihue, which is the main city on Kauai. The railway is located at Kilohana Plantation next to Kauai Community College. Just look for the white picket fence.

**LOCATION:** 3-2087 Kaumualii Highway, Lihue
**PHONE:** 808-245-7245
**WEBSITE:** kauaiplantationrailway.com
**E-MAIL:** train@hawaiilink.net

**ALBERTA**

1 Alberta Prairie Railway Excursions

2 Alberta Railway Museum

3 Aspen Crossing Railway

4 Edmonton Radial Railway

5 Fort Edmonton Park

6 Galt Historic Railway Park

7 Heritage Park

8 Royal Canadian Pacific

9 VIA Jasper-Prince Rupert Route

**BRITISH COLUMBIA**

10 Alberni Pacific Railway

11 BC Forest Discovery Centre

12 Cranbrook History Centre

13 Fort Steele Heritage Town

14 Fraser Valley Heritage Railway

15 Kamloops Heritage Railway

16 Kettle Valley Steam Railway

17 Kwinitsa Railway Station Museum

18 Nelson Electric Tramway

19 Railway & Forestry Museum

20 Revelstoke Railway Museum

21 Rocky Mountaineer

22 West Coast Railway Heritage Park

# ALBERTA

## Alberta Railway Museum

The museum's collection of railway equipment and buildings focuses on the Canadian National Railway and the Northern Alberta Railway. It includes more than 75 locomotives and cars, three stations, a telegraph office, and a water tank. The museum is open weekends from Victoria Day through Labor Day. You can take a walking tour, ride a speeder, and on long holiday weekends, ride a passenger train.

LOCATION: 24215 34th Street NW, Edmonton
PHONE: 780-472-6229
WEBSITE: albertarailwaymuseum.com
E-MAIL: form on website

## Edmonton Radial Railway

The Edmonton Radial Railway operates streetcars in Fort Edmonton Park and in Old Strathcona. At Fort Edmonton Park, the 1-mile streetcar rides are included with admission. In Old Strathcona, the trolley crosses High Level Bridge over the North Saskatchewan River. The Strathcona streetcar barn contains a museum with exhibits on streetcar history. Streetcars operate from May into October, and the museum is open Saturdays.

LOCATION: 103 Street and 84th Avenue, Edmonton
PHONE: 780-437-7721 or 780-496-1464
WEBSITE: edmonton-radial-railway.ab.ca
E-MAIL: info@edmonton-radial-railway.ab.ca

# Fort Edmonton Park

Nestled in Edmonton's river valley, Fort Edmonton Park is a living history museum that represents four historical periods between 1840 and 1920. It contains more than 75 buildings. A 1919 steam train takes you through the park, and caboose rides are available. A streetcar also travels along the historic streets. The park is open from Victoria Day weekend through Labor Day.

LOCATION: Fox Drive and Whitemud Drive, Edmonton
PHONE: 780-496-7381
WEBSITE: fortedmontonpark.ca
E-MAIL: info@fortedmontonpark.ca

# Galt Historic Railway Park

The park exhibits artifacts from the steam and coal eras in southern Alberta, focusing on the Galt Railway system. It includes the restored 1890 depot that stradled the Canada–U.S. border near Sweetgrass, Montana. Speeder rides are offered during special events. The park is open Tuesdays through Saturdays June through August.

LOCATION: 65032 Range Road 19-4C, Stirling
PHONE: 403-756-2220
WEBSITE: galtrailway.com
E-MAIL: gcprs@telus.net

# Royal Canadian Pacific

The Royal Canadian Pacific, an arm of the passenger department of Canadian Pacific Railway, offers periodically scheduled all-inclusive luxury-train ride packages on CPR's route through the spectacularly scenic Canadian Rockies. Ride aboard vintage, heavyweight CPR sleeping, observation, and dining cars with lavishly restored interiors.

LOCATION: 7550 Ogden Dale Road SE, Calgary
PHONE: 877-665-3044
WEBSITE: royalcanadianpacific.com
E-MAIL: form on website

# Alberta Prairie Railway Excursions

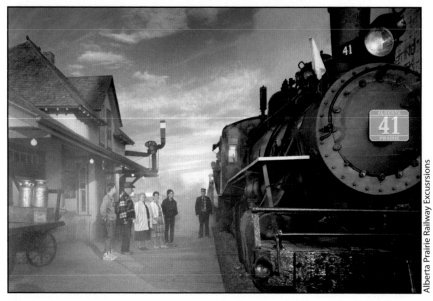

Alberta Prairie Railway Excusrsions

A trip aboard the Alberta Prairie conjures up visions of what a central Alberta wheat line must have been like 100 years ago. Traveling from the well-developed community of Stettler, it passes through stands of trees and fields before reaching Big Valley, where the ruins of a roundhouse and a restored depot remain.

**CHOICES:** The railroad offers an extensive schedule of excursions and specials throughout the year. All excursions include a buffet meal, which is served in Big Valley, onboard entertainment, and possibly a train robbery. Specially themed rides include live dinner shows, steak barbecues, country dinner trains, Polar Express rides, and teddy bear trains. The trains are pulled by Baldwin 2-8-0 steam engine No. 41 or by General Motors diesel No. 1259. Several times a year, usually for special events, such as on Canada Day, historic steam engine No. 6060 is in operation.

**WHEN TO GO:** Summer excursions begin in May and continue until mid-October each year.

**GOOD TO KNOW:** The railway was once part of a vast grain railroad network belonging to the Canadian Northern. Be sure to chat with the train crew. Many of the veteran railroaders on this line have great stories. And if you get the right conductor, he might just sing you a song or recite a poem for you en route.

**WORTH DOING:** In Big Valley, the restored station and several railcars display railroad and local history artifacts. You can take a self-guided tour of the five-stall roundhouse remains and former rail yards, view a wooden grain elevator, and visit the Jimmy Jock Boardwalk, which is modeled after a frontier town's street.

**DON'T MISS:** For an added prairie experience, you can take a 20-mile covered wagon trip along historic rail rights-of-way.

**GETTING THERE:** Stettler is about 3 hours northeast of Calgary on Highway 12.

**LOCATION:** 4611 47th Avenue, Stettler
**PHONE:** 800-282-3994 or 403-742-2811
**WEBSITE:** absteamtrain.com
**E-MAIL:** info@absteamtrain.com

# Aspen Crossing Railway

Aspen Crossing Railway

This railway takes you back to a simpler time. Along a 28-mile, 3-hour round trip, passengers get to enjoy serene prairie views, pass historic wooden elevators, learn about the area's agriculture and the railroad—or simply relax to the soothing sounds of the rail.

**CHOICES:** In addition to regular Sunday excursions, there is a large variety of special event trains, including twilight departures, elevator tours, wine tasting trips, or brunch trains. Many of the trains include musical entertainment and/or a train robbery.

**WHEN TO GO:** Trains run from May through September. During May, June, and September, trains operate on Saturdays, Sundays, and most Fridays. July and August see trains Fridays through Sundays, with the addition of a circus train on Wednesdays. October weekends and the days before Halloween are dedicated to the Train of Terror. The Polar Express runs in December.

**GOOD TO KNOW:** Some 1-hour mini excursions are available during the season. In August, look for the Southern Alberta Music Festival to take place at Aspen Crossing.

**WORTH DOING:** While at the station, you can dine in a restored 1887 Pullman railcar. The restored car was once the private business car of former Prime Minister John Diefenbaker. If you want to make your visit an extended stay, you can stay in the railway's 85-site modern campground or one of three caboose cabins. The cabooses are from the Union Pacific, Canadian Pacific, and Northern Alberta Railway.

**DON'T MISS:** On the Prairie Tour, you'll see the Mossleigh grain elevators, some of the rare original elevators left in Canada. In the 1930s, there were more than 5,000 grain elevators, and now less than 350 remain across the prairie provinces.

**GETTING THERE:** Aspen Crossing is located about an hour's drive southeast of Calgary. It is 1 mile west of Mossleigh on Highway 24.

**LOCATION:** Highway 24, Mossleigh
**PHONE:** 866-440-3500 or 403-534-2129
**WEBSITE:** aspencrossing.com
**E-MAIL:** info@aspencrossing.com

# Heritage Park

Heritage Park

Discover what life was like in the Canadian West between 1864 and 1914 by visiting this re-created village framed by the Rockies. More than 150 exhibits, including many buildings transplanted from Calgary and other locations throughout Alberta, bring the past to the present.

**CHOICES:** The park includes a roundhouse and turntable along 30 locomotives and cars. A train ride is an excellent way to see the park. Make a day of your visit and wander from building to building, paying particular attention to the transplanted railway stations, rolling stock, and re-created carbarn. If it's too hot, take a cruise on the water aboard the replica sternwheeler SS *Moyie*. Heritage Town Square represents a street scene from the 1930s to '50s, complete with an automobile museum and a replica train station.

**WHEN TO GO:** All of Heritage Park is open daily from mid-May through mid-October. Historical Village is open weekends during September through mid-October. Then over the winter, Gasoline Alley Museum is open Tuesday through Sunday.

**GOOD TO KNOW:** A short streetcar line connects the outer parking area to the main entrance. It's well worth it to park out there, view ex-CPR 2-10-4 No. 5931 and S2 No. 7019, and then ride over to the gate in a replica Calgary or Winnipeg trolley.

**WORTH DOING:** Calgary's 10-day annual Stampede, which can draw more than one million people, is the world's largest rodeo. The event also features chuck wagon racing, agricultural exhibits, entertainment, and a parade.

**DON'T MISS:** During Railway Days in September, the park celebrates Canadian railways and rolls out much of its collection. You can also take a caboose ride, ride a handcar, and tour a steam locomotive cab.

**GETTING THERE:** Heritage Park is approximately a 20-minute drive southwest from downtown Calgary. A shuttle service operates during park hours from the Heritage light rail stop.

**LOCATION:** 1900 Heritage Drive SW, Calgary
**PHONE:** 403-268-8500
**WEBSITE:** heritagepark.ca
**E-MAIL:** info@heritagepark.ca

# VIA Jasper-Prince Rupert Route

VIA Rail

The VIA Rail Canada train between Jasper and Prince Rupert, British Columbia, is one of the scenic highlights of any trip to western Canada. The 2-day, 725-mile trip, which includes an overnight stop in Prince George, takes you from the Rocky Mountains in Jasper National Park to the Pacific coast.

**CHOICES:** Travelers can opt for either economy or touring class. Budget-minded vacationers can relax in the leg-rest seats found in economy class. Those with a voracious appetite for scenery may want to spend a little more for touring class, which puts you in a dome car with its upper observation deck and panoramic views. Touring class also provides meals. Economy class has access to the dome during the off-peak months of October through May.

**WHEN TO GO:** The train operates Wednesday, Friday, and Sunday year-round. The shorter days and deep snows of winter give way to a plethora of spring flowers in May. Hot summer days morph into colorful, cool fall days by October. Economy class is offered year-round, and touring class is available only from mid-June through September.

**GOOD TO KNOW:** Don't forget to book a hotel room for your overnight stay in Prince George. When arriving in Prince George, you may want to take a taxi, even though accommodations are a few blocks away as the area around the VIA station may be considered rough. Prince Rupert is a port of call on the Alaska Marine Highway.

**WORTH DOING:** In Jasper, you can explore Jasper National Park, the northernmost park in the Rocky Mountains, and leave feeling hot or cold. You can experience a glacier close up and soak in a hot spring. In Prince Rupert, you can visit the Kwinitsa Railway Museum and the First Nation Carving Shed, where artists produce works in wood and metal.

**DON'T MISS:** Just west of Jasper, Mount Robson, the highest peak in the Canadian Provinces, is visible from the train for only a few cloudless days a year. You may also see moose, bear, elk, wolves, seals, and eagles along the way.

**GETTING THERE:** VIA Rail operates the Vancouver-Toronto *Canadian* three times a week during summer and twice a week the rest of the year. Jasper is also served by bus from Edmonton and other points.

**LOCATION:** 607 Connaught Drive, Jasper
**PHONE:** 888-842-7245
**WEBSITE:** viarail.ca/en/explore-our-destinations/trains/rockies-and-pacific
**E-MAIL:** form on website

# BRITISH COLUMBIA

## BC Forest Discovery Centre

The most relaxing, and most scenic, way to take in this 100-acre site is by riding the train, which is pulled by a steam-powered 1910 locomotive or a gas-powered locomotive. Speeder rides are also offered. The site's collection features Shay, Climax, and Vulcan locomotives. Other exhibits include an operating sawmill, a lookout tower, and antique logging trucks. The site is open April into October, daily June to September, and for special events.

LOCATION: 2892 Drinkwater Road, Duncan
PHONE: 250-715-1113
WEBSITE: bcforestdiscoverycentre.com
E-MAIL: info.bcfdc@shawlink.ca

## Fort Steele Heritage Town

Fort Steele Heritage Town is a restored 1890s pioneer town complete with railway. A Montreal Locomotive Works 2-6-2 Prairie type locomotive takes you on a 20-minute scenic ride that includes a stop at a viewing platform. You can also examine a variety of rail equipment and steam engines displayed by the engine house. Fort Steele is open year-long, and the railway operates daily during summer.

LOCATION: 9851 Highway 93/95, Fort Steele
PHONE: 250-417-6000
WEBSITE: fortsteele.ca
E-MAIL: info@fortsteele.bc.ca

## Fraser Valley Heritage Railway

The railway runs a heritage interurban car, No. 1225, and speeders on the original BC Electric Railway route. Cars leave from the replicated Cloverdale station along the line through Surrey. It operates weekends from May to October.

LOCATION: 176A Street and 56th Avenue, Cloverdale
PHONE: 604-574-9056
WEBSITE: fvhrs.org
E-MAIL: q@fvhrs.org

## Kwinitsa Railway Station Museum

Located in Prince Rupert's waterfront park near the Museum of Northern BC, this restored station house is an excellent example of the small stations once found along Canada's northern railway line. Photographs, videos, and detailed restorations depict the life of station agents and linemen who worked for the Grand Trunk Railway at the turn of the 20th century. It is open daily June through August.

LOCATION: Bill Murray Way and First Avenue, Prince Rupert
PHONE: 250-624-3207
WEBSITE: museumofnorthernbc.com

## Nelson Electric Tramway

Streetcar 23 runs from the park to Prestige Lakeside Resort along the beautiful west arm of Kootenay Lake. The 2.5-mile round trip takes about 20 minutes and includes some street running. The streetcar operates from May into October. Car 23 ran in Nelson more than 60 years ago and was restored after being turned into a dog kennel (and a chicken coop). The trolley barn contains historical exhibits.

LOCATION: Rotary Lakeside Park, Nelson
PHONE: 250-352-7672
WEBSITE: nelsonstreetcar.org
E-MAIL: info@nelsonstreetcar.org

## Railway & Forestry Museum

The museum displays historic railway and forestry exhibits in a park-like setting. The extensive rail collection dates to 1899 and includes two stations and a turntable. It also contains both steam and diesel locomotives and more than 40 pieces of rolling stock. The museum is open daily May to September and Tuesday through Saturday the rest of the year.

LOCATION: 850 River Road, Prince George
PHONE: 250-563-7351
WEBSITE: pgrfm.bc.ca
E-MAIL: trains@pgrfm.bc.ca

## Revelstoke Railway Museum

This railway museum focuses on the history of the Canadian Pacific Railway in western Canada. You can walk through Business Car No. 4 and view steam locomotive No. 5468, various railcars, and artifacts. You can also try a train simulator. The museum also operates a small facility at Craigellachie, 28 miles west of Revelstoke, where the last spike of the Canadian Pacific Railway was driven. The museum is open year-round.

LOCATION: 719 Track Street West, Revelstoke
PHONE: 877-837-6060 or 250-837-6060
WEBSITE: railwaymuseum.com
E-MAIL: railway@telus.net

# Alberni Pacific Railway

Alberni Pacific Railway, Ken Rutherford

The Alberni Pacific offers passengers a chance to visit the former McLean Paper Mill, 6 miles east of Port Alberni over the former Canadian Pacific Railway Port Alberni Subdivision. The mill is a National Historic Site that commemorates the history of logging and milling in British Columbia.

**CHOICES:** Trains to the mill are pulled by a 1929 Baldwin 2-8-2T steam locomotive, and passengers ride in converted former Canadian National transfer cabooses, three of which are open and two are covered. The 35-minute trips leave (and return) from a restored 1912 CPR station. Cab rides in No. 7 are also available.

**WHEN TO GO:** Runs are made over this scenic trackage Thursdays through Sundays between the end of June until September. Special events occur throughout the year including special steam trains in fall as well as wine trains, train robberies, and Santa trains.

**GOOD TO KNOW:** The McLean Mill is the only steam-operated sawmill in Canada. This historic site and the railway are part of the Alberni Valley Heritage Network that celebrates the area's history and culture. Also included are the Alberni Valley Museum and Maritime Discovery Centre.

**WORTH DOING:** Visit Port Alberni's quaint harbor, which offers a mix of restaurants, galleries, tours, and shops. You are also within minutes of numerous outdoor activities including seeing Delta Falls, the tallest waterfall in Canada.

**DON'T MISS:** At the mill, you can explore the site on your own or take a guided tour. It has been laid out as an early 20th century logging camp with restored buildings and original pieces of logging equipment, including an operating steam donkey.

**GETTING THERE:** Bus service is available from Vancouver Island to Port Alberni. Ferry service operates between the mainland and various points on Vancouver Island including Port Alberni.

**LOCATION:** 3100 Kingsway Avenue, Port Alberni
**PHONE:** 855-866-1376
**WEBSITE:** albernisteamtrain.com
**E-MAIL:** info@alberniheritage.com

# Cranbrook History Centre

Cranbrook History Centre

The centre's rail collection is a magnet for anyone interested in Canadian passenger rail travel as it once was. The centre is home to the only surviving train set of equipment from the 1929 *Trans Canada Limited* as well as the beautifully reconstructed Royal Alexandra Hall.

CHOICES: Visitors can choose from several different guided tours that examine the trains in the museum's collection, including the *Soo-Spokane Train Deluxe* and *Trans Canada Limited*. Various business cars, cars of state, and historic structures are also included. Guides explain the history of the equipment and bring to life the beautifully restored railcar interiors. Be prepared to walk. Depending on the tour, you could cover a half mile or more.

WHEN TO GO: The museum is open daily July and August. During the remainder of the year, it is open Tuesday through Saturday.

GOOD TO KNOW: Cranbrook is a gateway to the Canadian Rockies, which are a short drive away. Enjoy the sun and a hot soak. Situated at an elevation of 3,000 feet, Cranbrook also is one of the sunniest spots in Canada. After a walking tour of the museum, you can soak in several hot springs in the area.

WORTH DOING: Fort Steele is less than 20 minutes away. Once a thriving mining town, Fort Steele became a ghost town when the railroad bypassed it for Cranbrook. It is now a heritage town, where visitors can experience its boom-town history.

DON'T MISS: Visit the exquisitely re-created Royal Alexandra Hall from the Canadian Pacific Railway's Royal Alexandra Hotel that once stood beside CPR's Winnipeg Station. The hall was the grand cafe of the hotel and features Edwardian architectural style. Other exhibits are located on the lower level of the original CPR's freight shed, including working model railway displays.

GETTING THERE: Air service to Cranbrook is available with direct flights from Vancouver and Calgary. Greyhound also operates daily scheduled service to the city. It is about a 3.5-hour drive from Spokane, Wash.

**LOCATION:** 57 Van Horne Street South, Cranbrook
**PHONE:** 250-489-3918
**WEBSITE:** cranbrookhistorycentre.com
**E-MAIL:** form on website

# Kamloops Heritage Railway

John Godfrey

This steam-powered tourist line's regular excursion is a 7-mile round trip on the Canadian National's Okanagan Subdivision that features mountain vistas, lakeside scenery, and an occasional train robbery.

**CHOICES:** On the Spirit of Kamloops' 70-minute excursion, you can ride in a restored 1930s air-conditioned coach or in an open-air car. Along the way, masked riders reenact the famous 1906 train robbery by the Bill Miner gang. The train departs from a restored 1927 CN station and crosses the South Thompson River over a 1927 steel trestle bridge, where the train stops and allows you to photograph the scenery.

**WHEN TO GO:** The Spirit of Kamloops operates Thursday and Friday evenings and during the day on Saturdays in July and August. Illuminated with hundreds of lights, the Spirit of Christmas is a 1-hour holiday special, complete with candy canes, hot chocolate, and caroling. Halloween trains also operate.

**GOOD TO KNOW:** The former courthouse in Kamloops, where train robber Bill Miner was tried and convicted, is now a popular hostel.

**WORTH DOING:** At the Secwepemc Museum in Kamloops, you can discover the history of the Shuswap people. Visit Heritage Park and go through the incredible 2,000-year-old winter village and the summer pit houses.

**DON'T MISS:** Railway Heritage Park is the base of operations for the passenger train, and you can view equipment on display in the yard and take a guided tour of the backshop. You may even get an up-close look at locomotive 2141.

**GETTING THERE:** Kamloops is about a 3.5-hour drive from Vancouver. You can follow the Trans Canada Highway east or take the scenic Fraser Canyon route, but allow time for viewing the vistas along the way. The ticket office is located just outside the main door of the station building at Station Plaza.

**LOCATION:** 510 Lorne Street, Kamloops
**PHONE:** 250-374-2141
**WEBSITE:** kamrail.com
**E-MAIL:** info@kamrail.com

# Kettle Valley Steam Railway

Kettle Valley Steam Railway

The Kettle Valley Steam Railway operates over the only preserved portion of the famed Kettle Valley Railway, which was completed in 1915. Passengers can enjoy the rural landscapes of Summerland's Prairie Valley, and take in the mountains and views of Okanagan Lake from the Trout Creek Bridge, a major feature of the original line.

CHOICES: The KVR offers regular excursions over a 6-mile route. The 90-minute trip winds through Prairie Valley and its scenic vistas. A century-old steam locomotive, No. 3716, or a backup diesel engine supplies the power. You can ride in two 1940s vintage passenger coaches or three open-air cars. Special events are scheduled throughout the year and include Easter, Mother's Day, and Christmas trains. About a dozen train robbery and barbecue events take place.

WHEN TO GO: The KVR operates on a varied schedule. In May and June, and during September and October, regular excursions run Saturday through Monday. In July and August, they run Thursday through Monday.

GOOD TO KNOW: Summerland is situated in the Okanagan Valley amid lush orchards and vineyards, and the valley is home to more than 50 wineries.

WORTH DOING: Take a side trip into nearby Penticton and tour the former CP ship SS *Sicamous*. This steel-hulled sternwheeler was built in 1914 as a multipurpose vessel that provided first-class passenger service as well as delivering cargo and daily mail.

DON'T MISS: The Trout Creek bridge, at the current turnaround point south of Summerland, sits 238 feet above the canyon floor and provides spectacular views.

GETTING THERE: The Prairie Valley station is located off Highway 97 from either Rosedale Avenue or Prairie Valley Road. It is about a 10-minute drive from the highway.

LOCATION: 18404 Bathville Road, Summerland
PHONE: 877-494-8424 or 250-494-8422
WEBSITE: kettlevalleyrail.org
E-MAIL: form on website

# Rocky Mountaineer

Rocky Mountaineer

This premier rail tour company offers more than 65 unique rail experiences through the wild beauty of the Canadian Rockies and the Pacific Northwest. In addition to its signature destinations of Banff, Jasper, and Lake Louise, the company offers service to Seattle on its Coastal Passage route.

**CHOICES:** Rocky Mountaineer offers 2-day (or longer) all-daylight journeys over four routes. On First Passage to the West, you follow the route of early explorers over the Rockies from Vancouver to Banff or Lake Louise in Alberta. On Journey through the Clouds, you experience coastal mountains, Fraser Canyon, Hell's Gate, Pyramid Falls, and Mount Robson on the journey from Vancouver to Jasper, Alberta. The Rainforest to Gold Rush route takes you from Vancouver to Whistler through Gold Country to Quesnel for an overnight stay and then along the Fraser River to Jasper. The Coastal Passage route provides passengers with a 3-day trip from Seattle to the Canadian Rockies (or the opposite direction).

**WHEN TO GO:** Service begins in April and runs to October.

**GOOD TO KNOW:** The Jasper and Banff/Lake Louise trains are combined between Vancouver and Kamloops. Trains operating on the former British Columbia Railway north of Greater Vancouver arrive and depart from the vicinity of the former BCR station in North Vancouver.

**WORTH DOING:** Go for the gold and take advantage of the fancy digs and pampering with GoldLeaf service. It is a luxury train, after all. GoldLeaf service features bi-level dome coaches with full-length windows above, and gourmet cuisine served in the exclusive dining room below. You can also try SilverLeaf service, which is featured in a single-level, glass-domed coach.

**DON'T MISS:** All trips run both eastbound and westbound, and either direction offers spectacular scenery.

**GETTING THERE:** Scheduled motor coach service connects Jasper, Banff, and Whistler to the outside world. VIA Rail Canada provides rail service to and from Jasper, Kamloops, and Vancouver. Seattle is a stop on the Amtrak rail network.

**LOCATION:** 1755 Cottrell Street, Vancouver
**PHONE:** 877-460-3200 or 604-606-7245
**WEBSITE:** rockymountaineer.com
**E-MAIL:** reservations@rockymountaineer.com

# West Coast Railway Heritage Park

West Coast Railway Heritage Park

Heritage Park provides a home to the West Coast Railway Association's large collection of locomotives and rolling stock. Located in a beautiful 12-acre mountain valley setting, the museum offers visitors a chance to learn about railway history from 1920 to 1960 in Canada's westernmost province.

CHOICES: The park features a variety of railway stations and other buildings. You are also able to see railway equipment in various stages of restoration in the 1914 PGE car shop. The collection of more than 90 vintage railway cars and locomotives includes cabooses, snowplows, a restored 1890 business car, and the only surviving Pacific Great Western steam engine. A mini train ride circles the park.

WHEN TO GO: The park is open year-round, with a shorter schedule during winter. Summer months provide the least likelihood for an encounter with the area's famous "wet sunshine." The park holds various special events including days out with Thomas the Tank Engine and the Polar Express.

GOOD TO KNOW: The West Coast Railway Association also operates the Locomotive 374 Pavilion in Vancouver, which houses historic CP locomotive 374. The locomotive, built in 1886, brought the first transcontinental passenger train into the city.

WORTH DOING: Incorporate a visit to the museum with a scenic drive along the Sea to Sky Highway for a nice day-long family outing. The Sea to Sky Highway travels through five different biogeoclimatic zones, from coastal rain forest to mountain forest. This predominantly two-lane road goes from Vancouver to Whistler.

DON'T MISS: The park's 21,000-square-foot roundhouse displays various exhibits including Royal Hudson No. 2860, one of the last Royal Hudson locomotives built for the Canadian Pacific Railway by Montreal Locomotive Works in June 1940.

GETTING THERE: From Vancouver, it is about an hour's drive north on Highway 99 along spectacular Howe Sound, North America's southernmost fjord, to Squamish. Turn left on Industrial Way until Queens Way and then turn right and follow the signs.

**LOCATION:** 39645 Government Road, Squamish
**PHONE:** 604-524-1011 or 604-898-9336
**WEBSITE:** wcra.org
**E-MAIL:** info@wcra.org

# MANITOBA

## Prairie Dog Central Railway

Mark Perry

This railway's round trip over the former CN Oak Point Subdivision from the north side of the Manitoba capital to the towns of Grosse Isle or Warren offers a glimpse into prairie railroading of the past.

**CHOICES:** The train takes a leisurely trip through rural Manitoba, and you can travel in either open-vestibule or closed-vestibule coaches. The wooden coaches, built between 1901 and 1913, are fully restored and air-conditioned—when the windows are open. Power is provided by ex-CPR 4-4-0 steam locomotive No. 3, ex-BNSF GP9 No. 1685, or diesel No. 4138. Special events, including train robberies, take place throughout the season. You can also ride in an ex-CPR wood caboose or be an engineer for a day on a diesel. Vintage equipment can be seen around the shops, notably two ex-CPR G5 steam locomotives and a GE 35-ton diesel.

**WHEN TO GO:** Trains operate on Sundays during May and June, on Saturdays and Sundays July through September, and on weekends in late October for Halloween trains. Special runs also operate on Victoria Day, Canada Day, and other holidays.

**GOOD TO KNOW:** Ex-Winnipeg Hydro 4-4-0 No. 3 was built in 1882 by Dubs in Scotland and is one of the oldest operable engines in North America. The railway's station, constructed in 1910 by the Canadian Northern Railway, is a Canadian Heritage Railway Station. It was moved from St. James Street and renamed Inkster Junction Station.

**WORTH DOING:** During the stopover at Grosse Isle, take time to examine the displays of local crafts and home-baked goods and tour the old school. Grosse Isle is home to the 72-mile Prime Meridian Trail, a recreation trail built on an abandoned rail line.

**DON'T MISS:** Secure a ticket in either combine No. 104 or coach No. 105. These beautifully maintained relics are rolling time machines to another century.

**GETTING THERE:** Inkster Junction Station is located immediately north of Winnipeg's airport on Prairie Dog Trail. It is on the north side of Inkster Boulevard between Route 90 and Sturgeon Boulevard.

**LOCATION:** Prairie Dog Trail, Winnipeg
**PHONE:** 204-832-5259
**WEBSITE:** pdcrailway.com
**E-MAIL:** info@pdcrailway.com

# Winnipeg Railway Museum

Mark Perry

The Winnipeg Railway Museum takes visitors back to the historical first days of railroading across the vast western Canadian prairies. The museum's two tracks, located under the train shed at VIA Rail Canada's Union Station, host a variety of equipment, exhibits, and displays for all enthusiasts to enjoy.

CHOICES: The museum operates in the train shed of the grandiose Canadian Northern 1911-built Union Station. It contains various displays of both vintage steam and diesel locomotives, railbuses, passenger coaches, freight cars, cabooses, and many other Canadian Railway artifacts. A pair of restored vintage fire trucks that came from nearby CNR and CPR backshops are displayed. Various spreaders, snow dozers, and other equipment round out the collection.

WHEN TO GO: The museum is open year-round. It is open daily April through October. During the rest of the year, it is open Monday, Thursday, Saturday, and Sunday.

GOOD TO KNOW: Located in the heart of downtown Winnipeg, Union Station is still actively used by VIA Rail Canada's passenger trains. The CN's busy two-track Rivers Subdivision runs right next to the train shed.

WORTH DOING: A historic gathering place for centuries, the fantastic shopping, dining, and entertainment development is Winnipeg's number-one tourist attraction. Formerly, The Forks was a CNR rail yard, and the remaining historic railway buildings have been well preserved and upgraded. Railway equipment is preserved on the grounds, and a pristine CNR F unit is displayed inside the Children's Museum.

DON'T MISS: The museum features some notable railway equipment on display including the first steam engine in Manitoba, Canadian Pacific's wood-burning Baldwin *Countess of Dufferin*, and the unique CN GMD-1 1900, a steam generator equipped GMDL diesel that switched passengers cars around Union Station.

GETTING THERE: Winnipeg is 60 miles north of the North Dakota border on Highway 75. VIA Rail operates a cross-country passenger train from Vancouver and Toronto that stops in Winnipeg. Union Station is at the corner of Main Street and Broadway Avenue in downtown Winnipeg.

LOCATION: 123 Main Street, Winnipeg
PHONE: 204-942-4632
WEBSITE: wpgrailwaymuseum.com
E-MAIL: wpgrail@mts.net

# SASKATCHEWAN

## Rusty Relics Museum

Rusty Relics Museum portrays pioneer life in Saskatchewan. Housed in Carlyle's 1910 station, its collection features several buildings, machinery, and artifacts. Railway items include a caboose, a jigger, a tool shed, and a working telegraph. It is open Monday through Saturday June to September.

**LOCATION:** 115 Railway Avenue West, Carlyle
**PHONE:** 306-453-2266 or 306-453-2363
**WEBSITE:** rustyrelicsmuseum.com
**E-MAIL:** rustyrelicmuseum@sasktel.net

## Saskatchewan Railway Museum

This 7-acre museum contains more than 10 buildings, including a station, express shed, interlocking tower, and tool sheds, from the Canadian National, Canadian Pacific, Canadian Northern, and Grand Trunk Railways. On display are a variety of freight cars, passenger coaches, streetcars, cabooses, and a CPR S3 diesel locomotive. You can take a guided tour or explore the museum on your own. It is open Fridays through Sundays and holiday Mondays late May to September.

**LOCATION:** Highway 60, Saskatoon
**PHONE:** 306-382-9855
**WEBSITE:** saskrailmuseum.org
**E-MAIL:** srha@saskrailmuseum.org

## Western Development Museum

The WDM in Moose Jaw focuses on transportation, and it displays a passenger coach, Canadian Pacific station, and CPR locomotive 2634. It also offers train rides pulled by a Vulcan steam engine, the only operational steam locomotive in the province. The museum is open daily year-round, except for Mondays January through March.

**LOCATION:** 50 Diefenbaker Drive, Moose Jaw
**PHONE:** 306-693-5989
**WEBSITE:** wdm.ca
**E-MAIL:** moosejaw@wdm.ca

# Southern Prairie Railway

*Southern Prairie Railway*

**Located in southern Saskatchewan, this railway offers excursions across the prairies, not unlike the ones early settlers would have taken. The train features a 1922 Pullman passenger coach and a 1945 GE diesel locomotive.**

**CHOICES:** Trains leave from a restored Canadian Pacific station, and several uniquely themed excursions are available. The 2.5-hour round-trip Heritage Train runs west along an old CP branch line to Horizon, where tour guides take you through a 1920s grain elevator. On the fourth Saturday of the month, you can ride to Pangman for a trip to a farmers market.

**WHEN TO GO:** Heritage Trains operate Saturdays and Sundays from mid-June through September. On select dates, you can sample a one-of-a-kind pitchfork fondue meal or a turn-of-the century settler's supper. Other specials include brunch trains, train robberies, 1920s rum runner trains, and an all-day train.

**GOOD TO KNOW:** The CP train station was built in 1912 and moved 150 miles from Simpson, Saskatchewan, to Ogema.

**WORTH DOING:** About an hour's drive south of Ogema, you'll find the Big Muddy Badlands, which features cone-shaped hills, steep cliffs, caves, and unique weathered formations, highlighted by Castle Butte.

**DON'T MISS:** The nearby Deep South Pioneer Museum features 30 buildings that re-create a pioneer village. The museum also includes more than 150 tractors and pieces of farm equipment. You can also take a stroll down Ogema's historic Main Street.

**GETTING THERE:** Ogema is about 90 minutes south of either Moose Jaw or Regina and about 4 hours northwest of Minot, N.D.

**LOCATION:** 401 Railway Avenue, Ogema
**PHONE:** 306-459-7808
**WEBSITE:** southernprairierailway.com
**E-MAIL:** form on website

# YUKON

## Copperbelt Railway & Mining Museum

Located in copper country, the museum's exhibits focus on the area's mining and rail history. You can take a ride through the 10-acre park on a passenger car pulled by a diesel mining engine. The museum is open daily mid-May until September, and the train ride runs every 30 minutes.

**LOCATION:** Mile 91928 Alaska Highway, Whitehorse
**PHONE:** 867-667-6198
**WEBSITE:** yukonrails.com
**E-MAIL:** copperbelt@yukonrails.com

## Whitehorse Waterfront Trolley

In downtown Whitehorse, you can ride a restored 1925 trolley along the city's waterfront. The trolley departs from Rotary Peace Park and travels to Spook Creek. Along the way, you can stop at the MacBride Museum of Yukon History, White Pass & Yukon depot, visitor information center, and SS *Klondike* National Historic Site. You'll also hear stories about the area's history. The trolley operates daily mid-May into September.

**LOCATION:** 1127 First Avenue, Whitehorse
**PHONE:** 867-667 6355
**WEBSITE:** yukonrails.com
**E-MAIL:** trolley@yukonrails.com

Le cheval de

The iron horse

La ruée vers l'oues

Go west young ma

# REGION 12

**NEW BRUNSWICK**

1   McAdam Railway Station

2   New Brunswick Railway Museum

3   Shogomoc Historical Railway Site

**NEWFOUNDLAND**

4   Railway Coastal Museum

5   Railway Society of Newfoundland Train Site

**NOVA SCOTIA**

6   Museum of Industry

7   Sydney & Louisburg Railway Museum

**ONTARIO**

8   Agawa Canyon Tour Train

9   Canada Science and Technology Museum

10  Canada Southern Railway Station

11  Chatham Railroad Museum

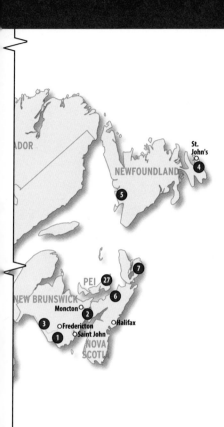

# NEW BRUNSWICK

## McAdam Railway Station

Built in 1900, the McAdam Railway Station has been restored and is a heritage railway station that contains a telegraph office, rail artifacts, and photos. Guided tours are available July through September. You'll hear about German spies, early rail travel, and a shooting in the waiting room. Also be sure to try a slice of railroad pie.

**LOCATION:** 96 Saunders Road, McAdam
**PHONE:** 506-784-3101
**WEBSITE:** mcadamstation.ca
**E-MAIL:** info@ mcadamstation.ca

## New Brunswick Railway Museum

The museum contains more than 20 pieces of rolling stock that includes locomotives, passenger cars, freight cars, maintenance-of-way equipment, and cabooses. Some of the cars are open for viewing. The museum also displays a speeder car, telegraph office, and smaller artifacts. It is open June through September.

**LOCATION:** 2847 Main Street, Hillsborough
**PHONE:** 506-734-3195
**WEBSITE:** nbrm.ca
**E-MAIL:** info@nbrm.ca

## Shogomoc Historical Railway Site

In the French Fry Capital of the World, you can take a guided tour of a 1914 restored CPR train station, which contains railway artifacts and displays. Three renovated CPR passenger cars are on site. One displays additional artifacts and another is a restaurant. The station is open June to September, and the dining car is open all year.

**LOCATION:** 9207 Main Street, Florenceville-Bristol
**PHONE:** 506-392-8226 or 506-392-6763 (off season)
**WEBSITE:** florencevillebristol.ca
**E-MAIL:** tourism@florencevillebristol.ca

# NEWFOUNDLAND

## Railway Coastal Museum

The Railway Coastal Museum is housed in the restored 1903 Riverhead station and contains a large collection of items relating to Newfoundland's rail and coastal boat services. You can walk along the platform where passengers boarded the *Newfie Bullet* and examine the rolling stock displayed in the train park. The museum is open year-round, daily during summer.

**LOCATION:** 495 Water Street West, St. John's
**PHONE:** 866-600-7245 or 709-724-5929
**WEBSITE:** railwaycoastalmuseum.ca
**E-MAIL:** info@railwaycoastalmuseum.ca

## Railway Society of Newfoundland Train Site

The society maintains a collection of narrow gauge rolling stock from the Newfoundland Railway. Several trains are displayed including the *Newfie Bullet*, once Newfoundland's fastest passenger train. Steam locomotive No. 593 is displayed with a representative selection of cars. A snowplow train is also featured. You can walk through all the railcars. The museum is open daily during the summer.

**LOCATION:** Marine Drive and Station Road, Corner Brook
**PHONE:** 709-634-2720 (in season)
**WEBSITE:** cornerbrook.com

# NOVA SCOTIA

## Museum of Industry

Through its artifacts, big and small, the museum tells the story of how Nova Scotia changed through industry and technology. It features demonstrations of a steam engine, printing press, and sawmill. On display are nine locomotives, including *Samson* and *Albion,* two of the oldest surviving locomotives in the world. *Samson* was built in 1838 by Thomas Hackworth. It is open daily May through October and weekdays November through April.

**LOCATION:** 147 N. Foord Street, Stellarton
**PHONE:** 902-755-5425
**WEBSITE:** museumofindustry.novascotia.ca
**E-MAIL:** industry@gov.ns.ca

## Sydney & Louisburg Railway Museum

The museum features rolling stock, artifacts, and photographs relating to the Sydney & Louisburg Railway. Housed in an 1895 S&L station, the museum also contains historical exhibits about Louisburg. An original freight shed and roundhouse also contain displays. You can also view Nova Scotia's oldest passenger coach. It is open weekdays in June and daily during July and August.

**LOCATION:** 7330 Main Street, Louisbourg
**PHONE:** 902-733-2720
**WEBSITE:** facebook.com/slrailway
**E-MAIL:** slrailwaymuseum@gmail.com

# ONTARIO

## Canada Science and Technology Museum

The museum is scheduled to reopen in November 2017. (Check the website for updates.) It will feature 80,000 square feet of new exhibition space and contain five galleries. The museum's rail collection features 1,000 artifacts ranging from photos to locomotives and dates back to the early days of Canadian railway history.

**LOCATION:** 2421 Lancaster Road, Ottawa
**PHONE:** 866-442-4416 or 613-991-3044
**WEBSITE:** cstmuseum.techno-science.ca
**E-MAIL:** contact@techno-science.ca

## Canada Southern Railway Station

Built in the 1870s, this restored Italianate-style station houses the North America Railway Hall of Fame, which features exhibits on its various inductees. It also includes artifacts from the station's history. Rail-related and other events take place at the station throughout the year. Tours are available weekdays.

**LOCATION:** 750 Talbot Street, St. Thomas
**PHONE:** 519-633-2535
**WEBSITE:** casostation.ca
**E-MAIL:** tourismandevents@narhf.org

## Chatham Railroad Museum

Housed in a retired 1955 Canadian National baggage car, the Chatham Railroad Museum includes interactive exhibits and photos on local as well as national and international railroad history. Located across from the VIA rail station, the museum is open Tuesdays through Saturdays during the summer.

**LOCATION:** 2 McLean Street, Chatham
**PHONE:** 519-352-3097
**WEBSITE:** chathamrailroadmuseum.ca
**E-MAIL:** crms@mnsi.net

# Fort Erie Railway Museum

This museum site features the restored Grand Trunk's Ridgeway station, which houses historic furnishings, telegraph equipment, tools, and other artifacts. Canadian National Railway steam engine No. 6218, a 4-8-4 Northern type, is the museum's centerpiece. Also on display are a fireless engine, a CN caboose, and other equipment. The CN's B-1 station that monitored traffic over the International Railway Bridge is also on site. It is open daily Victoria Day weekend to Labor Day.

**LOCATION:** 400 Central Avenue, Fort Erie
**PHONE:** 905-894-5322
**WEBSITE:** forterie.ca/pages/museum

# Komoka Railway Museum

Komoka's restored Canadian National station houses a collection of artifacts and photos dedicated to rail history in the area. It includes tools, lanterns, and a tiny flag stop station. Also on display are a 1913 Shay locomotive and a steel-sided baggage car. The museum is open Friday through Monday July to September and on Saturdays the rest of the year. It is closed January through March.

**LOCATION:** 133 Queen Street, Komoka
**PHONE:** 519-657-1912
**WEBSITE:** komokarailmuseum.ca
**E-MAIL:** station-master@komokarailmuseum.ca

# Memory Junction Museum

Memory Junction features several structures including an 1857 Grand Trunk station, a baggage shed, and an unloading depot. A rare N-4-a locomotive is on display along with a restored 1929 wooden caboose and other railcars. The museum includes local historical and railway artifacts. It is open Thursday through Saturday June through September.

**LOCATION:** 60 Maplewood Street, Brighton
**PHONE:** 613-475-0379
**WEBSITE:** memoryjunctionmuseum.ca
**E-MAIL:** re.bangay@sympatico.ca

# Muskoka Heritage Place

Muskoka Heritage Place contains the Muskoka Museum, Pioneer Village, and Portage Flyer, which can be pulled by a restored 1902 steam locomotive or a diesel engine. After boarding at the train station, you travel along the Muskoka River to Fairy Lake. The train station doubles as a museum with exhibits focusing on local steamships and locomotives. You can enjoy the entire site or just ride the Portage Flyer. The museum is open year-round, while the village and train operate mid-May into October.

**LOCATION:** 88 Brunel Road, Huntsville
**PHONE:** 705-789-7576
**WEBSITE:** muskokaheritageplace.org
**E-MAIL:** form on website

# Northern Ontario Railroad Museum & Heritage Centre

This museum emphasizes railroading history in northern Ontario and includes additional exhibits on mining and lumbering. Artifacts are displayed in the Museum House, which was used by the Canadian National as a superintendent's residence. In nearby Prescott Park, it displays a U-1-f bullet-nosed steam locomotive, Temiskaming & Northern Ontario steam locomotive No. 219, a wooden CNR caboose, and other equipment.

**LOCATION:** 26 Bloor Street, Capreol
**PHONE:** 705-858-5050
**WEBSITE:** normhc.ca
**E-MAIL:** info@normhc.ca

# Port Stanley Terminal Rail

Excursion trains depart from a historic station next to the King George lift bridge. Early diesel locomotives pull open and closed coaches, some that have been converted from cabooses. Regular 1-hour excursions run to Whytes Park. A variety of special trains run during the season, and some travel the entire line into St. Thomas. You can view the fleet of equipment in the yard just north of the station. Excursions operate April through December, with an expanded schedule during July and August. Trains travel along the entire line to Parkside on Saturdays in July and August.

**LOCATION:** 309 Bridge Street, Port Stanley
**PHONE:** 877-244-4478 or 519-782-3730
**WEBSITE:** pstr.on.ca
**E-MAIL:** info@pstr.on.ca

# Railway Museum of Eastern Ontario

This museum is housed in a restored 1914 Canadian Northern Railway station that contains artifacts relating to the Canadian Pacific, Grand Trunk, Canadian National, and other railways. The national historic site displays a 1912 steam locomotive, a CP diesel, passenger cars, a CN snowplow, and a unique dental car. You can spend a night in a caboose, take a train ride, or partake in other activities. The museum is open daily mid-May through mid-October.

**LOCATION:** 90 William Street West, Smiths Falls
**PHONE:** 613-283-5696
**WEBSITE:** rmeo.org
**E-MAIL:** info@rmeo.org

# School on Wheels Railcar Museum

This car was one of seven railway schools that served children and adults along northern Ontario railways. When touring the car, you will walk through the classroom and living quarters and view historical videos, children's activities, artifacts, and photos. It is open Thursdays through Sundays and holiday Mondays Victoria Day weekend through September.

**LOCATION:** 76 Victoria Terrace, Clinton
**PHONE:** 519-482-3997
**WEBSITE:** museumsontario.ca
**E-MAIL:** cnrschoolonwheels@gmail.com

# Toronto Railway Museum

The museum features a variety of railroad components including the John Street roundhouse, an interlocking tower, and operational turntable. In addition to viewing historic rail equipment and displays, visitors can check out the cab of a steam locomotive, tour Roundhouse Park, and ride on a miniature railway. It is open Wednesdays through Sundays.

**LOCATION:** 255 Bremner Boulevard, Toronto
**PHONE:** 416-214-9229
**WEBSITE:** trha.ca
**E-MAIL:** info@trha.ca

# Waterloo Central Railway

The railway operates excursion trains through southern Ontario behind a 60-ton diesel locomotive. The railway's restored steam engine may also run. You can take the entire 12-mile round trip or detrain at St. Jacobs, where you can look around, visit the railway museum, and take a later train back. Market trains run Tuesdays, Thursdays, and Saturdays April through October. The railway also operates various special trains throughout the year.

**LOCATION:** 10 Father David Bauer Drive, Waterloo
**PHONE:** 888-899-2757
**WEBSITE:** waterloocentralrailway.com
**E-MAIL:** form on website

# York-Durham Heritage Railway

The railway operates excursions on Sundays from June through October between Stouffville and Uxbridge. Diesel locomotives pull passenger coaches built between the 1920s and the 1950s. The Uxbridge station, which was built in 1904, contains displays of rail artifacts. There are numerous special events, and extra trains run in fall. Caboose rides are also available. Trips leave from both stations.

**LOCATION:** 6176 Main Street, Stouffville
**PHONE:** 905-852-3696
**WEBSITE:** ydhr.ca
**E-MAIL:** ydhr@ydhr.ca

# Agawa Canyon Tour Train

Agawa Canyon Tour Train

The tour train offers the chance to ride into unspoiled Canadian wilderness from Sault Ste. Marie more than 100 miles north into Ontario as far as the spectacular Agawa Canyon. Along the way, you journey over tall trestles, alongside mountain lakes and rivers, and through granite rock formations and breathtaking forests.

**CHOICES:** The tour train takes you to Agawa Canyon and back on a one-day round trip. En route to the canyon, the beauty of the area will unfold through the large windows of the recently refurbished coaches. In the canyon, you'll have 90 minutes to explore: take a scenic walk on trails to several waterfalls, climb 300 stairs to the inspiring lookout perched 250 feet above the canyon floor, or enjoy a picnic lunch. Packages with Sault Ste. Marie accommodations are available.

**WHEN TO GO:** The train runs from late June through the long weekend in October. Most trains are full throughout the season, and fall color in the region is a huge tourist draw, so it is best to plan ahead for any trip.

**GOOD TO KNOW:** Aboard the train, a GPS-triggered narration, available in five languages, highlights points of interest and shares some of the rich history of the region. Also, locomotive-mounted cameras provide an "engineer's eye view" on monitors installed throughout the coaches.

**WORTH DOING:** There is much to do in Sault Ste. Marie, such as strolling along the boardwalk, visiting a casino, or touring the locks.

**DON'T MISS:** Find a good vantage point at mile post 19, where the railroad crosses the Montreal River on a huge curving trestle perched atop a dam. Then when the train descends into the canyon, keep a lookout as you travel 500 feet down to the canyon's floor.

**GETTING THERE:** Sault Ste. Marie is located at I-75 and Highway 17. The train leaves from the depot downtown, and signs will point the way to the depot.

**LOCATION:** 129 Bay Street, Sault Ste. Marie
**PHONE:** 800-242-9287
**WEBSITE:** agawatrain.com
**E-MAIL:** agawacanyontours@cn.ca

# Credit Valley Explorer

Credit Valley Explorer

The Credit Valley Explorer offers a scenic round trip between Orangeville and Brampton over a route that was completed in 1879. The ride, aboard 1950s rail coaches, takes you through rolling hills and deep valleys, over the Credit River, and across a 1,146-foot-long trestle bridge.

**CHOICES:** The regular 3-hour excursion departs Orangeville and travels through the Caledon Hills, Cataract, and the forks of the Credit River to Inglewood and Brampton before returning. Tours include meal service with complimentary refreshments, interpretive commentary, and a mile-by-mile printed guidebook.

**WHEN TO GO:** Scenic excursions operate year-round, and different times of year offer different experiences. Late spring and early summer give you a chance to see the countryside before the foliage becomes dense. Autumn is busy, and the trains are full, but the fall colors are spectacular.

**GOOD TO KNOW:** You can take a walking tour through Orangeville's historic downtown or examine the unique Art Walk of Tree Sculptures.

**WORTH DOING:** The Hills of the Headwaters is a great area for experiencing the great outdoors, no matter what the season. Hiking trails abound, and you can also fish, golf, and ski in a variety of locations.

**DON'T MISS:** Most mid-day trips stop in Inglewood, so you can explore this quaint rural community.

**GETTING THERE:** Orangeville is about an hour's drive from Toronto in southern Ontario. Trains depart from the railway yard on Town Line Road. From Highway 10, take Broadway to Town Line Road and turn left. Follow Town Line Road to the entrance.

**LOCATION:** 49 Townline Road, Orangeville
**PHONE:** 888-346-0046
**WEBSITE:** creditvalleyexplorer.com
**E-MAIL:** form on website

# Elgin County Railway Museum

Elgin County Railway Museum

The railroad has been a part of life in St. Thomas since 1856. Over the years, a total of 26 railways have passed through town, helping it garner the moniker of the Railway Capital of Canada. Located in the former Michigan Central locomotive shops, the Elgin County Railway Museum helps preserve and display the railway heritage of St. Thomas and the surrounding area.

**CHOICES:** As a working museum, equipment restoration is ongoing, and you can occasionally catch a glimpse of the volunteers in action. The museum displays a variety of equipment including locomotives, cabooses, and passenger cars. Highlights are a CP diesel locomotive, a CNR Hudson, a Grand Trunk Western caboose, a Pullman sleeper, and an electric-powered car that transported children to school in the 1920s. In St. Thomas, the BX interlocking tower is available for touring during special events.

**WHEN TO GO:** The museum is open year-round. It is open Tuesday through Sunday between Victoria Day and Labor Day weekends. From September to Canadian Thanksgiving, it is open Wednesday through Saturday. The rest of the year, it is open Saturdays only. Thomas the Tank Engine stops by several weekends in July, and the museum hosts various events during the year.

**GOOD TO KNOW:** A short drive from the regional center of London, St. Thomas is a small town with all services. Its Iron Horse Festival takes place in August.

**WORTH DOING:** Combining a visit to the museum along with a ride on the nearby Port Stanley Terminal Rail makes for an interesting day of exploring the preserved rails of southern Ontario.

**DON'T MISS:** Climb aboard the legendary 1930 CN Hudson 5700 steam engine that is on display.

**GETTING THERE:** VIA Rail Canada offers scheduled passenger service through London to the north. If driving, the museum is 2 hours from Toronto, 2 hours from the U.S. border at Detroit, Buffalo, or Niagara Falls, and 1 hour from Sarnia and Port Huron. Once in St. Thomas, you will find the museum on Wellington Street between Ross Street and First Avenue.

**LOCATION:** 225 Wellington Street, St. Thomas
**PHONE:** 519-637-6284
**WEBSITE:** ecrm5700.org
**E-MAIL:** thedispatcher@ecrm5700.org

# Halton County Radial Railway

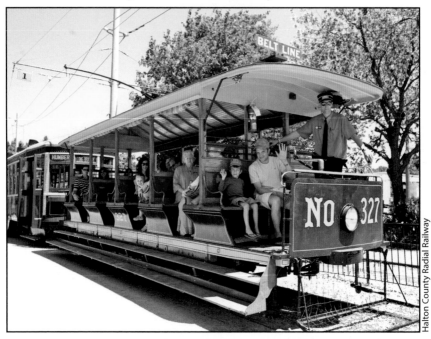

Halton County Radial Railway

Canada's preeminent trolley museum brings the streetcar era to life with the help of the largest collection of operable streetcars in the country. Its streetcars, radial cars, and work cars operate over a rebuilt portion of a long-abandoned interurban railway.

**CHOICES:** Streetcars, such as Toronto Transit Commission No. 2894, travel over a short track on a 20-minute ride through a hardwood forest. The railway features four display barns filled with 75 pieces of equipment that, in addition to streetcars, includes freight cars, passenger coaches, buses, and a locomotive or two. Most of the streetcars were built in the early 20th century.

**WHEN TO GO:** Streetcars operate on weekends and holidays from May to October and daily during July and August. A number of special events are incorporated into the operating season.

**GOOD TO KNOW:** Admission includes unlimited streetcar rides and access to the exhibits displayed in the carbarns and Rockwood Station, which was built in 1912 for the Grand Trunk Railway. You can also enjoy a picnic lunch on the railway's grounds.

**WORTH DOING:** On Labor Day weekend, steam fans can take in Milton's steam-era event that features steam-powered equipment in action, a parade of tractors and antique autos, and tractor pulls.

**DON'T MISS:** Take a break on your trolley ride with a stop at the ice cream shop at the outer loop and return to the main grounds on a different car.

**GETTING THERE:** Milton is 25 miles west of Toronto on Highway 401. From Highway 401, take Exit 312 and go north on Guelph Line until you reach the museum. It is also the the terminus of Toronto's Milton commuter train line.

**LOCATION:** 13629 Guelph Line, Milton
**PHONE:** 519-856-9802
**WEBSITE:** hcry.org
**E-MAIL:** streetcar@hcry.org

# South Simcoe Railway

South Simcoe Railway

The South Simcoe Railway operates over 4 miles of former Canadian National trackage through rolling countryside north of Toronto. Excursions are powered by a 1948 diesel locomotive or steam locomotive No. 136, which was built in 1883.

**CHOICES:** Regular excursions from Tottenham to Beeton and back take about an hour. As the train rolls through Beeton Creek Valley, the conductor provides an informative commentary. Passengers ride in restored 1920s steel heavyweight coaches. Special trains include the Easter Express, Haunted Halloween Adventure, and Santa Claus Express.

**WHEN TO GO:** The railway runs multiple trips on Sundays and on holiday Mondays between Victoria Day weekend and Canadian Thanksgiving. It also operates on some Mondays and Tuesdays in July and August and weekends in October for viewing the fall colors.

**GOOD TO KNOW:** The town of Tottenham has a variety of quaint shops and eateries. Across the road from the railway is Tottenham Conservation Area, a park that offers swimming, camping, fishing, and hiking.

**WORTH DOING:** For a unique combination rail-water excursion, the RMS *Segwun*, the oldest operating steamship in North America, sails July and August on the Muskoka Lakes, about a 2-hour drive north to Gravenhurst.

**DON'T MISS:** Take one rail trip and then follow another for some great photos. The engine faces south into the sun, and the relatively slow pace of the train makes it easy to follow.

**GETTING THERE:** No public transit is available to this neck of the woods. Tottenham is about an hour's drive north from Toronto. From Highway 400, take Highway 9 west 9 miles to Tottenham Road and turn right. Continue into downtown Tottenham and turn left onto Mill Street to reach the station.

**LOCATION:** Mill Street West, Tottenham
**PHONE:** 905-936-5815
**WEBSITE:** southsimcoerailway.ca
**E-MAIL:** info@southsimcoerailway.ca

# PRINCE EDWARD ISLAND

## Elmira Railway Museum

The museum offers a look at railroading on the island in the early 1900s. It features a station house with a re-created station master's office and waiting room as well as displays and artifacts. A miniature train operates around the museum, and various special events take place on the outdoor stage, which was built from the base of a flatcar. The museum is open weekdays June and September and daily during July and August.

**LOCATION:** 457 Elmira Road, Elmira
**PHONE:** 902-357-7234 or 902-368-6600 (off season)
**WEBSITE:** peimuseum.com
**E-MAIL:** elmira@gov.pe.ca

# QUEBEC

## Exporail

The largest collection of railway equipment in the country is well worth a stop for anyone interested in Canadian railways and rail transit. Locomotives, rolling stock, and streetcars from many parts of the country tell of the evolution of both industries.

**CHOICES:** The museum's collection boasts 160 railway vehicles. Special events and exhibits are scheduled throughout the year geared toward modelers and transit enthusiasts. The museum has several train ride options. A streetcar runs daily between May and October. On Sundays May to October, you can take a short ride on a passenger train. The main building contains only a portion of the collection, and you can explore the rest of the site from stops along the streetcar loop. You'll be able to see Barrington Station, a restored, rural flag stop station from southwestern Quebec.

**WHEN TO GO:** The museum is open daily between mid-May and early September. During September and October, it is open Wednesday through Sunday. The remainder of the year, the museum is open on weekends, for spring break, and around Christmas.

**GOOD TO KNOW:** Stop, Look, Listen: Incoming Train? is a new permanent exhibition on railway safety that provides an interactive, educational, fun and preventative railway safety experience for young visitors and their parents.

**WORTH DOING:** There is much to see and do in Montreal. You can discover centuries of history in Old Montreal, explore Olympic Park and Mount Royal, or take in one of its many festivals and international events.

**DON'T MISS:** Walk through an observation pit under a CP Royal Hudson and an LNER A4 Pacific in the Grand Gallery of the Angus Pavillion.

**GETTING THERE:** The museum is located 12 miles from downtown Montreal. Amtrak's *Adirondack* connects the city with the rest of its network in Albany, N.Y. CIT Roussillon provides bus service near the museum, and AMT provides commuter rail. On Saint-Pierre Street, a locomotive marks the entrance to Exporail's parking lot.

**LOCATION:** 110 Saint-Pierre Street, Saint-Constant
**PHONE:** 450-632-2410
**WEBSITE:** exporail.org
**E-MAIL:** info@exporail.org

# Orford Express

Orford Express

Enjoy the eye-catching scenery of Quebec's eastern townships from the only dinner train in the province as it travels Central Maine & Quebec rails between Magog and Sherbrooke.

**CHOICES:** The dinner train is made up of a pair of converted RDCs and a dome car led by either an FL9 or a unique M-420 TR locomotive. Service options include dining in the main car, the salon section of the lounge, and the panoramic section of the lounge car. In addition to dinner outings, brunch and lunch excursions are also offered. Trains begin running in mid-May and go through mid-October, and on summer days, Wednesday through Sunday, you'll find at least one type of train in operation.

**WHEN TO GO:** While the long days of summer offer the maximum daylight viewing, the often spectacular fall colors in the surrounding hills are a delight to behold.

**GOOD TO KNOW:** A variety of packages including local accommodations is available, lessening the chance of nocturnal large wild-life encounters after evening trips.

**WORTH DOING:** You can incorporate the dinner train into a long weekend of exploring the region, while including stops at Exporail in suburban Montreal or the hot air balloon festival in St Jean that takes place each August.

**DON'T MISS:** Upper level dome seating offers an unparalleled view of the surrounding countryside, not regularly seen since the days when the Canadian Pacific's Atlantic Limited traveled these same rails.

**GETTING THERE:** Located at the head of Lake Memphramagog, the Orford Express station in Magog is 75 miles from greater Montreal via Highway 10 and is also served by intercity bus. Magog can also be reached from upstate Vermont across the lake by private boat.

**LOCATION:** Quai MacPherson Pointe Merry, Magog
**PHONE:** 866-575-8081 or 819-575-8081
**WEBSITE:** orfordexpress.com
**E-MAIL:** info@ orfordexpress.com

# Index

# G

# H

# I

# S

## TOURIST RAILROADS AND MUSEUMS

## RAILROAD ASSOCIATIONS

## RAILROAD EQUIPMENT SALES & SERVICES

## TRAVEL

# A Beautiful Mountain Adventure by Rail...

*A partnership of:*

HISTORY Colorado **&** Historic Rail Adventures

# MONTICELLO
# RAILWAY
# MUSEUM

Monticello, IL • www.mrym.org

## RIDE VINTAGE TRAINS
### *in Central Illinois*

For more details and complete schedules go to ***www.mrym.org***. "Like" us on Facebook!

The museum is located at I-72, Exit No.166; take the frontage road (Iron Horse Place) to the museum, or for fuel and the Best Western Gateway Inn. Parking is free and downtown Monticello has lots of good dining.

Charter a whole train or one of our dining cars for your group. Our popular "Throttle Time" lets you run a diesel locomotive as the engineer.

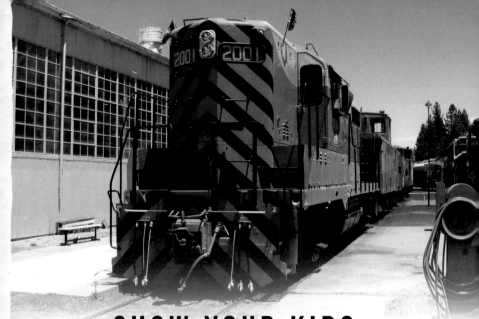

# SHOW YOUR KIDS
## NOT ALL TRAIN SETS COME IN A BOX

Discover the Western Pacific Railroad Museum, where you can experience hands-on rail history. Home to North America's largest and most complete collection of Western Pacific trains, the Western Pacific Railroad Museum has over 150 pieces of rolling stock. Tour the vintage passenger cars, and climb aboard to ride the trains and even operate a locomotive.

Located in California's beautiful Feather River Country, the Western Pacific Railroad Museum offers train rides each weekend from Memorial Day to Labor Day, and features Pumpkin Trains in October and Santa Trains in December. Reservations are recommended for Run-A-Locomotive. For more information, call 530-832-4131, or visit www.WPLives.org.

### ADMISSION
Adults 19 and up $ 8.00
Youth 4-18 $ 4.00
Children under 3 FREE
Family Pass $20.00

### MUSEUM HOURS
Shop the museum store and visit the museum
April 1 – 30 Thursday – Sunday, 10 AM – 4 PM
May 4 – Sept 9 Daily 10 AM – 4 PM
Sept 10 – Oct 13 Thursday – Sunday, 10 AM – 4 PM

**WPRM**
Western Pacific Railroad Museum
PORTOLA

www.wplives.org
700 Western Pacific Way near Old Town, Portola, California
Western Pacific Railroad Museum is operated by the Feather River Rail Society

# The Galveston Railroad Museum
## www.galvestonrrmuseum.com

**FREE PARKING!**

### 2602 Santa Fe Place • Galveston, Texas 77550
### (409) 765-5700

Location of the original Gulf, Colorado, and Santa Fe Passenger Union Depot in Downtown Galveston, Texas. The museum features five acres, including 50 pieces of rolling stock, model trains and numerous exhibits. Home of the Santa Fe Warbonnets, the largest railroad museum in the Southwest.

- Open Seven Days A Week
- Summer: 10 AM-5 PM
- Winter: 9 AM-4 PM
- Train Rides Saturdays
  11 AM-2 PM
  *Weather Permitting*

# RIDE THE TRAIN

Take a 55-minute, 7-mile round-trip journey through rural Wisconsin countryside aboard century-old railcars!

View the FREE museum with railroad displays and restored railway equipment!

| | | |
|---|---|---|
| OPEN 7 DAYS/WEEK: | June 3–Sept. 4, 2017 | |
| OPEN WEEKENDS: | May 13–Oct. 15, 2017 | **20 MILES FROM WIS. DELLS** |
| DEPARTURES: | 11 am, 1 pm, & 3 pm | |
| MUSEUM HOURS: | 9:30 am – 5:00 pm | |
| | *on days trains operate* | |

*Schedules subject to change. Times vary during special events.*
**Call or visit website for latest schedules**

**Also join us for these events:**
Vintage Railcar Tours
Autumn Color Weekend™
Pumpkin Special™
Santa Express™
Snow Train™
*and Onboard Dining trains*

# MID-CONTINENT RAILWAY MUSEUM
### (608) 522-4261 -or- (800) 930-1385    www.midcontinent.org
### E8948 Museum Road North Freedom, WI 53951

# ·1880 TRAIN·

*The best vacations are*
# POWERED BY STEAM.

CELEBRATING
**60**
SIXTY YEARS

BLACK HILLS CENTRAL RAILROAD

**RESERVATIONS - 1880TRAIN.COM**

*Departures daily from Hill City & Keystone, SD   Early May - Mid October*
*Book early- trains sell out!*

OLDEST CONTINUOUSLY OPERATING STANDARD GAUGE EXCURSION TRAIN IN THE WORLD

# Travel Through Time On Indiana's Most Scenic Railroad

## Whitewater Valley Railroad
### Grand Central Station
### 455 Market St., Connersville, IN 47331

# 765-825-2054

Celebrating over 40 years of Operations. The Whitewater Valley Railroad is an operating railroad museum dedicated to the preservation of a historic branch line railroad, to the restoration of railroad equipment, and to the conduct of railroad educational programs operated by trained volunteers.

The Whitewater Valley Railroad is a Not For Profit 501c3 Organization.

Ride the train, rain or shine, as it departs Grand Central Station in Connersville, IN at 12:01 pm every Saturday, Sunday and Holidays between May and October. Two hour layover in Metamora.

 Find us on **Facebook**   **You Tube**

**FOLLOW US ON** twitter

Train Excursions and Special Events are available throughout the year. Our trains are also available for charter. contact us for more information.

Come and see where the Red Diamonds still work the rails. Ex Cincinnati Union Terminal #25, the last remaining 750 hp unit in existence and only one of four Lima-Hamilton diesels to survive.

www.officialbestof.com

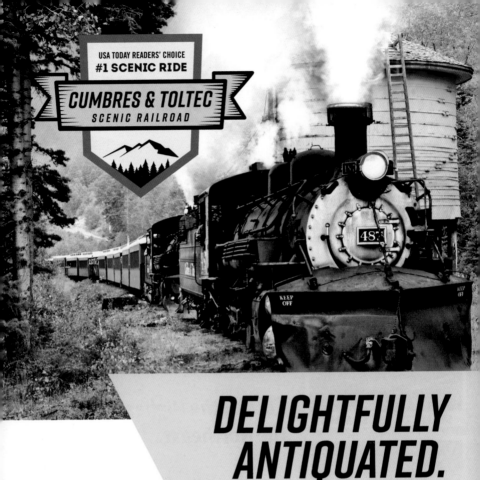

**USA TODAY READERS' CHOICE**
**#1 SCENIC RIDE**

**CUMBRES & TOLTEC**
SCENIC RAILROAD

# DELIGHTFULLY ANTIQUATED.

Let our coal-fired steam engine take you to another century and beyond.
Into an unspoiled West of simplicity, natural beauty, and authenticity.
Climb aboard our national historic landmark and you'll zig zag along
the Colorado and New Mexico border through steep mountain canyons,
the high desert, and lush meadows. It's an experience that's completely
at odds with the modern world. And better for it.

**BOOK NOW AT CUMBRESTOLTEC.COM   1-888-286-2737**

*Cumbres & Toltec*

ride the world famous

# SKUNK TRAIN

SKUNKTRAIN.COM | 707.964.6371 | FORT BRAGG & WILLITS, CA

# MODERN DAY RAIL ADVENTURES
## for the Historic Train Lover

# PROUD MEMBERS OF THE
# AMERICAN HERITAGE RAILWAYS FAMILY

Durango & Silverton Narrow Gauge Railroad | *Durango, CO*
Great Smoky Mountains Railroad | *Bryson City, NC*
Mt. Rainier Railroad | *Elbe, WA*

AMERICA'S RAILROAD
DURANGO & SILVERTON
NARROW GAUGE RAILROAD & MUSEUM
*Established 1881*

888-872-4607
DurangoTrain.com

The D&SNGRR was named the
**BEST TRAIN EXPERIENCE**
by *Sunset Magazine* in 2016

The Best Way to see the
Great Smoky Mountains of
Western North Carolina

Charles Snodgrass

GREAT SMOKY
MOUNTAINS
RAILROAD

800-872-4681
GSMR.com

Experience Living History
at Mt. Rainier Railroad and
Logging Museum

MT RAINIER RAILROAD
AND LOGGING MUSEUM

888-STEAM-11
MtRainierRailroad.com

Bob Harbison

# AMERICA'S
# ILLINOIS RAILWAY MUSEUM
## LARGEST

# SEE, RIDE AND EXPLORE AMERICA'S LARGEST RAILWAY MUSEUM!

The **Illinois Railway Museum** is composed of many collections representing different aspects of railroading in the United States. Locomotives and cars, artifacts such as buildings, signals and much, much more!

- Over 400 Railroad & Transportation vehicles operating and on display!
- Ride trolleys, interurbans, & coaches on our railroad!
- Explore the displays in car barns and open railyards

*Hours of Operation:*
*Sundays: April - October:*
*10:30 a.m. to 5 p.m.*
*Saturdays: May - October:*
*10:30 a.m. to 5 p.m.*
*Weekdays: Memorial Day*
*- Labor Day: 10 a.m. to 4 p.m.*

ILLINOIS RAILWAY MUSEUM

For Information: Call **1-800-BIG-RAIL** or visit: **www.irm.org**
7000 Olson Rd., Union IL 60180 (Take I90 to Hwy 20 Exit— Follow the Signs)

# THE SCENIC RAILWAY OF THE WORLD

**WHITE PASS & YUKON ROUTE**

GATEWAY TO THE YUKON

Built in 1898 during the Klondike Gold Rush, this narrow gauge railroad is an International Historic Civil Engineering Landmark.

Experience the breathtaking panorama of mountains, glaciers, gorges, waterfalls, tunnels, trestles and historic sites from the comfort of vintage parlor cars.

🐦 whitepassrail
f 📷 whitepassrailroad

wpyr.com
1-800-343-7373

# RIDE THE RAILS INTO THE BEAUTIFUL
# LEHIGH GORGE STATE PARK

Trains run into the state park May through December

Train excursions are 16 miles round trip

Special family-friendly train rides include:

* Winterfest Train Rides
* Easter Bunny Specials
* Bike Trains
* Hometown High Bridge Excursions
* Santa Claus Specials

Additional special train excursions available in partnership with the Reading and Northern Railroad, please visit www.rbmnrr-passenger.com.

Pick Between Open Air Seating, Standard Coach Seating, Caboose, or Cab Rides During Summer Months.

All Standard Coaches are Heated in Winter Months.

Clean Men's & Women's Restrooms are on Standard Coaches.

www.LGSRY.com    570-325-8485    info@lgsry.com

# ALL ABOARD FOR FAMILY FUN!

## Take a Nostalgic 22-mile trip aboard L&N's Historic Lebanon Branch

### KENTUCKY RAILWAY MUSEUM

**www.kyrail.org**

136 South Main St. • New Haven, KY 40051 • 800.272.0152

## Folkston Funnel
Funnel Street, Downtown Folkston, GA

The "Folkston Funnel" is CSXT's double track line which serves as the main artery for ninety percent of the railroad traffic into and out of Florida. From the Train Viewing Platform visitors can watch upwards of 60 trains a day pass through this charming southeast Georgia town. The platform is equipped with scanner, fans, electricity, internet, & floodlights for night train watching. Diagonally across the street is the restored Train Depot, home to our Train Museum, featuring the "Cookie" William's Model Train Room. Don't miss the new radio exhibit & museum gift shop. The Depot has a covered pavilion perfect for a picnic or cookout. There are plenty of open areas for taking pictures or video. If you love trains, you'll love Folkston.

For more information visit our website at
**www.folkston.com** or call **912-496-2536**

# We've Got the Inside Track on Fun.

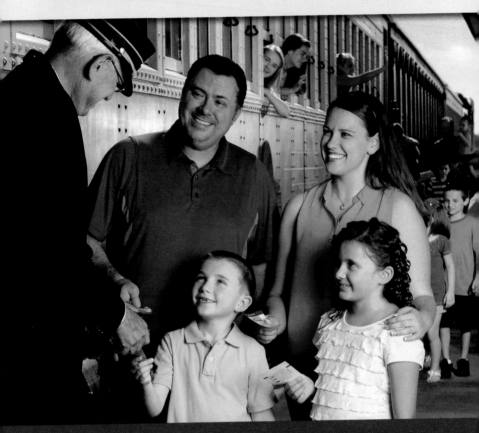

**HOP ABOARD** the Grapevine Vintage Railroad, centrally located between Dallas and Fort Worth. Travel in authentic 1920s Victorian-era coaches from Grapevine's Cotton Belt Depot to the Fort Worth Stockyards, or on the Stockyards Trinity River Ride.* There is an array of attractions and fun waiting for you in Grapevine. Come and make it a weekend.

705 S. Main St., Grapevine, TX 76051
130 Exchange Ave., Fort Worth, TX 76106

For tickets, schedules and train information, visit
**www.GVRR.com** or call **817-410-3185**

*Stockyards Trinity River Ride departs from Fort Worth Stockyards Station.

From the Railroad Museums commemorating steam trains of the past to the Main Line Excursions of the 21st century, from Short Line Railroads to Railroad Contractors, McRail provides the insurance coverage that keeps the rail industry on track and moving swiftly.

# McRAIL

A Borden Perlman Salisbury & Kelly Company

800-486-6984   www.mcrail.com

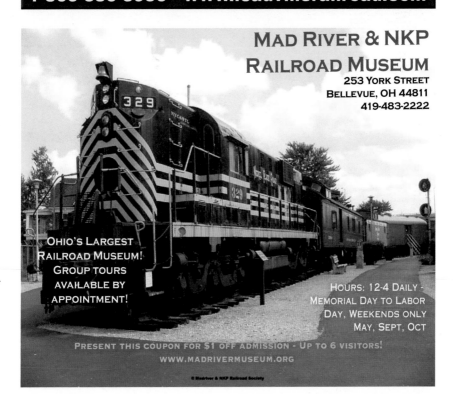

# *Always an impressive site to see...*

Get the best seat in the house overlooking Bailey Yard –
the world's largest railroad classification yard.

From atop the Golden Spike Tower, you'll watch the action
as the crews of Union Pacific Railroad sort and connect
nearly 10,000 cars daily on two classification hump yards
and 120 bowl tracks. There's no place else to see it than
right here at Golden Spike Tower. Enjoy our indoor
train displays and a large train gift shop.

NorthPlatteRailDays.com
GoldenSpikeTower.com

**NORTH PLATTE RAIL DAYS**
GOLDEN SPIKE TOWER

**Sept 15th-17th, 2017**

More trains than you can keep track of:

**GOLDEN SPIKE TOWER**
A panoramic view of the world's largest rail yard.
**Open Daily**

Minutes from I-80, Hwy 30 and Hwy 83
1249 N Homestead Rd.  North Platte, NE